THE SECESSION MOVEMENT
IN VIRGINIA, 1847-1861

A Da Capo Press Reprint Series

THE AMERICAN SCENE
Comments and Commentators

GENERAL EDITOR: WALLACE D. FARNHAM
University of Illinois

THE SECESSION
MOVEMENT
in Virginia
1847-1861

By
HENRY T. SHANKS

DA CAPO PRESS • NEW YORK • 1970

A Da Capo Press Reprint Edition

This Da Capo Press edition of
The Secession Movement in Virginia, 1847–1861,
is an unabridged republication of the first edition
published in Richmond, Virginia, in 1934.

Library of Congress Catalog Card Number 70-109545

SBN 306-71899-5

Copyright, 1934, by Garrett & Massie, Incorporated,
Richmond, Virginia

Published by Da Capo Press
A Division of Plenum Publishing Corporation
227 West 17th Street
New York, N. Y. 10011
All Rights Reserved

Manufactured in the United States of America

THE SECESSION MOVEMENT IN VIRGINIA, 1847-1861

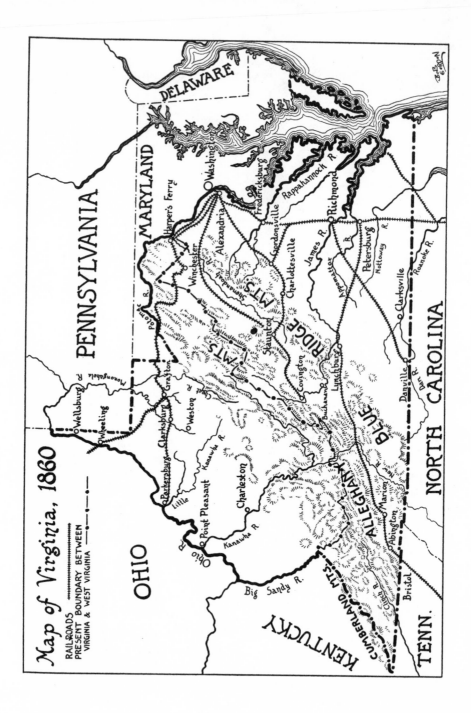

Map of Virginia, 1860

RAILROADS ....
PRESENT BOUNDARY BETWEEN
VIRGINIA & WEST VIRGINIA — ·· — ·· —

PENNSYLVANIA

OHIO

MARYLAND

DELAWARE

Washington

Harper's Ferry

Winchester

Fredericksburg

Rappahannock R.

Alexandria

Gordonsville

Charlottesville

James R.

Richmond

Petersburg

Appomattox R.

Nottoway R.

Roanoke R.

Clarksville

Danville

Dan R.

NORTH CAROLINA

Staunton

Covington

Lynchburg

Buchanan

Wellsburg

Wheeling

Monongahela R.

Parkersburg

Clarksburg

Grafton

Weston

Point Pleasant

Little R.

Kanawha R.

Charleston

Kanawha R.

Ohio R.

Big Sandy R.

Marion

Abington

Bristol

Clinch R.

CUMBERLAND MTS.

KENTUCKY

TENN.

ALLEGHANY

BLUE RIDGE

S. W. MTS.

E. MTS.

Shenandoah R.

Potomac R.

THE SECESSION MOVEMENT
in *Virginia*
1847-1861

By

HENRY T. SHANKS

Professor of History in Birmingham-Southern College

RICHMOND

GARRETT AND MASSIE · PUBLISHERS

TO
MY MOTHER AND FATHER

PREFACE

MANY have written about the secession of Virginia, but no one, so far as I know, has published a comprehensive and, at the same time, critical study of the subject. Several years ago Dr. Douglas S. Freeman prepared, but did not publish, his doctor's dissertation on *The Attitude of Political Parties in Virginia Towards Slavery and Secession*. Other historians have examined the topic briefly in connection with their treatments of kindred problems. With the exception of Dr. Freeman, these neither placed their emphasis on the story of Virginia's withdrawal from the Union nor had access to material now available. This book is an attempt to fill this gap in historical writing.

The inception of the study was a term paper prepared for Dr. William E. Dodd's seminar at the University of Chicago in 1926. Three years later much of the first six chapters in the present treatment was presented as a doctor's dissertation at the University of North Carolina. Since then new material necessitating a revision has been found, and the last five chapters have been added to complete the story.

In collecting the data for this book I found Dr. Freeman especially kind and helpful. He very generously turned over to me his notes and unpublished dissertation. The frequent references in the notes of my study to these will partially indicate how valuable they have been. For their use I am sincerely grateful. I owe also a special debt to the librarians and their staffs of the Virginia State Library, Library of Congress, the Department of Archives and History of the State of West Virginia, McCormick Agricultural Association, Boston Athenæum, Confederate Museum, and the libraries of the universities of North Carolina and West Virginia for accommodations and assistances in gathering my material. I wish to acknowledge special obligation to Miss Lilly Hagan of Morgantown, for access to her large Waitman T. Willey collection; to Mr. George Coleman of Williamsburg for the use of his valuable Nathaniel Beverly Tucker manuscripts; to Dr. Lyon G. Tyler for help in locating descendants of the leaders of the secession period; and to the late Mr. Armistead C. Gordon for the privilege of examining the rare newspaper files in the Augusta County courthouse, and for his advice on several controversial points.

I desire also to express my appreciation to Dr. C. C. Pearson, Dr. Marcus W. Jernegan, Dr. A. C. McLaughlin, and especially Dr. William E. Dodd for inspiration and guidance in my early historical training. Dr. J. G. de Roulhac Hamilton has patiently and generously directed me throughout the preparation of this book. His assistance in locating material and his constructive criticisms of the manuscript have been an invaluable asset. For these and innumerable other aids and kindnesses I owe to him most and am deeply indebted. Miss Maude H. Woodfin of Westhampton College and Mr. William R. Abbot of the College of the City of Charleston have read the entire manuscript and made helpful suggestions for improving the content, style, and punctuation. Professors W. W. Pierson, R. D., W. Connor, and H. M. Wagstaff, who with Professor Hamilton directed my later graduate study, have read and indicated important changes of different parts of the treatise. To all of these I wish to acknowledge my special gratitude. Any mistakes which may remain, however, are mine rather than theirs. Finally to my wife, Anne Graham Shanks, I am particularly obligated for her help and encouragement in preparing the manuscript for the press.

Henry T. Shanks.

March, 1934
Birmingham-Southern College

CONTENTS

MAPS

THE SECESSION MOVEMENT IN VIRGINIA, 1847-1861

CHAPTER I

SOCIAL AND ECONOMIC BACKGROUND

IN THE movement for a Southern confederacy Virginia's course was of singular significance. Her population, resources, and wealth were greater than those of any other slave state. Because of her history and prestige, the Old Dominion's influence, not only with the border and cotton states but also with most of the free states, was probably stronger than that of any other commonwealth. Since this state extended from the Atlantic to the Ohio River and bordered upon the free states of Ohio and Pennsylvania on the northwest and upon the national capital on the north, her location was of strategic importance. Union with the South would offer the Confederates a channel of invasion into the free states or a line of defense against a Northern attack. On the other hand adherence to the Union would protect the Federal Government and the North from a Southern attack as well as provide a route of invasion into the South. In either case her territory would be the chief battle-ground during a war between the two sections of the country. Even more important in the minds of the two contestants was the fact that if Virginia did not secede, Kentucky, Maryland, North Carolina,[1] and Tennessee would probably remain in the Union, thereby confining the Southern Confederacy to the lower South.

In considering the course to follow, Virginia's leaders were guided by economic and social interests as well as by the traditions and bonds which held their state to the respective sections. As a background, therefore, for a study of the secession movement in Virginia, a brief sketch of the geographic, economic, social, and political features as they existed in 1850-1861 is necessary.

The surface of Virginia consisted of two uneven but parallel plains which sloped in opposite directions, and a centrally located Valley.[2] The eastern plain extending from the Atlantic to the Blue Ridge was subdivided into the Tidewater and Piedmont. Stretching from the fall line, which practically corresponded to the present Richmond, Fredericksburg and Potomac, and the Atlantic Coast Line railroads, the Tidewater with an elevation rarely exceeding three hundred feet was generally level. The valleys of its numerous navigable streams and a few sunken pockets were usually fertile and suited to the production of staple crops and to the plantation system. The soil between these streams, however, was frequently sandy and of little agricultural value.[3]

The other half of the plain east of the Blue Ridge formed a right triangle with the North Carolina line as a base, the Blue Ridge as the hypotenuse, and the fall line as the perpendicular.[4] Here the streams were shallow and rapid, thereby offering power for grist, saw, and textile mills. Its soil made of decomposed rocks, which contained gneiss, mica, granite, porphyry, and iron, was suitable for the production of wheat, corn, fruits, and tobacco.[5] Because of its rolling and hilly surface, the soil in most of the Piedmont wore out rapidly, especially when careless methods of cultivation and drainage were used and exhaustive crops were grown.[6] It included, however, some very fertile belts such as the red sandstone lands of the Potomac counties[7] and the gray and red soils of the Blue Ridge foothills in Bedford, Franklin, Albemarle, and Greene.[8]

The second main division of the state, the central district or Valley, extending northeast and southwest between the Blue Ridge and Alleghany mountains, was not a continuous valley but a depressed and uneven surface several hundred feet below the ranges on each side. It included the fertile and beautiful Shenandoah, New, and Holston valleys which extended northeast and southwest. The James, emptying into the Atlantic, and the Great Kanawha, flowing west into the Ohio, broke across the inclosing ridges at the center of this middle division of the state to make east and west valleys. Nevertheless, in spite of the fact that this whole district was not connected by a common river system, its soil and general topography gave it common characteristics. Generally speaking, its soil included limestone and sand loam, and its surface was for the most part rugged and uneven.

The third main division of the state, the western plain, was subdivided into the Alleghany highlands, the Cumberland plateau, and the Ohio River district.[9] The whole division sloped towards the Ohio, and its rivers generally flowed to the west.[10] The Alleghany highlands, the most eastern of these subdivisions, lay close to the western side of the mountains which divided the western plain from the Valley, and stretched across southwestern and western Virginia to the Pennsylvania line. Because of the unevenness of the surface, these highlands were sparsely settled. The valleys were narrow and the rivers were not navigable. Most of the cultivation was on the top or sides of these mountains.[11]

To the west of the Alleghany highlands and extending in a similar direction was the Cumberland plateau. Beginning as a mountain range in Tennessee, it spread out into a table-land covering virtually the whole of western Virginia. Its elevation was generally 1,000 to 2,000 feet above sea level. Like the Alleghany highlands it had a rough and rugged surface, rapid streams, narrow valleys; and it was almost as thinly populated.[12]

Along the Ohio River was the narrow strip sloping from the Cumberland plateau to the west. Though uneven in surface, its rolling hills and its numerous fertile valleys made it the most prosperous farming section of western Virginia.[13] Its many navigable streams gave outlets for minerals, and for wheat, corn, rye, oats, and buckwheat as well as for the products of the small manufacturing plants in the river towns.[14]

This brief survey of the physical features as they existed in 1850-1861 shows the possibilities of the sectionalism and economic differentiation. Within the respective larger divisions there were minor units. In the Alleghany highlands, for instance, the southwestern slave section on the Clinch River was cut off from the region to the north and connected with the southwestern Valley. In the Cumberland plateau, the inhabitants on the Great Kanawha had little natural contact with those to the north in Lewis and Barbour counties. Likewise the soils and resources of the small units varied. But the similarities of the features within the respective main geographic units justify the original division.

The divisions varied almost as much economically as they did geographically. By 1860 the Piedmont and Tidewater had become a unit in political interests, markets, crops, and social institutions. In the early days of the state, the planters of the Tidewater had "looked down on" the German and Scotch-Irish small non-slaveholding farmers of the interior. The succeeding half-century, however, had carried the eastern slave system to the hilly upcountry. With the slave system implanted, the Piedmont soon accepted the economic and political tenets of the older region. Consequently, in 1829-1832 and again in 1850-1851, when the constitutional and slavery issues arose in the legislature and conventions, the Piedmont and the Tidewater were fighting together against western social and political innovations.

These two sub-divisions which made up the eastern plain and which were the centers of the secession movement in 1860-1861 were mainly agricultural in their economic activities. A few counties around Norfolk and Washington cities began in the thirties to engage in trucking.[15] Even large planters became interested and were soon devoting their time to

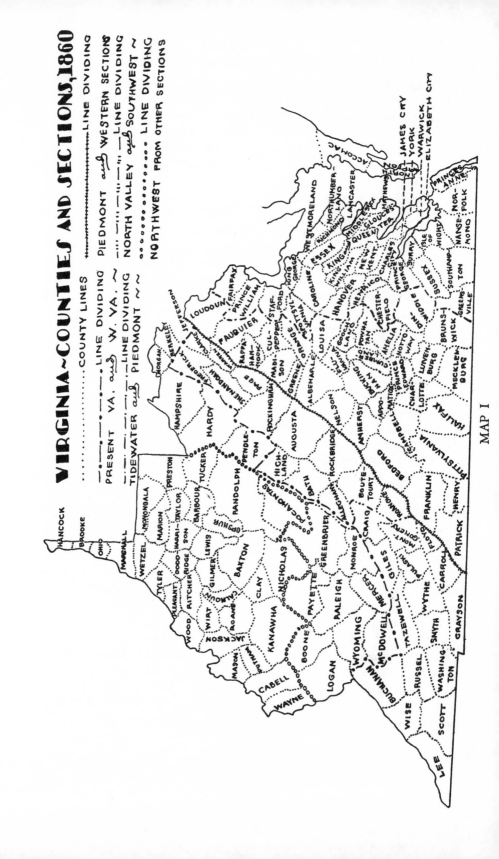

VIRGINIA~COUNTIES AND SECTIONS, 1860

.... COUNTY LINES

——————— LINE DIVIDING PRESENT VA. and W. VA.

~~~~~~~ LINE DIVIDING TIDEWATER and PIEDMONT

———·——— LINE DIVIDING PIEDMONT and WESTERN SECTIONS

—··—··— LINE DIVIDING NORTH VALLEY and SOUTHWEST

·········· LINE DIVIDING NORTHWEST FROM OTHER SECTIONS

MAP I

the production of the garden products.[16] Their markets were Baltimore, Washington, New York, Boston, and Philadelphia.[17] Settlers from the free states came in and white labor often supplanted slaves.[18] But most of the people in the Tidewater continued to produce staples, such as wheat, corn, oats, tobacco, and, to a limited extent, cotton.[19] In the Piedmont, the middle, southern, and southwestern counties comprised the great tobacco belt.[20] Besides tobacco, they produced wheat, corn, and livestock for domestic consumption and exportation. After being transformed into flour and meal by the mills at Richmond, Petersburg, Danville, and Lynchburg, their grain products were shipped to the cotton states, Brazil, and the North.[21] The red land district on the Potomac was even more important in the production of cattle and wheat.[22]

Because of the broad fields, the climatic conditions, and the adaptability of the soil to the production of staple crops, this eastern plain was the heart of the plantation system. Of the 490,865 slaves in Virginia in 1860, 428,351 were from east of the Blue Ridge,[23] and of the 14,551 planters with more than ten slaves each, 12,796 were in the same division.[24] Five and six-tenths per cent of its farms included over five hundred acres each, whereas in the Valley, the next largest plantation section, only three and four-tenths per cent of the farms had as many as five hundred acres each.[25]

Although tobacco, the main crop in the Piedmont and to a less degree in the coastal plain, had through constant cultivation of the same lands worn out much of the soil, the eastern plain remained the wealthiest of the three main divisions of the state.[26] The increased demands of the lower South, the opening of the Texan lands, and the favorable economic conditions of the decade prior to 1860, when slaves, tobacco, and wheat were bringing good prices, brought this comparative prosperity. Besides, Edmund Ruffin, through the *Farmer's Register,* the Virginia Agricultural Society, lectures and addresses to the planters, and through his own farm as a sort of experimental station, initiated the system of fertilization, rotation of crops, drainage, and scientific soil study which deserves the name of an "agricultural revolution."[27]

In addition to this comparative agricultural wealth, the eastern plain possessed practically all the larger towns and cities. Some of these, such as Portsmouth, Norfolk, Alexandria, and Richmond, were shipping and receiving posts for the planters' exports and imports. Others, in addition to being distributing centers, turned the tobacco, cotton, wheat, and corn into finished products for exportation to the lower South, the West Indies, the East, Europe, and Brazil.[28] Richmond, Petersburg, Danville,

Lynchburg, and Clarksville manufactured the snuff, chewing tobacco, and smoking tobacco, much of which was consumed in the cotton states.[29] Along with numerous smaller towns, these cities ground $15,-851,866 worth of flour and meal.[30] There were also in this eastern plain many small factories engaged in the production of textiles, firearms, farming implements, and other commodities to the amount of $25,-000,000 out of the total $39,000,000 worth in the whole state.[31] Richmond, Danville, Lynchburg, and Petersburg produced about three-fifths of the state's manufactured products.[32]

With respect to transporting the surplus agricultural and manufactured commodities to their destination, the eastern plain was comparatively fortunate in its river and railroad systems. As most of the streams were navigable to the fall line, the people had good outlets through their own ports. By 1860 the James River and Kanawha Canal, originally intended to connect the Middle West with Richmond, had been completed as far as Buchanan in the Valley, nearly two hundred miles west of Richmond;[33] and before the railroads were built, it afforded the tobacco and wheat growers of the Blue Ridge foothills a channel for transporting their bulky crops.[34] The Dismal Swamp Canal, likewise, enabled Norfolk to carry on much trade with North Carolina.[35] The railroads which were built in the forties and fifties afforded even greater means for getting these commodities to ports of Virginia, Maryland, and Pennsylvania. Indeed, the Piedmont and Tidewater were tied together with a network of railroads which practically corresponded to the present system there.[36] Local jealousies and rivalries, however, prevented railway coöperation; so the Canal remained, until the war, the largest channel for freight.[37]

Across the Blue Ridge in the middle district or Valley, economic conditions were becoming more like those in the eastern plain than those west of the Alleghanies, but sufficiently different to warrant separate treatment.[38] Portions of this division, such as the rugged and thinly populated counties of Grayson and Carroll in the south, and Highland, Pendleton, Hardy, and Morgan in the north, were not united to the plantation type of agriculture. On the other hand, the valleys of the New, Holston, and tributaries of the James and Kanawha rivers, and the fertile limestone soil of the Shenandoah produced some tobacco, many cattle, and large quantities of grain. In the central part of the Valley, counties along the James, where slaves were almost as numerous as they were in some of the eastern sections, produced staples, such as wheat, corn, and cattle.[39] South of this river, tobacco was added to these.[40]

Although the plantation system was not so deeply intrenched here as it was across the Blue Ridge, several counties had an appreciable number of slaves and planters. With a few exceptions a single row of counties, beginning with Washington in the southwest and extending to the Potomac on the north, had from fifty-five to one hundred and seventy-one planters with over ten slaves each to the county—a number large enough in that sparsely settled area to influence the attitude toward the plantation system.[41] In Clarke over fifty per cent, in Jefferson more than thirty per cent, and in Pulaski, Roanoke, Botetourt, Rockbridge, Augusta, Bath, and Warren over twenty per cent of the farmers owned slaves.[42] In the Shenandoah Valley slavery was declining, but in the New River section it was on the increase.[43]

In spite of the fact that the transportation system of that day did not link the Valley so closely to the eastern part of the state as many desired, it provided some contact. The Virginia and Tennessee Railroad, which passed through the southwestern counties and which connected Lynchburg and Bristol, offered the only direct outlet for Virginia products to the cotton states.[44] In the counties along the James as far west as Botetourt, the James River and Kanawha Canal offered contact with the markets of the Tidewater. Inhabitants of Augusta and the Shenandoah sections had connections with the West over the Covington and Ohio Railroad and the Kanawha and Ohio rivers, with Richmond and Norfolk over the railroad which later became the Chesapeake and Ohio, and with Baltimore and the North over a road to Strassburg, Alexandria, and Washington. The rich slave counties of Clarke and Jefferson and the less fertile small farm districts of Hampshire and Morgan were linked to the West and East by the Baltimore and Ohio and by the Winchester and Potomac.[45] These northern counties, which in 1861 consistently opposed secession, were in direct contact with Alexandria, Baltimore, and Washington but not with Richmond and the eastern part of the state.

The western plain with some exceptions had few economic features similar to those of eastern Virginia and the South. Although some of its round-top mountains were conducive to the production of such staples as wheat and corn, and, to a limited extent, tobacco, it had few large farms and almost no slaves. Instead it was a country of small farmers. Only in Russell and Tazewell of the southwest, Monroe and Greenbrier on the Greenbrier River, and Kanawha County on the Great Kanawha River were there as many as ten per cent of the families slave owners.[46] And only in thirteen other counties west of the Alleghanies were five per cent of the farmers slaveholders.[47] McDowell and Hancock were without any slaves.[48] Most of the slaves were found along the Greenbrier, Kanawha, and Clinch rivers.[49] The mountainous interior and fertile as well as prosperous Ohio River district were non-slaveholding.[50] In this whole area the number of slaves was increasing less rapidly than the white population.[51] Except for a few counties along the Baltimore and Ohio Railroad where there never were many slaves, the territory north of the Great Kanawha and west of the Alleghanies had fewer slaves in 1860 than in 1850; whereas in the southwest the reverse is true.[52]

In 1860 this western plateau was the mining section of Virginia. Its tonnage in iron was nearly three times as great as that of the territory east of the Alleghanies.[53] Mason on the Ohio River mined about one-third of the state's coal,[54] and Ohio County produced an equal percentage of the bar iron.[55] In the Kanawha Valley and Panhandle around Wheeling, the gas and oil which were discovered in the forties and fifties offered great promise to the capitalists.[56] The latter district because of these commodities and the iron plants located there was, next to Richmond, the largest manufacturing center of the state.[57] Between the small farmers, manufacturers, and miners of the western section and the planters of the eastern plain, there was not the same unity of interests which prevailed between the latter and the Valley.

Unfortunately for the coöperation of these sections, this dissimilarity was increased by the lack of communications between them. The James River and Kanawha Canal was chartered to extend to the Ohio, but it was never completed beyond the Valley. Shortly before the Civil War the Covington and Ohio Railroad was chartered to follow the proposed route of this canal and to connect with the Central Railroad to Staunton. In 1861, however, the former railroad had not been finished.[58] In the northern portion of the western plain the Baltimore and Ohio and the Northwestern railroads, built by private subscription and companies without state aid, offered excellent connections to Washington, Baltimore, Pittsburgh, and the west.[59] But, few people in the northwest had business acquaintances with Richmond, for their connections were elsewhere. Added to these non-Virginia outlets were the Ohio River and its many tributaries.[60] The eastern Virginians had done little for the internal improvements of the west, partly because of the sectional feeling but more particularly because of the fear that railroads would hinder the development of the canal.[61] Such eastern leaders as Henry A. Wise saw the advantage of linking the west to the east; hence in the fifties they chartered road and turnpike companies.[62] In 1860 the legislature generously appropriated money for making the Kanawha River navigable and for completing the Covington and Ohio Railroad.[63] Out of gratitude for these belated appropriations the people of Charleston had a great celebration.[64] These efforts to placate the west were too late, and in 1861 when the secession issue arose most western people had no contacts with those of the Richmond district.

Added to the economic differences and similarities in the divisions of Virginia were the social features. The respective sections of the state were inhabited by different races or at least by settlers from various parts of the United States. With the exception of Fairfax near Washington city and the trucking district around Norfolk, the eastern plain had few foreigners and Northerners.[65] Its people were Virginians in origin and tradition. By 1860 the Valley had also made over the Pennsylvania Germans and Scotch-Irish into "good" Virginians;[66] settlers from western Maryland, Ohio, Pennsylvania, and New York had moved into western Virginia. In the Panhandle and the Ohio Valley as well as in the northern stretch of present-day West Virginia were people from the North and the non-slaveholding sections of Maryland.[67] Along with these had come a few "dangerous" New Englanders.[68] South of the Little Kanawha, the Panhandle, and Doddridge and Randolph counties were colonies of anti-slavery Germans.[69] In 1860 the foreign-born population in the whole state was less than two and one-half per cent of the entire population.[70] This was divided largely between the Irish and Germans.[71] There were, however, from the other states of the Union 68,340, one-half of whom came from Pennsylvania, Ohio, and Maryland. The District of Columbia, New York, New Jersey and Massachusetts, as well as Kentucky and North Carolina, furnished the next largest number, over one thousand each.[72] The rest came mainly from other Northern states.[73]

Similar sectionalism was noticeable in the churches and educational institutions and policies. The Democratic west and much of the Valley favored free public schools, and eastern planters continued to oppose this innovation.[74] The east urged larger appropriations for state colleges; the west tried to reduce such expenditures.[75] Most of the students from the west attended institutions of Ohio and Pennsylvania rather than those of eastern Virginia. In 1860 twice as many college students from the Trans-Alleghany counties were in attendance at the free state colleges

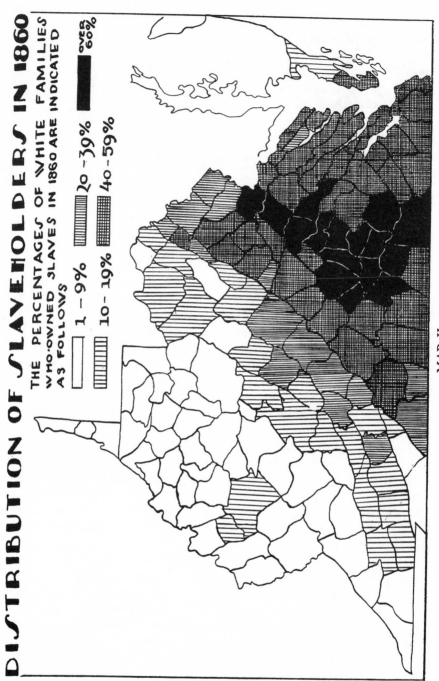

DISTRIBUTION OF SLAVEHOLDERS IN 1860

THE PERCENTAGES OF WHITE FAMILIES WHO OWNED SLAVES IN 1860 ARE INDICATED AS FOLLOWS

1 - 9%
10 - 19%
20 - 39%
40 - 59%
OVER 60%

MAP II

as at their own state institutions.[76] Out of three hundred and seventy Virginians at the University of Virginia in 1859 only seventeen were from west of the Blue Ridge;[77] whereas as early as 1839 there were fifteen from the same area at Marietta College (Ohio) alone.[78] The Valley and southwest patronized the eastern institutions.

Although the church differences were less marked, they were evident. Most Episcopal, Quaker, German Reformed, and Lutheran congregations were located east of the Alleghanies.[79] The Methodists, Baptists, and Presbyterians were numerous in all sections.[80] But ever since the division of the Methodist and Baptist churches in 1844-1845, Virginia had been the battleground between the Northern and Southern branches of these respective churches.[81] The Methodists furnished the best example of this contest. Their line of separation began at the mouth of the Chesapeake Bay and extended up it to the Rappahannock River. Following that stream to its source and continuing to the Blue Ridge Mountains, the line ran along their crest to a point southwest of Lynchburg. From there it extended to the source of the Big Sandy River which it followed to the Ohio.[82] This line, while not permanent since the Southern Methodists soon expanded their activities to the Pennsylvania boundary, indicated to a certain extent the secession and Union votes in 1861.[83]

The large plantation system was not so prevalent in Virginia in 1860 as it was in the cotton states. In Georgia, Louisiana, Mississippi, Alabama, and South Carolina, five per cent of the landholders owned more than fifty slaves each; whereas in Virginia only one and six-tenths per cent had that many slaves. In the same five states 35.7 per cent of the slaveholders owned more than ten slaves each, but in Virginia the percentage was only 27.9.[84] In fact, slavery was apparently declining in Virginia from 1830 to 1860, particularly in certain sections of the state. In 1790, 39.2 per cent of her population were slaves. This remained the approximate ratio until 1840 when it was 36.2 per cent. By 1850 this percentage had decreased to 33.2. Ten years later it was 30.1 per cent;[85] yet in the lower South the ratio of slaves to total population had increased.[86] In like manner the total number of slaves in Virginia remained about the same during these years. From 1840 to 1850 the increase there was only 5.21 per cent against 28.91 per cent for the whole country.[87] During the same period the white population of Virginia grew 14.6 per cent. In the next ten years the state's slave population was enlarged 3.73 per cent.[88]

The main slaveholding area of Virginia was the eastern plain. It was stated above that 428,351 of the 490,865 slaves in the state were in the counties east of the Blue Ridge; that 12,796 planters with more than ten slaves each out of 14,551 for the whole commonwealth were in the same section; and that its farms were larger than those elsewhere.[89] In the Valley and southwest there were some counties with many slaveholders, but in the northwest and the northern Alleghanies there were virtually none.[90] These differences were more marked in 1860 than in 1850. During this period there was an actual decline in the number of slaves in the northwest and the Shenandoah Valley; but there was a slight increase in the Tidewater, a larger growth in the Piedmont, and an appreciable increase in the southwest.[91] Within these respective regions there were some exceptions. In the Tidewater there was a decline in Norfolk, Accomac, Northumberland, Essex, Southampton, New Kent, and Mathews.[92] In the Piedmont there was a considerable increase of slaves in the southwestern corner, where the newly constructed Danville and Richmond Railroad was located, and in the Richmond district; but there was a decline in the Potomac region around Warrenton.[93] In the Shenandoah Valley, Augusta, Rockingham, Pendleton, and Highland had a ten per cent increase. The last two counties had only 646 slaveholders in all. This increase was probably due to the completion of the Virginia Central Railroad west of Staunton. West of the Blue Ridge, a few counties along the newly constructed Northwestern Railroad had an increase.[94] There was also a growth in Jackson on the Ohio, and in Braxton, Nicholas, and Fayette on the Kanawha.[95] Most of the northwest, however, had a decided decline, especially in the Panhandle and in the counties near the Pennsylvania line and the Ohio River.[96] Here was found the limited anti-slavery sentiment which existed in the state.

This decline in the number of slaves in certain districts and the total decline in ratios of increase in the whole state does not mean that Virginia was losing her ardor for the institution of slavery. In the Revolutionary period many Virginia leaders accepted it as an unfortunate evil.[97] Although some defended slavery rather early, not many offered arguments in its support until after the Nat Turner insurrection and the beginning of the Garrison movement.[98] After that insurrection the Virginia legislature seriously considered emancipation. Political leaders from east of the Blue Ridge, led by W. O. Goode of Mecklenburg, tried to keep down this discussion, but the Richmond *Enquirer* and the petitions from the eastern as well as western counties forced the General

Assembly to give the problem its attention.[99] In the debate which followed, the democratic western representatives, who felt that their political and economic interests were threatened by the aristocratic slave-holding easterners, argued that slavery was economically unsound—they were little concerned with the moral issue.[100] They contrasted Virginia with the Western free states and emphasized the backwardness of the former, attributing this to slavery.[101] Goode replied that this depression was not due to the "peculiar institution" but to the removal of slaves to the Southwestern cotton states.[102] Even some from the east admitted in this debate that the system of labor was an economic handicap. The controversy was settled by the House of Delegates agreeing that "for the present" it was inexpedient to adopt measures of emancipation.[103]

This condemnation of slavery soon underwent a great change. Professor Thomas R. Dew in his able review of this debate not only proved to the satisfaction of such leaders as Thomas Ritchie, editor of the Richmond *Enquirer,* who was not previously a strong pro-slavery advocate, that emancipation was impractical but also that slavery was a "good" institution.[104] This system of labor soon spread into the southwestern part of the state and the Kanawha district, where there were broad and fertile fields for cultivation and salt mines to be worked by untrained hands.[105] Everywhere the increased price of slaves brought on by the expansion into the Southwestern cotton lands made the domestic slave trade more profitable.[106] Improved methods of farming — thanks to Ruffin and the agricultural societies and journals—the new lands which the railroads and other internal improvement projects opened up, and the factories in the towns enhanced the value of slavery in the state.[107] Added to this economic motive for changing the sentiment in Virginia was the planter's fear of the attacks from the abolitionists. Dr. R. L. Dabney, a noted Presbyterian minister of Richmond, writing to a friend in 1840 said that before these radical Northerners began their crusade the general impression was that "domestic slavery was at least injudicious, as far as the happiness of the master was concerned. I do believe that if these mad fanatics had let us alone in twenty years we should have made Va. a free State." But their attacks on the South, he continued, had caused more careful study; consequently "slavery is considered a positive good."[108]

By 1840 many may not have been so certain of this change as Dr. Dabney, but his view was an expression of the revolution in sentiment which was then going on.[109] In the Constitutional Convention of

1850-1851, the western leaders not only expressed the same hostility as the easterners to the abolitionists, but, in the same words of the latter, promised fidelity to the "peculiar institution."[110] In the congressional campaign of 1857 all Democrats were elected on the slogan of "anti-abolitionism."[111] After denying that the Northern radicals had a following west of the Blue Ridge, the *Kanawha Valley Star*, in 1858, maintained that "the people of the west are pro-slavery from principle," and were as devoted to the institution as the people of the planter region.[112] In all sections of the state both political parties were careful to pledge their loyalty to slavery.[113] Even in the Secession Convention, John S. Carlile and other western members who were pro-Union emphasized their adherence to the Southern labor system and their disapproval of the radical New Englanders. They declared, at that time, that the best way to preserve this system was in the Union rather than out of it.[114] After the war began John C. Campbell, president of the Northwestern Bank of Virginia at Wheeling, wrote Willey: "I trust you will be able to keep abolitionism & everything touching slavery out of this war,—I doubt very much whether you could hold even western Va., with her strong devotion to the Union, if anti-slavery is made to become a prominent feature in carrying on the war."[115]

In spite of these statements of loyalty to slavery, there was some anti-slavery sentiment in western Virginia. Constant reports of the activities of anti-slavery leaders and societies were made in the papers of the times; especially was this true of the reports from the counties along the Ohio River.[116] Moreover, many new supporters of the institution were not thoroughly converted to this cause.[117] John Letcher, who as late as 1847 with other Rockbridge leaders endorsed the Henry Ruffner pamphlet against slavery and who was attacked in the east in the campaign of 1859 on the ground that he was not "sound" on this issue, wrote J. D. Davidson, July 20, 1852, "I have no fancy for buying and selling that sort of property—never wishing to own more of them than were absolutely necessary for the convenience of my family."[118]

✓   ✓   ✓   ✓

In the early forties* after John Tyler and the regular Whigs had quarreled, many of the Virginia states' rights followers of the President went back to the Democratic party.[119] This gave the latter party an even stronger hold on the state than it already had. In addition to its many

---

*Chapter III treats party politics from 1851 to 1859. Here an attempt is made to indicate the party alignments as they existed in 1847 in order to lay the background for the struggle of 1847-1851.

supporters in the west, it had the ablest political leaders of the eastern part of the state. There developed, however, as early as 1844 a division within the party that until 1861 widened under different leaders. Thomas Ritchie, the master of the Jacksonian wing, had long since created the Richmond "junto" which, with the aid of the powerful Richmond *Enquirer,* the patronage, and the prestige of success, dominated the Democratic party of Virginia.[120] Young members, styling themselves "States' Rights Democrats" under the leadership of R. M. T. Hunter of Essex County, J. M. Mason of Winchester, Lewis E. Harvie of Amelia, and James A. Seddon of Goochland, were determined to make the party an organization for protecting Southern rights. To reach their goal these leaders wished first to elect Calhoun, President; consequently, in 1843 they earnestly set to work to gain Virginia's support for their candidate. As a result a newspaper, the Petersburg *Republican,* was established; a life of Calhoun was written and distributed by Hunter; and war was made on Ritchie.[121] Since the latter wanted the state to support Van Buren, he compromised with them by allowing them to write a strong pro-Southern platform in the state party convention on the condition that they accept his candidate.[122] He then promised not to attack Calhoun. Soon thereafter this old nationalist began singing the South Carolinian's praises. The Hunter wing expected, therefore, to see its candidate elected President in 1848.[123] The same faction was strengthened the next year when Ritchie left Virginia to edit Polk's organ, the Washington *Union.*[124] Finally in 1848 by warring on "King Caucus" these Southern Democrats, or as they were labeled by their enemies "Young Fogies," aided by the Whigs, elected Hunter and Mason to the United States Senate.[125] They failed, however, to gain the control of the Democratic party, for in the state convention of that year was passed over their protest a resolution endorsing Polk in such language as to reflect on Calhoun.[126] This marks the split of the party. Consequently, in spite of the Ritchie wing's effort to conciliate the Hunter faction by offering to support Mason for the vice-presidency in 1848, strife within the party almost threw the state's vote to Taylor.[127]

The Whigs were not entirely harmonious in the late forties. John Minor Botts of Richmond led the supporters of Clay in their fight against Taylor. John S. Pendleton, T. S. Flournoy, and W. B. Preston, who were inclined to the states' right view, saw in this military hero, on the other hand, a possibility of carrying Virginia and the country for the Whigs. Out of this contest grew the two wings of this party, but it was only a personal division until the Kansas-Nebraska bill.[128]

The Democrats usually won in the state elections. In 1844 and in 1848 Virginia's electoral votes were cast for the Democratic candidates. An analysis of the presidential and congressional ballots for 1844-1848 reveals the fact that the Democrats were strong in the western counties, and the Whigs' strength was in the east. Of the six Whig congressmen from the state in 1847, four were elected from districts east of the Blue Ridge, one from the Valley, and one from the Kanawha area.[129] With the exception of four out of nine Ohio River counties, the cluster of five in the Kanawha Valley, and six between the Alleghanies and the Blue Ridge, all counties west of the latter ridge went for Polk in 1844.[130] East of the Blue Ridge several counties in the tobacco belt south of the James and other scattering ones in the north Piedmont remained Democratic. The others in this eastern plain supported Clay in that year. Towns like Richmond, Norfolk, Alexandria, and Petersburg along with the southwestern portion of the state, the region to the east of Richmond, and the red lands around Fauquier, Albemarle, and Bedford, usually voted for Whig candidates.

From the general survey of this chapter it is evident that Virginia was, in 1860, sectional in her economic and social institutions, in politics, and in industries.[131] But there were bonds of internal unity and ties which held the different parts of the state to the lower South at the same time that other forces attached them to the Union. In 1850 and 1860 the chief money crop in Virginia, as well as in Kentucky and Tennessee, was tobacco. In the later year this product brought the Virginia growers about $10,000,000.[132] About three-fourths of the raw product was turned into snuff, plug tobacco, and smoking tobacco at the Richmond, Petersburg, Danville, Lynchburg, and Clarksville plants. From these a large portion of their products was shipped directly or through the Northern ports to the South for consumption by the cotton planters and their slaves.[133] Many of the poorer "upcountrymen" and mountaineers transformed their oats, rye, and corn into liquors, which they peddled among the "rich" tobacco growers of Virginia or the cotton planters of the South.[134] "And the cattle raisers, pork pochers, and drovers of mules also turned south for their best markets."[135] Many planters of the Old Dominion owned plantations in the cotton belt. The political, social, and cultural bonds, likewise, connected many Virginians with those of the lower South. Both possessed the plantation system and, as will be shown later, by 1860 a consciousness of common interests and aspirations characteristic of a Southern nationalism had developed in Virginia as well as in the cotton region.[136]

At the same time there were other forces fully as strong which bound many Virginians to the North. Economically, tobacco was by no means the only important agricultural product of the state, although it was the most concentrated of the many crops. The stock slaughtered for market amounted to $11,491,027; and the livestock was valued at $33,-656,659 in 1860.[137] One-ninth of the country's wheat and corn crops was produced in Virginia in 1860.[138] Although much of these were consumed at home or shipped South, great quantities of the two commodities were shipped to Northern and foreign ports. Garden and orchard products valued at a million and a half, 2,510,019 pounds of wool, 930,000 pounds of maple sugar, and a large supply of buckwheat were sold in the North.[139] The railroads tied western Virginia, in particular, to the North and Northwest; so Baltimore, Pittsburgh, Cincinnati, and Philadelphia were more familiar to many settlers west of the Blue Ridge and north of the James than Richmond and Norfolk. Governor Pierpoint later said, "Secession and annexation to the South would cut off every outlet to our productions."[140]

CHAPTER II

VIRGINIA AND THE COMPROMISE OF 1850

DURING the period from 1847 to 1851 the South, for the first time in her history, seriously considered secession as a practical remedy for her grievances. The agitation of those years was continued and increased until the dissolution of the Union was accomplished in 1860-1861. Consequently, 1847 has been selected as an appropriate year with which to begin a study of the secession movement in Virginia. But since secession was used as the means of dissolution, it seems advisable first to trace Virginia's early adherence to the doctrine of state sovereignty on which the right to withdraw rested.

States' rights and state sovereignty were old ideas in Virginia. In ratifying the Federal Constitution in 1788 the state convention resolved that the "powers granted under the constitution, being derived from the people of the United States may be resumed by them whensoever the same shall be perverted to their injury or oppression, and that every power not granted thereby remains with them and at their will."[1] It would seem from the debate on this resolution that the phrase "people of the United States" referred to the people of the separate states as political entities rather than to the people of the United States as an entity.[2] In 1861 the secessionists and many moderates interpreted this clause as justifying the right of secession.

Whether or not the Virginians accepted this right in the period following the ratification of the Federal Constitution, they certainly opposed the centralization program of Hamilton and the Federalists. This opposition came to a head in the famous Virginia and Kentucky resolutions of 1798 and 1799. Although declaring loyalty to the United States, the Virginia resolutions expressed the view that since the Constitution was a compact the states "have the right . . . to interpose, for arresting the progress of the evil, and for maintaining within their respective limits, the authorities, rights and liberties appertaining to them."[3] John Taylor of Caroline, who was always zealously warning the country against centralization, recommended that Virginia and North Carolina secede.[4] Jefferson discouraged such a radical step, however, on the

18

ground that it was inexpedient.[5] As a Virginian of Taylor's school was soon in power, the doctrine of state sovereignty was not put to a test.

Under Jefferson and Madison, Virginia became a champion of nationalism. When some New Englanders in 1803, 1808, and 1814 threatened separation, Virginians denounced the Puritans as traitors. Thomas Ritchie, the new editor of the Jeffersonian Richmond *Enquirer,* began to extol the "Holy Union" which "is our pillar of Peace, our Safety, our Prosperity," and to insist that the theory of secession should not be discussed.[6] In one editorial he denied the right itself.[7] He, along with other Virginians, condemned the Hartford Convention not only for its "treasonable" efforts in time of war but also for its dangerous doctrines.[8]

The nationalistic program of the young Westerners, with Marshall's Federalistic decisions and the deplorable economic conditions in the state, soon turned Virginia back to the doctrine of 1798. John Taylor in Congress and Spencer Roane at the head of the Virginia Court of Appeals, neither of whom had ever been a nationalist, buckled on their armor to defend the rights of the state. In 1814 Taylor had already published his *Inquiry into the Principles and Policy of the Government of the United States* which opposed the centralization caused by the Supreme Court decisions.[9] In 1823 he added his *New Views of the Constitution.*[10] Roane, under the name of "Hampden" in a series of letters for the Richmond *Enquirer* in 1816, reviewing Marshall's decision in *Hunter v. Martin,* declared that the state courts were not inferior to the Federal courts, and that the doctrines of the resolutions of 1798 and 1799 should be adhered to.[11] By 1819 even the former nationalist, Thomas Ritchie, was boasting that "whenever State's rights are threatened or invaded Virginia will not be the last to sound the tocsin."[12] These three leaders continued throughout 1819-1823 to write against the growing centralization of the Federal Government.[13]

While they were actively teaching the younger Virginians the "true" states' rights tenets as rebuttals to Marshall's doctrines, the legislature now in the control of the particularistic school was confirming the same view in resolutions. By a vote of 138 to eighteen the House of Delegates in reply to Marshall's decision in *Cohen v. Virginia* resolved "that the Supreme Court of the United States have no rightful authority, under the Constitution, to examine and correct the judgment for which the Commonwealth of Virginia has been cited and admonished to be and appear at the Supreme Court of the United States."[14]

In the midst of this controversy over the courts, the Missouri question, which Jefferson considered "the knell of the Union"[15] and the settlement of which John Randolph labeled "a dirty bargain,"[16] arose. The state legislators resolved that they would coöperate with them [the people of Missouri] in resisting with manly fortitude any attempt which Congress may make to impose restraints or restriction, as the price of their admission, not authorized by the great principles of the Constitution, and in violation of their rights, liberty and happiness."[17]

On the tariff and internal improvement questions of the twenties and early thirties, the states' rights view was expounded in greater detail. W. F. Gordon, a friend of Jefferson and a leader of the particularistic party, in December, 1825, wrote to the latter that the proposals of Adams left "little room to hope that we shall be able to save even a vestige of the Constitution."[18] Jefferson, whose letters to Madison in 1824 and 1825 show great concern over the growth of the Federal Government's powers,[19] replied to Gordon that although the tendencies were towards consolidation into a "single government without limitations of powers 'we must not, like the hot-headed Troup' of Georgia, 'stand on our arms at once.' "[20] In accordance with these ideas, the General Assembly passed in 1826, 1827, and 1829 several sets of resolutions on the tariff and internal improvements. Those of 1826 against internal improvements repeated the preamble of the resolutions of 1798-1799.[21] Those of 1829 against the tariff maintained that the United States Constitution was a "federation compact between sovereign states," and that each state had the right to "construe the compact for itself."[22]

Eastern Virginia, like South Carolina, was hostile to the tariff, but western Virginia, because of her wool-growing, mining, and to a limited degree manufacturing interests, was inclined to the "American System."[23] But since the district east of the Blue Ridge controlled the state government, Virginia voiced an opinion against it.[24] Connected with the hostility to the tariff was the antagonism of the Leigh-Tazewell-Floyd-Gordon states' rights faction which hated Jackson more than it did the duty on imports. In 1832 a paper to carry on the fight of this group was established under the editorship of R. K. Cralle in Petersburg.[25] Jackson's bitterest enemy, Governor John Floyd, rejoiced in South Carolina's nullification ordinance.[26] On the day that he heard of South Carolina's action he recorded in his diary: "I, as Governor of Virginia, will sustain South Carolina with all my power."[27] Two and a half weeks later when he saw the President's proclamation, he characterized it as the "most extraordinary document which has ever appeared in the United States," but "I think I shall be able to check him."[28] Had the states' rights wing controlled all branches of the government, it would have probably taken sides with the nullifiers.

Jackson, because of Ritchie's powerful support, was too strong for the South Carolina friends to offer much comfort to Calhoun and his followers. To the disgust of Floyd, the House of Delegates for more than a week debated mild resolutions to send to their sister state.[29] The result was a compromise providing for sending B. W. Leigh as a peace commissioner to check the Palmetto State in her threatened drastic course. When he arrived he found that the little state had amended her course.[30] Consequently there was no test in Virginia. Many resolutions from the Valley and the western part of the state indicated that those regions would have remained loyal to Jackson and his proclamation.[31] Led by John Randolph, who left his sick bed to stir the people to action, the inhabitants of the Piedmont and the Tidewater, although considering the South Carolina doctrine inexpedient, were bitter against Jackson's proclamation and the force bill.[32] Ritchie, more than likely, expressed the view of most of his wing of the party when he declared the South Carolina doctrine "mischievous and absurd heresy . . . as seeking to place a State, *in* the Union and *out* of it *at the same time*," but as a last resort his state would be for secession.[33]

At the same time that Virginians denied the doctrine of nullification, the legislature declared the resolutions of 1798 and 1799 the "true interpretation of the constitution," pledged the state to the doctrine of state sovereignty, and denied the right of the Federal Government to use force as Jackson's proclamation proposed.[34] In a letter to Van Buren, June, 1832, Ritchie stated that Virginia was determined not to send "a man or musket to put down South Carolina."[35] George P. Blow, a local politician of Southampton County, in a letter to John Y. Mason declared that if the general government applied force South Carolina would secede, and that common interests and principles would force Virginia, North Carolina, Georgia, Florida, Alabama, and possibly Mississippi to follow. He insisted, therefore, that "the friends of the President should prevent such a calamity by checking his mad policy."[36]

✦   ✦   ✦   ✦

The first attempt at secession, which received any appreciable backing in the South and which seriously threatened disruption, was in connection with the territorial and slave questions arising out of the Mexican War. Since the debate in Congress on the abolition petitions in the thirties, the Southern leaders had tried to keep slavery out of congressional discussions. In order to avoid such a debate the Southern Whigs even opposed the acquisition of Mexican territory.[37] In their county meetings of January and February, 1848, the Virginia Whigs insisted on such a policy.[38] The thirst for new lands, however, stimulated expansion since slavery must expand or die, as J. M. Mason told Webster a little later in the United States Senate.[39]

The controversy opened in August, 1846, when David Wilmot of Pennsylvania introduced his famous Proviso in the House of Representatives. At first the South was not particularly concerned.[40] But when the Northern press and legislatures began expressing their earnest approval and slavery was again made the issue, the slave region was aroused.[41] Even those Whigs who had opposed the acquisition of Texas and the Mexican cession felt that it was now a social question. "A right denied made an evil into a good; the use of false and irrelevant charges by a 'hostile section' made necessary the arousing of the deepest fear a people were capable of knowing."[42] Calhoun sounded the alarm, February 19, 1847, by introducing in the United States Senate resolutions which declared that territories were the common property of the several states and that the Federal Government must protect slaves there.[43] The Virginia legislature expressed its view soon thereafter by refusing to receive New Hampshire's resolutions endorsing the Wilmot Proviso.[44] The Richmond *Whig* took this occasion to warn the North that whenever the South should be called on to act she "will present an undivided, stern, and inflexible front to its fanatical assailants."[45] At the same time the organ of the administration Democrats, the Richmond *Enquirer,* which at first was alarmed because the Wilmot Proviso would destroy Democratic harmony and prevent the successful prosecution of the war, began to see in it danger to the South.[46] For the first few weeks of 1847 it argued for Southern unity, and warned the North of the inadvisability of bringing the measure up at that time. While urging the South to take no drastic step, it appealed to the Northern conservatives to come to the rescue of the slave states and to save the Constitution and the Union.[47] Soon, however, the radical wing of the Democratic party forced this paper to take "more advanced ground."[48]

The "Southern Rights" party made a more direct protest when on February 17 one of its members, Lewis E. Harvie, introduced into the House of Delegates strong resolutions on the subject.[49] With slight modifications these were adopted on March 8, 1847, thereby making them the first legislative protest from the South.[50] They declared that the United States Government had no legal control over the institution of slavery, and that in assuming such jurisdiction it "transcends the limits of its legitimate functions by destroying the internal organization of the sovereignties who created it"; that since any territory acquired by the United States "belongs to the several states of this Union, as their joint and common property, in which each and all have equal rights," the enactment of a law preventing the citizens of one state migrating to that region would be a violation of the Constitution and the rights of citizens of those states, and "would tend directly to subvert the Union itself; that a violation of the Missouri Compromise and the passage of the Wilmot Proviso will force the people of Virginia to follow the only alternative that will then remain of abject submission to aggression and outrage, on the one hand, or determined resistance on the other, at all hazards and to the last extremity."[51]

These resolutions, the model for the protests of the other slave states,[52] were the foundation of Virginia's position throughout the struggle. The Democrats and, until Taylor came into power, the Whigs persistently maintained that the application of the Wilmot Proviso would mean disunion. To satisfy the Hunter-Mason wing, the state Democratic convention in 1848 endorsed Yancey's "platform" which asserted that it would not support any candidates for the presidency and vice-presidency who would not "openly and avowedly declare themselves opposed to prohibiting slavery in the territories by continuing the municipal laws of Mexico, or by act of Congress."[53] While objecting to this "gasconading" the Whigs advised calmness and moderation in order to gain the assistance of the Northern conservatives. At the same time they assured the Democrats that they would support them "at all hazards and to the last extremity" if the Wilmot Proviso passed.[54]

Throughout 1847 and much of 1848, the Virginia Democrats preached Southern unity as a means of protection against the Wilmot Proviso. Taking its cue from Thomas Ritchie's Washington *Union*, the Richmond *Enquirer*, now edited by Ritchie's sons, continued to guide the Democratic opinion even though the Hunter-Mason wing felt that this pace was too slow. On April 17, 1847, the *Enquirer* declared: *"Let the South unite, and the North will divide; but let the South divide, and the North will be together."* The Missouri Compromise, it continued, having been agreed to by sovereign states, should not be broken, and the union of states being only a confederation, citizens of one state had the same rights as citizens of other states to take their property into the territory. For "whatever may be the fate of slavery, our own destiny is united with it, and no hands but ours must touch it."[55] Likewise, J. R. Tucker expressed the view that the Wilmot Proviso was but one of a series of aggressive steps being used by Northern abolitionists for attaining their ultimate object—the destruction of slavery in the whole South.[56] Throughout January and February before the state Democratic convention met, the county meetings denounced the Proviso as dangerous to the Union and unfair to the South.[57] When the Democratic convention met at Richmond, February 29, it resolved that Wilmot's proposal was a "wilful assault on the rights and interest of one portion of our Confederacy."[58]

The Whigs, formerly almost as outspoken as the Democrats against the Proviso, changed their position after Taylor's election. In contrast to the Democrats, they attempted after that event to show that Wilmot's proposal was really not an issue; that it was merely a party maneuver in the North; and that for party purposes the Southern Democrats were over-estimating its gravity. To the Richmond *Times* (Whig) it had become a mere abstraction, for slavery could never exist in the territories any more than it could in Massachusetts. Besides, it continued, General Taylor would quiet the excitement which party intrigue had conspired to create. [59] The Richmond *Whig* even labeled the Wilmot Proviso an "exploded humbug."[60] Along with other conservative Whigs of the South, it considered Calhoun's attempt to unite the slave states a Democratic trick to split their party and destroy the effects of Taylor's election.[61] In keeping with the same view this staunch Union paper severely attacked the South Carolinian's disunion activities.[62]

When Congress convened in December, 1848, the California and New Mexico bills were introduced. They opened the slavery discussion which both parties had attempted to keep out of the presidential campaign. The agitation for the preceding year in Congress, on the stump, and in the press, however, was already making the territorial and slavery issues a sectional contest,[63] a thing all Southerners were afraid of.[64] In the midst of this excitement, the Governor of Virginia in his annual message to the General Assembly in December declared that if the Proviso or a kindered measure passed Congress "then indeed the day of compromise will have past, and the dissolution of our great and glorious Union will become necessary and inevitable," but that he hoped that a united South would diminish the danger. He concluded by recommending that the legislature pass another set of resolutions similar to those of 1847.[65] In accordance with these recommendations, John B. Floyd, later Secretary of War under Buchanan, on December 23 presented to the House of Delegates resolutions which declared that the Proviso was contrary to the Federal Constitution. They provided further that if this measure should pass Congress, the Governor should convene the legislature in extra session to take the necessary steps for redress.[66]

These resolutions provoked a spirited discussion. The Richmond *Times* (Whig) asserted that the resolutions implied a want of confidence in President-elect Taylor. Moreover, it continued, the heated contest in the House of Representatives, then going on, did not reveal what Congress would do, for the Senate would check radical action; that, in fact, much of the noise made by Northern politicians had been made for the sake of squaring their accounts with their constituents rather than for securing the adoption of the measures introduced.[67] The *Enquirer* replied that the Floyd resolutions were only intended to unite the South in order to bring the North to her "senses."[68]

Robert E. Scott, a member of the House of Delegates from Fauquier and a prominent Whig, on January 1, 1849, proposed to replace Floyd's drastic resolutions with more moderate ones. Scott's recommendation provided that whether or not the Wilmot Proviso were constitutional it was unwise and unjust to the South, but that there was no occasion for disunion over a "mere abstraction." Interference with the slave trade or slavery in the District of Columbia, on the contrary, would be a direct attack on the Constitution and should be resisted.[69]

The debate over these two sets of resolutions continued for nearly a month. At the same time the discussion in Congress was extended to include slavery and the slave trade in the District of Columbia as well as the territorial question. Extreme Southern congressmen tried to check the course of affairs by drawing up an address. At their first meeting eighty were present, some for the purpose of checking the extremists.[70] In the latter part of January, three—two Whigs and one Democrat—of the twelve Virginians present voted for the conservative address to the people of the United States drawn by Berrien, seven—all Democrats —supported Calhoun's address, and two Whigs refused to vote on either because they felt that the whole affair was improper and uncalled for.[71]

In the controversy within Virginia over these meetings of the Southern congressmen and the General Assembly's resolutions, which were closely linked together in the minds of the people, the Democrats repeated their former position that the acceptance of the extreme Floyd resolutions and the Calhoun address would unite the South so effectively that the North would give in. The *Enquirer* even insisted that Floyd's resolutions did not tend towards disunion. It further declared that if the Wilmot Proviso or Gott's resolutions restricting slavery in the District of Columbia should pass, it would not favor immediate disunion but a Southern conference and a protest, and would resort to secession only when the liberties of the South could not be guaranteed in other ways.[72] These proposals would serve the same purpose that the resolutions of 1798-1799 did,[73] but Scott's propositions would only give the Northern fanatics confidence.[74] The Lynchburg *Republican* argued that the North's great economic interest in the Union would bring her to terms if she were impressed with the dangers of the movement.[75]

The Whigs, on the other hand, returned to the party contention that both of the measures were unnecessary, disrespectful to the President-elect, and would lead to disunion or nothing.[76] The Alexandria *Gazette* thought the resolutions went too far, and that, while Scott's were in principle satisfactory, there was no occasion for any.[77] Some Whig papers, however, were sympathetic to the ideas of the drastic recommedations. Of these the Fredericksburg *Recorder* maintained that Scott's resolutions yielded ground.[78] The Winchester *Virginian* held that since the Proviso was a step towards abolition, drastic action should be taken.[79]

For the purpose of obtaining a large vote, compromise resolutions less severe than Floyd's were presented. After reaffirming those of 1847, they declared that interference with slavery or the slave trade in the District of Columbia would be considered "a direct attack" upon the institutions of the Southern states, to be resisted "at all hazards," and that if such measures or the Proviso should pass Congress, the Governor should call an extra session of the General Assembly to decide at once the course for Virginia to take.[80] Both parties in the committee of the House of Delegates accepted this compromise.[81] The Whig leader, R. E. Scott, announced that although he considered the new resolutions too drastic, he would, for the sake of uniformity, give his support;[82] and the Democratic organ asserted that, since there was no great difference in these and those of Floyd and since the change was for the sake of harmony, it would give its full approval.[83] All, however, were not as easily reconciled to the alteration. The representative in the House of Delegates from Alexandria maintained that Congress had the power to legislate on slavery in the territories, and therefore he would not support the new propositions;[84] and Harrison of Loudoun contended that the proposals were "braggadocio and unbecoming of a state."[85] In the midst of the legislative debate, the Richmond *Times* stated that although the General Assembly was in a stir the people were not worried.[86] This opposition did not defeat the new resolutions, but it did delay their passage until they were too late to affect the Calhoun address then under consideration by Southern congressmen.[87]

In the light of the response of the county meetings and the elections which followed, it would seem that these resolutions met with the people's approval.[88] The Democrats tried to make them the issue in the approaching congressional election.[89] Some Whigs, however, insisted that their party did not oppose them.[90] In February the Fredericksburg *News* (Whig) declared that the Scott resolutions were "an insult to the people of this commonwealth."[91] In the election which followed, the Democrats were advised to vote for a pro-Southern Whig where the Democratic candidate had no chance for election.[92] Consequently, in order to defeat the administration Whigs, the Democrats did not nominate candidates in the districts where they were weak.[93] As a result most of those who were lukewarm on the Proviso, such as Goggin, Flournoy, Pendleton and Botts in Congress and the able R. E. Scott in the House of Delegates, were defeated by Democrats or independent Whigs.[94] The most noted of these turnovers was in the Orange district where Jeremiah Morton, an independent Southern rights Whig, won from the regular party nominee, John S. Pendleton, although the district had given Taylor a majority of 1,569 out of 6,953 votes.[95] In the legislature the change was not very noticeable. The Democrats lost one seat in the senate and gained one in the house.[96]

It would seem from these results and the drastic resolutions that Virginia was ready for a determined stand. In presenting the resolutions to the United States Senate, R. M. T. Hunter said that, even though they were presented in the spirit of compromise, they were a warning of the "fearful alternatives between which she must choose if she cannot be permitted to retain her position of equality in this Union, even by the sacrifice of a portion of her rights and interests."[97] J. M. Mason, his colleague, on February 28, 1849, declared that if the Wilmot Proviso or the resolution on the slave trade in the District of Columbia were passed, the Northern leaders would see that Virginia would be placed "beyond the reach of further aggression."[98] Hunter was under Calhoun's influence and Mason was a "fire-eater" who by no means represented the majority sentiment of Virginia. R. K. Cralle probably estimated the true position of Virginia when he wrote Calhoun, July 25, 1849, that these were merely resolutions and did not mean that Virginia would live up to them in case the Wilmot Proviso were passed. "After a few patriotic groans," he continued, the state "will submit."[99] Inasmuch as the Wilmot Proviso was never passed, the Virginia resolutions were never tested.

Throughout the summer and autumn of 1849 both Virginia parties awaited the action of the President, who in a speech at Mercer, Pennsylvania, in August, had declared that the "people of the North need have no apprehension of the further extension of slavery,"[100] and who was already urging California to form a state government preparatory to admission when Congress should convene in December.[101] Awaiting an opportunity to attack him and his "pro-Northern" policy, the Virginia Democratic organ declared, October 19, that California should not be admitted because she was too large and that she had not gone through the territorial stage.[102] In reply the *Whig* contended that although this new state acted unwisely by including the anti-slavery clause in its constitution, it was a legal organization and was eligible for admission without going through the territorial stage in the same sense that Texas had been.[103] Going a little further than the *Whig*, the Richmond *Republican* (Whig) rejoiced in the anti-slavery clause in this constitution because it removed "one of the most formidable stumbling blocks to the continued peace and integrity to the Union. There is no longer any field for agitation, either by fanatical abolitionists or power-hunting demagogues."[104] Weakened in its argument, the *Enquirer* replied that it was afraid this concession was but the first act in the drama, and that encouraged by their success there the Free Soilers would be heartened to prohibit slavery in New Mexico, to abolish it in the District of Columbia, and to extinguish the slave trade between the Southern states. As proof of this contention the paper quoted the New York *Tribune's* editorials which endorsed such a program.[105] A little later it urged Southern congressmen to make their fight on the admission of California and check the abolitionists at the threshold.[106]

When Congress, with a membership of 112 Democrats, 105 Whigs, and thirteen Free Soilers, convened on December 3, 1849, every one foresaw a contest. The South realized that her "peculiar institutions" and "rights" were in danger. In his message, Taylor advised that California should be admitted under her constitution, but that New Mexico should be left alone until ready for admission.[107] Because of the President's refusal to commit himself, the Southern Whigs were still uncertain as to the course to take in case the Wilmot Proviso should pass Congress.[108] The Toombs Whigs, therefore, decided to make a test on the election of the Speaker.[109] When the caucus nominated John Winthrop of Massachusetts, Toombs and five other Southerners, including Jeremiah Morton of Virginia, refused to vote for him because of his stand on the Proviso.[110] In the course of the balloting the Democrats shifted to Brown of Ohio whom the Free Soilers supported, and who, an investigation showed, had promised to appoint committees which would assist in the passage of the Wilmot Proviso.[111] The excitement which followed caused R. K. Meade of Virginia to make such a pro-Southern speech that Duer of New York called him a disunionist. The lie was passed and, except for interference, a fight would have followed.[112] A deadlock ensued until three weeks later when a rule was adopted permitting the candidate receiving a plurality to become Speaker. The result was the selection of Howell Cobb, a Georgia Democrat.

During this controversy over the election of Speaker and while feelings were being stirred by the continued agitation of the Wilmot Proviso, the problem of slavery and the slave trade in the District of Columbia again came up. So long as it had been merely a matter of territories which were by nature unfitted for slavery, many Virginia Whigs had been moderately indifferent. But now that the question was more pertinent they became alarmed. This party's organ for instance declared: "Believing as they [Southern people] do, that the act of abolishing slavery in the District of Columbia would . . . be . . . dangerous, and unconstitutional, they already ask themselves, if we submit now, what can we expect hereafter? Can we have any security for the observance of any of the guaranties of the constitution?"[113] In the midst of the congressional fight which this provoked, the movement for a Southern convention developed.

The heated contest in Congress and the press war in the autumn and December of 1849 caused many extremists, whose Southern unity program of the year before had been threatened by the Whigs,[114] to look to a Southern convention as a means of gaining redress either in or out of the Union. Consequently, encouraged by South Carolina, Mississippi in October, 1849, issued a call to the other slave states to hold such a gathering at Nashville.[115] At first this plan was enthusiastically received by most of the slave states. Even Maryland's House of Delegates expressed its willingness to send representatives.[116] In Virginia the Richmond *Enquirer* on October 16, 1849, declared that the Mississippi proposal offered the best means for saving the Union as well as the preservation of Southern rights. Moreover, it continued, a declaration of a united South would gain the support of the masses in the North.[117] Certainly, it stated in a later editorial, the times demanded redress of some kind, for Virginia was losing around $300,000 annually through the escaping fugitive slaves, and her institutions would be less secure if the proposed abolition of slavery in the District of Columbia went through.[118]

While this organ of the conservative Ritchie wing of the Democratic party was advocating adherence to the Nashville Convention as a means of warning the North and of saving the Union, a small group of extremists such as Edmund Ruffin,[119] M. R. H. Garnett, J. M. Mason, Governor John B. Floyd, and Nathaniel Beverly Tucker were intent on gaining complete satisfaction in Congress; otherwise they would support separation.[120] Tucker probably preferred a dissolution of the Union to redress.[121] For some time he had been urging J. H. Hammond and William Gilmore Simms, with whom he carried on a continuous correspondence, to lead South Carolina on and Virginia from necessity would follow.[122] Calhoun seems to have expected Virginia to coöperate at Nashville, for in a letter to Hammond, January 4, 1850, he stated that the congressmen from Virginia "speak with confidence that delegates will be appointed by the State."[123]

Two days before Calhoun wrote this letter, J. H. Claiborne of Franklin County offered in the House of Delegates a resolution calling for a committee on Federal affairs. This was amended so as to provide for the appointment of delegates to the Nashville Convention.[124] At the same time, in presenting the Vermont resolutions which called for the restriction of slavery in the territories and for abolition in the District of Columbia, Governor Floyd declared to the legislature that "the time has already passed for the discussion of the question between us; no human reason or eloquence can stop the headlong career of injury and wrong which the North is pursuing towards us." Consequently, he recommended that the South should defend herself and that as a move in that direction Virginia should send delegates to Nashville.[125] Claiborne's report as amended was referred to a joint committee which on January 30 recommended a more moderate set of resolutions.[126] The original plan provided for the appointment of four delegates by the legislature, the selection of others by congressional districts in the regular spring election, and the payment of all expenses by the state;[127] those of the joint committee directed that in case the Wilmot Proviso were passed or slavery were abolished in the District of Columbia, the Governor should have delegates elected to a state convention which would "take into consideration the mode and measure of redress, . . . appoint delegates to a Southern convention, and . . . adopt such measures as the crisis may demand." The latter neither required that under the existing condition representatives to Nashville should be elected, nor provided for the state paying their expenses. It only "recommended" the selection of delegates to the congressional district conventions and advised that these gatherings elect representatives from each party to go to Nashville.[128] This alteration was made by the Whig leaders who considered the whole affair useless but who wanted to satisfy their eastern constituents.[129]

As a result of this change even the Richmond *Whig* said that no harm could be done.[130] With little opposition the measure passed the senate by a vote of twenty to seven and the house by an even larger majority.[131] When Cook of Greensville introduced other resolutions providing for the state's paying the expenses of the delegates, his motion for their adoption was indefinitely postponed.[132]

In the contest over the original Claiborne resolutions, the Democratic speakers and press consistently maintained in reply to the Whigs' cry of "disunion" that the purpose of the Southern convention was not to dissolve the Union but to unite the South in defense of her rights in the Union. It would, they said, "exert a moral influence in satisfying the North *that we are in earnest.*"[133] *The Tenth Legion* in Shenandoah County declared that few were for secession, but that the permanency of the confederacy depended "upon a *bold, decided, and patriotic policy, on the part of the South,* for the Union, the Whole Union, and nothing but the Union."[134]

At first the Whigs were afraid of the movement. Their organ contended that a Southern convention would do no good; it might do harm; and it would at least be an expense to the state.[135] Before the joint committee's report supplanted the Claiborne plan, the Lynchburg *Virginian* added: "Disguise it as you will, the object of this Convention is to familiarize the public mind with the idea of dissolution."[136] After this report, however, the Whigs felt that the Nashville Convention's decision would not be binding on Virginia; and so if some wanted to kill their political future by taking part in it, they should be free to attend.[137] This quieted the tremendous opposition in the northwestern part of the state.[138] The *Republican Vindicator* (Democrat) of Staunton, at first as outspoken in its opposition as the *Whig*, was reconciled after the joint committee's report, for it did not think any harm could be done under the new arrangement.[139]

The Nashville Convention, however, was already an anathema to all except the pro-Southern Democrats. In his paper, the Washington *Union*, "Father" Ritchie, setting an example which most conservative Virginia Democratic papers from the *Enquirer* down followed, began on January 29 his campaign for conciliation. Reviewing the "glories" of the Union and pointing to the "hopes" of the future, he called upon the "patriots" of Congress to save the country from dissolution.[140] Henry Clay, Ritchie's archenemy, came forward with his proposals. Through a conference of February 10, arranged by friends of the two, a reconciliation was brought about. From this time on, these two leaders of opposite parties worked together to put through a compromise.[141] The extremists of Virginia as well as those of the lower South were indignant. J. M. Mason wrote Beverly Tucker, March 1, 1850: "After years of forbearance the South had just presented so determined a front as at least to satisfy those meddlers, that they would have to choose between separation or backing out, and were fast preparing for the latter when our people here have been cajoled to listen to terms of treaty."[142] This agreement between Clay and Ritchie was later followed by Webster's "Seventh of March" speech, which, in the minds of many Virginians, guaranteed the passage of the Clay proposals. As a result Tucker wrote Hammond, March 13, that Clay's measures were growing "here" and on March 26 that "our politicians have gone over to the compromisers."[143]

Although these tendencies killed the Nashville Convention movement in Virginia, several leaders continued to urge that delegates be sent. The *Enquirer* in an unenthusiastic tone supported this idea, and even the *Whig* did not object.[144] In a series of open letters to the *Enquirer* one writer begged the people to elect representatives in order to check the radicalism of the lower South at Nashville, for whatever course that gathering should take would affect the Old Dominion. Such a proposal in itself shows how weak the appeal had become in Virginia.[145]

In accordance with the joint resolution passed by the legislature, the Virginia delegates were to be selected at the May congressional district conventions by leaders chosen for that purpose in the county "primaries."[146] Although three such county meetings were held in February[147] before Webster's speech, most of them did not meet until the latter part of March and April. Only in the eastern part of the state were delegates finally selected. There the election of these delegates was limited generally to the regions between the James and the York in the first congressional district, south of the James in the second, and along the lower Rappahannock in the eighth. There were scattered county meetings in the Charlottesville, Portsmouth, and Mecklenburg districts.[148] Even in this eastern section not half the counties sent representatives to the conventions.[149] In some of them, instructions, in fact, were given to their representatives that, if the compromise measures should pass Congress before the Nashville Convention met, the delegates were not to attend.[150]

Several county meetings, on the other hand, not only refused to send delegates but also criticized the calling of a Southern convention. After declaring that there was no crisis which demanded such an assembly, the meeting in Albemarle County expressed its love for the Union;[151] Loudoun's reply was of a similar character.[152] After several postponements, the Richmond city "primary," by a vote of 214 to 105, agreed that it was unwise to send delegates; but to pacify the extremists, led by James A. Seddon, it resolved that a state had the right to secede.[153] In several counties which took no official action the pro-Southerners held extra-legal "primaries" and sent representatives to the district conferences.[154] West of the Blue Ridge only one county, Jefferson, the home of J. M. Mason, elected representatives to the district conference.[155]

The congressional conferences were held in May. In March and April, Congressman W. O. Goode expressed the view that, so far as Virginia was concerned, Webster's speech had destroyed the Nashville Convention, but that the pro-Southern Democrats should exert themselves to have full representation from the eastern section of the state even though they could not hold the Valley and the western portions.[156] Such was the attitude of several leaders of this faction.[157]

The first district conference was held, May 3, at Hampton, Elizabeth City County. With a moderately full delegation from Williamsburg, Lancaster, New Kent, York, and Northumberland, this was one of the best attended conventions. It elected Nathaniel Beverly Tucker and R. H. Claybrook.[158] Four days later the fifth district held its meeting at Charlottesville with only nineteen county representatives present — twelve from Albemarle who were elected extra-legally, three from Madison, two from Greene, and one each from Bedford and Amherst.[159] Orange had selected representatives, but none appeared; and Nelson held no county meeting.[160] Of the nineteen present at the Charlottesville convention only one was a Whig despite the fact that this was one of the strongest Whig centers.[161] William F. Gordon and B. F. Barbour were selected to go to Nashville.

The following day the second district convention met at Lawrenceville in Brunswick County. Although Brunswick and Greensville alone had selected sixty-one representatives, there were only forty-nine from all counties present—twenty-seven Whigs and twenty-two Democrats.[162] William Goode made a strong states' rights speech which, although not advocating a division of the Union, some considered too radical.[163] In spite of his extreme views, however, he was selected to go to Nashville as the Democratic representative. With him Thomas S. Gholson, a

Whig, was chosen.[164] The other congressional district conferences were as poorly attended as the ones already referred to.[165]

Of the fourteen delegates selected from the seven out of the fifteen districts in the state, only six appeared at Nashville—Newton, Claybrook, Gordon, Goode, Gholson, Tucker.[166] Henry A. Wise and James Lyons refused to go.[167] In an open letter of May 25, Lyons explained that he expected the compromise measures to pass Congress and until those were voted upon the Nashville Convention should not act.[168] Of the six Virginia delegates present Nathaniel Beverly Tucker, a states' rights Whig, was the only out-and-out disunionist.[169] Less rabid than Tucker were W. O. Goode who favored protecting the South in the Union if possible and who rejoiced that Webster's speech gave a hope for further concessions, Willoughby Newton a Whig and extreme states' rights man who in the later fifties became a strong proponent of secession but who in 1850 felt that the Southern rights could be preserved in the Union, William F. Gordon of Albemarle, the only Virginia delegate to appear at the second session of the Nashville Convention, and R. H. Claybrook.[170] T. S. Gholson of Brunswick County, a capitalist, lawyer, and judge, was in 1850 strongly pro-Union in his sympathies. He balanced Tucker's radicalism.[171]

The Nashville Convention held its first session on June 3, while the compromise measures were being discussed in Congress. Its members realized that the half-hearted support of the several states in selecting delegates, along with the progress of the compromise measures, would prevent radical accomplishments. Consequently, after drawing up resolutions which set forth the grievances of the South and after agreeing to R. B. Rhett's address to the Southern people, which expressed the belief that sooner or later disunion must come because of the diversity of interests between the sections, the convention adjourned to await the action of Congress.[172] All the Virginia delegates signed the resolutions and all except Gholson approved Rhett's address.[173] Of the speeches made by the Virginians two stand out, Gholson's for the conservatives and Tucker's for the extremists. The former declared that he desired to use every effort "under heaven" to save the Union; he believed that it could be preserved "without sacrifice of rights or honor"; he "loved the south more than the union and would never agree that she should be subjected to shame or humiliation"; and, therefore, he wanted amendments to Clay's compromise, but he thought the original resolutions would serve as a basis for a settlement which would guarantee the South's safety.[174]

Following Gholson's conservative speech, Tucker in his address satisfied even the secessionists of South Carolina. He maintained that amendments to Clay's plan could not be put through; that delay only meant further degradation to the South; and that disunion would not bring war, because the value of cotton and Southern trade to the Northern manufacturers and shippers was too great. He felt that if the cotton states would withdraw, the border states would follow. Let Virginia be told, he said, that "she must fight somebody, and she will not be long in deciding whom she will fight."[175] Finally he ended with a picture of the "glories" of a Southern confederacy.[176]

The resolutions and address of the Nashville Convention received slight attention in Virginia. The people were too concerned over the discussion in Congress to retain interest in resolutions of a discredited gathering. In order to retain harmony in their party, the Ritchie Democrats attempted to justify the convention by insisting that its purpose from the beginning had been to gain a united South and not to split the Union. They contended, furthermore, that the South had not gained from Clay's compromise all that she deserved, but that in the circumstances Virginia Democrats would consent to it, "not only as saving their honor, giving peace to the agitated elements, and crushing the fanatical free-soilers, but as securing much that would be otherwise lost."[177] In its approval of the resolutions of the Nashville Convention, this Democratic organ emphasized the statement of principles and grievances in the address and overlooked the part which declared dissolution inevitable.[178] It regretted, furthermore, "the inflamatory character of some of the speeches."[179]

The Calhoun party in Virginia made a severe attack on the *Enquirer* for its change of front from an earlier championship of the Nashville gathering and an insistence that delegates should be sent. William O. Goode and the Lynchburg *Republican* felt that the South should never have given in until 36° 30′ had been gained, and blamed the *Enquirer* for not holding up the Southern cause. In reply to this attack, the latter stated that it had changed only when the people had refused to send a delegation, and that with other Southern leaders it had turned to Congress to obtain, through a compromise, the best that it could. But, it asserted, if the compromise measures should fail to pass it would be for an "extreme" course.[180]

As the organ of the Whig party, on the other hand, the Richmond *Whig* declared that Virginia would have nothing to do with the Rhett disunionists' idea, and that it was fortunate for many elected delegates that they could not go to Nashville as it would be a dishonorable attachment. "Treason," it asserted, "can find no foothold here: no man can rise in a public assembly, avow himself a Disunionist, and live, politically, one moment after it."[181] Later in an editorial on Tucker's rabid speech, the *Whig* declared that his position was not even that of the delegates who attended the convention and certainly not that of Virginia as a whole. It regretted that this came from a professor at William and Mary College for it was dangerous for the minds of the Virginia youth to be "polluted by political poison" and "their hearts alienated from the love of that Union which from our cradles we are taught to cherish with almost religious devotion."[182]

Their refusal to coöperate whole-heartedly at Nashville did not mean that Virginia leaders were indifferent to the complaints common in the South. Instead, it indicates that they thought the best means of gaining guarantees was through Congress; so it was there that they exerted their influence.

In the resolutions of 1847 and 1849 Virginia had taken "high ground."[183] When Clay first introduced his measures of adjustment, she had not been enthusiastic for them. The *Enquirer*, February 5, 1850, stated that "all the ravings of Northern fanatics, together with the aggressive spirit constantly exhibited by Congress put together, have not filled our minds with such a feeling of despondency, as these Resolutions of Mr. Clay's." There was not "one controverted question," it continued, "between the North and the South, which is not fully surrendered to the North by the terms of these resolutions."[184] The Lynchburg *Republican*, a pro-Southern organ, maintained that the South could not make a more dangerous concession, and that if these resolutions were adopted "southern rights will be a mere empty name, and southern property in slaves a thing, that *has* been but *is* not."[185] At first even the papers which supported Taylor were hostile to Clay's plan.[186] The orthodox Richmond *Whig*, February 1, 1850, declared these proposals embraced "no compromise, or rather, that all the compromise is on one. side."[187] Only the Lynchburg *Virginian*, a strong Clay and nationalistic paper, supported them from the beginning.[188]

But when Ritchie and the Whig leaders threw their weight on the side of conciliation, sentiment in Virginia began to change.[189] Only the Hunter faction of the Democratic party and a few pro-Southern Whigs like Tucker continued to fight the Compromise. To the followers of Hunter, Ritchie was a traitor to the Southern cause. Nevertheless, a majority sentiment was created for the measures.

Clay introduced his resolutions in the Senate January 29. At the same time by a vote of 105 to seventy-five, the House tabled the Wilmot Proviso, thereby causing the South to be less outspoken for secession.[190] Webster's speech in March increased the possibilities of a settlement. Even Calhoun Democrats in Virginia praised this effort.[191] Ritchie was already writing editorials on the "glories" of the Union and emphasizing the compromise character of the past relations of the states in the Union.[192] On February 10 he made peace with Clay. Thereafter the two were at the same time exerting their influence and appealing to other "patriots" to assist in saving the "Union of the Fathers."[193]

In accordance with the suggestion of Ritchie and Senator Foote of Mississippi, the Clay reports were referred to a committee, on which the pro-Southerner, J. M. Mason, represented Virginia.[194] This committee reported May 8. Taylor opposed the California boundary, the territorial bills for New Mexico and Utah, and the boundary claims of Texas in the Clay program.[195] As long as Taylor lived the Compromise was in danger. Even the conservative Richmond *Whig* was unenthusiastic in its support of Clay until Fillmore came into power.[196] Consequently, after July 9 when Taylor died, pressure was exerted by several factions to make Virginia congressmen vote for the measure. Ex-President Tyler who still had a limited amount of influence threw in his support,[197] and meetings were held in different counties to bring public sentiment to bear.[198]

In the United States Senate both Virginia Senators, Hunter and Mason, were of the Calhoun wing of the Democratic party. Naturally, therefore, they opposed most of the Compromise. On the admission of California August 13, the Texas boundary August 9, and the restriction of the domestic slave trade in the District of Columbia September 16, they voted in the negative;[199] but they supported the New Mexican territorial bill and the fugitive slave act.[200] Along with eight other Southern Democrats they signed a protest against the admission of California as a free state.[201] For this they were accused of disunion activities, an accusation that Hunter denied.[202]

In the House of Representatives the Virginia congressmen gave a majority of their votes for all the provisions except the admission of California and the restriction of the slave trade in the District of Columbia. On the last two all but one Whig, T. H. Haymond, and one Democrat, J. M. H. Beale, both from west of the Alleghanies, voted in the negative with the other Southern Democrats.[203] But on the Utah, Texas boundary, New Mexico, and fugitive slave provisions the majority were in the affirmative.[204] The pro-Southern members, including A. R. Holla-

day, R. K. Meade, and James A. Seddon, opposed even the Utah measure.[205] T. H. Averett, John S. Millson, and Paulus Powell joined them in
opposing the Texas boundary and New Mexican proposals which were
voted on together.[206] Holladay, Meade, Seddon, Averett, Millson, and
Powell were from east of the Blue Ridge. T. H. Bayly of the Eastern
Shore joined those from the Valley, the Albemarle Whig district, and
those from west of the Alleghanies in their support of most of the measures. These votes in the House were in the main sectional. They show
that the extreme eastern, the northern, and the western parts of the state
were for the Compromise and that nearly all the Piedmont and the Tidewater were against most of its provisions.[207]

Shortly after the Compromise had been passed most Virginians seemed to be reconciled to its distasteful provisions. The *Enquirer* explained
that all that it had desired had not been obtained, but that under the
existing conditions the South had gained as much as was possible.[208]
Congressman Bayly explained to his constituents that the South had
really profited by the agreements.[209] By reminding the voters that those
Virginians who had voted in the negative were Democrats and that their
leadership, had it been adhered to, would have brought disunion, the
Richmond *Whig* hoped to strengthen its party's position.[210] This powerful mouthpiece insisted that all candidates should swear their ac-
quiescence.[211] In support of this recommendation several party county
meetings pledged to vote for no one who was opposed to it.[212] At the
state convention, September 25, resolutions endorsing the agreement of
the sections and denouncing "any attempt to disturb those measures of
peace *as* a blow aimed at the integrity of the Union" were adopted.[213] So
certain were the Whigs that sentiment was for the Compromise and
against disunion, they made the right of secession the issue in the next
congressional campaign.[214]

The Democrats were not united in their acceptance of the measures.
While the Ritchie conservative wing rejoiced in the settlement, it could
not afford to disregard openly the feelings of the Hunter group. The
Enquirer, therefore, advocated the acceptance of the Compromise only
as a necessity and not as a fair adjustment.[215] But the attachment of
these conservatives to the sectional agreement was so strong that J. M.
Mason, in order to regain his nomination when a candidate for reëlection to the Senate in December, 1850, had to declare that even though
he disapproved the settlement he would follow the dictates of Virginia.
At the same time, he expressed his loyalty to the Union.[216] Many Democrats supported him because they thought he would uphold the Com-

promise, and because his election would convince the North that Virginia expected that section to live up to the fugitive slave law.[217] In January of the next year considerable excitement arose when a member of the House of Delegates stated that at the time of this senatorial election Mason looked upon his reëlection as an endorsement of his opposition to the Compromise. Resolutions to the effect that Virginia would support this settlement were introduced. By a vote of fifty-nine to fifty-five these were postponed indefinitely on the ground that they would "merely bring up feeling when there should be quiet."[218] The Lynchburg *Republican*, which remained hostile to the Compromise, declared that these resolutions were not only an attempt to commit Virginia to "one of the most infamous measures of plunder and outrage that ever disgraced the statute books of our country," but also a scheme of the Whigs to furnish capital for the congressional elections in the spring.[219]

A few of the Hunter wing continued to disapprove of it. At heart J. M. Mason was hostile. In a memorandum written in August, 1851, he declared that this "pseudo compromise . . . will, in its consequences, be found fatal, either to the Union of the States, or to the institution of slavery."[220] M. R. H. Garnett, the author of a forceful pamphlet on the points at issue in 1850,[221] in a letter to W. H. Trescott of South Carolina, May, 1851, advised South Carolina to secede, and if force should be applied, Virginia would probably come to her rescue.[222] Others in this faction were dissatisfied.[223] Nevertheless, the majority of all parties concurred.

Although both political parties outwardly accepted the Compromise, the controversy did not end in Virginia with the passage through Congress of these measures. The continued threats of secession in South Carolina and the repudiation of the fugitive slave law by many in the North kept the feeling alive.[224] In reply to South Carolina's invitation to a second Southern conference, the General Assembly, after expressing its sympathies for Calhoun's state, declared that the people of Virginia were "unwilling to take any action . . . calculated to destroy the integrity of this Union."[225]

On the fugitive slave law and its reception by the North there was considerable uniformity of sentiment in Virginia. Even the western Democrats and eastern Whigs felt that the North had been unfair on this issue. Speaking in the House of Delegates, December 15, 1848, C. J. Faulkner stated that in the preceding month Berkeley County alone had lost forty-two "valuable slaves" through the abolitionists' influence; that Jefferson, Clarke, and Frederick counties had suffered slightly less;

and that Virginia's loss from this source amounted to "fully $90,000" annually. In comparison with this the Wilmot Proviso was unimportant.[226]

Among the Compromise measures, Mason's fugitive slave bill had caused many border-state people to feel that it would guarantee the safety of their property.[227] The expression of hostility to the measure by many prominent Northerners, the increased activities of the underground railroad, and the rescue of slaves in Boston and other Northern cities in 1851, however, tended to disabuse the South of this hope. Departing from his usual course of refraining from entering into political discussions, the conservative editor of the *Southern Literary Messenger,* John R. Thompson, declared: "We say to the people of the North then not as alarmists, but as those who love the Union of our fathers, in no spirit of menace but rather in that of expostulation, that in our judgment *the continued existence of the United States as one nation, depends upon the full and faithful executions of the Fugitive Slave Bill.*"[228] Even the Union-loving Richmond *Whig* declared that if the Northern states attempted to repeal this law "then in our humble opinion the value of the Union will be speedily calculated. If a majority of the people deliberately violate a right secured to us by the Constitution, it will be impossible to maintain with them peaceful and fraternal relations."[229] In censuring the Boston mob in the "Shadrach case," this paper reminded the North that the violation in this way of Southern constitutional rights "will not be suffered to pass or submitted to with impunity."[230] Even the northwestern Parkersburg *Gazette* preferred disunion to submitting to a repeal of this law.[231] The *Enquirer* recommended that if this hostility to the Constitution continued, retribution through the seizure of Boston ships should be resorted to.[232]

As a retaliation for the Northern hostility to the fugitive slave law, a considerable element in Virginia advised the boycotting of Northern goods. This idea, suggested in the Proviso period, was frequently offered as a remedy throughout the whole controversy. In February, 1849, a correspondent of the *Enquirer* proposed the levy of a license fee of $1,000 on retail merchants and $10,000 on wholesalers trading in goods manufactured in any state which refused to suppress abolition societies.[233] Believing that "the patriotism of the Yankee lies almost exclusively in his pocket," the Lynchburg *Republican* endorsed the *Enquirer's* program.[234] In his special message to the legislature on Ohio's refusal to return a fugitive slave, Governor John B. Floyd, March 12, 1850, recommended a tax on Northern goods as the only means to secure redress.[235] In December of the same year he repeated the recommendation.[236] Others also advised the fostering of Southern economic independence.[237]

From this sentiment developed the Southern Rights Association whose purpose at first was retaliation and resistance. Soon this organization was changed into an agency for agitating economic independence as the only hope of the South. Such agitation particularly marked the Prince George County association, founded by Edmund Ruffin.[238] In compliance with these purposes it resolved in its November meeting to buy no goods manufactured in the North, until the free states' "aggression on our rights and property ceases, and also use our most strenuous efforts to build up Southern commerce and manufacturers."[239] Before the year was over, a central association, including the counties around Richmond and such leaders as Governor Floyd, James A. Seddon, and D. H. London, had been formed.[240] In its meetings in December and January this body advocated steamship lines from Virginia to Europe, to the West Indies, and to South America.[241] It petitioned the legislature to levy a tax on Northern goods as a means of developing Southern manufactures and urged merchants to buy Southern or foreign goods rather than Northern.[242] Nothing, however, came of this. The Whigs opposed the movement on the ground that the association was too closely tied to disunion agitation and that a tax on Northern goods would be unwise and unconstitutional. Even Democrats from western Virginia refused to join eastern members of their party in passing the tax and license bill. Consequently, about all the association accomplished was to perfect an organization which was later used for economic retaliation against the North.[243]

The secession and disunion discussions which were common in the lower South during the controversy over the Proviso received, as has been indicated, little attention in Virginia as an immediate remedy. Most of the expressions about dissolution had been more in the nature of threats than programs. Since their chief aim was to gain redress through Congress, they gave little attention to the right of secession. As the tension of the struggle lessened, a contest involving this abstract right of secession developed throughout the South.[244] It was the plan of the "Southern Rights" Democrats to regain the support of the Union Democrats which they had lost in the Compromise discussion.[245]

In Virginia before the congressional campaign opened, the *Enquirer* had made the issue by suggesting that the second session of the Nashville Convention should content itself with an affirmation of the "right of secession—a conservative principle of our Confederacy, which cannot properly be denied, and which can alone save us from consolidated tyranny."[246] The Richmond *Whig,* quickly accepting this as an issue for the campaign, pretended at first to doubt the sincerity of the Democratic organ and to wonder at the meaning of the doctrine. Beginning by admitting that if the right of secession meant "that ultimate and inalienable right which every oppressed people have to redress by the sword the evils they suffer at the hand of Government," it would not be denied by anyone; but if it "is a principle lying *within* our Confederacy, and which may be exercised in accordance with the great charter that holds it together, we . . . are not able to comprehend the proposition. . . . No government is ever so suicidal as to provide for its own demolition."[247]

The *Enquirer,* in reply, thought it strange that the Whig paper did not remember what "nearly every one in Virginia accepted." It reminded the *Whig* that states were sovereign before the Union was formed, that under the Articles of Confederation the sovereignty of the states was recognized by all, and that in ratifying the Federal Constitution, Virginia had specifically declared her adherence to the right of a state to withdraw. Moreover, it continued, in 1798 and 1799 Virginia had very definitely stated her acceptance of state sovereignty. The doctrine that "secession is the basis of, inherent in, and inseparable from the idea of compact, conferring a right, when the compact is broken, of peaceable withdrawal from the confederation, does not directly and necessarily involve . . . calamitous consequence" as some seemed to think. Instead, it was the only means of guaranteeing local rights.[248]

To the *Enquirer's* argument that the Virginia ratification ordinance and the resolutions of 1798-1799 justified secession, the *Whig* replied that the ratification ordinance was merely a matter of form and had no intrinsic value, and that if it were granted that these resolutions were correct, it should be remembered that they were approved by only one state. Besides, these resolutions were drawn up by Madison who in a letter of 1833 stated: "I do not consider the proceedings of Virginia in 1798-1799 as countenancing the doctrine that a state may *at will* secede from its constitutional compact with the other states. A rightful secession requires the consent of the others, or an abuse of the compact . . . ."[249]

When the South Carolina invitation to Virginia to join in a Southern convention came up for consideration in 1851, the debate shifted to the powers of the Federal Government to enforce laws in a seceded state.

The *Enquirer* argued that sovereign states could not be forced. In support of this it referred to Virginia's position upon receipt of Jackson's proclamation against South Carolina in 1832.[250] The *Whig,* on the contrary, contended that if South Carolina seceded the Federal laws would still prevail in that state for the central government rested on individuals and not on states; consequently, the President in performing his constitutional duties would not deal with the state in its corporate capacity but with individuals who violated such laws—[251] a doctrine later repudiated by many Whigs.[252] Furthermore, "secession, without the assent of other parties to the compact, is revolution. . . . It will be proper to consider, that there are involved in the compact between the states, reciprocal rights growing out of the results of our political association" and so "there can be no secession which does not implicate or impair the relative rights of others; and that is in itself revolution."[253]

In the political campaigns for which this issue had been raised by the two party organs, the Whigs selected strong nationalists such as John M. Botts for Congress and G. W. Summers for Governor. The Democrats, however, were careful to endorse the Compromise, to pledge their loyalty to the Union, and to declare that there was no occasion, as South Carolina seemed to think, for disunion.[254] They selected conservative Democrats for their candidates. Judge John Caskie, for instance, replaced the extremist James A. Seddon, a former congressman from the Richmond district.

T. S. Bocock, Democratic candidate of the Lynchburg district, was called on by his party to explain the conservative character of the Democratic position. He declared that he sympathized with South Carolina's complaint, and that he would therefore entreat her to refrain from radical steps that would lead to dangers which no one could measure, and if it came to the point of surrendering "the Union or our liberty . . . then we too will appeal to our reserved rights."[255] In his contest with Bolling in the Lynchburg district he added a defense of the right of secession. Bolling, on the other hand, did not hold to the extreme view of the Botts school. He denied, instead, that peaceful secession was possible, although he did not commit himself on its legality. His emphasis was on the contention that no cause for dissolution existed. He admitted that as a last resort a state should judge for herself "whether she would submit to or resist such action of the United States Government, as in her judgment was oppressive and tyrannical." To him the extent of the grievance determined the justification for disunion. He dodged the legal issue.[256] In the Shenandoah district Henry Bedinger, the states' rights Democrat, after declaring his acceptance of the Compromise of 1850, expressed his "unqualified acceptance of the right of secession" as a last resort.[257]

The congressional contest in which this constitutional question was the chief issue was between John Minor Botts, the Clay nationalist who remained loyal to the Union in 1861-1865, and Judge John Caskie, the conservative Democrat who replaced Seddon. This contest was in the Richmond district which because of the large city vote was usually carried by the Whigs. In the several joint debates Caskie, after first declaring his adherence to the Compromise and his love for the Union, repeated the arguments advanced by the *Enquirer* before the campaign began.[258] Botts not only denied the right of secession, but also declared that it was the duty of the President to enforce the Federal laws in South Carolina should she attempt to withdraw from the Union.

As for 'peaceful secession' [he said], I look upon that as one of the most ridiculous, abstract humbugs ever talked about upon earth— The idea that any one State in this Union has a right to dissolve this Confederacy after entering into this perpetual compact—the idea that South Carolina, which has a right to claim protection from every other State in the Union, can withdraw from the Union and form a league with Great Britain or any other foreign power without the power on the part of the rest of the States, for self-protection, to coerce her into submission—is the most ridiculous abstraction ever entertained by human mind, . . . [and a President who would not enforce the laws in a state when Federal laws were resisted] would be a foresworn felon.[259]

In all the eastern congressional contests where the right of secession was made the issue by the nationalistic Whigs, the Democrats won. Even the normally Whig districts of Charlottesville and Richmond went Democratic.[260] Success, however, was not entirely due to the constitutional question for this was only one of the issues.[261] In Richmond the Democratic victory was partly due to the dislike of many Whigs for Botts, who had antagonized the younger leaders in the Clay-Taylor campaign.[262] Furthermore, the defeat of the Whigs in Virginia was only a part of a general decline of the party throughout the South.[263] They were too closely allied to the Seward anti-slavery Whigs in the North to retain support there.

The nationalistic Whigs, with G. W. Summers as their candidate, continued the fight in the gubernatorial contest against the right of secession. Hoping to gain the western part of the state, Summers repeated the Botts argument.[264] In this he was disappointed, for the popular Joseph Johnson of the northwest won by a six thousand majority.[265]

The nationalistic and anti-secession position of the Whigs in the campaign of 1851 did not represent the feeling of the states' rights faction. From this latter group Jeremiah Morton, congressman from Orange, and C. W. Russell of Wheeling went over to the Democrats. The Norfolk and Portsmouth *Herald* and the Richmond *Republican* in their editorials openly criticized the Richmond *Whig's* position.[266] This campaign marked another step in the division of the party.[267]

CHAPTER III

PARTY POLITICS, 1851–1859

I N THE decade following the Compromise, the question of Southern safety was ever present in the minds of Southern leaders. Radicals, such as Yancey and Rhett from the lower South and Ruffin and Tucker from Virginia, insisted that there was no security for their institutions in the Union. After each sectional controversy of this period, these agitators emphasized with renewed vigor this contention. Their crusade* had its effect on party history, so that in each party there were factional quarrels centering in the issue even though personalities frequently overshadowed it. In this chapter a review of these political struggles within Virginia will be made, partly with a view to giving a background for the more serious sectional strife of 1860-1861 and partly with a view to tracing the growing Southern unity in politics.

Party history in Virginia from 1851 to the Brown raid in October, 1859, is divided into two distinct periods. The first extends from 1851 to the presidential election of 1856. During it the slavery issue except for the Kansas-Nebraska debate was dormant; the Democrats were more or less harmonious and all-powerful; and the Whigs were disorganized and split into factions. The second period covers the years, 1857 to 1859. In it the personal feud between Henry A. Wise and Senator Hunter was so influential a factor that until the Charleston Convention it overshadowed other Democratic party problems; whereas, the Whigs reorganized and consolidated their forces. At the same time, there appeared in the North a new party which, with the Kansas problem, kept alive the slavery and disunion discussions. These in turn became an important part of party history in Virginia.

In the introductory chapter of this study, party alignments as they existed in 1847 were briefly surveyed, and in the discussion of the years 1847-1851 the position of the respective parties and factions on the issues of the succeeding period was indicated. It was noted in the latter connection that both parties declared their acceptance of the Compromise. Even the "Southern Rights" Democrats, in form at least, ac-

---

*This is discussed in chapter IV.

quiesced. The Whigs not only endorsed it but, being under the domination of the nationalistic Botts-Summers wing, denied the right of secession in the campaign of 1851.

In that year, Thomas Ritchie, who with the Richmond "junto" had for many years controlled the organization of the Democratic party, and who by checking the Nashville Convention movement in Virginia had kept his party safe for the Compromise, retired from public life.[1] This left the old wing without a leader to hold it together. Ritchie's chief support had come from the western section of the state, and this region became more important in politics after the constitutional changes of 1850-1851.[2] In the election following these changes, Joseph Johnson was elected Governor, the first candidate from west of the Blue Ridge to win this honor. Johnson, however, did not attempt to assume Ritchie's former position as party director.

The contest between the Ritchie element, commanded by the remnant of the "junto" which was fast breaking up, and the Hunter "Southern Rights" faction continued after Ritchie's withdrawal from politics. Into this struggle of the early fifties, first as a supporter of Hunter and later as his rival, came Henry A. Wise. Wise was an aggressive leader who frequently changed sides but, regardless of his stand on issues, carried many followers with him. A Tyler Whig in the Jackson period, he went over to the Democrats in the forties. Upon his return in 1848 from Brazil, where he had served as minister, he supported the "Southern Rights" faction in the contest of 1848-1851. He was elected to the Nashville Convention, but he did not attend. In a letter to Hunter, February 13, 1851, he accused Ritchie of selling out on the Compromise and of deserting the South.[3] In spite of Wise's leaning to this wing of the party, he was distrusted by its leaders. In 1852 some even expected Wise to oppose Hunter for the Senate.[4] Because of the fact that he alone of the eastern men had defended the western program in the Constitutional Convention of 1850-1851, Wise had a large following in the west.[5] In this struggle for controlling the party after Ritchie's withdrawal, therefore, Wise was an important person. Neither the "junto" nor the Hunter wing wanted his support because of his insatiable ambition, but neither faction could afford to let him go to the opposite side.

These two Democratic leaders in 1852, when Wise sought to have the state party agencies instruct the delegates to the national convention to vote for Buchanan, began their first contest for party leadership.[6] In the hope of nominating a Southern man for the presidency, Hunter's supporters opposed this plan. Inasmuch as the former position was in accord with the traditional policy of the Virginia Democrats, it was carried through.[7] After the nomination of Pierce the leaders of both elements joined to carry the state for the ticket. In the following year by a system of "gerrymandering" all congressional seats were won by them.[8]

Wise without consulting Hunter announced in 1854 his candidacy for Governor. In his effort to gain this nomination he enhanced his prospects by a popular attack on the American movement. Since the defeats of 1851 and 1852, the Whigs had been discredited and disorganized, and in 1852, as a means of regaining their lost strength, they joined the Know-Nothings. Taking advantage of this situation, Wise in one of his most effective open letters, September, 1854, attacked the movement as an abolitionist and fanatical undertaking.[9] His letter not only won for him the title of "tribune of the people" but also strengthened his candidacy. He had the state convention to meet early—November, 1854 —at Staunton, near his western supporters; and in that body he had the traditional two-thirds rule abolished.[10] The minority not only refused to make his nomination unanimous but several of the Ritchie wing, such as John Letcher, Fayette McMullen, and Ex-Governor William Smith, refused to support him in the campaign that followed.[11] The Hunter faction remained loyal,[12] and Wise was elected by a majority of 10,180, which was smaller than that given to Pierce before and to Buchanan after him; but it exceeded the normal gubernatorial majority.* As Governor and titular head of his party, Wise had the usual control of the party machinery and state appointments.[13] At the same time, by supporting internal improvements, he increased his popularity in the west.[14]

During the years 1851-1856 the Whigs were divided into two groups, not entirely unlike those of the Democrats before Wise returned to state politics. This Whig division began in the presidential campaign of 1848 when John M. Botts and John Janney continued to support Clay after seeing that the majority of the Virginia Whigs were for Taylor.[15] In defending his position, Botts carried on a heated controversy through the Whig newspapers with John S. Pendleton, T. S. Flournoy, T. Fulton, and W. B. Preston, the champions of Taylor.[16] This conflict probably cost the Whigs Virginia's electoral vote in 1848.[17] As a result, the supporters of Taylor disciplined Botts by permitting the Democratic candidate, Judge John Caskie, to defeat him for Congress

---

*The vote in the election is analyzed on pages 95-96.

in 1851. This Whig division which began as a personal conflict soon resulted in nationalistic and states' rights wings with Botts, Summers, and Janney leading the former, and W. B. Preston, T. S. Flournoy, and W. L. Goggin leading the latter.

In the controversy over the Compromise these two groups had worked together. Although some Southern-rights-Whig leaders and newspapers had opposed the position taken by the party in the canvass of 1851, the majority of both factions, outwardly at least, remained loyal and delayed the breach in the party.[18] The Kansas-Nebraska bill completed the division. Botts and his followers opposed this measure on the ground that it abrogated the Compromise of 1850;[19] whereas the majority of the Whigs along with the Democrats maintained that it merely carried out that settlement.[20] This bill, also, split the Virginia Whigs from the Northern branch.

In the latter part of 1854, they looked to the Know-Nothing movement as a means of restoring the national organization of their party and of strengthening their position in the South. One of the Whig leaders advised the South to insist on the restriction of immigration because it endangered slavery.[21] William C. Rives, on the other hand, thought Know-Nothingism rested on too narrow a basis to build a party. It was, he maintained, merely an expression of disapproval of the Pierce Democrats and "Seward's Whiggery." Out of this disapproval, he added, might come a new party.[22] But such hopes were short lived, for Wise's complete victory in 1855 soon destroyed their hopes of success. This failure of Know-Nothingism left the Whigs without a national organization.

The Whigs and Democrats, during the period 1852-1856, differed little on the questions affecting the South. In the beginning both, outwardly at least, accepted the Compromise of 1850, although the Democrats, influenced by the "Southern Rights" element, were less outspoken in their endorsement than the Whigs. In 1851 the Democratic party championed the right of secession; but the Whigs were afraid to admit this right lest such an admission might encourage South Carolina to secede.[23] At the same time, they reminded the Northern people not to mistake their position, for they would not "tamely submit to any outrage."[24]

In the Democratic state convention of 1852, the "Southern Rights" wing led by Seddon succeeded in defeating a resolution of the "Administration Democrats" to endorse as a permanent settlement the compromise measures of 1850. He had adopted in its place propositions which adhered to the doctrine of 1798-1799 as a "fundamental principle" of the party.[25] In the same year seven of the thirteen Democratic congressmen refused to approve a resolution accepting the Compromise as a finality.[26] The Seddon element had apparently won. But in his campaign for reëlection as United States Senator, Hunter had to permit the endorsement of this settlement of 1850 before he felt confident of defeating his opponent.[27]

In spite of those various resolutions of the Democrats, the slavery issue was given little publicity during the years 1852-1853. All factions were apparently ready to stop with resolutions. But in the first months of 1854, when the Kansas-Nebraska bill was introduced, old feelings were again stirred.

Douglas reported his original bill on January 4, 1854.[28] Twelve days later Senator Dixon, a Whig of Kentucky, offered his famous amendment expressly repealing the Missouri Compromise. A few days later Douglas accepted this proposal.[29] At first the two parties of Virginia were indifferent. Neither the *Whig* nor the *Enquirer* was enough concerned to carry editorials of any force until Douglas's substitute was offered. The Winchester *Virginian* expressed the view which the Democratic papers held prior to Douglas's substitution of Dixon's proposal when it declared, "Mr. Dixon's amendment . . . is *calculated for no earthly end than the excitement of bitter and prolonged agitation.*"[30] At the same time the Richmond *Whig* declared that Douglas's maneuver was that of a "free-soiler," and expressed the fear that the bill would stir the old strife of slavery.[31] The Parkersburg *Gazette* stated that it was afraid that the gift to the South would be another wooden horse from which would issue "all sorts of plagues to torment the recipients"; that because of climatic conditions slavery would not go into the region; and that the repeal of the Missouri Compromise would only give the North an excuse to break her contract on the fugitive slave law.[32] After early February, however, the Whig papers became outspoken in their defense of the Kansas-Nebraska bill.[33] The Democratic papers had already become defenders of the measure.[34]

From early February, then, the positions of the two parties were not essentially different. In spite of some disagreements,[35] the majority in each agreed that the act only carried out the settlement of 1850. In the contest of 1848-1850, the *Enquirer* and the *Whig* had constantly argued that the Missouri Compromise was never constitutional or just, but for the sake of preserving the Union the South had acquiesced in it.[36] They held that the North, in the case of California, did not respect the Missouri Compromise;[37] that the New Mexican and Utah territorial bills by their principle of nonintervention superseded the Missouri agreement;[38] and that the territorial settlement of 1850 was intended as a final adjustment of slavery in all territories.[39] Even Henry Clay, the Virginia press reminded the North, had told Ritchie in 1850 that he considered the Compromise a revocation of the agreement of 1820.[40] While the South did not expect to gain any territory from this particular bill, she was anxious to have the principle of Southern rights in the territories recognized.[41]

It had become a sectional contest before the vote was taken in Congress. Consequently the Virginia press, as well as that of the lower South, was "greatly concerned." The *Enquirer* on March 3, 1854, declared, "There has never been a dispute between the South and its enemies in the North, which has excited so intense and universal an interest among the people of the South"; and that it wanted to "hang, draw and quarter without judge or jury, the southern traitor that skulks now."[42] The Petersburg *Southside Democrat* advised that the opponents of the bill should "be hanged in chains as an example and warning to traitors."[43] Nevertheless there were not so many county protests as there had been in the Wilmot Proviso period; and Millson, the only Virginia congressman to vote against the measure, continued to hold his seat in Congress down to disunion in 1861.

Instead of quieting the slavery question the Kansas-Nebraska bill increased the discussion. In the North a political party built partly on hostility to the Southern institution was organized. Leaders and organizations of both sections began sending settlers to Kansas to make that territory free or slave. Soon thereafter open war was evident in the new region, and governments representing the two factions were set up. After a protracted contest over the election of Speaker, the House of Representatives in February, 1856, began discussing the new Kansas situation. Petitions, resolutions, and reports of conditions kept alive a heated debate throughout the spring and summer. The famous "Crime against Kansas" speech of Charles Sumner indicates the hostile feelings which pervaded the halls of Congress during that period. Then came Brooks's attack on Sumner. Though many Virginians condemned this South Carolinian's method, they commended the purpose back of the attack.[44] The *Kanawha Valley Star*, June 11, 1856, for instance, declared: "It was a glorious act . . . and we must ardently hope this good and great work will be kept up, until every foulmouth slanderer of Southern institutions will know that if he does abuse and

villify the South, *he does so at the peril of his hide."* Likewise some
approved meeting "Sharp's rifles with Sharp's rifles" in Kansas.[45]

The election of 1856 came in the midst of the excitement. Wise and
Hunter were aspirants for Virginia's support at the forthcoming conclave. Wise's chances of the state's endorsement rested on his popularity in the west and his control of the party organization. Unfortunately, he had almost no following in other states. Realizing this
handicap, he soon threw his support to Buchanan.[46] Hunter's friends,
on the other hand, were willing to go with Wise until this Pennsylvanian's nomination seemed impossible. After that they would turn
to a conservative Southerner. To accomplish this purpose, many of
Hunter's friends were selected as delegates.[47] At the national convention, however, the "Southern Rights" faction did not have a chance to
desert Buchanan.

In spite of this factional quarrel both wings—by now Wise controlled most of the old Ritchie conservative wing—campaigned for the
national Democratic candidate. Since Wise had already destroyed
Know-Nothingism in Virginia and since the Whigs were disconsolate,
there was little doubt as to Virginia's electoral vote. The state Democrats, however, were deeply concerned about the nation. Fayette Mc-
Mullen, Democratic congressman from the southwestern part of the
state, declared in an open letter, April 8, 1856, to his constituents that
since the "avowed purpose" of the Republican party "is to carry on a
warfare against the institutions of the South" the election of the Republican candidate would dissolve the Union.[48]

Because of this peculiar interest in the outcome, John B. Floyd and
Hunter were sent into New York on a speaking tour. At Poughkeepsie
on October 1, Hunter in his calm and logical style explained the South's
position on slavery. Slavery, he said, was a practical solution of a more
serious race problem: destroy slavery and the race difficulty would still
keep the negro in economic servitude. He then tried to show that the
abolition of this institution would be the first step towards the destruction of all property; and finally he indicated what he felt the North
would lose by the disunion that would follow the election of a Republican President.[49] Floyd on the following day in a more sectional speech
at New York declared: "There is no essential difference between an
election of a President by sectional combinations, which exclude over
half the union from all participation [in] the canvass and the direct
usurpation of the office without the form of the election at all. The

usurpation differs only in degree; the spirit and intent of the Constitution are alike violated in both instances."[50]

Governor Wise went further than these two leaders. In a campaign speech at Richmond, October 20, he said:

Sir, to tell me we should submit to the election of a black Republican, under circumstances like these, when the election would be an open, overt proclamation of public war, is to tell me that Virginia and her fourteen sister slave States are already subjugated and degraded. . . . Yes, you will find hundreds that will say: . . . Oh! Wait!—Wait for some overt act— Wait for him to do some wrong! Tell me, will any person entertaining feeling of self-respect, having the spirit and courage of a man, wait to prepare for war while its cloud is on the horizon, until after the declaration is made?[51]

In a letter of August 15 he explained further that the people of Virginia were very distrustful of the North, "since the people have seen the tone of the North to be that of arrogance . . . . I tell you the country was never in such danger . . . . I shall be ready, the South will be united."[52] A little later Wise wrote that if Fremont were elected he could "arm and equip 50,000 men the next morning, ready for revolution!"[53]

In keeping with his impulsive nature, Governor Wise invited the governors of all the Southern states, except Kentucky and Missouri which did not have Democratic executives, to meet him in conference at Raleigh on October 13 to decide on a course to follow in case Fremont were elected.[54] Several years after the war he explained to Senator Henry Wilson of Massachusetts that his purpose in calling this conference was to guard against disunion, but failing in that he was for protection.[55] As a part of his plan he asked Jefferson Davis, the Secretary of War, to exchange percussion for flint muskets.[56] In submitting this request, Senator Mason urged Davis to comply. If Fremont were elected, he said, the South would secede at once and he himself would be a "candidate for the first halter."[57] Wise's conference proved a complete failure. Only the executives from South Carolina and North Carolina met him.[58] No action was taken.[59] The Richmond *Whig* declared, "True it was a miserable fizzle, the greatest of Gizzard's [Wise's] innumerable failures . . . ."[60]

These radical views of Wise were shared by Mason and Garnett.[61] But most leaders, even though they thought that the secession of the lower South might result from Fremont's election, were not ready to commit themselves to such a step.[62] The conservatives of both parties, on the other hand, although discrediting much of the "crisis cry" and asserting that the election of Fremont would not justify the secession of Virginia, were alarmed.[63] Early in the campaign the *Whig* had reminded the North that it could not "conceive of a Union after . . . the election of Fremont has been accomplished."[64] A little later this paper was frightened to find the Northern press as hostile to the South as if the two regions were at war with each other.[65] On August 12 the editor thought that if the agitation continued "disunion is only a question of time . . . . The feeling in the North towards the South is of a more angry character than ever existed between countries, not at open war."[66]

The fear that Fremont's election would produce the secession of the lower South and a contest in Virginia led the preachers of Richmond to issue a public letter to the citizens of that city entreating them "by the memory of our fathers . . . to follow the things which make for peace."[67] John Tyler wrote his son, Robert, that the Democrats of Virginia were prepared to meet "the danger in the face, . . . but there is a large minority who are entirely indisposed to any action. They wish to see the inaugural, and to await some hostile movement."[68]

With the passing of the crisis of 1856, the political parties of Virginia again turned their attention to internal party matters. The rivalry of Wise and Hunter for control of the Democratic machinery continued; and the Whigs tried to reorganize their party. In the Democratic party each group attempted to increase its strength in the other's territory—Hunter tried to hold the pro-Southern element and to gain the western part of the state; whereas Wise hoped to gain recognition among the pro-Southern element as well as to hold the western followers. The issues in which most of their struggle centered were Kansas and the territorial question.

As soon as the election was over, Wise wrote a friend that Buchanan's victory was only a respite for the South, and that preparations should be made for 1860.[69] In keeping with this view the *Enquirer,* edited by one of Wise's sons, began advocating slavery extension to all the territories of the country in order that the South might retain equality in the Senate.[70] "The South," it maintained, "must insist on the legitimate expansion of its institution."[71] The other Democratic papers, on the contrary, seemed little concerned.[72] The Richmond *Examiner* felt that the North and South should have equal representation in the Senate, but that slavery should be extended only under the terms of the Kansas-Nebraska bill.[73]

When Buchanan came to power, R. J. Walker was selected as territorial governor for Kansas.[74] Walker's policies soon provoked a heated debate between these two factions in Virginia. The Richmond *South*, recently established by Roger A. Pryor to defend the cause of the Hunter wing, disapproved this appointment even before the new governor reached Kansas.[75] The *Enquirer* shifted to a more conservative position and upheld Walker.[76] It even declared that, if the new territorial governor by guaranteeing a "fair" election should produce a free state in Kansas, he would do the South no injury.[77] At the same time the Hunter organ contended that the loss of Kansas would force the South to "relinquish all hopes of extending its institutions and of regaining its lost equality in the Union."[78] In this contention the *South* was backed by the Lynchburg *Republican* which advised Buchanan that if he wished his administration to be a success he should risk "little of his reputation upon Walker."[79]

In the controversy Wise was posing as the leader of the national administration and conservative Democrats of Virginia. Hunter's friends saw the advantage of remaining, outwardly at least, loyal to the administration even though they liked neither Walker's program nor Wise's leadership. Consequently, they decided not to attack the President but to show their disapproval of Walker and await events.[80] In accordance with this plan, Hunter wrote the editor of the Norfolk *Argus* that he had never said or done anything against the administration. Pryor was advised to direct his editorials against Wise to show that the latter wished to unite Virginia to the Northern Democrats and to sever her connection with the Southern wing.[81] To aid the *South* the Richmond *Examiner*, edited by John N. Hughes, was won over, thereby leaving the *Enquirer* as the only important paper opposed to Hunter.[82]

Hunter, in his senatorial campaign which came in the midst of this personal contest, was not afraid of Wise alone; but he and his friends were concerned over a combination of leaders who were trying to control the party. This combination included Judge William Daniel of Lynchburg, a highly respected member of the old Ritchie wing, Secretary of War John B. Floyd, and Representative C. J. Faulkner. These leaders, it was supposed by Hunter's friends, agreed to defeat him for the Senate with Judge Daniel as their candidate, to give Mason's seat to Floyd, to make Faulkner the next Governor, and to support Wise as Virginia's candidate for President in 1860.[83] But if such a combination ever existed it fell to pieces in short order. Judge Daniel was won over by the popular Democratic congressman from the Valley, John Letcher, who disliked Hunter's associates but who had a greater dislike for Wise.[84] Faulkner also refused to oppose the Hunter wing.[85]

In the latter part of 1857, the "Southern Rights" party found its position strengthened within Virginia by the outcome of the Walker-Buchanan quarrel. Ever since Walker had gone to Kansas, this faction had objected to his interference in the Lecompton Convention's plan of voting. Wise, on the other hand, had taken the position that since natural conditions would eventually make Kansas a free state, Democratic interests demanded that the territorial governor's plan should be carried out.[86] He championed the idea that the whole constitution should have been submitted to the people. At the same time Hunter upheld the view of most Southern Democrats, namely, that Congress should admit Kansas with the Lecompton Constitution.[87] This corresponded with Buchanan's position; consequently Hunter had no trouble retaining the support of the "Southern Rights" and administration Democrats in the senatorial election of December, 1857.[88]

Shortly thereafter Buchanan definitely expressed his agreement with the Southern Democrats by recommending the admission of Kansas under the slave constitution.[89] Douglas bolted the administration and defeated the President's recommendation. The Hunter element in Virginia denounced Douglas as a traitor to "Democracy"; while Wise, although disagreeing with the latter's argument, contended that the "Little Giant's" motive was good.[90] The legislature agreed with the administration and discredited Wise.[91]

By April, 1858, the Hunter element, now the orthodox Democratic wing, favored the English bill. If this measure should not make Kansas a slave state, the leaders argued, it would at least keep their free state representatives out of Congress until 1861, by which time the South might be able to regain that state.[92] When the people there rejected the plan of the English bill and returned to the territorial stage, the Hunter element accepted the result with equanimity.[93] As a result of this bitter conflict, Hunter had supplanted Wise as the leader of the administration Democrats, had discredited though not crushed him, and had consolidated his own hold on the "Southern Rights" element.

With the Kansas and territorial question temporarily settled, the two wings of the Democratic party prepared for the gubernatorial campaign. Both leaders were looking to 1860. Hunter lacked the support of the nationalistic west, where Wise was still strong. Wise began bidding for the radical "Southern Rights" element which had previously supported Hunter. Hunter's followers picked for their candidate a western man who had not been "sound" on slavery very long; while their opponents backed one who was "safe" on this institution. This fight marks the change in the policies of the two factions. Contrary to its earlier position, the Richmond *South* since the defeat of the English bill's proposal by the Kansas voters was carrying editorials to show that slavery in the territories was of little immediate interest—for once this organ even became national.[94] Apparently it felt that Kansas was lost and the Southern states should make the best of an unfortunate situation. This change of policy, it was thought, would please western Virginia as well as strengthen Hunter's chances with the Northern delegates in the Democratic convention of 1860. Hunter himself, by nature conservative in conduct, began courting the western section of the state.

"Honest" John Letcher, congressman and influential leader of the Democratic stronghold in the Valley, was selected as their gubernatorial candidate. He had distinguished himself in 1855 by his opposition to Wise's nomination, and, although he had little in common with Hunter, he was willing to work with the "Southern Rights" Democrats in order to defeat Wise. In the summer of 1858 he had his candidacy for Governor announced from Washington by his fellow-congressmen.[95] Immediately the Wise organ, the Richmond *Enquirer,* attacked this step on the ground that Letcher's record on slavery was not commendable.[96] At the same time the "Southern Rights" organ at Richmond and the western leaders and papers were enthusiastic in their endorsement.[97]

In order to defeat Letcher and nominate Judge John Brockenbrough or some other pro-slavery easterner, the *Enquirer* brought up the "Ruffner Pamphlet" of 1847. In that year Henry Ruffner, president of Washington College and an opponent of slavery, addressed the Franklin Literary Society of Lexington on the advantages of moving the slaves from western Virginia. John Letcher, S. McDowell Moore, James A. Hamilton, John Echols, and other members of the society were so pleased with the views expressed that they asked Ruffner to publish them.[98] According to Letcher, however, Ruffner changed the address from "a calm argument on the social and political influence of slavery upon agricultural and mechanical development of Western Virginia" to one which "contained many things so exceptional that those (with one exception, I believe,) who called upon him to publish the speech refused to contribute to the cost of the publication of the pamphlet."[99]

In June, 1858, Letcher admitted that, like many others, he had believed in 1847 that slavery was a social and political evil, but that he did not regard it then or afterwards as a moral evil.[100] As proof of this he cited the fact that he had then and ever since owned slaves acquired through purchase rather than through inheritance.[101] Since 1847, because of the abolitionists' attacks, he had studied the question, and as a result he had come to the conclusion that his former views on the political and social evils of the institution were wrong.[102]

This explanation satisfied the *South,* the *Examiner,* and their followers.[103] Until the nomination, however, the Wise element continued its hostility. The latter maintained that even if Letcher were "sound" this pamphlet would make him a poor candidate against the reorganized "Opposition."[104] To strengthen this attack which would be effective in the planter region, the *Enquirer* appealed to the Democrats of the northwest to vote against Letcher on the ground that he was opposed to internal improvements.[105] On the very eve of the state convention Letcher's friends were afraid of the combination against him.[106]

In the convention at Petersburg the contest became more than a factional one. Several speakers declared that Letcher's nomination at this time would be hazardous to the party and to the best interests of the state.[107] Not even all of the Hunter group backed him.[108] Nevertheless, out of a total of 86,225 votes in the convention he won 16,115 more than the other five candidates together.[109] His support came from all sections except the southwest,[110] where he had the backing of only two and a half counties.[111] Of the sixty-seven counties east of the Blue Ridge he received a majority in forty-six and half of seven others.[112] On the other hand, he carried only twenty of the fifty counties which today make up West Virginia.[113] It would seem, therefore, that he was not so much the choice of the western as the eastern members of his party.* These results show the strength of the new combination between the "Southern Rights" and northwestern elements—a combination that made Hunter almost as powerful in the Democratic party as Ritchie had been prior to 1850.

In the convention which nominated Letcher, the Wise faction, led by Henry A. Wise's son, tried to put through a resolution rejoicing in Douglas's defeat of Lincoln in the Illinois senatorial race.[114] Yet because of Douglas's Freeport position and his break with the administration in February, 1858, the Hunter group was able to defeat the resolution.[115]

This division within the Democratic party gave the Whigs their first

---

*The vote in the election is analyzed on pages 61-62.

chance to elect a Governor after the constitutional change of 1850-1851. Even in 1856 they had attempted party reorganization.[116] The failure of the American movement caused them to return to their old principles. They began again preaching against slave agitation and sectional parties.[117] But these efforts had little effect at first, for in 1857 the Democrats carried every congressional district.[118] The Whigs were more hopeful in 1858-1859 because of the division of the Democrats, the nomination of Letcher, and the improved organization of their own party. In their state convention at Richmond on February 10, 1859, the Botts nationalists joined the new leaders with the hope of defeating Letcher. They nominated W. L. Goggin of Bedford, a states' rights man inclined towards the pro-Southern view and "sound" on slavery, for Governor, and Waitman T. Willey of the northwest for lieutenant governor.[119] Resolutions condemning "squatter sovereignty" and "alien suffrage" as practiced in Kansas, declaring that Letcher was in favor of exterminating slavery, and expressing loyalty to the Union were adopted.[120]

The campaign which followed was a peculiar one. In the eastern sections the Whigs tried to make the most of Letcher's supposed unsoundness on slavery; while in the west they put a soft pedal on this issue. They circulated many copies of the "Ruffner Pamphlet" supplemented by Letcher's speeches on slavery, particularly those that supported the constitutional amendment for the taxation of slaves under twelve.[121] This practice provoked such hostility among the Whigs of the west that F. H. Pierpoint threatened to cease campaigning. To appease him and others of his section, therefore, they were careful not to distribute this pamphlet in their region, or to let Goggin speak there.[122] They left that territory to Willey who disregarded the slavery issue and attacked the Democratic indifference to western desires for internal improvements.[123] The Democrats in like manner carried on a twofold campaign. Montague, their candidate for lieutenant governor, campaigned in the east, and Letcher never crossed the Blue Ridge.[124] This party insisted in the planter sections that Letcher's explanation of his stand on slavery was satisfactory, and that Goggin's and Willey's records on the issue were not beyond reproach.[125] Letcher and Goggin were outspoken in their defense and pledges of loyalty to slavery.[126] The Wise element and a few of the "Southern Rights" Democrats, hoping all the time that Letcher would be defeated, either remained silent or campaigned in a half-hearted way.[127]

Most of the Whigs carried on a vigorous campaign, not only with the

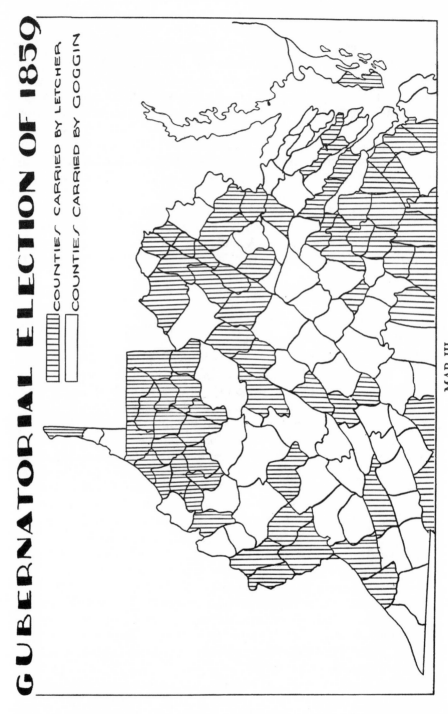

GUBERNATORIAL ELECTION OF 1859

COUNTIES CARRIED BY LETCHER
COUNTIES CARRIED BY GOGGIN

MAP III

hope of electing Goggin, but also with the view of preparing for 1860.[128] Old leaders joined the young ones to stump the state and spread party pamphlets to a greater extent than the Whigs had done since 1848.[129]

As a result of this intensive campaign, Letcher received a majority of only 5,569, the smallest of any Democratic candidate since 1848. His greatest strength was in the northwest, the Valley, and portions of the east. Goggin carried the region east of the Blue Ridge and the southwest. Consequently, the Richmond *Whig* declared: "We repeat that Letcher owes his election to the tremendous majority received in the Northwestern Free Soil counties, and he owes his tremendous majority in those counties to his anti-slavery record."[130] The *Blue Ridge Republican* and the *Kanawha Valley Star* denied that the *Whig's* position was correct, and insisted that instead of slavery, party disloyalty had been responsible for the small margin.[131]

The "Ruffner Pamphlet" probably had weight in this election, particularly in turning votes from Letcher but not in gaining votes for him in the west. There is danger, though, of giving it too great an emphasis, as a study of the result will indicate.[132] Goggin carried the counties east of the Blue Ridge by only 1,389 majority out of 67,399 votes; whereas in the same region in 1860 Bell had a plurality of 3,348 and came within 2,414 of having more than Douglas and Breckinridge together.[133] The Valley, with more slaves than any section west of the Blue Ridge, gave its popular leader a majority greater in proportion than the northwest.[134] In the southwest where slaves were moderately numerous, Letcher received his smallest vote; but it must be remembered that this was the center of Wise's strength and of the opponents of the Hunter group.[135] In the northwest where Letcher was strong, Ohio County gave Goggin a majority of three hundred, despite the fact that in 1856 it had gone Democratic. Halifax, on the other hand, the largest slave county in the state, gave Letcher a majority of four hundred.[136] In the counties which gave Letcher majorities and in which he gained on Wise's vote of 1855 there were 258,490 slaves; whereas, in the counties which gave Goggin majorities and in which he gained on the vote of the Whig candidate of 1855 there were 204,038 slaves.[137] In the part of the west where Letcher gained most there were 50,000 slaves, and in that section where Goggin gained most there were only 10,000.[138] It may be concluded, therefore, that although some Democrats refused to vote for Letcher because of his anti-slavery leanings, Wise's hostility was the chief reason for the small vote. Probably the

Blue Ridge *Republican* was correct when it concluded that most people felt that both Letcher and Goggin were "sound" on slavery.[139]

The returns of this election reveal the growing strength of the Whigs. In the congressional contest at the same time they succeeded, in spite of the gerrymandering, in electing one Whig and four independent Democrats. From this period until the Brown raid the Whigs or "Opposition," as they were often called, were hopeful of carrying the state in the presidential election on a program of union with the conservative Northern forces including some Republicans.

The Democrats, on the other hand, continued their factional quarrel. In the gubernatorial campaign, Wise had lost the support of the Valley and the northwest, but he had retained the southwest; consequently his strength was not very great. Letcher and Hunter had molded the pro-Southern and conservative states' rights easterners and the nationalistic westerners into a strong body which, should the disunion question be kept down, would be able to control Virginia's stand at the National Democratic Convention in 1860. In preparing for that convention, therefore, this strong party established a paper to take the place of the *South* which had gone out of existence in November of 1858. As new editors, William Old and Patrick Henry Aylett tried to make the Richmond *Examiner*, instead of the Richmond *Enquirer*, the organ of the party.[140]

After the rejection by the people of Kansas of the plan in the English bill and after the nomination of Letcher, the Hunter group tried to quiet the discussion of slavery extension. In the summer of 1858 when W. L. Yancey and Edmund Ruffin began advocating the "League of United Southerners" as a means of forcing the parties "to hold the Southern issue paramount," Pryor as editor of the *South* declared the attempt unwise and unnecessary. He maintained that with the Democrats controlling the government and with the Supreme Court upholding "our rights" there was no occasion for alarm.[141] Moreover, he continued, "it is time enough to prepare for secession when secession is . . . inevitable."[142] Later the editor of the *Examiner* dropped the slavery issue and returned to the old arguments against the centralization of the Federal Government.[143]

While the Hunter wing was becoming more conservative, Wise and his friends were making a bid for the support of the "Southern Rights" faction of Virginia as well as that of the lower South. Although he had taken a position in 1857 and 1858 on the territories not unlike that of Douglas, and had tried to get the Virginia Democratic convention of 1858 to congratulate Douglas on his victory over Lincoln for the United States senatorship,[144] Wise and his friends by the summer of 1859 were taking an extreme position on slavery in the territories. In a long letter to William F. Sanford of Alabama he contended that Congress had the power to protect slavery in the territories not only as property but as persons.[145] This was published as a sort of feeler of Southern sentiment.[146] As soon as the Southern press expressed its disapproval, Wise's organ, the *Enquirer*, placed at its head the "Cardinal Democratic Principles on the Slavery Question." Among these were the following: first, Congress could not introduce or interfere with slavery in the territories; second, Congress could not discriminate either in favor of or against slavery in the territories; third, Congress must protect slavery in the territories; and fourth, the territorial legislature previous to statehood must afford adequate protection to persons and property under the Constitution of the Union.[147] Along with these principles it published the journal of the caucus of the state's delegation at the Cincinnati Democratic Convention of 1856 where Seddon, a Hunter delegate, had introduced the third resolution of these cardinal principles.[148] In this way the *Enquirer* thought it would be able to show that the hostile element had once favored this new position.[149]

The *Examiner* had prepared for such an attack by its editorial of June 16, 1859, a week before the *Enquirer* published the journal of the Cincinnati caucus. In this editorial it maintained that Congress had the abstract right to protect all property in the territories, but the protection of slavery was as property and not as persons.[150] Yet it was unwilling to force an "abstract truth upon a body [referring to Charleston Convention] of men whose . . . aid is essential to the maintenance of rights practically endangered."[151]

From this time until Brown's raid, the Hunter leaders urged that the slavery issue should be dropped, and that the "Southern Rights" Democrats should accept at Charleston a restatement of the Cincinnati platform's provision on slavery in the territories.[152] They were trying in this way to gain the followers of Douglas in the North and to hold the lower South. Wise's friends, however, insisted that the Charleston platform should specifically guarantee congressional protection to slavery in the territories.[153] It appeared to them that Hunter's supporters were sacrificing the interests of the South in order to gain their leader's nomination at Charleston.[154] In reply, the Lynchburg *Republican*, a Douglas paper, agreed with the Hunter wing and reminded the *Enquirer* that its policy would bring about the election of a Republican and disunion.[155]

As a result of this territorial debate, Hunter was greatly strengthened within Virginia. The western part of the state, which had disapproved of Wise's break with the national administration and his opposition to Letcher, rejoiced to see Hunter's friends trying to quiet the slavery issue.[156] Some of the conservative Democrats even looked upon Douglas as the only candidate capable of winning.[157] But Douglas's article on slavery in the territories in *Harper's Monthly* in August, 1859, destroyed his chances in Virginia.[158] The supporters of Wise and Hunter were hostile to the view of this article.[159] Thus was Hunter left master of the Democratic party in Virginia and apparently strong in other sections of the country.[160]

While this personal rivalry within the Democratic party was growing, the Whigs were more harmonious in their preparation for a strong come-back in 1860. In the Letcher-Goggin and congressional elections of 1859, they had shown a strongly organized and confident party as contrasted with the factional and disconsolate one in the period prior to 1857. Leaders, such as Preston and Stuart in the Valley, Willey, Carlile, and Summers in the northwest, and Goggin and Flournoy in the Piedmont, were working continuously for a new spirit in their party.[161]

These leaders proceeded in the summer of 1859 to comply with the request of Northern conservatives that all parties except the "abolitionists" join against the Democrats.[162] In a series of articles the *Whig* tried to convince its readers that the one issue, slavery, which kept the conservative Republicans and Whigs apart, was dead. As proof of this contention it pointed to the Kansas situation.[163] This slavery question, it stated, had always been used for party purposes. "In the North, the ignorant have been made to believe that the 'slave power' was preparing to trample into the dust the great interests of freedom; and in the South, the credulous have been persuaded, that all the North is united in a crusade against slavery!"[164] When the state "Opposition Convention" met in Staunton in late August, 1859, it resolved: first, that it deprecated further agitation of this question; second, that many, for political purposes, kept the slavery issue before Congress; third, that the "Kansas-Nebraska policy and all the measures which were its accessories and incidents were in no wise beneficial to either section of the Union, and in our judgment were, so far is the South was concerned, 'a delusion and a snare' "; and fourth, that the question of Congress' interference with slavery in the territories ceased to be a practical question.[165]

At the same time that they were declaring the slavery issue dead, the

Whigs were contending that the other differences with the conservative Republicans were not great.[166] They tried, too, to strengthen their position by showing that the lower South was preparing for a dissolution of the Union, and that the coöperation of the opposition factions was necessary to defeat the disunionists.[167] In reply to the Democratic charge that the Republicans were abolitionists, the Richmond *Whig* said that, although individuals in that party had championed the radical abolition position, the majority of them "have never made public" intentions to expel slavery, and that such a view was "only imaginary."[168]

As a practical step in carrying out this plan of uniting the conservative Republicans and the Whigs, the Richmond *Whig* advised "the Southern Opposition members of Congress . . . not to hesitate a single moment" in coöperating with the Republicans in the organization of the House of Representatives. It preferred a Republican to a Democrat because the former would be more effective than the latter in the investigation of the corruption in the Federal Government.[169] Before Congress met, however, the John Brown raid occurred. This incident created such hostility in Virginia against the North and Republicans that the Southern Whigs had to abandon their plan.

CHAPTER IV

SECESSIONISTS AND SOUTHERN NATIONALISM, 1850-1860

IT HAS been pointed out already that in disregarding the Nashville Convention, Virginia indicated her disapproval of disunion.[1] In chapter III it was also noted that the two political parties during the succeeding period, 1851-1859, did not reveal any decided leanings toward the secessionists' view except in 1856, when the threats were apparently more for effect in the election than for explaining a position. Even in that year the Whigs frankly opposed the discussion of any plan for the dissolution of the Union in case of Republican success; and the eastern Democrats did not specifically recommend that if secession should come Virginia should join the lower South.[2]

The Union feeling seemed stronger in 1858 and 1859 than in any period after 1854. The Hunter wing of the Democratic party and the two branches of the Whigs began advising that the slavery issue be ignored. The Richmond *Dispatch,* a non-partisan penny paper with a circulation greater than that of all other Richmond papers combined, stated on August 23, 1858, that ninety-nine out of every hundred men in eastern Virginia were loyal to the Union; and that "as for Western Virginia there never was a time when it dreamed of disunion. There is probably no part of the United States where the Union has greater and firmer adherers than Western Virginia."[3] Even the "Southern Rights" Democratic Richmond *South* in the summer of 1858 was hostile to the Yancey-Ruffin "League of United Southerners," for, it stated, there was no occasion for agitation as long as the Democratic party controlled the government.[4] This Union feeling continued to dominate the political parties until the Brown raid in October, 1859.[5]

During most of this decade, though, there was an aggressive faction or group of intellectuals and agriculturists who were constantly trying to bring Virginia around to the position where her people would be ready to follow the lower South whenever that section should secede. Among these agitators there was obviously no expectation that their state would lead the way. Consequently, their chief efforts were to familiarize the people with dissolution possibilities, so that when secession became a practical issue it would not be disregarded through fear. These extremists continuously reminded the people that their interests and civilization bound them to the South, and that for this reason, if the cotton states should withdraw, Virginia would find it to her advantage to follow. In this undertaking these propagandists were aided by others who worked for Southern economic and intellectual solidarity, not so much with the view to gaining Southern political independence as to developing the slave region within the United States. Whatever the purpose of this latter group, its efforts helped to prepare the way for the decision when the question of which side to take presented itself to the Secession Convention in 1861.

In the critical years 1847-1851, while South Carolina and Mississippi were advocating a Southern confederacy built on slavery, a few bold spirits of the Old Dominion began the "educational campaign" in their state. The most outspoken of these were M. R. H. Garnett who had just completed a brilliant record at the University of Virginia, and the elderly Judge Nathaniel Beverly Tucker. The former in his pamphlet, *The Union, Past and Future,*[6] which soon ran through several editions and also appeared in the newspapers and *DeBow's Review,* and which Henry Clay called "the most dangerous pamphlet he had ever read,"[7] attempted to show that the South's wealth would enable her to maintain her independence and that the North would decay should disunion come. "The South," he concluded, "loves the equal union of our forefathers for its historical associations and the worldwide glory of its stars and stripes. But she will not tamely submit to see *her* stars changed into satellites. . . . No power may stay her onward march to Equality or Independence."[8] One year later while in the constitutional convention, he wrote William H. Trescott of South Carolina that secession would increase the state's wealth because of the release from Federal taxes; that "the prestige of the Union would be destroyed; and [that] you would be the nucleus for a Southern Confederation at no distant day."[9]

Tucker was more direct in his appeal for the development of Southern unity and "nationalism." Beverly Tucker, son of the eminent jurist and professor, St. George Tucker, and half-brother of the erratic John Randolph of Roanoke, was reared in the atmosphere of the Virginia states' rights school. After graduation at William and Mary College he became a successful lawyer in Charlotte County. Following a short stay in Missouri in the twenties, he returned to Virginia to become professor of law at his alma mater. He held this post until his death in 1852.[10]

During this time he became a popular teacher, a close friend of the South Carolina secessionists, and a leader of the Virginia radicals.[11] His influence on his students for the "Southern cause" must have been great, for J. H. Hammond, who was favorable to the disunion movement, wrote him in 1849, "When I see anything good in Virginia, I set it down to your pupils."[12]

As early as the nullification controversy Tucker passed for a disunionist.[13] In 1836 as a campaign document against Van Buren and his "anti-Southern" program, he published his famous novel, *The Partisan Leader*.[14] Published under the date of 1856, the book pretended to be a record of events which were supposed to have occurred in the late forties. In 1848, according to the story, Van Buren had just been elected President for the fourth time. Through free distribution of the Federal patronage to political leaders of his party in Virginia, he had succeeded in holding the Old Dominion in the Union; but the other slave states had formed a Southern confederacy in which the tariff and centralizing policies were not allowed. With the beginning of Van Buren's fourth term many "patriotic" Virginians revolted and attempted to join the South. The story ends with a battle between the Van Buren supporters and the "patriots," but without any explanation of whether Virginians succeeded in joining the cotton states.[15]

In the controversy of 1849-1850 over slavery in the territories acquired from Mexico, Tucker, as was noted above, attempted to place his state in line with Southern unity and secession. He contributed, along with M. F. Maury, Senator Hunter, and George F. Holmes, to William G. Simms's radical *Southern Quarterly Review*.[16] Likewise his correspondence with "Southern Rights" leaders of Virginia and South Carolina indicated his interest in disunion.[17] In letters to Hammond and Simms, he recommended that the Democratic party be made a sectional one in order to gain the Southern Whigs.[18] Through letters, personal visits, and newspaper articles, he worked for coöperation in the Nashville Convention.[19] He tried to get Hammond and other South Carolina leaders to help the Southern cause in Virginia by writing articles for the Richmond *Examiner* which under the control of one of his former students was ultra-Southern in its leaning.[20] Later when he found that the Nashville Convention would fail, he advised South Carolina to secede in order that Virginia would be forced to follow.[21] At Nashville he was one of the extremists.[22] When the Richmond *Whig* declared that his speech there did not represent any perceptible Virginia sentiment,[23] Tucker rejoiced in the stand he had taken. In a letter to Simms on February 14, 1851, he proudly declared that since 1820 he had considered the Union a curse.

I vowed then, and I have repeated the vow, *de die in diem,* that I will never give rest to my eyes nor slumber to my eyelids until it is shattered into fragments. I strove for it in '33; I strove for it in '50, and I will strive for it while I live, and leave the accomplishment to my boys. Time was when I might have been less desperate, because I could have sought refuge under some emperor or king. But all such refuges are broken up, and there is now no escape from the many-headed despotism of numbers, but by a strong and bold stand on the banks of the Potomac. . . . If we will not *have* slaves we must *be* slaves.[24]

He was agitating in this strain until his death in 1852.[25]

The popularity of the Compromise of 1850, the determination of leaders in both parties to keep the slavery issue under cover, the revival of prosperity, and the interest in internal improvements caused the people of Virginia in the early fifties to disregard the advice of the alarmists. Although for political purposes mainly, constant demands for the unity of the South were made in the early fifties, no new pamphleteers and agitators were actively campaigning for secession again until the election of 1856. From 1856 to 1861 while disunion threats were constant, the proponents of secession went over much of the ground covered by Garnett and Tucker. Through pamphlets, newspaper articles, addresses before college and agricultural societies, speeches at county and state fairs, and through the *Southern Literary Messenger* and *DeBow's Review,* these later propagandists for a Southern confederacy were probably more effective in their efforts to create a disunion sentiment than those of the earlier period.

Just as there was one conspicuous agitator, Tucker, in the early fifties, so was there a great crusader, Edmund Ruffin, in the later peroid. Until the middle of the decade he devoted his major effort to agriculture. In addition to making a financial success of his own plantation through methods of farming introduced and advocated by him, Ruffin wrote numerous pamphlets and made even more speeches to Virginia and Southern audiences. He hoped thereby to encourage the application of his agricultural discoveries by others.[26] From 1833 to 1842 he edited the *Farmer's Register.* At other times he served as president of the Virginia Agricultural Society. Because of these various activities, he became a widely known and respected person, not only in his own state but also throughout the South.

By nature Ruffin was a reformer with the seriousness akin to that of the abolitionists. He was in the North only once; and, even before he became an ardent supporter of the Southern cause, he distrusted the "Yankees." This feeling soon grew into an intense hatred. He believed everything the politicians said and was convinced by 1855 that the sectional conflict was an "irrepressible" one.[27] In his early manhood he had considered slavery a moral and social evil;[28] but gradually as he continued his study of agriculture and slave labor, he altered his views until he became as enthusiastic in his defense of the "peculiar institution" as Garrison was bitter in his opposition to it. In the period of the Wilmot Proviso, he wrote pamphlets and interviewed Southern leaders with a view to preparing for the "inevitable" separation;[29] but it was not until 1855 when he retired from his agricultural pursuits that he began his crusade for a Southern confederacy.

In his copious diary which covers the years, 1855-1865, he explains his new purpose in this manner: "My zeal made me desirous to treat this subject [secession] before the public—in as much as no one in Virginia yet advocated such extreme action."[30] Here he had more fervor and confidence than in his fight of the forties. In the earlier period he simply defended slavery and Southern rights, but in the late fifties he was working to create a new nation and a new society in which the "false theory of democracy" would be discarded and slavery would be made a corner stone. In keeping with this purpose, he joined Yancey in 1858 at the close of the Montgomery Commercial Convention in an effort to organize a "League of United Southerners." This was intended to function in the old parties within the Union as a means of nominating "Southern Rights" men.[31] Although only six chapters were formed and all of these were in Alabama, the effort indicates the fervor of the founders.[32] When John Brown made his notorious raid, Ruffin in his childish enthusiasm seized upon this episode to further his cause. He hastened to Harper's Ferry, gathered up the pikes intended by Brown for his slaves, and sent some of them to the Southern governors with this inscription on each pike: "Sample of the favors designed for us by our Northern Brethren."[33] Finally in the period of the Secession Convention he "stumped the state" for separation.[34]

Ruffin was not a successful speaker, but he was a very effective pamphleteer. He personally distributed many of his tracts at the agricultural societies' meetings and at the sessions of the Southern Rights Association. He used the "franking" privileges of Mason, Goode, and Hammond for mailing others.[35] In addition he wrote extensively for newspapers and magazines, especially for the *Enquirer,* Richmond

South, Charleston *Mercury, Southern Planter,* and *DeBow's Review.*
The most widely circulated of his articles were those published in the
Enquirer, December, 1856, and in *DeBow's Review* for the same year.[36]
Later these were combined into a book entitled *Anticipations of the
Future.*[37] In this volume he maintained that abolitionists could not be
trusted; that secession was the only redress for Southern wrongs; that
the dissolution of the Union would bring economic prosperity to the
South and bankruptcy to the North; and that secession would not likely
produce war, but if war came "cotton is king" and the resistance of
the united slave states would guarantee Southern success. After presenting rather forceful arguments to sustain these contentions, he proceeded to predict the course of events. These later essays were merely
speculations of what would happen to the country in the next few
years. The earlier ones, however, were logical and highly commended
by DeBow and other secessionists who looked upon Ruffin's reasoning
as sound.

Assisting Ruffin in his efforts to create sentiment in Virginia for a
Southern confederacy were: Willoughby Newton, a former congressman
who by 1857 enjoyed the reputation of being a "political philosopher"
of local note; George Fitzhugh, author of numerous articles in defense
of slavery and the Southern civilization; George F. Holmes, after 1857
professor of history and literature at the University of Virginia; political leaders, such as Roger A. Pryor, James A. Seddon, and John Scott
of Fauquier; and A. T. Bledsoe and J. P. Holcombe, members also of
the faculty of the University of Virginia.

These agitators repeated many of the arguments of Tucker and Garnett but added some new ideas and refreshed the minds of Virginians
with the earlier contentions. After rehearsing the old pro-slavery views
of Dew,[38] many of these, especially Fitzhugh and Newton, extolled the
conservative character of Southern society and condemned the Northern
civilization for its democratic inclinations. They denied the principles
of equality embodied in the Declaration of Independence and emphasized the value of recognizing the "sanctity of property."[39] Newton opposed the support of schools by the public on the ground that such a
practice was socialistic and would interfere with private rights.[40] Fitzhugh's attack on the abolitionists was based on the feeling that they
were enemies of conservatism and all society. He linked the anti-slavery
movement with atheism, socialism, and communism.[41] He maintained,
furthermore, that the propertied classes of the North and South should
champion slavery as the only defense against radicalism. Anything in-

terfering with the permanency of this institution and agriculture should be discarded. Manufacture and commerce, he believed, should supplement rather than undermine the South's economic system, for the latter alone could preserve property rights and individual liberty.[42] In order that this "peculiar institution" and the plantation system might survive, he advocated the endorsement of slavery in all forms rather than just negro slavery, the acquisition of more slave territory, and the reopening of the African trade in negroes.[43]

Most of these agitators did not go so far in their demands as Fitzhugh for they were more practical. Instead, they attempted to educate Virginians to see that secession was the only available means of guaranteeing "Southrons" the permanency of slavery, their social system, and their rights; that a Southern confederacy would be of economic and social advantage to Virginians; and that dissolution would be accomplished without war. In support of the first of these contentions, they maintained that their section's "interests" were not obtainable and secure in a union with the North. The Southern civilization, they continued, was based on a system of labor which could not be permanent unless it had perfect security "in its present and *future existence*" and unless it had assurances of its natural expansion and development.[44] They felt that such guarantees could be had under the Federal Constitution as long as friends of the South controlled the government, but that when this administration passed to her enemies the Constitution would fail to serve as a protection.[45] They were convinced that the people of the free states were becoming more and more anti-slavery in their views, and that their control of the government was only a matter of time.[46] Ruffin explained, for instance, how the South might be crippled without the party in power violating the letter of the Constitution. The North through her rapidly increasing population, he said, would secure a stronger hold on the House and, with the increasing free states resulting from larger immigration, the Senate and presidency. The Supreme Court would then pass under Northern control; and, eventually, the Constitution itself would be altered through the assistance of the new states which immigration and a division of the old ones would produce.[47] The Republican defeat of 1856 gave Ruffin little comfort; for he saw no chance for the South to protect herself "unless by another declaration of independence of, and separation from, a despotic party, whose wrongful and oppressive acts have already far exceeded, and threaten to exceed much more in the future, all the acts of actual and prospective oppression of our mother country.

. . . And still many of the South continue to recommend patience, and endurance, and submission to every wrong and evil, rather than meet the evil of disunion!"[48] "Every year," he later wrote, "adds to the strength of the North"; hence the safety of the South "must be secured by the more southern states seceding first, and speedily."[49]

Closely linked to the security argument of these agitators was the contention that separation would bring great economic advantages to Virginia and the cotton states. As a background for this contention, agitators insisted that, since the lower South was destined to secede, Virginians must make up their minds as to which civilization they would attach themselves. Beverly Tucker in the Nashville Convention of 1850 had contended in his impressive speech that the people of his state, Tennessee, and Kentucky might not be prepared to join the cotton states at first, but they would feel that their interests identified them with the lower South. Even if secession should not bring war, the border states, he continued, would soon follow, for they would not tolerate the misgovernment of the North, while the cotton states were prospering under their tariff "for revenue only."[50] Other secessionists contended that as long as Virginia remained in the Union after the other slave states had withdrawn, slavery would be insecure. "But after dissolution the abolitionists would not have free access to slaves as they do today." By a careful examination of Northern immigrants and by severe punishment to those caught encouraging fugitives, a more effective means for preventing slaves' running away would be secured. It would make slavery permanent and its benefits were "known to all Southerners."[51]

Great advantages would, in like manner, result from the development of manufacture and commerce, if these propagandists were correct. Garnett, in his *Union, Past and Future,* argued that until 1850 the South through the tariff duties had paid most of the Federal expenses, while she had received in return only a small per cent of the central government's expenditures.[52] Furthermore, Willoughby Newton maintained:

A tariff for the support of the new government would give such protection to manufacturers that all our waterfalls would bristle with machinery, and the hum of manufacturing industry would be heard in all the inland towns of the State. The spindles of Lowell, Lawrence, and Manchester would be transferred to the falls of the Potomac, Rappahannock and the James, and the industrious artisans of the North would be transferred with them. . . . Under judicious revenue and navigation laws, the ships of all nations would crowd the ports of the South, and the products of other lands be brought directly to our own shores, in exchange for our own. . . . Norfolk would become the emporium of foreign commerce.[53]

Even conservatively minded Hunter predicted that, if secession were accomplished, Virginia as a member of a Southern confederacy would supplant New England as the manufacturing section for the South.[54] Randolph Tucker, state attorney-general in 1860, held a similar view.[55] In his correspondence on this subject printed in the New York *Herald,* November 28 and December 22, 1860, he maintained that in addition to manufacturing advantages Virginia would receive great commercial gains from a Southern confederacy. "With the command of the Southern trade, with her extended Southern connections, with her commercial facilities, Virginia would be the great commercial, manufacturing and navigation State of the South. Her bottoms would replace those of New England . . . her factories those of the free states."[56]

These propagandists gave greatest attention to the defense of their third contention that secession would not result in war. Ruffin devoted practically two-thirds of his *Anticipations of the Future* to this phase of the subject. Ruffin, like R. H. Glass of Lynchburg,[57] argued that secession would not be considered a cause for war, but that if the North should deny the right to dissolve the Union the free states would not be so "foolhardy" as to undertake the subjugation of the South, for war would impoverish the North.[58] Beverly Tucker maintained that war would throw the South into the hands of Europe, and European manufactured goods and commerce would supplant those of the North.[59] War would mean the loss of cotton, and the lower South could "make its own terms with the world."[60] A short time before he had contended:

The mind of man has not conceived the wretchedness which the failure of one cotton crop would produce. Universal bankruptcy—universal ruin—the prostration of the wealthy, and the uprising of the suckling masses, violently snatching from their beggar employees a portion of their scanty remnant of former abundance, to satisfy the wants of nature. . . . Like Sampson the South can pull down the pillars on the Phillistines without injuring herself by refusing to grow cotton. . . . If you take away the South's cotton the New England ships would lie rotting at the wharves; the factories would tumble into ruins; and, skulking in corners of their marble palaces, the merchant princes, like those of Venice, would live meagerly on contributions levied on the curiosity of troublers.[61]

Laborers would go to the West; Boston would be like Venice; and England would be forced to take sides with the cotton states in order to keep her three million textile workers from starving. If the North tried to interfere in the South, he continued, the power of wealth in Europe "would oppose it—the cry of famine would forbid it—the united voice of the civilized world would command the peace." Even conservative John Tyler felt that the thesis, "cotton is king," would prevent war.[62]

But suppose the North should make war, what would be the outcome? Ruffin contended that the fifteen slave states united under a separate government could repel all invasions; that if only the cotton states withdrew, the border states would not permit an invasion across their borders; and that invasion from the sea would be impossible. The slaves would remain loyal as they had in the War of 1812 when the British tried to stir them to insurrection. "Slavery, in fact, lends itself to a military system. It produces leaders." "A blockade would not be effective. Privateering on Northern commerce, blockade runners, and foreigners in order to obtain cotton would destroy any blockade." Besides, for the period of war, the South could produce her necessities.[63] Willoughby Newton pointed out, furthermore, that the slave states were decidely stronger in proportion than the thirteen colonies were when they successfully revolted against the greatest power of their time.[64]

Some of these agitators predicted not only that a Southern confederacy would succeed without war, but also that Pennsylvania, because of New England's competition within the Union, would eventually join a Southern confederacy where a tariff policy would aid her industries. Even the Northwest would be influenced by the bonds of the Mississippi River to do likewise.

While these propagandists were familiarizing the people of Virginia with the probabilities and "advantages" of a Southern confederacy, the growing differences between the sections of the country and the common efforts in the slave states to create a feeling of unity in their midst were producing a Southern nationalism.[65] If it is agreed that a nation is made up of spiritual rather than material parts and that one of the most essential elements in it is the consciousness on the part of its "component atoms" that it is a nation,[66] then the South was rapidly becoming one in 1860. Since the Colonial days there had always been sectional differences of an economic, social, and political character; and in spite of the increased bonds of unity in the Revolutionary and Jeffersonian eras, these regional antagonisms constantly came to the surface in the early years of the Republic. After the rise of the tariff and especially the abolitionist issues, sectionalism increased until the expansion crisis of the forties made it the most conspicuous factor of the period.[67] From 1849 to 1860 this idea was ever present in politics.

Goaded by outside attacks, Southern leaders emphasized the similarities of the slave states and ignored their dissimilarities. As a result there was created a sentiment for Southern unity, although the Civil War showed that instead of one South there were many Souths. As a part of this nationalistic movement, attempts were made to create and develop a Southern literature, a Southern educational system, Southern economic independence, Southern denominations, and even a Southern political party. Southern social habits and manners were extolled, and many writers, such as Newton and Fitzhugh, were convinced that this civilization, in addition to being the greatest in modern times, was so different from the North's that the two were not compatible.

This feeling of nationalism was more evident in some parts of the South than in others. In the newer portion—Alabama, Mississippi, and Louisiana—the local bonds and attachments were less than the larger feeling for the whole South, but in the older section the reverse was probably true. In the border states the consciousness of common interest was probably not so pronounced as in the lower South. In western Virginia, for instance, the people had little in common with Alabama. In eastern Virginia, on the other hand, there were numerous expressions of the nationalistic attitude, and the Virginia agitators made the most of this fact. They argued that there were two nations in the United States and that it was impossible for both of them to continue under one government. Garnett, in his congressional campaign for 1856, held that "from Plymouth Rock and Jamestown down to the present time two systems of civilization were established, one at Plymouth, the other at Jamestown."[68] In 1857 the Richmond *South* contended that even if the slavery issue were settled the two sections would be unable to live together peacefully, for they had little in common. "There is a Government between them; but it is no token of unity or bond of peace. They are different people, contrasted in fact in their institutions, their ideas, their modes of society and their manners."[69] Shortly after this a writer of a series of articles in the *Southern Literary Messenger* insisted that the ruling people of the South were of different blood from those who controlled in the North—the former were descendants of the Normans who were elected to rule, while the latter were descendants of the Britons, Saxons, dissenters, and commercial classes.[70] The people of the North, therefore, were concerned primarily with material affairs, money, and trade; while the "Southrons" were "chivalrous & idealistic, and genteel" descendants, in taste, of the Roman nobles and English gentry.[71]

In the same manner, Glass argued that in the latter part of the eighteenth century necessity held the two sections together, but that with the passing of this the cohesive power of the Union was removed, "and the two grand sections of our country have each, ever since played to its separate and diverse magnets. . . . The dissolution of the Union . . . will be the necessary fruit of . . . strife and discord arising from sectional differences, which are, in their natures, peculiar and irreconcilable."[72] Ruffin was a crusader for Southern unity and independence;[73] so was John Scott of Fauquier. After ably reviewing the equilibrium of the sections as established by the "Constitutional Fathers" and after sketching the process by which the Federal Government and the North had grown at the expense of the Southern states, Scott in his *Lost Principle* said that the "North and South had come virtually to two nations under one government." To him independence seemed inevitable.[74]

Whether or not this idea of a Southern nationality was accepted by a large number of Virginians prior to 1861, there was a consciousness of a unity of interest with the cotton states.[75] These ties which centered around the institution of slavery were zealously defended by extreme leaders who saw in its defense an opportunity to keep alive a strong Southern sentiment. After explaining that the "massive Doric that sustains and supports the social edifice of the South is slavery," a writer in the *Southern Literary Messenger* in 1857 urged the unity of the South, "heart and hand, soul and body, as those who have a common destiny, common principle, and the same interests involved in the momentous issue," in order that "she can go out of a Union with safety."[76]

As a part of this Southern nationalistic movement, Virginia agitators as well as leaders of the other slave states tried to bring the press and the educational institutions to their support. As early as 1847 the Richmond *Whig* advised against sending Southern boys to Dickinson College since it had an "abolitionist" on its faculty.[77] In 1853 the Southern Commercial Convention of Memphis urged that the boys and girls of the South be educated at home and that periodicals and watering places of the slave states be patronized.[78] Moreover, while the Kansas-Nebraska bill was before Congress, the *Whig* called attention to the fact that the discussion of this measure showed the "utter unreliability of Northern men of all parties, creeds and professions in reference to the institutions of the South." Professors and clergymen, the editor continued, had left their appropriate spheres and become agitators and fanatics.[79] In keeping with this position the people of Richmond re-

solved: "That in the opinion of this meeting, it is becoming and right
. . . to encourage and patronize Southern schools, colleges, or institutions; and a just respect requires that Southern literature, in all its
branches, should meet with the hearty support of all Southern men, in
view of the gross slanders and misrepresentations which are dissemi-
nated by Northern periodicals and newspapers."[80] The movement thus
begun in 1854 was increased by the scare of 1856 and the exciting years
which followed.[81]

In education the University of Virginia partly because of this effort
was the leading institution in the slave states.[82] As a result its enrollment of 163 students in 1846-1847 increased to seven hundred in
1858. This gave it the largest student body in the country.[83] The *Kanawha Valley Star* in 1859 said that the boys at the University and the
preparatory schools of Albemarle County were being "instructed in like
manner . . . united with a common devotion to Southern rights, Southern institutions, Southern manners, and Southern chivalry. In a word,
the University is shaping and molding the minds of the educated youth
of Virginia and the entire South; it is uniting the young men of the
South together, making them more and more attached to the peculiar
institutions."[84] This idea was carried out in the colleges under the
guidance of such pro-Southern professors as Tucker at William and
Mary, James P. Holcombe and A. T. Bledsoe at the University of Virginia, and W. A. Smith at Randolph-Macon.[85] Likewise in the acade-
mies, public and private, as well as in the grammar grades, the students
were taught by Southerners if not by states' rights teachers—a fact
which increased the attachment of the young people to the South.[86]
Western Virginia, however, was not greatly influenced by this sectional
movement, for as late as 1857 only thirteen of the 333 Virginians at
the state's university were from the counties later included in West Virginia; and only seventeen of the 370 Virginians there in 1859 were
from west of the Alleghanies.[87] In the western counties, though, there
was not the same hostility to Northern teachers.[88]

Many Virginians coöperated with the leaders of the cotton states in
their attempt to create a Southern literature, partly as a defense of
slavery and partly as a salve to their sectional feelings. In keeping with
this motive, a Virginian wrote in the *Southern Literary Messenger* that
a local literature was of "vital importance" to the South's "social and
political interests, a question on which hangs the integrity of her
peculiar institutions, and on which is based the preservation of her
social and political independence."[89] Magazine editors, such as John

R. Thompson and George W. Bagby of the *Southern Literary Messenger,* and William Gilmore Simms of South Carolina, exerted great effort to produce a sectional literature. Upon assuming the control of the *Messenger* in 1847, Thompson appealed to local pride "to show our Northern brethren that Southern learning can think for itself."[90] In spite of this appeal, he was little concerned at first with developing a feeling of Southern nationalism;[91] instead, he wanted to capitalize on this sentiment in order to stimulate for its own sake literary activity.[92] With the appearance in 1852 of *Uncle Tom's Cabin,* Thompson began making the magazine a regional organ for defending slavery and for advocating "the development of a literature that would reveal to the world the beauties of Southern life and manner."[93] As long as he was editor he kept the *Messenger* out of politics, the advice of Simms to the contrary notwithstanding. But Bagby, as much as he disliked the South Carolina "sophomoric" glorification of the South, in 1860 made it a political medium, and after December 20 turned it into one of the most ardent secession journals within the slave states.[94] Non-literary persons in the commercial conventions attempted to aid this and other Southern publications by recommending that books, magazines, and newspapers printed within the section be patronized;[95] and the *Kanawha Valley Star* carried in its columns a list of school books and recommended that Virginians use them.[96]

These efforts to create a literature failed. Northern magazines and books continued to dominate the Southern markets.[97] Because of the sectional appeal the Southern critics were not severe in their reviews of books written by authors from the slave states. The themes were mainly sectional—nearly every Virginia writer from 1830 to 1860 wrote in glorification of his native state or his section of the country.[98] The writings of J. P. Kennedy, W. A. Caruthers, Beverly Tucker, St. George Tucker, P. P. Cooke, and even J. E. Cooke, the most noted of these, are proof of such a contention. The result was sentimentalism without art. The emphasis itself, nevertheless, indicates that the regional and, possibly, Southern national feeling was back of these efforts.

While the educational and literary leaders of Virginia were attempting to develop sectional institutions and literature which would defend and bolster up their civilization and interests, some of the churches were becoming more Southern in character. The Episcopalians, and until 1861 the Presbyterians, succeeded in keeping the sectional divergences from splitting their churches into Northern and Southern wings. The two larger denominations, the Baptist and Methodist, however, were not so easily held together. In 1844-1845 they had already formed separate units. Since the organization of the Baptist church permitted each congregation to control its own affairs, it never had the open conflict experienced by the Methodists. Individual Baptist ministers and particular congregations expressed views on slavery, the Southern civilization, and the abolitionists; but as a Southern church they had few points of contact with the Northern branch of the same denomination.[99]

The contest in the Methodist denomination was carried on with intense feeling. Splitting into the Northern and Southern branches in 1844 over the issue of bishops' owning slaves, these two wings carried on a bitter struggle in the border states over the church's property and the boundary of each's supervision.[100] The tentative line of division placed practically one-half of Virginia in the Northern church.[101] Both branches soon determined to push their boundaries into the other's territory. In 1848 the Northern church created the "Western Virginia Conference" in order to strengthen its position in that state. Two years later the Southern Methodists organized a similar division. Like political discussions, however, churches were calm in the early fifties.[102] With the renewed slavery agitation arising out of the Kansas-Nebraska bill, the contest between the two branches within Virginia was revived. In the years 1854-1855 the Southern church decided to carry its boundary up to the Mason and Dixon line. One of its ministers at Charleston on the Kanawha in 1855 stated, "Our prayer is O Lord! revive thy work, until the North shall give up, and the South will not keep back, so long as sons and daughters are born unto God."[103] And a local paper added "Let the good work commenced continue till the whole valley and Western portion of Virginia are cleansed of this foul leprosy of anti-slavery Methodism!"[104] In reply to this move the other church sent missionaries where the Southerners were in control.[105] One of their leaders, "Wesley Smith," expressed their position when he said, "We expect to add an additional ship [conference] on slave territory every four years."[106] In spite of this growth the membership of the Southern church increased in the Western Virginia Conference from 10,707 to 11,275 in one year.[107] As a result of these activities both churches by 1861 had representatives far within the other's territory.

At the general conference of the Northern church in 1856, the radicals tried to force through measures prohibiting slaveholding among the laymen.[108] Although the border conferences—thanks to the two-thirds rule—prevented the passage of this recommendation until 1860, the abolitionists succeeded in getting the church to use the Sunday school literature for spreading anti-slavery views.[109] From 1856 to 1860 the anti-slavery forces continued to strengthen their control in the Northern church. By the latter year the Northern Methodists declared their opposition to members owning slaves,[110] thereby leaving northern and western Virginians who were affiliated with this branch in a quandary; they were labeled abolitionists by the Southern church and supporters of slavery by the other body. A member of this conference explained, "We occupy the unenviable position of being between two fires; but the Southern pro-slavery fire is nearest us, and against this our chief efforts are needed."[111] Out of deference to this element, the ruling of 1860 was not strictly enforced in the border states, [112] yet this made some go over to the Southern Methodists.[113]

In addition to their attempt to extend the northern boundary, the Southern Methodists revealed their sectional character by openly defending the institution of slavery. After the Northern general conference in 1856 agreed to use the Sunday school literature for spreading anti-slavery views, the Southerners who until then had used the same "tracts" gave up their support of this literature.[114] At the same time they tried to show that their Northern brethren were abolitionists in sentiment.[115] In Botetourt County in the Valley a debate between the ministers of the two churches was held in October, 1857, and at its close resolutions were drawn up to the effect that the "Discipline and Literature of the Methodist Episcopal Church, North, on the exciting subject of slavery, are at war with the best interests of the people of Virginia."[116] For this stand they were commended by politicians who were not members of the church.[117]

The Presbyterians, as stated above, did not split until 1861. In their general assemblies slavery was constantly brought up, but on each occasion during the fifties Southern churchmen in control of the organization managed to table all proposals against the ownership of slaves.[118] Outside of the general assemblies there was considerable feeling aroused in Virginia among Presbyterian churches against the attempt of Northern members to bring up this issue. A layman, writing to the Richmond *Whig* in 1856, urged the able Presbyterian ministers, Moore, Read, and Hoge, to assist in dividing this church as the Baptists and Methodists had done.[119] The next year the Virginia Synod contended that the resolutions and testimonies of the assembly were hostile to the slaveholders. It recommended, therefore, that since "there is no prospect of the cessation of this agitation of slavery," all the presbyteries in the church opposing this attack on the "peculiar institution" should "appoint commissions to meet at Knoxville for the purpose of organizing a general synod."[120] At the same time, the Southern branch of the "New School Presbyterians" split from the Northern group on the ground that the Cleveland assembly had adopted a paper which made "slave holding a cause for discipline by the church court."[121] This did not represent a division of the whole church but it was an indication of what would come in 1861.

The divisions in the churches did not prove that the Northern and Southern people were separate nationalities in 1860, but they did show the growing sectional animosities of the two people. The intense feeling stirred between these churches, especially between the branches of the Methodist church, was carried over into the political contests. The ties by which the sectional church organizations held their members together, moreover, would naturally influence people's decisions as to which side they would align themselves when separation became a fact. In the Southern Methodists' territory sectional ideas were advocated and spread through religious literature designed for the purpose. In the portions of western Virginia where the other branch of this church was in control, the sentiment in 1861 for the Union was overwhelming— a fact that was partly due to the circulation of their "literature."[122]

In the fields of commerce and manufacture there were efforts made during the fifties, not unlike those exerted in the churches and among literary men, to use this sectional consciousness for producing economic independence. Concerted efforts which led to Southern commercial conventions advising diversified industries and direct trade with Europe had been tried without success in the thirties and forties.[123] In the excitement of 1849-1851 the economic agitation was revived. First as a means of gaining redress, attention was given to boycotting Northern goods.[124] In this period Southern Rights Associations were more concerned with developing Southern industries than with fostering independence.[125] No material advantage came from these early efforts.[126] Western Virginia even thought the whole movement unwise and suicidal.[127]

In the late fifties this method of retaliation with slightly more success was revived. Fitzhugh advocated a tariff wall against the Northern goods not only as a means of benefiting the South economically, but as an agency for keeping out the evils and "isms" of the manufacturing section of the country.[128] The Richmond *Whig* advised leaders of the South to drop their interest in politics and make their people economically independent,[129] but nothing came of this agitation until the Brown raid.[130]

More direct activities in connection with a united economic South were exerted through the commercial conventions which were again revived in the fifties. These gatherings had been held in many Southern states prior to 1850,[131] and while these of the fifties were imitations of the earlier ones, in many respects they were more sectional in their enthusiasm. As in the early period direct trade with Europe, the development of Southern railroads, and diversified industries were considered. In addition the questions of the Pacific railroad, the reopening of the African slave trade, and the disunion agitation were introduced.[132] The conventions began anew in 1852 and continued to meet annually until the war. Those of the years, 1852-1855, were composed almost entirely of business men or political leaders with commercial interests. These members confined themselves to the discussions of purely economic problems such as the Pacific railroad and direct trade with Europe.[133] Such men as James Lyons and D. H. London of Richmond ardently urged the latter trade as a special benefit to Virginia. Their efforts resulted in resolutions but had little influence on legislatures.[134] After the rise of the Republican party and the Kansas issue, the commercial elements lost control to men interested in politics.[135] In the Savannah Convention of December, 1856, measures recommending the organization of Southern emigration to Kansas were adopted.[136] The year before a motion for the reopening of the African slave trade was made. From this time on, the issue remained a subject of heated discussion, and Virginians usually opposed it.[137]

Beginning with the Savannah Convention these commercial bodies became agencies for promoting Southern unity and political "rights." In such discussions Virginians took an active part. James Lyons, president of the Savannah body, declared that the recent presidential election did not settle the rights of the South. Instead, the same struggle would arise again in 1860. This convention, therefore, should have for its chief purpose the making of plans which would prevent the endangerment of "our homes . . . our liberties."[138] In the following year at Knoxville, a committee of five declared that these assemblies enabled the Southern states to become acquainted and united in sympathy for each other; that recent events led them to believe that they would soon have to attempt political independence; and that the South should develop her commerce as a preparation for this.[139] In the Montgomery Convention of 1858, Pryor promised, in the course of a speech against the reopening of the slave trade, that Virginia would follow the cotton states into secession if they would select some honorable issue which would produce a united South.[140]

Virginia, like the other slave states, was by this time sending to these conventions such men as Pryor, Harvie, Scott, Preston, and Ruffin. With the exception of Preston all of these were of the "Southern Rights" faction. In the Montgomery body Ruffin offered a resolution suggesting that a permanent committee of these conventions be appointed so that it could mold the opinion of the South on important matters as they arose, thereby producing a solidarity of sentiment.[141] Although few tangible economic results came from these later conventions,[142] they were rather important in creating a sense of Southern unity.[143]

CHAPTER V

THE JOHN BROWN RAID

B Y October, 1895, the Kansas question was temporarily without influence in the political parties in Virginia. Most Democrats and Whigs were ready to accept Southern defeat there. The followers of Hunter even advised that in the approaching campaign the issue of slavery in the territories should be abandoned; and the Whigs talked of uniting with the conservative Republicans as a means of defeating the "corrupt" party which was then in control of the Federal Government. Among the nationally known political leaders of the state, only Wise desired to keep the slavery issue alive; and his desire was stimulated by the hope that a continuation of its agitation would enable him to gain the support of his party's Southern wing. Such radicals as Ruffin were disconsolate.[1] In fact most Virginians seemed to be satisfied with the Union and the existing status of slavery. This contentment, however, was short lived, for the Harper's Ferry episode made conservative as well as radical Virginians so distrustful of Northerners, for the moment at least, that there was grave consideration of disunion. John Brown, already noted for his Kansas atrocities and supported by a fanatical group of Boston abolitionists, on October 16 and 17 with the assistance of eighteen devoted followers crossed the Potomac River into Virginia from Maryland at Harper's Ferry, seized the Federal arsenal, and sent out parties in the neighboring district to free the slaves and to make captives of their masters.[2] Throughout the day which followed the raid, wild and absurd rumors spread over the country; while the people of the vicinity, aided by the militia which Governor Wise had hastened to the scene, bottled up the little band of "conspirators" in the engine room of the arsenal. On the morning of the eighteenth, Colonel Robert E. Lee with a contingent of United States marines captured Brown and all his followers, except the few who had escaped from the armory or the Kennedy Farm, where Brown had made his headquarters before the attack. In the mêlée one marine and four civilians were killed, and one marine and ten civilians were wounded.[3] After a trial in the county court —a remarkably fair one when the state of mind of the time is considered—Brown was sentenced on November 2 to be hanged a month later. Between those two dates constant rumors of contemplated rescues were current;[4] consequently the people of this vicinity remained in a state of great uneasiness.[5] Such unrest gave the Governor just cause for retaining the troops at Charlestown, where Brown was imprisoned, and for taking other precautions.[6]

Nevertheless, with the exception of the people in the Harper's Ferry neighborhood, a few politicians who wanted to use this incident to further their interests, and sincere alarmists like Edmund Ruffin,[7] the first reaction of most Virginians to the raid seems to have been that of incredulity. They looked apparently upon the episode as that of an imbecile and felt that after his punishment the whole affair should be dropped.[8] On the morning following the raid the Richmond *Dispatch* expressed doubt that the newspaper reports of the incident were true.[9] Two days later it declared that there never was a more exaggerated account of anything than the current one of the Harper's Ferry trouble. It wondered how sensible people could have been so panic-stricken for twenty-four hours.

Such a feeling as that expressed by the *Dispatch* did not prevail long. Upon hearing of the raid, Senator Mason hurried to the scene of the "outrage" and learned that Brown's attempt to free the slaves had been backed by respectable Northern abolitionists. When he gave this information to the press the episode assumed larger proportions. The fact that many Northern newspapers and leaders were inclined from the first to sympathize with Brown increased the alarm of Virginians.[10] For some time Wise and his organ, the *Enquirer,* had been trying to wrest the support of the "Southern Rights" wing of the Democratic party from the now conservative Hunter. The Brown raid offered the former the opportunity to accomplish this purpose; and being a shrewd politician he took advantage of it.[11] This incident within itself was an object of great concern to the Virginia planters and, especially, to the non-slaveholding whites who bore a greater hatred for the abolitionists than the conservative slaveholders. A slave insurrection was always greatly feared by Southern whites, and Virginians had the memory of the Southampton tragedy to impress them with the horrors of such uprisings. In 1859 many could recall that terrible "nightmare" of the thirties. This fear had been revived and kept alive by several rumors of contemplated insurrections hatched by abolitionists.[12] After the Brown raid there were constantly other scares to keep the people on edge. On December 10 near Ruffin's home riders "carried word of a 'body of negroes, headed by several public men,' who were about to march through the country. The women hurried to central homes for protection. The men, mounted and armed, gathered to meet the terrible facts which never came."[13]

The loyalty which the slaves displayed toward their masters at first gave much comfort to Virginians, yet the enlarged reports of Brown's schemes caused them to think more seriously of their peril.[14] The constitution of the "conspirators" and Brown's frank confession after his arrest convinced many that the "outrage" was only a small part of a larger plot.[15] The Richmond *Enquirer* looked upon the "*amount of money* with which these wretches at Harper's Ferry were supplied" as evidence that "the Northern fanatics mean more than words, and are determined to wage with *men and money* the 'irrepressible conflict' to its bitter end."[16] At the same time the conservative *Whig* called the raid a "regular Abolition conspiracy, extending throughout the North, and embracing a body of twelve or fifteen hundred men, who were pledged to active personal participation in the invasion, and how many others who only rendered 'aid and comfort' to the enterprise, we have no means of knowing."[17] To the Petersburg *Express* it was the "fruit of those Satanic doctrines which are inculcated by the rabid and unprincipled teachers of the Garrison, Greely and Seward schools."[18]

More important than the raid itself in consolidating public sentiment in Virginia for "determined action" was the reaction of the North to the raid. As Brown's body was carried through the free states on its way to Boston, bells were tolled, prayers were offered, and public meetings condemning Virginia's action were held. The Massachusetts senate came within three votes of adjourning in honor of Brown. At a public gathering in Boston, Ralph Waldo Emerson, Jacob M. Manning, Wendell Phillips, and Governor John A. Andrews spoke in commemoration of him,[19] a fact which Virginians could not excuse because to them Brown was not only a conspirator but a murderer of the most cruel type and an archenemy of their social system. Parker, Thoreau, Emerson, and Phillips likened his hanging to the crucifixion of Christ.[20] Northern papers, such as the *Journal of Commerce* and the New York *Herald* which were usually friendly to the South, advised Wise to pardon Brown for effect.[21] At the time, Ruffin felt that all reports indicated that "the great mass of the people of the North, even embracing many who have been deemed . . . our friends, are more or less enemies of the South."[22] Governor Wise received from Northern people—some from leaders whom the South respected—over five hundred letters threatening or advising him to free Brown.[23] State newspapers carried full reports of the radical reaction in the North. In order "to show to the people of Virginia and the South what are the views of the press—Whig, Democratic, Republican, Abolitionist, and Independent—concerning so atrocious and diabolical proceeding," the *Whig* promised to report various editorials and accounts of meetings in the North.[24] In accordance with this program it published the editorials of the New York *Times,* New York *Tribune,* New York *Herald,* and the speeches of Wendell Phillips to represent the views of the conservative Republicans, radical Republicans, Northern Democrats, and the abolitionists, respectively.[25] At the same time it called on its Northern friends to bring pressure on their radicals so as to save the Union.[26] It evidently enlarged the reports of the dangers of disunion in order to arouse its friends.[27]

Although Wise's attempt to place the blame for the raid on the whole Republican party[28] may have caused many from the free states to express friendliness to Brown, the fact remains that the Northern response influenced Virginians to demand a drastic course. The latter overlooked the fact that the friendly forces in the free states were ready to offer them assistance should a crisis arise. Instead they looked upon the speeches of Phillips, Brooks, and Emerson as representative of that section's position.[29] While the Whigs of the Old Dominion were trying to distinguish between the radicals and conservatives in the nonslaveholding states and induce the latter to check the former, the rabid Southerners were attempting to convict the whole North for the Brown raid. They maintained that the sentiment there was so hostile to slavery that even their friends had been forced to remain quiet, thereby giving the radicals a free hand.[30]

As a result of the Northern sympathy, or supposed sympathy, for Brown's crime, all factions in Virginia were united in their resentment. To the *Enquirer,* Brown's undertaking was as "nothing compared with the manifestations of undoubted sympathy displayed by thousands at the North."[31] A month later this same paper reminded the New York *Times* that the "Opposition and Democratic parties no longer dispute about dividing issues; a common wrong unites all parties in a common defence. . . . Such unanimity of sentiment never before, within our knowledge, pervaded the State; there is no paper of either party, of the least respectability of influence, but what has given expression to the prevailing feeling that now absorbs the people. . . ."[32] In the United States Senate, Hunter expressed the view of his faction when he declared that the South was not so startled by the action of Brown as by the conduct of the Northern people.[33]

Because of Northern approval and the fear caused by the raid itself, the state was in great excitement for the remainder of the year—an excitement which was not created by politicians, for the response of the people was too spontaneous. Around Charlestown the concern of the people was extreme until after the execution of Brown.[34] In the Tidewater, Piedmont, the Valley, and to a limited extent, in the northwest, public meetings were held, military companies were formed and drilled, and preparation was made "to let the 'nigger worshipers' know that Virginia intends to maintain her institutions, peacefully if possible, but with force if necessary."[35] In a personal letter John Tyler wrote that "Virginia is arming to the teeth—more than fifty thousand stands of arms already distributed, and the demand for more daily increasing. Party is silent, and has no voice. But one sentiment pervades the country: *security to the Union,* or separation. An indiscreet move in any direction may produce results deeply to be deplored."[36] An entire edition of the Richmond *Whig* was devoted to the reports of military maneuvers in the different counties; and its editorials commended the warlike attitude.[37] In the issue of December 6 the editor stated that the reports of county meetings indicated that "never before, in the history of this commonwealth, were the people so aroused, and so bent on maintaining their rights and honor, *at any cost!*"[38] In several counties "vigilance committees" were appointed to watch for abolitionists and suspicious characters,[39] in other counties committees of correspondence were created.[40] The *Kanawha Valley Star* advised housekeepers to examine their premises, their stables, and barns "to see that none of these incendiary wretches are secreted for mischief."[41] Rockingham County's public meeting ordered George Rye, a "suspicious character," to leave immediately.[42] Likewise the newspaper *Flag* recommended that persons in Prince William County who received the twenty copies of the New York *Tribune* should be presented before the grand jury and fined heavily.[43] At a public meeting in Fauquier the people suggested that free negroes should be moved from the state, and that the manumission of slaves by will or deed should be prohibited.[44] Some of these gatherings resolved that a Southern convention should be called in order that some uniform means of gaining redress from such "outrages" as the Brown raid might be devised. Others declared that the election of a Republican as President of the United States would be a just cause for secession. Nearly all of them advised boy-cotting Northern goods.[45]

Little was discussed in the newspapers throughout October, November, and December except the Brown raid and the sentiment which it created. Entire issues of the Richmond papers were devoted to reports of the Northern reaction to the raid itself, to accounts of the military preparations then going on in the state, and to communications from the county meetings. Although secession as an immediate remedy was not widely discussed prior to the arrival of the South Carolina commission in January, the antagonism towards the free states was so pronounced in this period that Union leaders of Virginia were afraid that dissolution would become a practical issue. The Richmond *Enquirer*, October 25, said: "The Harper's Ferry invasion has advanced the cause of disunion, more than any other event that has happened since the formation of its Government; it has rallied to that standard men who formerly looked upon it with horror."[46] A month later the *Whig* declared:

Recent events have wrought almost a complete revolution in the sentiments, the thoughts, the hopes of the oldest and steadiest conservatives in all the Southern States. In Virginia, particularly, this revolution has been really wonderful. There are thousands upon top of thousands of men in our midst, who, a month ago, scoffed at the idea of a dissolution of the Union as a madman's dream, but who now hold the opinion that its days are numbered, its glory perished.[47]

Governor Letcher who opposed secession until after Lincoln's call for troops in 1861 wrote Hunter on December 9, 1859, that disunion would be near at hand unless Northern sentiment were radically changed.[48] The Central Southern Rights Association at its meeting in December drew up for the legislature a memorial which declared that the United States Constitution had been broken, that the churches had been severed, and that "we are put in daily peril of our lives. . . . Therefore it behooves us . . . to take prompt and thorough measures for remedy and redress—under the constitution, if we can—beyond it, if we must."[49]

The excitement created by the Brown raid would probably have declined around the first of the year had two other incidents not occurred to keep it alive—the heated contest over the election of Speaker for the House of Representatives, and the refusal of the Ohio and Iowa governors to surrender participants in the Brown raid. When Congress met December 5, 1859, the new House included 109 Republicans, eighty-eight administration Democrats, and twenty-seven Americans or

Whigs.[50] From the first session slavery became an issue. Southerners of both parties tried to force the House to agree that no one who had endorsed Helper's *Impending Crisis* should be eligible for the speakership. Prior to the Brown raid the Richmond *Whig* had advised Southern Whigs or Americans to support a conservative Republican in preference to a Democrat.[51] By December when Congress convened, however, this paper was ready to support a Democrat rather than a "Black Republican."[52] A. R. Boteler, the only "Opposition" member from Virginia, followed the *Whig's* advice.[53]

The debate from December until after the election of the Speaker on February 10 was one of the most exciting in the history of Congress. Personal encounters in the House were frequent; social intercourse between the Northern and Southern Senators ceased and rumors spread that every man in Congress carried a revolver.[54] In April while slavery was still being debated, Pryor of Virginia challenged Potter of Wisconsin to a duel.[55] Such "fire-eaters" as Pryor, Garnett, and Leake from Virginia joined men of similar dispositions of the cotton states to repel all attacks on the South and slavery. Garnett's speech on December 7, 1859, illustrates the feeling of this group. On that occasion he told the Northerners, "You must go home to your people and you must put down this abolition spirit. You must repeal the laws" which abrogate the fugitive slave law. "Unless you do pass such laws [condemning the abolition plotters against the South], unless you do put down this spirit of abolitionism, the [life of the] Union will be short."[56] In the Senate, Mason who had succeeded in creating a committee to investigate the Brown raid apparently tried to prove that the Republican party was responsible for the crisis.[57] This congressional excitement reacted on Virginia in such a way that the conservative W. C. Rives wrote J. J. Crittenden: "We are looking with disappointment to the course of events at Washington. I have never known the public mind in Virginia filled with as much anxiety as it is at the present moment."[58]

While this congressional contest was being waged, Governor Letcher who had succeeded Wise in January was reporting to the state senate, February 13, that the governor of Iowa had not only refused to surrender Barclay Coppac, one of Brown's companions at Harper's Ferry, but in his inaugural address had justified the Brown "outrage."[59] About the same time the governor of Ohio refused to give up another of Brown's accomplices to the Governor of Virginia.[60] To Letcher this was an evidence of the uncertainty of his state's rights in the Union. "We must cease to be surprised," he said, "when we see the Constitution, and laws enacted for the protection of life, liberty and property, disregarded, condemned and trampled upon. We must meet this spirit of oppression upon the slaveholding States sternly and resolutely, and to this end union and harmony is indispensable to success. We must have a united South."[61]

When the legislature met in December, 1859, the Harper's Ferry incident came up for consideration. In his message to that body Governor Wise declared:

. . . [an] entire social and sectional sympathy has incited their crimes [crimes of abolitionists], and now rises in rebellion and insurrection to the height of sustaining and justifying their enormity. . . .
And since their [abolitionists'] violation it has defiantly proclaimed aloud that 'insurrection is the lesson of the hour'—not of slaves alone but of all who are to be free to rise up against fixed government, and no government is to be allowed except 'the average common sense of the masses,' and no protection is to be given against that power. . . . There can be no compromise with them. . . . They must be met and crushed, or they will crush us, or our union with non-slaveholding States cannot continue.[62]

In conclusion he recommended that Virginia should "organize and arm," and demand of each commonwealth in the Union "what position she intends to maintain for the future in respect to slavery and the constitution." When he had heard from all the states, he said, he would have the Old Dominion act and "not resolve."[63]

Before following Wise's advice, however, the General Assembly appointed a joint committee from the House of Delegates and the senate to investigate the causes and significance of the raid. Late in January this committee submitted its report.[64] After relating the story of the raid, the report summarized the accounts of Northern sympathy for Brown, expressed the belief that "respectable" abolitionists were partners in the crime, reviewed the enactment of "personal liberty laws" in the free states, pointed to the offensive tone of the Northern pulpit and to the activities of the intellectuals in the free states, and pledged Virginia's attachment to the Union. The report recommended the following: first, encourage domestic manufactures, promote direct trade with foreign countries, and establish sectional commercial independence, so far as possible under the United States Constitution; second, "Organize, arm and equip the militia for active and efficient service"; and third, enact bills for "more prompt and effectual punishment of all foreign emissaries and others, who may be found guilty of conspiring against the peace of our community, or seeking to incite our slaves to insurrection."[65]

Radicals outside of the legislature had hoped to use the Brown raid as a means of consolidating Southern sentiment in favor of dissolution.[66] A correspondent in the Richmond *Enquirer* urged immediate secession without awaiting a united South.[67] Within and without the legislature, however, most discussions centered in a later proposal for a Southern convention.

The first of the committee's recommendations relative to commercial and economic retaliation had long since been an object of agitation.[68] In the crisis of 1847-1851 Southern Rights Associations had been formed, and the press and leaders had considered non-importation the most effective weapon against the North.[69] In less pronounced form such a policy had been advocated throughout the fifties.[70] The Brown raid revived the earlier fervor of these associations. Beginning probably with Ruffin's resolutions of 1859, which urged the renewal of the old associations,[71] the idea was shortly thereafter championed by the newspapers and endorsed by the county meetings throughout the Tidewater and Piedmont.[72]

Recalling the effect of Colonial non-intercourse against England in the pre-Revolutionary years and the assumed effect of a similar movement against the North, in 1850-1851, the advocates of this plan of redress argued that since the North could not prosper without Southern markets "this is the string upon which the South must plan to bring the North to her senses."[73] At first even the *Whig* joined the extremists in advising that Northern goods should be taxed and foreign trade encouraged.[74] Soon, however, when it had seen the dangers of a tax on goods from the free states, this paper recommended the establishment of voluntary associations

bound together by a common pledge among themselves [the members of such an association] neither to eat, drink, wear, buy or use any article whatsoever manufactured at or imported from the North. Our fathers in the Revolution made and carried out a similar pledge in regard to importations from the mother country, and thus evinced a patriotic self-denial which has no parallel in history. . . . We of the South must imitate their glorious example, if we would not be longer tributary to those who are fast getting to be our worst enemies.[75]

The *Enquirer* wished to follow this plan not only as a means of retaliation and redress, but as a preparation for self-sufficiency in case a dissolution of the Union should come after March 4, 1861.[76]

In accordance with these general recommendations the Southern

Rights Association began a crusade for carrying through non-intercourse with the North and the development of home manufactures.[77] In a public meeting at Manchester in the eastern part of the state, resolutions were adopted pledging those present "to use, eat, drink, wear or buy nothing under the sun from north of the Mason and Dixon line."[78] An Amelia County gathering urged the legislature to pass laws discriminating against Northern products until the people there suppressed "their agitation and movements against us and our interests."[79] Women wore "homespun" dresses at their parties and balls.[80] In its issue of December 20 the *Enquirer* declared that in "nearly all the cities and towns throughout the State 'Homespun Clubs,' the members of which pledge themselves to dress in no other than Virginia fabrics, are being organized. The clubs seem to be very popular, and are patronized by the most prominent people of Norfolk, Richmond, and Alexandria."[81] As an expression of this spirit Senator Mason appeared in the Senate dressed in homespun.[82] In their meeting on November 30, 1859, the members of the board of directors of the Richmond and Danville Railroad decided that since it was a Southern enterprise it was their duty to support the cause of the South. Therefore, they said, they would not purchase material for their road from the North whenever the same equipment could be obtained in the South at a reasonable rate.[83] Richmond merchants decided that, as far as practicable, they would buy their goods directly from Europe rather than from the free states.[84] Because of these numerous resolutions, a Richmond firm prepared a trade directory listing Northern merchants sympathetic to the South.[85] Along with other Southerners, many Virginia medical students attending Northern colleges transferred to Southern institutions.[86] In keeping with this retaliatory spirit, moreover, the long-drawn-out efforts exerted throughout the fifties to gain direct trade with Europe were realized within a month after the Brown raid.[87]

The boycotting resolutions apparently affected the trade of Northern manufacturers and merchants. On November 25, 1859, the *Whig* joyfully announced that "we hear of various instances in which Northern 'drummers' have been flatly notified that it was altogether useless to solicit 'orders' here."[88] In December the Bridgeport *Farmer* (Connecticut) declared that one manufacturer of that city had to reduce the working hours because the usual Southern orders did not come in. A similar complaint was made by a firm in Worcester, Massachusetts.[89] At the beginning of 1860 the Philadelphia *Evening Journal* reported that one hundred laborers in a factory in that city had been dismissed because of Southern conditions;[90] The New York *Journal of Commerce* stated that the Harper's Ferry incident had caused Northern textile workers to move South;[91] and the New York *Herald* said that New York City had lost "considerable trade" because of the Brown raid.[92] Although the country was in a more prosperous condition in 1860 than in 1859, New England's shipment of shoes which were designed mainly for slaves declined from 717,991 pairs in 1859 to 653,047 in 1860— a nine per cent loss.[93]

Some Virginians felt that, as in 1849-1851, the legislature should aid the volunteer boycotting of Northern products by placing a special tax on goods from the free states. This idea, although at first backed by the *Whig* and *Enquirer,* was given little support in the legislature. A bill was introduced providing for a special license for those who sold Northern goods within Virginia. Wyndham Robertson of Richmond dealt this a severe blow when he showed that it would injure Virginia's trade with friendly states of the North. He said, furthermore, that unless other slave states coöperated it would have little effect; that the home manufacturers produced only two per cent of the textiles used in Virginia; and that above all the bill would violate the interstate commerce clause of the United States Constitution. Along with others, therefore, he recommended dependence on the voluntary associations.[94] Before the measure came up for a vote the sentiment of the state had become calm again, and as a result the bill was defeated.[95]

The second method for gaining redress, military defense, was more successful in the legislature. The news of the Harper's Ferry raid led Governor Wise, in October, 1859, to call out several regiments of the militia. As reports and rumors of contemplated rescues spread in October, November, and early December, people became more alarmed. This unrest was indicated by the fact that the military activities within the state were in keeping with those in time of war. In most counties volunteer companies were organized,[96] young men drilled daily, and the newspapers rejoiced in the war spirit displayed. As an expression of such a spirit, the Portsmouth *Transcript* declared that there was something "grand in it, that . . . hides the horrible from our vision, and asks the recognition of our noblest sentiments. . . ."[97] The *Whig* urged "the citizen-soldiers of Virginia, as they value their homes and the blessings of good government . . . the instant necessity of making the secular arm of the State all that it can possibly welcome by down-right, practical, thoroughgoing training. If we needs must be soldiers, let us be soldiers in earnest."[98] On the Eastern Shore, in the Valley, at Richmond College, at the University of Virginia, and in various other parts of the state, military companies were enthusiastically drilling during the autumn and winter of 1859-1860.[99]

This outburst of military enthusiasm convinced the leaders that a better equipped militia was needed as a protection. Wise, in his last message to the legislature in December, and Letcher, in his inaugural in January, advised the General Assembly to increase the military force of the state in order that the borders could be defended against future raids.[100] Likewise, the joint committee, appointed to investigate the Brown raid, advised the legislature to "organize, arm and equip the militia for active and efficient service."[101] In accordance with these recommendations the General Assembly passed a law providing $500,000 to establish a public armory, and to purchase arms for the purpose of defending the "most exposed parts of the state."[102] Twenty thousand dollars extra were appropriated for the Virginia Military Institute to take care of the increased demand for officers.[103] Regulations affecting the organization and discipline of the militia were altered so as to meet the new emergency.[104]

The third measure of redress recommended by the committee was taken up by local authorities. In its place the legislature considered the proposed Southern convention. In the excitement immediately following the Brown raid, the "Southern Rights" party in Virginia insisted that secession was the only remedy. The most rabid of these, Ruffin, rejoiced in Brown's "outrages" since they might "stir the sluggish blood of the South."[105] From Harper's Ferry where he had uttered "disunion views" on "every available opportunity," he went to Washington.[106] There, in conference with congressmen from South Carolina, North Carolina, Alabama, and Virginia, he advised these members of the national legislative bodies to "agitate and exasperate the already highly excited indignation of the South," lest slavery be doomed.[107] He wrote articles for the press and pamphlets for distribution, and exerted all the influence he was capable of at the Southern Rights Associations' meetings.[108] Despite the fact that he exercised at this time little political weight, his former reputation and services in agriculture caused some people to respect his views.[109]

Men more conservative than Ruffin expressed considerable anxiety over the growing secession sentiment.[110] In his inaugural address Letcher said that " 'if the aggressions to which we have been subjected for so many years are to be repeated, if mutual distrust and suspicions are to continue, and if the election of a Republican candidate to the presidency in 1860 is to be superadded, it is useless to attempt to conceal the fact that, in the present temper of the Southern people, it cannot and will not be submitted to.' "[111]

Because of these outspoken secession sentiments and the general unrest in Virginia, the South Carolina legislature in December, 1859, determined to try again its coöperation plan. It selected C. G. Memminger, a Unionist in 1852 and a moderate in 1859, to express the "cordial sympathy of the people of South Carolina with the people of Virginia," and to recommend that the Southern states unite "in measures of defence."[112] If Virginia responded favorably to the invitation, the other slave states would be asked to join a Southern convention.[113] Mississippi joined in the scheme and sent Peter B. Starke to advise that "some remedy consistent with their interest and honor" in the Union "be devised."[114]

This was not an entirely new plan of redress even for Virginians, for several county meetings and one important newspaper, the *Enquirer*, had recommended Southern and national conventions.[115] The Hunter element expected to call a Southern conference if concessions could not be obtained from the North through a national body, or through special commissioners of Virginia to be sent to the respective free states.[116]

Memminger arrived in Richmond on January 12. After delivering the resolutions from his state he proceeded, upon the invitation of the Virginia legislature, to address that body. He reminded his hearers that in 1833 and 1852 South Carolina had modified her course because of Virginia's requests, and now that the Old Dominion was in distress his state had come to the rescue; that there was no safety for the slave states in a union where Republicans controlled; and finally that the Harper's Ferry episode was merely a forerunner of graver invasions. The South, he said, had already lost her controlling power in the government, and as the North continued to increase her hold, the South's safety would be imperiled even more since the abolitionists would gradually enlarge their power over the Northern parties.[117]

Memminger soon found that there was a great difference between the expressed disunion sentiment of November and December and the actual consideration of what some labeled a "secession plot." His plan was bitterly opposed by the extreme Unionists who maintained that the Harper's Ferry incident had never been a cause for alarm and that the uncalled-for excitement prevalent in the state had been manufactured by politicians for party purposes,[118] and by moderates who were afraid of any conference with the lower South. Unionists, such as Timothy Rives of Prince George, R. M. Bentley of Loudoun, Edwin Watson of Pulaski, and George M. Porter of Hancock, began extolling in their speeches in the legislature the "glories" of the Union. At the same time they advertised the growing friendly sentiment of the North as expressed in meetings at Boston, Philadelphia, and New York.[119] The *Whig* and the independent Richmond *Daily Dispatch* also took a similar position.[120] Even the Democratic press had become lukewarm in its support of a Southern convention. When the sectional conference was first proposed by South Carolina, the *Enquirer* declared that while it would do no harm it might have a wholesome effect on the North. This paper insisted that the purpose of the conference was not to gain disunion, but to unite the South in her efforts to obtain redress for grievances at the hands of the North.[121] At least it would be a way to defeat the Republican candidate in the presidential election.[122] The Hunter faction felt that a Southern conference would be dangerous to its candidate's chances for President in 1860.[123] In its place it advised that the appeals of Virginia to the Northern states should be made independently and that a Southern convention should not be resorted to at this time.[124]

Unfortunately for Memminger his proposal came up for discussion at the time when all factions were looking to the presidential campaign. The Whigs tried to show that the South Carolina scheme was designed solely to bring about disunion and that because of that fact it had the backing of many "Southern Rights" Democrats.[125] Stuart wrote Crittenden on January 22, 1860, and urged him to issue the party's address in order to save their pro-Southern element from going over to the Democrats. "You see," he continued, "Memminger is here — for God's sake give us a rallying point or disunion may follow."[126] In a personal letter to R. B. Rhett on January 28, Memminger explained the party wrangle going on in the legislature.

It is extremely difficult to see through the Virginia Legislature. The Democratic party is not a unit and the Whigs hope to cleave it with their wedge, wherever dissensions arise. Governor Wise seems to me to be really with us as well as Mr. Hunter's portion, but he seems to think it necessary to throw out tubs to the Union whales. The effect here of Federal politics is most unfortunate. It makes this great state comparatively powerless. . . . I see no men . . . who would take the position of leaders in a Revolution.[127]

In the latter part of January the legislature began debating the proposal for a Southern conference. After much wrangling, committees were appointed in each house to consider not only South Carolina's invitation but also Mississippi's. They were directed to take cognizance also of Letcher's recommendations for a national convention and special commissioners who would request the Northern states to repeal their "personal liberty laws."[128] Before these committees reported, the discussion in the press and among leaders had practically killed the chances of success for any of the radical schemes. The Richmond *Whig* declared that most Virginians were "neither ready nor willing to appeal to that last *resort* [secession] . . . on account of any aggression or pretended aggression of the North, down to the present hours."[129] Since the United States Constitution would be satisfactory if it were enforced, a Southern convention or a national convention would be useless.[130] The Democratic Staunton *Vindicator* agreed with the *Enquirer* that these proposals from the cotton states did not involve disunion. It felt that for courtesy's sake South Carolina's invitation should be accepted.[131] As in the debate over the Nashville Convention in 1850, the question of disunion became an issue; and the Democratic press failed to convince most legislators that the proposals did not involve a dissolution of the Union.

In this contest virtually all newspapers west of the Alleghanies— the *Kanawha Valley Star* was a noticeable exception[132]—and even the county Democratic and city Whig papers of the east counseled moderation. The few papers which supported the Southern conference insisted that their purpose was not secession.[133]

In the legislature the committees delayed matters. For the first two weeks after its appointment, the senate committee did not meet. Consequently before a vote came, Memminger, without hope, had returned to his native state to report to Governor Gist that "the apprehension that the proposed conference must lead to disunion has . . . been the hindrance to its adoption."[134] On March 8 the plan was defeated in the senate by a vote of thirty-one to eleven and in the House of Delegates by ninety to forty-two.[135] The overwhelming majorities in both houses included Democrats as well as Whigs in spite of the halfhearted advice of the *Enquirer, Examiner,* and Richmond *Index* to the contrary.[136] For the sake of pacifying the radicals the resolution declining to coöperate in the Southern conference was made as courteous as possible. It stated: "We hail with lively gratification this renewed manifestation of that fraternal regard and affection which has heretofore characterized" the relations of South Carolina and Mississippi with Virginia. In its conclusion, however, the resolution definitely stated that "efficient coöperation will be more safely obtained by such direct legislative action of the several states as may be necessary and proper, than through the agency of an assemblage which can exercise no legitimate power except to debate and advise."[137] This refusal to coöperate caused the Charleston *Mercury* to become so bitter towards Virginia that the Alexandria *Gazette* reminded the *Mercury* that a continuation of such abuse would drive many to the Union side.[138]

The Brown raid went far towards preparing Virginia for secession in 1861. Although an overwhelming majority in the state felt that the incident itself was not a sufficient cause for disrupting the Union, it increased the number of secessionists and decreased the faith of a larger number in the advantages and permanency of the Union. It caused many Union leaders to wonder if continued association with the free states would be possible. John C. Rutherfoord, for many years chairman of the State Democratic Committee and a member of the legislature, very forcefully expressed this change of view when on February 21, 1860, he declared in the House of Delegates:

Public opinion is king in the nineteenth century. It makes laws, decides court cases. . . . If Northern public opinion were already fatally imbued with a spirit of active and fanatical hostility to the institution of slavery, I should regard the Union as even now dissolved in fact, if not in form. A common government could not long bind those together whom insults, injuries and mutual hatred had already disunited and divided into two hostile nations. . . .

Northern sentiment has reached an alarming state . . . . [Out of this hostile sentiment has grown] nullification of a constitutional compact for the security of our property; the denial of our equal rights in the territories; the insecurity of our property in the states; the unfriendly action of the federal government; the hostile legislation of Northern states, and even the bloody invasion of our soil. It is this anti-slavery sentiment which has severed, between the sections, the bonds of party and of religion, and threatens now to close the channels of trade and sever the bonds of interest, which has honored, with high office, admirers of Brown and endorsers of Helper; and which has even driven, by hundreds, true-hearted sons of the South from Northern seminaries of learning. . . . Here [in this anti-slavery sentiment] lies the danger of disunion.[139]

Rutherfoord, therefore, felt that the Union could be saved only by a change of sentiment in the North.[140] Similarly, Governor Wise declared to the medical students, who returned to the South from Northern institutions as a protest against the Northern sympathy for Brown,[141] that the disruption of churches was not so dangerous as the present separation of "our people."[142] Even the *Whig* maintained:

For twenty-five years the Northern people have been keeping up a continual agitation in the Union concerning the institution of slavery. . . . Our connection with the North, is a standing instigation of insurrection in the South. . . . Congress is a vast abolition conventicle, and the Union itself a powerful organization by which domestic disquietude is created. . . . The Harper's Ferry invasion therefore, if wisely considered, is of vast significance, and should bid the people of the South to prepare for those future events, of which this is only the premonition.[143]

For the first time such conservative independent papers as the Richmond *Daily Dispatch* were inclined to speak sarcastically of the Union's value "except to the North."[144] The radicals who had been in ill repute were now listened to, and even conservatives demanded guarantees in the territories which they had not formerly asked for.[145]

Earlier "crises" had scarcely, except for a brief period in 1849-1850, alarmed more than the political leaders in Virginia. The Brown raid stirred the people. Davidson, for instance, wrote on December 19 that "a short time ago" he thought it "treason almost even to speak of disunion. . . . But late events & developments foreshadowed for years back, have taught the South to look to its own interests & stand on its defence. And now that word Disunion, is in the mouth of almost every man, and as common, as household words."[146] It convinced the farmers and planters that Republican control was synonomous with abolition rule.[147] Dr. Douglas Freeman, who in 1908 obtained the opinions of many prominent survivors of the period, maintains that those opinions were unanimous in the conclusion that the Brown raid more than any other one event convinced the people that secession was a smaller evil than the avowed hostility and continued aggression of the North.[148]

A more tangible result of the Brown raid related to the political parties. It has been observed that prior to the Harper's Ferry incident the Whigs and Hunter Democrats were ready to drop the slavery issue from politics.[149] The Whigs had even considered uniting with the conservative Republicans.[150] After the Brown raid, however, the friendship was completely changed, and in its attacks on the Republicans this party organ became as bitter as the Democrats.[151] In fact, by December the *Whig* was advising the "Opposition" congressmen to vote for a Democrat as Speaker of the House of Representatives in preference to a Republican.[152]

This alteration of political affairs necessitated a new program for the "Opposition Party." The Virginia Whigs had planned to hold their state convention before Christmas but were forced to postpone it until after the excitement declined.[153] What Crittenden of Kentucky,

Everett of Massachusetts, Bell of Tennessee, and Stuart of Virginia had hoped to make a strong "Opposition Party," based on non-slavery issues and hostility to Democratic corruption, now became the "National Union Party"—a name which W. C. Rives of Virginia urged Critten-den to change to the "Constitutional Union Party" because of Southern hostility to the word "national."[154] In the legislature, Stuart tried to use the fight on the Memminger proposal as a means of strengthening his party in Virginia, thereby setting the example for other states.[155] When the state convention finally met February 22, Washington's birth-day—a date which was selected to aid their purpose of making it the Union party—what had formerly been a Whig organization became "the" Union one.[156]

The influence of the raid on the Democrats was more noticeable on their factions than on the party as a whole. Before October 17 the supporters of Hunter had virtually absolute control of the party. In order to gain support in the West and North they had become con-servative in their views on slavery in the territories. After the raid they found that in order to keep pace with Wise, who had suddenly become the most popular leader in Virginia, Hunter had to restate his extreme Southern views. In a private letter William Old said that the nominee at Charleston should have a "thorough Southern endorsement . . . to get the popular vote. . . . The vote of this state [Virginia] . . . will be cast for the man who is more distinctly with the popular sentiment on the slavery question."[157] Wise, on the other hand, found the senti-ment stirred by the Brown raid in keeping with his radical territorial program. He emphasized the significance of the Brown incident and tried to make himself the hero of the Southern cause.[158] As a result of his activities the Hunter leaders felt that the fiery ex-Governor was too strongly entrenched to defeat in the state Democratic convention. There-fore, they postponed the contest with him until the election of delegates in the congressional districts. They hoped that by that time Wise would have impaired his chances for the support of Virginia.[159]

CHAPTER VI

THE PRESIDENTIAL ELECTION OF 1860

THE Brown raid altered the Virginia political parties' plans for the election of 1860. The preparations of the Whigs to discard the slavery issue and unite all the conservative factions of the country into the "Opposition Party" were made valueless by this incident, for the Harper's Ferry "invasion" tended to consolidate the Republicans and to separate the Northern and Southern Whigs. The Whig leaders in Virginia, therefore, postponed the "Opposition State Convention" which should have met before Christmas, and awaited the passing of the storm.

The Brown episode and the election of a Speaker emphasized the differences within the ranks of the Democratic party to such an extent that many began to doubt the possibility of holding the factions together for the election of 1860. In addition to this national danger the Virginia Democratic leaders had to deal with a controversy between their two aspirants, Wise and Hunter, for the nomination in the Charleston Convention. Prior to the raid Hunter was almost certain that the vote of the Virginia delegation would go to him. This incident, however, gave Wise an opportunity to regain much of his lost popularity. By a defense of Southern rights and by his defiant replies to the Northern petitions for the release of Brown, he greatly increased his prestige and influence within his own state and throughout the South. As much as they disapproved of the Governor's policy, the supporters of Hunter found that it was not advisable to attack him until after the excitement abated.[1] During the remainder of the year they said little about the approaching presidential campaign, and they ceased their tirades against Wise. Instead they returned to the extreme Southern views which had been abandoned in 1858. It was felt that such a course would strengthen Hunter in the lower South as well as in Virginia.[2] In order to give Wise a chance to destroy or dissipate his recently acquired popularity, they had the state Democratic convention postponed until February 13, the latest date it could conveniently be held.*

---

*After the state convention adjourned the county "primaries," followed by the congressional district conventions, had to be held before the delegates left for Charleston where the national convention would convene on April 23.

As the excitement caused by the Brown raid began to subside in January and February, the political leaders again turned their attention to party matters. Under the new name of "Constitutional Union Party" the Whigs went into their state convention in the early part of February with a united spirit, hoping that with their new strength they might hold the balance of power in the country as a whole and save Virginia from the unharmonious Democrats. The resolutions, accepted as a platform, declared that the Federal Government had no right to interfere with slaves in the states, and that the South would stand by the non-intervention idea as propounded in the Compromise of 1850.[3] Before adjourning they "expressed 'an immovable attachment for the Union' and urged all parties to unite in the endeavor to preserve the Union of their fathers."[4] Contrary to the friendly feeling held by many Virginia Whigs for the Republicans in the summer and early fall of 1859, this convention showed considerable bitterness towards them.[5]

In the Democratic party, while Wise was profiting from the county meetings which continued to excite the anti-Northern sentiment, the supporters of Hunter led by William Old, Lewis Harvie, and B. B. Douglas were shrewdly maneuvering to gain control of the Charleston delegation. They decided that since Wise was too strong to defeat in the state convention, they would first prevent that body from expressing its preference for a presidential candidate; and then in the district conventions they would select delegates friendly to Hunter.[6] In this they succeeded.[7] Aided by the supporters of Stephen A. Douglas, they influenced the state convention simply to reaffirm the "Cincinnati Platform" on congressional control of slavery in the territories, although Wise's friends sponsored resolutions similar to those which were later championed by the delegates from the cotton states at Charleston.[8] In the latter part of February and early March as the extreme Southern sentiment declined, Wise's popularity dwindled away. Consequently after the first defeat in the district conventions he withdrew his name.[9] As soon as they saw that Hunter would control the state's delegation, many followers of Wise turned to Douglas in order to defeat their old rival and to have part in the nomination of a successful candidate.[10] Some extremists among this faction even wanted the "little giant" nominated so that they would have "an excuse and an incentive to independent action."[11] Douglas's followers, on the other hand, hoped that after a few complimentary votes had been cast for Hunter, Virginia's delegation would support their candidate.[12] Many for different reasons, therefore, joined in the district convention to elect delegates who were either hostile or unenthusiastic in their support of Hunter.[13] Nevertheless, a majority of those selected were loyal to him.[14]

Just before the meeting of the Charleston Convention, Hunter's advisers were encouraged by their candidate's chances for nomination. Such national party leaders as Howell Cobb and Robert Toombs of the lower South, Charles Levi Woodbury of Massachusetts, George Fisher of Illinois, and T. L. Kane and W. H. Winder of Pennsylvania had already expressed their willingness to support the Virginia Senator.[15] Kane wrote on March 30, 1860, that the majority of the representatives from Pennsylvania had told him that if Douglas failed at the convention they would work for Hunter.[16] John M. Johnson made the same promise for Iowa.[17] Hunter was conservative, a loyal administration man and, except for the tariff, acceptable to the business interests.[18] He was not a popular candidate but his friends hoped that his conservative tenets and nature would satisfy the Northern Democrats, and that he was sufficiently Southern to please the people of the cotton states.

Douglas's chances of nomination lay in the possibility of his carrying the North in the election; while Hunter's hopes rested on the unity of his Southern supporters aided, after Douglas was checked, by the Northwest. The Virginians planned to force the Northern delegates "to yield to the pertinacious vote of the united South."[19] As a preparation Old explained to Hunter:

> We should . . . make the impression that we intend to meet the Black Republicans, in their sectional character, and in their most Northern aspect, that we mean to make the presidential election one of the issues with the antislavery party, and to make them all distinctly, and that we do not want a victory won by any means that cast doubt on the character of the contest.[20]

When the Charleston Convention convened the delegation from Virginia was not united on the course to follow.[21] The supporters of Hunter felt that they must gain the backing of the "united South" or their candidate would lose. At the same time they could not afford to antagonize Douglas's delegates from the North. They hoped to keep the representatives of the lower South quiet on the platform—their concession to the North—and to win the nomination for a Southern man; consequently they would have the nomination first. The Virginia delegates who were friendly to Douglas agreed to the suggestion on the platform, but they wanted their candidate rather than a Southern man as the party's nominee because they felt that he was the best chance for a successful campaign in the North. The few followers of Wise were for an endorsement of Senator Jefferson Davis's resolutions on slavery in the territories, even to the extent of splitting the party.

The adherents of Hunter tried in the early days of the convention to carry out their idea of nominating the candidate first,[22] but the Yancey and the Northern extremists were determined to fight out their platform differences before making nominations. Since Hunter's success depended primarily on the support from the cotton states, he could not antagonize that region. With much misgiving, therefore, his supporters went into conference with the other Southern delegates for the purpose of agreeing on the sectional demands.[23] The decision to confer was reached by a vote of thirty to four in the state delegation's caucus, Wise and Hunter's friends voting in the affirmative and Douglas's in the negative.[24] Finally on April 25 by a vote of twenty-seven to three —several were absent—it was decided to support the lower South in her demands.[25] Contrary to the resolutions of the state Democratic convention which endorsed the Cincinnati platform, the delegation agreed to insist on the specific congressional protection to slavery in the territories. The followers of Douglas reminded those friendly to Hunter that, although this position was legally right, the embodiment of the principle in the Southern demands would result in the destruction of the Democratic party and the election of a Republican as President.[26]

In the convention the adoption of the Douglas platform led to the withdrawal of the delegations of Alabama, South Carolina, Mississippi, Florida, Texas, Arkansas, and Georgia.[27] As a result of this withdrawal, the representatives from Virginia were puzzled as to the course they should follow. Many supporters of Hunter were indignant because those from the cotton states had destroyed the chances of nominating their candidate,[28] but they could not afford to attack the seceders. After receiving the promise of the New York delegation that at any time they would support the Tennessee resolutions, all but one of the representatives of Virginia, along with those from the other border states, decided to remain in the convention.[29] At the same time they agreed that as long as they attended they would be bound by every vote and the nomination.[30] It was their hope that in order to prevent a permanent split of the party, the Northwest would grant some modification in platform or nominate a candidate acceptable to the South.[31] Throughout the remainder of the convention Virginians tried to prepare the way for reconciliation between the seceders and the Northern element. In this effort they attempted to gain the adoption of the Tennessee resolutions[32] and to have a Southern man nominated.[33] After these efforts failed, Russell, the chairman of Virginia's delegation, recommended that the body adjourn to meet at Baltimore June 18. He hoped that the period between the two sessions would aid in the conciliation of the wings of the party.[34]

The reaction in Virginia to the conduct of the Southern delegates varied in different sections and among different factions. A few eastern papers, friendly to Wise, not only exonerated the seceders but also condemned the delegation of Virginia for not doing likewise.[35] At the other extreme, those supporting Douglas criticized the representatives of the cotton states for seceding and the Virginians for agreeing with the Yancey element to press the radical platform of the convention.[36] Davidson even wrote Letcher that he was "inclined to fear . . . that Southern men have brought this thing about to secure the election of a Black Republican—so as to have a pretext for disunion."[37] The papers which were supporting Hunter's candidacy excused the action of the state's delegation and condemned those who withdrew.[38] From the first the *Examiner* tried to restrain the attacks on the representatives of the lower South, for, it said, such attacks would diminish the possibilities of reconciliation.[39] In many "primaries" of the eastern counties the position taken by the seceders was commended; in a few, such as those of Chesterfield, Rockingham, and Dinwiddie, resolutions condemning the action of the cotton states at Charleston and pledging their support to the nominees at Baltimore were adopted; and in virtually no counties west of the Blue Ridge was the withdrawal commended.[40]

The Virginia Democrats' disapproval of the lower South's conduct at Charleston was further illustrated by their refusal to coöperate in the "Constitutional Democratic Convention," as the seceders' meeting was called. Only eight county "primaries" requested their delegates to attend this body; and these advised their representatives to go to the Richmond Convention not with the purpose of participating in the proceedings, but of entreating this body to join the convention at Baltimore.[41] Moreover, the Virginia press said little about the gathering at Richmond. The *Examier* was too much concerned with, conciliation to antagonize the cotton states by attacking it; so this paper practically ignored the gathering by placing the reports of its proceedings in a column headed "City Matters."[42] Because of its rabid Southern leanings the *Enquirer* was friendly but not actively engaged in trying to make this convention a success.[43] Under the editorship of Glass the Lynchburg *Republican*, a Douglas organ, openly attacked it. In one of his editorials he declared: "It is an attempt, without sufficient cause, to

disrupt the Democratic party, and eventually to disrupt the Union itself."[44] Governor Letcher also thought the object of the Richmond Convention was to overthrow the national party.[45]

Thus, on the eve of the National Democratic Convention at Baltimore
the different factions in Virginia were not united on a course to
pursue. The supporters of Wise endorsed the seceders' action and
urged the Virginia delegation to insist on the Alabama platform or
separate from the national party.[46] The Douglas element had no
sympathy for the seceders, the Richmond Convention, or the extreme
Southern platform. It was for accepting the Cincinnati platform and
for pledging the state Democrats to support the Baltimore nominee
whoever he should be.[47] Still hoping to nominate their candidate or to
modify the platform, the Hunter followers attempted at first to reconcile the Northern and Southern wings. They were playing their former
rôle of trying to convince the lower South of their loyalty to the latter's
interests and, at the same time, trying to induce the Northerners to
permit the seceders to be readmitted.[48] William Old advised that the
Virginia Democrats "must be the arbiters" at Baltimore and that the
attack on Douglas should have "most delicate management . . . [for]
we built him up in Virginia or *rather prevented his destruction*. We
must wait for action by his friends. . . ."[49]

The possibility of reconciliation lay in the readmission of these delegates and the acceptance of the Tennessee resolutions. In a series of
able editorials in May and early June, the *Examiner* tried to convince
the followers of Douglas that such a course would be the only way to
prevent a disruption of the Union.[50] At the same time Hunter, Mason,
and Garnett joined other Southern congressmen in "an address to the
National Democracy" urging harmony between all factions but actually
committing them to follow the Southern delegates in their separation
from the party should platform concessions, which would "proudly
vindicate the action of the seceding delegates," not be granted.[51] In
spite of criticism from C. W. Russell and Governor Letcher, two of his
most influential leaders in the Valley and northwestern part of the
state,[52] most of Hunter's supporters held to this extreme Southern position.

To decide on a course of action the state's delegates met in caucus
before the opening of the Baltimore Convention, and the supporters of
Wise and Hunter agreed to withdraw if the seceders were not readmitted. Under pressure from the lower South the followers of these
two leaders were now working together.[53] Even the *Examiner* was al-

most ready to go over to the extreme Southern view. It decided on the day the convention opened that the question at Baltimore was not the same it had been at Charleston, for in the earlier convention the preservation of the national Democratic party had depended upon the adoption of the Cincinnati platform, while at the forthcoming one the only way to save the party was to regain the coöperation of the lower South.[54] Two days later it declared:

> Indeed, apart from the safeguards it has given and secured, the Union is worse than worthless to the Southern States. Every day the evidence thickens that the guaranties of the Constitution are weakening, and that the time is coming when the powers of the Government are to be strained to the detriment of the South. Hitherto the only barrier to the advance of this calamitous tendency has been the Democratic party.[55]

On the fifth day of the National Democratic Convention at Baltimore when that body refused to seat the old Alabama and Louisiana delegates, Russell as chairman of the Virginia delegation led the Hunter and Wise men out of the hall.[56] They were followed by others until there were only thirteen states with full delegations left.[57] This withdrawal included twenty-three out of the thirty representatives from Virginia.[58] All the followers of Douglas except R. H. Glass remained,[59] and he withdrew although he did not take part in the "Seceders Convention."[60] Dillard, an alternate who did not secede, declared in an open letter explaining his position that his support of the Northern Democratic candidate did not mean that in a crisis he would be disloyal to the South and that, if dissolution of the Union should come, he would "be ready at once to unite, heart and hand, with the whole South in defence of our homes and section."[61]

Following their withdrawal from the National Democratic Convention, June 22, four-fifths of the Virginia delegates joined the 232 representatives of seventeen states in the "Seceders Convention" held at Maryland Institute Hall in Baltimore June 23. Here the "Majority Report" of the platform committee at the Charleston Convention was adopted. John C. Breckinridge of Kentucky and General Joseph Lane of Oregon were nominated for President and Vice-President, respectively.[62]

Before the two Democratic conventions had agreed on their tickets, the "Constitutional Union Party" in a more harmonious spirit had selected its candidates. Its conclave was held at Baltimore on May 9.[63] It was made up largely of representatives from the border states. Only three states from the Northwest sent delegates.[64] Instead of adopting a regular platform this body merely endorsed the "Constitution of the Country, the Union of the States and the enforcement of the laws." It was expected that each state would adopt a program to suit its own situation.[65] John Bell of Tennessee and Edward Everett of Massachusetts were selected for the presidential and vice-presidential candidates of the party.

In the early part of the campaign which followed, the chief interest in Virginia centered around the attempts to consolidate the Douglas and Breckinridge tickets. The first move in that direction was the calling of ratification conventions. On July 10, by a vote of six to three, the state Democratic executive committee decided to call a convention at Charlottesville for August 16.[66] Immediately thereafter two committeemen, J. E. Harman and Timothy Rives who objected to this ruling, advised the supporters of Douglas to meet in a mass gathering at Staunton on the same day.[67] Between these two dates the leaders in both camps discussed means of conciliation. R. H. Glass expressed the opinion that the only way to defeat Lincoln was for each state to have one set of Democratic electors who, after the popular election, should cast the vote for that particular candidate which "the best interests of the party and the country may to them [the electors] seem best at the time."[68] The *Enquirer* advocated the withdrawal of the Breckinridge ticket in New York as a means of defeating Lincoln.[69] The Charleston *Spirit of Jefferson,* a paper friendly to Douglas's candidacy, approved both these plans.[70]

When the two ratification conventions met on August 16 at Charlottesville and Staunton, Ex-Governor William Smith recommended that the former convention send a committee to the one at Staunton to work out a compromise. In spite of the opposition of such extremists as Mason and Harvie, the plan was approved by a vote of 111 to 105.[71] The Douglas body appointed a similar committee. Because of inconvenient train schedules, however, these committees never got together to discuss the fusion of the two tickets.[72] Instead, they negotiated by telegrams. In his telegram to the chairman of the Douglas committee, Smith proposed that the Democrats of the state vote for a single set of electors, "the voters designating on their tickets their preference for Breckinridge or Douglas, as the case may be, the electors to cast the vote of the State in conformity with the majority ascertained."[73] Realizing that Breckinridge would poll more votes in Virginia than Douglas, Harman declined this proposal.[74] As a substitute for Smith's plan, he suggested that each faction appoint seven electors who if elected "will pledge themselves to cast the vote of the State so as to beat Lincoln."[75] Since neither convention would accept the other's proposal, no agreement was reached.[76]

As the campaign developed both Democratic groups realized that Bell would probably carry the state if some plan of uniting the members of the party was not carried out; consequently another conference was proposed. Jacob Baylor, a supporter of Breckinridge, suggested that only one set of Democratic electors be placed on the ballots; and that, if elected, they should cast their votes for the respective party candidates in proportion to the popular votes for each. In other words, if there were eighty thousand popular votes in Virginia for Breckinridge and twenty thousand for Douglas, twelve electoral votes would go to the former candidate and three to the latter.[77] The Douglas executive committee approved this plan;[78] but the *Enquirer* announced for its faction that since Breckinridge would carry the state anyway and that since the followers of Douglas were denouncing "the Virginia Democrats as disunionists we would not feel justified in according to the proposition."[79] In the meetings of the two committees the Breckinridge elements defeated the Baylor plan, and the adherents of Douglas again rejected the Smith proposal.[80]

Already the hostility between the two factions was too strong for reconciliation.[81] Some of the supporters of Douglas weakened after their candidate declared in his Norfolk speech that, if he were elected President, he would use force against the seceding states.[82] Others went over to Breckinridge in order to defeat Bell.[83] On the other hand Governor Letcher, who openly aligned himself on the side of Douglas soon after the failure of Smith and Harman to combine the two wings of the party, doubtless carried many votes with him to the side of Douglas.[84]

At the same time that these efforts to join the tickets of the two Democratic factions were being made, the "Constitutional Union" leaders were playing a clever game. They waited until after the failure of the Charlottesville and Staunton conventions to work out a plan of coalition before opening fire on either Democratic element, for their attack on one of these might make the other join the attacked.[85] Stuart, one of the ablest Whig leaders, had written a number of editorials designed to promote the *"entente cordiale* between the friends of Bell and Douglas."[86] "This object," he wrote Blanton Duncan, "has been accomplished, and the Douglas men, if necessary would cheerfully support our ticket, to ensure the defeat of Breckinridge. This, however, will not be required, and we prefer that they should keep up their separate organization."[87] The speeches of campaigners for Douglas and the accounts of his activities were given prominent space in the Whig papers.[88]

In order to widen the breach in the Democratic ranks the leaders of the "Constitutional Union Party" portrayed the Breckinridge party as favoring disunion. In support of this contention they quoted from the speeches of radical Southerners such as W. L. Yancey, J. T. Morgan, and R. B. Rhett.[89] Although they conceded that Breckinridge himself was not a disunionist, they insisted that "his fortunes are too much and intimately associated with the schemes of the disunionists of the South" to justify his election.[90] At the same time, they emphasized their own love for the Union and begged the followers of Douglas to help them defeat the "enemies of the Confederation." The Whig county meetings were careful to express their hostility to secession; and speeches and letters of nationalists like Botts and Rives were circulated to strengthen the contention that theirs was the "Union Party."[91]

The adherents of Douglas also tried to prove the same thing about the Breckinridge party. They circulated a pamphlet of the national Democratic executive committee which included many passages from the speeches of Yancey.[92] In a speech at Richmond on October 17, Congressman Millson from the first district advised the people to cast a large vote against Breckinridge in order to insure the safety of the Union, for this would discourage the cotton states in their program.[93]

On the other hand, the Breckinridge Democrats, especially in the western part of the state, consistently denied that a vote for their candidate was a vote for secession. In fact, they insisted that the only way to prevent the Lincoln election and disunion was for the South to support their candidate.[94] In the eastern part of the state the argument for Southern rights was added. The *Examiner,* for instance, expressed the view that rather than a contest of union or disunion the campaign was a struggle for the rights of the states.

> The efforts on the part of the States Rights Democracy is to limit and restrain the power of this Federal Agent, . . . even though it be its agent of a despotic sectional majority, and does seek to suppress the rightful independence and sovereignty of the separate States. . . . It is nothing but the old contest between the friends of centralized, concentrated powers in the hands of a General Government, and the advocates of separate, distinct, conservative powers, in the limiting Constitution and the sovereign States authorities.[95]

After the Republican success in October in the state contests of Indiana and Pennsylvania, the election of Lincoln was made almost a certainty;[96] so the campaign in Virginia turned to the question of the course to follow when Lincoln became President of the United States. In 1856 and the latter part of 1859 several leaders had asserted that the election of a Republican would dissolve the Union.[97] In July of 1860 the *Enquirer* repeated this view by declaring that if the Republicans were successful at the polls slavery would eventually be destroyed and the South degraded.[98] In his campaign speech at Norfolk on September 27 in behalf of Breckinridge's candidacy, Wise said that although he felt that methods other than secession would be more effective for protecting Southern rights, he considered the election of Lincoln a justification for disunion.[99] Radicals, including Edmund Ruffin and John Tyler, Jr., even suggested that the South ought to secede if any candidate except Breckinridge were elected.[100] On the other side, Douglas's supporters, the Whigs, and especially many followers of Breckinridge in the western part of the state maintained consistently that the election of Lincoln would not be a just cause for breaking up the Union.[101] The *Daily Dispatch,* independent in politics, carried several editorials in August to show that secession would not be the best remedy for the South's grievances.[102] In a letter of August 15, 1860, to John B. Floyd, Buchanan's Secretary of War, Lincoln said that his recent communications from Floyd and Botts contained "one of the many assurances I receive from the South that in no probable event will there be any very formidable effort to break up the Union."[103] In the northwestern part of the state the talk of disunion was answered by threats to divide the commonwealth.[104]

In spite of this overwhelming attachment to the Union, the radicals led by the *Enquirer* kept the issue before the people in the latter part of the campaign when Lincoln's election seemed certain. On October 15 this paper provoked considerable discussion when it declared that, since Lincoln's victory was almost certain, the South should prepare to defend herself. Virginia, it continued, could not prevent the secession of the cotton states, and "hitched as she is to the Southern states, she will be dragged into a common destiny with them, no matter what may be the desire of her people. . . ." Believing that the majority of the people of Virginia realized that their destiny was connected with that of the South, this paper advised "the Slave States not to hesitate to strike an early blow from fear that Virginia may hesitate in her duty to the South."[105] The next day and until election it urged that one more effort ought to be made to save the Union by "uniting the South," for the alarm which the North would have from this unity would influence New York to vote against Lincoln and cause his defeat.[106]

In reply to the argument that secession by the lower South would necessitate Virginia's following, conservatives maintained that the Old Dominion was not "hitched" to the region of the South; and that such extreme ideas as those expressed by the *Enquirer* in the editorials just quoted not only misrepresented the sentiment of their state, but also encouraged the leaders of the cotton states to prepare for secession. Judge R. H. Field of Culpeper County in an open letter to the editor of this paper reminded him that such expressions of opinion were dangerous.[107] A county mass meeting in Rockingham denounced the *Enquirer's* position, as "a foul calumny and aspersion on this noble commonwealth and a gross insult to her people."[108] The *Whig* declared that "Virginia will *not* unite with them [the states of the lower South] in 'resistance' to the mere Constitutional election of Abraham Lincoln, or any other man. . . . The position of Virginia is, that she means to stand by the Constitution and Union to the last, and *demand* all her Constitutional rights *in* the Union, no matter who may be President."[109] In its reply to these conservative attacks, the *Enquirer* rather cogently argued:

This is all very well to tickle State pride. But is it true? Can Virginia take such an independent course, and separate her destiny from the cotton States?

If she can, as the 'Whig' intimates, separate from the cotton States, we may fairly conclude that Bell and Everett men will vote for her to make the separation. What then will be her condition—remaining in the Federal Union with the present border slave States, powerless to protect her slave property against the wild and reckless fanaticism of a dominant, unrestrained and uncontrollable free-soil party? Her condition would, in five years be more pitiable than that of St. Domingo. The Gulf States having dissolved their connection with the Federal Union, would, as foreign nations, prevent the importation of Virginia negroes, and here would begin the financial ruin that would soon culminate in a desolating and bloody servile war. Such would be the price of Virginia's boastful independence of the cotton States. No such independence exists,—institution of slavery binds all the States wherein it exists so intimately, that a common destiny awaits alike the planting and the farming States.[110]

Before the election was held on November 6, the *Enquirer* and some of its followers had gone further than the position of October 15. On the twenty-third of the month this paper took the position that the Union was already dissolved, for the Constitution as a contract had been broken by the North in her failure to carry out the fugitive slave law.[111] A military company was formed in Cumberland County in order to be prepared "to meet the first attack and not sit back and watch their people's property destroyed."[112] Under the influence of Wise, a Princess Anne mass meeting organized in each magisterial district a "Committee of Safety" similar to those in the Revolutionary times, and a body of "minutemen."[113]

After the October elections in Indiana and Pennsylvania, the Hunter wing of the Democratic party did not take such "advanced ground." It did not expect a dissolution of the Union;[114] therefore, it recommended that the South vote solidly for the "Southern Rights" candidate in order "to regain moral power, to assume a strong and respectable position before the country."[115]

It would seem from this survey of the presidential campaign that there was little disunion sentiment. Each party insisted that a vote for its candidate would be a vote for the Union. The Hunter wing dodged this issue and tried to elect Breckinridge on the ground that he was for Southern interests. It denied, however, that the Breckinridge party was for secession. The *Enquirer*, representing Wise, also maintained that Breckinridge was a Union man. Near the end of the campaign, however, it expressed the view that the election of Lincoln would justify secession, and that, if the lower South should withdraw from the Union, Virginia, because of her attachment to the cotton region, would have to follow. The Douglas faction and the supporters of Bell, on the whole, were pronounced in their Union views.

In the election Bell carried the state by the small popular plurality of 358.[116] He polled more votes than any other candidate in the counties of the Valley north of Roanoke and in those east of the Blue Ridge.[117] Breckinridge carried the northwestern and southwestern sections of the state.[118] Douglas's support came largely from the Shenandoah Valley, Richmond city, Chesterfield County, and a few counties in the northwestern section.[119] Lincoln polled 1,929 votes in the whole state. About twelve hundred of these came from the Panhandle around Wheeling.[120] The others came largely from the Northern Neck, Loudoun, Fairfax, and Prince William where New England anti-slavery people had settled.[121]

It is sometimes held that in the main the votes for Breckinridge were cast by secessionists and that the ones which went to Douglas and Bell came from the Unionists.[122] An examination of the election returns does not seem to warrant this generalization for Virginia. The northwest, the Valley, and some of the southwest were the Union sections of Virginia in the contest for secession in 1861;[123] and the Piedmont, Tide-

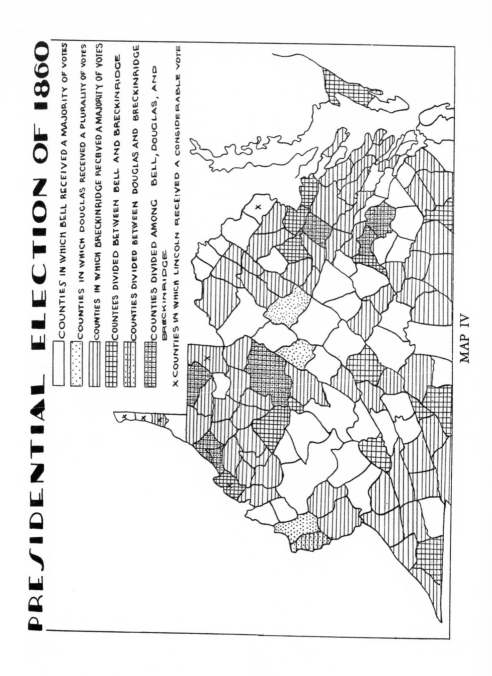

PRESIDENTIAL ELECTION OF 1860

☐ COUNTIES IN WHICH BELL RECEIVED A MAJORITY OF VOTES

⣿ COUNTIES IN WHICH DOUGLAS RECEIVED A PLURALITY OF VOTES.

▨ COUNTIES IN WHICH BRECKINRIDGE RECEIVED A MAJORITY OF VOTES

▤ COUNTIES DIVIDED BETWEEN BELL AND BRECKINRIDGE

▦ COUNTIES DIVIDED BETWEEN DOUGLAS AND BRECKINRIDGE

▩ COUNTIES DIVIDED AMONG BELL, DOUGLAS, AND BRECKINRIDGE

X COUNTIES IN WHICH LINCOLN RECEIVED A CONSIDERABLE VOTE

MAP IV

water, and a part of the southwest were the centers of disunion activities.[124] Breckinridge received 46.9 per cent of the total votes cast in the northwestern part of the state as against 46.4 per cent of those in the section east of the Blue Ridge.[125] If the support given the "Southern Rights" candidate in 1860 is compared with Letcher's in 1859, it will be seen that Breckinridge carried fewer counties of the Tidewater and no more than Letcher in the Piedmont. He had a majority in a smaller number of the counties in the northwest and in the Valley than did Letcher; but those were the districts where Letcher was extremely popular.[126] In proportion to the votes cast for Breckinridge, Douglas polled only a slightly larger number in the northwestern part of the state than he did in either of the counties east of the Blue Ridge or in the whole state.[127] In the district included today in West Virginia, Douglas polled only 5,112 as against 11,178 in what today constitutes Virginia.[128]

TABLE I

The distribution of votes among the different candidates in 1859 and 1860 were as follows:

	Letcher	Goggin	Breckinridge	Bell	Douglas	Per Cent of Total Votes of 1859 for Letcher	Per Cent Total Votes of 1860 for Breckinridge
Tidewater ..	15,809	16,404	15,233	18,232	3,091	50.6	41.6
Piedmont ..	17,196	17,890	19,891	20,240	2,661	49.0	46.4
Northern Valley	16,298	11,258	11,318	12,315	4,753	59.1	39.8
Southwest ..	10,152	11,474	10,456	9,578	857	47.0	50.0
Northwest .	17,567	14,517	17,425	14,316	3,946	54.8	46.9
Present W. Va.	25,362	20,283	21,961	21,175	5,112	55.5	44.2
Present Virginia ...	51,750	51,250	52,362	53,506	11,178	50.2	44.6

TABLE II

Number of counties in the respective districts of the state carried by the respective candidates in 1859 and 1860 were as follows:

	Tidewater	Piedmont	Northern Valley	Southwest	Northwest	Total
LETCHER	16	13	15	9	24	77
GOGGIN	19	19	5	15	10	68
BRECKINRIDGE ..	12	13	9	13	21	68
BELL	21	16	9	10	10	66
DOUGLAS	..	..	2	..	2	4

It would seem, then, that many Unionists did not consider Breckinridge the disunion and Bell and Douglas the Union candidates. This conclusion does not mean, however, that the supporters of Breckinridge did not include disunionists. The fact is that most of the members of the Secession Convention who favored a disruption of the Union had been supporters of Breckinridge in 1860.[129] Possibly some Democrats voted for Bell and Douglas rather than for Breckinridge because they considered the Southern Democratic candidate a secessionist.

More effective issues—effective so far as this campaign was concerned—than disunion seem to have determined the way most people of Virginia voted in 1860. A comparison of the returns from the counties in the elections of 1855, 1856, and 1859 with those of 1860 reveals the fact that most of the normally Democratic counties went for Breckinridge, and that most of the normally Whig counties went for Bell— that is, most people voted the regular party ticket. In this connection it should be recalled that the Whig party in Virginia had been reorganized in the years just prior to 1860 and that it almost won the election of 1859. Whereas in 1856 the Whigs or Americans polled only 60,310 votes, in 1859 they had 71,543, and in 1860, 74,681—a normal party growth.[130] In 1860 the Whigs, or "Constitutional Union Party," gained their full party support. The shift of votes was in the Democratic ranks, and in this party loyalty counted, especially in the west.[131] The organization, press, and most of the trusted leaders of the Democratic party supported Breckinridge. Party loyalty to most Virginia Democrats, therefore, required them to support him. In this connection it is interesting to note that wherever the party leaders and the local press supported Douglas, his popular vote was larger than in adjoining counties with similar interests, but without papers and leaders to change the voters from what they considered the orthodox Democratic ticket.[132] In addition to being guided by party loyalty, some Democrats supported Breckinridge because they thought he could carry Virginia, whereas Douglas could not.[133] Doubtless others felt that since the Northern Democratic ticket and the followers of Bell had little chance to win, they should support Breckinridge in order to defeat Lincoln in the electoral college or in Congress, and thereby save the Union. Moreover, Breckinridge himself was unusually popular in the western part of the state and in the Valley.[134]

The Douglas vote is not so easily explained on the ground of party loyalty as Breckinridge's. Yost, Moffett, Baylor, Harman, and Letcher maintained in the campaign that their candidate was the legal nominee of the Democratic party, and that, in spite of the contention of the party organization within the state, Breckinridge was nominated by those who had deserted the true Democratic principles and candidate.[135] In the districts where these men were active he received his largest vote.[136] Since the campaigners for this ticket emphasized the idea that a vote for their ticket was a vote for the Union, and since the vote for Douglas was strongest where these campaigners were most active, it is reasonable to conclude that some voted for Douglas because they considered Breckinridge a candidate of the secessionists. There were others, too, who wished to discipline the Southern Democrats for splitting the party at Charleston.[137] This element was afraid that the lower South would make it a Southern party, and thereby force the Northern element to join the Republicans. William G. Brown expressed this view when he said: "I hear every day, good, but I think mistaken, men preaching the doctrine that we must have a united South. I fear if that is effected it will tend to build up a like party in the North, and it seems to me that a united South and a united North in antagonism is disunion."[138]

Lincoln's vote came almost entirely from the regions where Northerners lived. In their state convention at Wheeling on May 2, 1860, the Republicans claimed that under the control of the cotton planters of the South and the tobacco planters of the border states, the Democratic and Whig parties had become enemies of manufactures. They also alleged that the eastern slave capital of Virginia, in its control of the state government, had distributed the taxes so that the slaveholders were exempt from their share of the financial burdens; and that the free farmers and laborers of the west had been oppressed by excessive capitation, income, license, and other forms of taxes. The money received from these sources of revenue, the convention asserted, was used for the construction of internal improvements in the east where the slaveholders could hire out their slaves to the state in its public work enterprises.[139] In their campaign in the northwestern counties they emphasized these economic and sectional grievances. Especially were they severe on slaveholders for the tax exemption of slaves under twelve years old and for listing older ones below market value.[140] In this connection F. H. Pierpoint's attack on the system was circulated widely.[141] Such Republicans, however, revealed no love or pity for the negro or desire for abolitionism.[142]

CHAPTER VII

PERIOD OF AGITATION

THE election of Lincoln created consternation among Virginians. A New York *Herald* correspondent wrote from Petersburg on the day following that event, "Every man feels that something terrible is impending."[1] With the exception of Henry A. Wise and the Richmond *Enquirer,* however, not even the "Southern Rights" faction had devised a plan to pursue.[2] Some of the extreme conservatives felt that the election of Lincoln would "put a stop to the slavery agitation more effectively than the election of either of the other candidates."[3] A review of the opinions expressed at the time by the press, political leaders, and county meetings will indicate how strongly attached to the Union most Virginians actually were.

The newspapers which supported Bell and Douglas in the campaign were, in the main, opposed to secession as a remedy for existing conditions. They felt that however "unpalatable the results may be to us of the South, our duty is plain." Since Lincoln was elected in a constitutional manner the South had no cause for "drastic action" until he violated in some way the Constitution.[4] They would await the "overt act" and " 'unite together to resist the aggressions of the dominant party upon their rights.' "[5] The ably edited Charlottesville *Review* (Bell) went further when it stated that Lincoln was connected with the conservative element of the Republican party; that he was explicitly for no interference with slavery where it existed; that he was opposed to the abolition of slavery in the District of Columbia unless a majority of the people there wanted emancipation; that he was in favor of an efficient fugitive slave law; and that he was opposed to negro suffrage.[6] Even if the President-elect, others held, should disregard his constitutional obligations, his restrictions were too great for him to injure the rights of the slave states.[7] The Senate, House of Representatives, and the Supreme Court were at hand to hold him in check; hence the Richmond *Whig* suggested that for the present the people "preserve a masterly inactivity."[8]

Many of these conservative papers not only maintained that Lincoln's

120

election was an insufficient cause for disunion, but they denied the right of secession itself. The *Valley Democrat* (Douglas) maintained that the "idea that a State has the legal right to withdraw from the Union, without a violation of the Constitution, is absurd, and would make our government the most unstable in the world, and convict the framers of the Constitution of weakness and inability to remedy the evils of the old confederation. . . ."[9] The Alexandria *Gazette* tried to strengthen this position by reproducing Thomas Ritchie's editorial of 1814 against the right of secession.[10]

The Breckinridge papers, although in the main opposed to a course which would lead to dissolution,[11] considered the election of Lincoln a step in that direction.[12] The most radical and probably the most influential of these was the Richmond *Enquirer*. Before the election it had urged the state to prepare for a dissolution of the Union[13] and, at the time of the balloting, it was the only influential paper in Virginia which championed immediate secession.[14] On November 10 the editor declared that the "idea of submission to Black Republican rule, under any pretext, is as dangerous as it is degrading." The course Lincoln should follow did not matter, for he was only a "cipher in the present count. . . . The significant fact which menaces the South, is not that Abe Lincoln is elected President, but that the Northern people, by a sectional vote, have elected a President for the avowed purpose of aggressions on the Southern rights. . . . This is a *declaration of war*."[15] The Petersburg *Bulletin* (Breck.) asserted that the election of a "Black Republican" had already destroyed the Union.[16] The Madison *Eagle* (Breck.) went into mourning not because Lincoln was elected, for that "event is rather a source of joy to every right-thinking Southron," but out of "due regard for the memory of our revolutionary fathers. . . ."[17]

Despite their hostility to Lincoln and their loss of hope in the permancy of the Union, these eastern Breckinridge papers did not advise that Virginia take the lead in a disunion movement. Instead, they felt that the cotton states would secede and that Virginia's interests would necessitate her following. The Lynchburg *Republican*, edited by R. H. Glass, stated: "When the cotton states do secede, we shall advocate secession with them. . . . We believe Virginia ought to be, and will be when the time comes, the North of the South, and not the South of the North."[18] Because of this belief, the Richmond *Examiner*, Hunter's organ, insisted that the right of secession was of minor significance, for such conditions would necessitate revolution if no other way could be found.[19] Consequently to prevent the Old Dominion being placed in this embarrassing position, both of these papers urged her to take the lead in securing concessions from the North before the lower South withdrew.[20] At the same time Mason's paper, the Winchester *Virginian,* agreed with the *Examiner* that the South was "one family . . . and if South Carolina secedes, and thus inaugurates a final issue with the North, we are necessarily forced to stand in defence of our homes, interests, and people."[21]

Of the eastern Breckinridge papers only the Portsmouth *Transcript* and the Tappahannock *Southerner* advised against following the lower South into secession if that section were to adopt such a radical course. The former paper maintained that although it expected the cotton states to secede, they would not be justified in taking that step.[22] The other organ expressed doubt that the Union could be divided. It felt, in fact, that an attempted division would provoke a civil war within the South.[23]

The positions of the leaders at this time were not different from those of the press. Only Edmund Ruffin and Wise publicly advocated immediate secession or its equivalent.[24] Before the election Wise had begun the formation of "minutemen" associations in the eastern counties.[25] Ex-President Tyler favored peaceful withdrawal.[26] Mason and Hunter, the two Virginia Senators, were non-committal until the latter part of November when they adopted a policy similar to that of the *Examiner.*[27] Ex-Governor William Smith urged Virginians to work for redress within the Union.[28] John B. Floyd, Secretary of War, endorsed the doctrine of secession but felt that an application of this right would be unwise and unnecessary, for he considered the Republican triumph only temporary.[29] A similar view was expressed by Congressman John S. Millson.[30] John M. Botts, on the other hand, was for remaining in the Union under all conditions.[31]

A more accurate estimate of the sentiment in Virginia at the time of the election can be obtained from a review of the resolutions drawn up in the county mass meetings. These gatherings were apparently non-partisan and occurred in all sections of the state. In most cases they "deplored the election of Lincoln as a terrible misfortune, but few of them held that this in itself constituted sufficient cause for secession."[32] In the northwestern portion of the state, these resolutions showed little sympathy for the disunion movement. A Preston County meeting denied the right of secession and declared that Southern interests could be protected in the Union.[33] In Harrison, the largest slaveholding county of this section, resolutions were adopted which favored exhausting all constitutional remedies for redress before resorting to violent means, and which maintained that the ballot box was the only agency they would resort to.[34] Taylor, a neighboring county, expressed its opposition to taking any steps which would lead to the disruption of the "glorious Union."[35] In Parkersburg on the Ohio River resolutions declaring that secession was nothing less than revolution were adopted.[36] Other northwestern counties and towns endorsed these sentiments.[37]

Between the Blue Ridge and Alleghany mountains the expressions of the public gatherings were almost as hostile to secession as those just considered; but many of this area felt that the slaveholding states ought to unite in an effort to gain from the North concessions which would keep the lower South in the Union. On November 12 a public meeting in Shenandoah County demanded the calling of a convention to confer with other slave states as a means of carrying out this program.[38] The people of Staunton pledged their loyalty to the Union and drew up resolutions decrying disruption and advising the lower South to take no hasty step and the Virginia legislature to "exert every effort to gain redress" in the Union.[39] A mass meeting in the adjoining county declared that "nine-tenths of the people of this state will be opposed to resisting the general government as long as it may be administered in conformity to the Constitution and the common benefit of all the states."[40] James B. Dorman, a Douglas leader at Lexington, wrote Governor Letcher that the "people here are thoroughly Union in feeling" and that they considered it absurd to follow South Carolina. He expressed, however, the fear that radicals such as Wise and those in the lower South would put the border states in an embarrassing position.[41]

East of the Blue Ridge the county meetings rarely supported secession as an immediate remedy,[42] but many looked upon Lincoln's election as such a great danger to Southern rights that withdrawal was justified.[43] They would preserve the Union by presenting a solid Southern front to the North, and thereby force concessions.[44] Others were for coöperation with the border states in a united appeal to the free states for guarantees of their "peculiar institution."[45]

As a result of this survey of the opinions expressed by the press, public leaders and meetings, it may be concluded that so far as the articulate classes represented the sentiment of Virginia a very small proportion of the people at the time of the election were for immediate withdrawal from the Union. The Richmond *Enquirer,* despite its own enthusiasm for separation, admitted that not one man in a hundred wanted to follow such a course.[46] Even among the more radical immediate action was championed in order to gain Southern unity and concessions.[47] Conservatives of all parties from the eastern part of the state conceded that the Southern interests would be in danger under a Republican President, and that guarantees must be obtained, but they did not feel that the existing conditions warranted drastic action.[48] J. B. Jeter, an influential Richmond minister, probably estimated correctly the attitude of many from this section when he wrote a friend in South Carolina that the sentiment of Virginia was decidedly for maintaining the rights of the South in the Union if possible, and, if not, for joining forces with the Southern states.[49]

By January 7 when the legislature convened in a special session, this almost universal sentiment against secession and for remaining in the Union, until all hope of compromise had gone, had changed to such an extent that the legislature was advised by a majority of the eastern and southwestern county meetings, and by some from other sections, to take steps which eventually led to dissolution. This revolution in sentiment was due to the aggressive campaign of the secessionists, to the course of events in the lower South and in Congress, and to the interpretations placed on the attitude of the Republican leaders. The remainder of this chapter therefore, will be devoted to these factors with a view to understanding the sentiment prevailing when the legislature met.

For nearly a month after the outburst produced by the election of Lincoln there was comparative quiet in Virginia. The conservative press advised against hasty commitments and the adoption of a rash policy. Instead, it advised that "with patience and dignity" the people should await the course of events;[50] while the radical press apparently looked to the lower South for leadership.[51] The editor of the Richmond *Whig* took this time for his vacation, and left the writing of editorials to younger men.[52] On November 15 the editor of the Richmond *Enquirer* wrote that he had been silent on the crisis "for the past week" because he wanted to reflect.[53] In like manner for several weeks the prominent political leaders were non-committal.[54]

In this brief period of comparative quiet on the part of most papers and leaders, a few agitators never let up in their efforts to bring the people around to their views. Among these was the venerable Edmund Ruffin[55] who rejoiced in the election of Lincoln, for he hoped that it would hasten the withdrawal of the South.[56] On the day following the election he went to South Carolina in order to participate in the secession of that state. At Charleston he enrolled in a company of "minutemen."[57] He made several speeches at public gatherings, and promised that if South Carolina would secede the Old Dominion and the border states would follow.[58] These speeches and articles written at the time were published in the newspapers and distributed rather widely by Ruffin himself.[59] Though his views were not those of many Virginians in the autumn of 1860 and though the political leaders had little respect for his opinions on such problems, many people, doubtless, listened to his arguments because of his agricultural reforms.[60]

Wise, too, was constantly agitating in this period. He did not recommend secession *per se,* but he probably did as much as any other leader to stir his followers—and he had many devoted supporters even though he had lost control of his party in the Buchanan-Douglas conflict—[61] for this cause. Before the election he induced a public gathering in Princess Anne County to adopt a series of resolutions. These declared that since the election of Lincoln would mean actual war, a committee of safety should be established for each magisterial district as a means of controlling "matters of policy for our safety and for organizing a body of 'minutemen.' "[62] Wise communicated this plan to many eastern counties and leaders, requesting that it be adopted, and advised that a convention of the committees meet to decide on measures for gaining safety within the Union.[63] At several such county meetings similar resolutions were drawn up and the companies of "minutemen" were organized.[64] In the general convention at Norfolk in early December only a few counties were represented.[65] But what this convention lacked in numbers was made up for in enthusiasm—secession speeches which would have done credit to the "fire-eaters" of the lower South were made.[66]

As a part of his program, Wise substituted for secession his unique idea of "fighting in the Union." By this he meant that since the Federal "government, army, navy, forts, treasury, etc.," belonged to the states which had not broken the Constitution and not to the violators, he would marshal the loyal forces with the ships and militias apportioned to states under the Constitution in time of peace, and seize the government from the hands of the Republicans.[67] Eventually when his plan seemed impracticable he supported outright secession.[68]

In the latter part of November and continuing until after dissolution was accomplished in April, Breckinridge leaders and papers supported these agitators in a most effective campaign for disunion. They had a strong party organization which controlled most of the state and national offices within Virginia, and an ably edited press to assist them.

Leading in this "crusade" were the Richmond *Enquirer* and the Richmond *Examiner*. The *Enquirer* had considerable influence because of its prestige gained under the masterful editorship of Thomas Ritchie and retained after his resignation by his own and Wise's sons. It was usually the official organ of the state administration and received the public printing contracts. In this campaign of education it was the mouthpiece of those favoring immediate secession.[69] The *Examiner* had been the paper of the Hunter wing of the Democratic party, but it was no longer restrained by that conservatively minded leader. Instead its position in this period seems to have been determined by Hunter's radical friends. The former hostility between these two papers was apparently forgotten. Differing in the details of their programs, the two enthusiastically worked together to obtain the coöperation of all the slaveholding states for gaining redress. When this failed they championed secession. The editorials, voluntary and solicited articles contributed by influential leaders, accounts of public meetings, full reports of happenings in the lower South, and the playing up of Republican statements which tended to show the impossibility of compromise were used to accomplish this purpose.

Assisting these organs were the many local Democratic papers which were accustomed to play up the editorials and news items in the *Enquirer* and the *Examiner*. Many of the leaders were also active in the "crusade." The activities of Ruffin and Wise continued in the course already discussed. Equally as enthusiastic were Roger A. Pryor, James A. Seddon, J. R. Tucker, and M. R. H. Garnett.[70] Other leaders who might have remained quiet were induced by the *Enquirer* to express their views. It sent a request to nine conspicuous leaders from all sections and all parties to outline their views on the crisis and to suggest how to meet it.[71] All of them except two conservative Whigs responded. Along with the opinions of others not specifically invited to contribute in this way, the replies were given considerable prominence in the secession papers.

In support of coöperation, these papers and leaders of their faith tried to persuade Virginians that since their interests bound them to the lower South every effort should be exerted to bring about a Southern convention with a view to devising means of keeping the cotton states in the Union, and, if this failed, to prepare for withdrawing with them.[72] They insisted that if the South should unite and present at once an ultimatum to the North, the free states would concede their demands, and thereby save the Union. Delay, on the other hand, would convince the North that the border states would not lend support to the demands of the lower South, and that, therefore, concessions would not be necessary.[73] Indifference on the part of Virginia would result in the secession of the cotton states, and when that had been consummated appeals for coöperation would be too late.[74]

By the middle of December these secessionists abandoned this plan, for it met with little success among the Virginia moderates, and even the lower South was unfavorably inclined toward it.[75] The leaders of the cotton states felt that this plan would cause delay, and that their "interests" were in such danger concessions from the North would be valueless.[76] They reminded the Old Dominion of their futile offer to coöperate with her after the Brown raid; consequently they would not be held back again by the border states.[77]

After this scheme seemed a failure, the Virginia secessionists proceeded to prepare the minds of the people for withdrawal. As a step in this direction they argued that Southern rights were not safe in the Union,[78] that the Republican party was well organized, well led, and was representative of the growing anti-slavery sentiment of the North. Although this party, they said, was not for abolition at the time its most aggressive leaders were, and the natural course for the Republican party to follow would be to accept the views of these leaders inasmuch as the majority of its members looked upon slavery as an evil. The election, they insisted, represented an endorsement by the North of an anti-slavery interest. The South, therefore, would be under the rule of those hostile to it.[79] Just how the Republicans would destroy slavery was not clear to these secessionists, but the hostility of this party and of the "Northern mind" to that institution would find a way to get rid of what they thought was wrong. The Republican rule would make "our property, labor and social systems" unsafe in the Union.[80] It would bring up the race question—a cause for alarm to most Southerners.[81]

When the Virginia conservatives in mid-December pointed to a Northern reaction against the "radical Republicans" and assured the South that she could depend upon her friends in the North to guarantee protection to Southern interests,[82] the Richmond *Examiner* replied that these reactions always came after elections when they would do no good, and that they only resulted in electing conservative mayors and other local officers. The South, it continued, was not encouraged by the fact that there were twenty thousand conservative men in Boston so long as the radicals there were in control of the government.[83] Shortly before this Senator Hunter tried to prove the Republicans' hostility to the South by pointing to the views expressed by Seward, Lincoln, Weed, and other important Republican leaders.[84]

The failure of the compromise measures in Congress at this time and the opposition of the Republicans to these proposals[85] were further evidences used by the secessionists to prove the impossibility of redress and the inevitability of the Union's disruption. Roger A. Pryor, congressman from Petersburg, in a public letter declared: "It is evident that the North will give us no guarantees. They are rather mending their hold; and the committee of thirty-three is more likely to report a plan of coercion than a system of pacification. The Black Republicans are beginning to be emboldened by the evidence of submission in certain Southern States." All Southerners in Washington, he continued, despaired of the Union, and "the efforts of patriots are directed exclusively to the end of rescuing the country from the horrors of civil war."[86]

The secessionists emphasized the fact that the lower South had already decided on forming a new confederacy, and so reconstruction was an impossibility. Virginia, therefore, should decide to which confederacy she would attach herself.[87] On November 29 Mason wrote that "the dissolution of the Union is a fixed fact. . . . There are those in the South who think (and I am one of them) that we have no choice but to accept the 'irrepressible conflict.' "[88] Immediate secession, they maintained, would prevent war.[89] Consequently they urged the Governor to call the legislature into extra session in order to provide for a state convention.[90]

In addition to familiarizing the public with the impossibility of redress and the inevitableness of disunion, the secessionists kept before the people the general reasons for joining a Southern confederacy.* They reviewed the arguments on the right of secession;[91] they tried to encourage others to join their ranks by showing how rapidly secession sentiment was growing;[92] they indicated what Virginia was losing by her dilatory policy;[93] they pointed out the economic advantages of a Southern confederacy to their state;[94] and they appealed to the "honor of Virginia" to uphold her "glorious and noble tradition of defending her rights."[95]

---

*These duplicated the contentions of the agitators as presented in chapter IV; consequently they will not be repeated here.

Opposing the secessionists' views in this period of agitation were the conservatives.* In a rather ineffective way they were attempting to stem the tide. Their negative rather than positive position had the disadvantage of trying to check a growing popular movement. They were not united like the secessionists, and their programs were as varied as the elements of the conservatives. Some of their papers and leaders that were ardent supporters of the Union insisted that there was no cause for alarm, and that the Southern institutions and "rights" would be safe during Lincoln's administration. They denied the right of secession and opposed all attempts to secure redress except those made through Congress.[96] Having no sympathy for the Southern movement, they poured out their wrath on South Carolina because of her leadership in this undertaking.[97]

Most of the conservatives, however, agreeing with the secessionists that the South had real grievances, differed in their methods of obtaining concessions. In reply to the radicals' policy, they first urged "delay, moderation and conciliation."[98] While Virginia was following this course they would advise the lower South not to act too hastily and the North to offer evidences of guarantees to the former's institutions. On December 14 the Richmond *Whig* begged the cotton states to await a conference with the other slave states in order that they might bring pressure to bear on the Northern people.[99] If no plan of action could be agreed to in such a meeting, no harm would be done.[100] To assist in carrying out such a program, the editor recommended that the legislature of Virginia send commissioners to the cotton states for consultation.[101]

At the same time that the conservatives tried to check the lower South, they asked their Northern supporters to come to their rescue.[102] In a letter to a Pennsylvanian, Governor Letcher pleaded with the free states to repeal their personal liberty laws "and show the South, that you really desire the preservation of the Union. You can do much to allay the excitement now existing, to restore concord and paternal feeling, to revive lost confidence between the sections. . . ."[103] In his first editorial after returning from his vacation, which began with Lincoln's election, the editor of the Richmond *Whig* on December 11 began his appeal:

Let, then, the Northern people, not only for the sake of the Union, but for

---

*The term "conservative" is used here in a rather general sense to include all factions which, in the fall of 1860, opposed secession. Later a more technical definition of the term will be given when it is applied to a party in the Secession Convention.

the sake of justice and truth and right, rise in the might and majesty of their patriotism and power, and heal the wounds which their own fratricidal, fanatical hands have inflicted upon the South. And whatever is to be done, let it be done cheerfully and quickly, for the revolutionary furor is increasing amongst us, and delay may result in irretrievable destruction to the Union and incalculable injury to all its parts.[104]

R. L. Dabney of Richmond tried to arouse the Christians of both sections "to their duty in staying the tide of passion and violence."[105]

While appealing for this assistance, the conservatives reminded the Southern people that many in the North were friendly and would help save the country from radical fanaticism.[106] The Charlottesville *Review* carried in its columns a long list of quotations from the papers in the free states which purported to show that a reaction against the Republicans had set in.[107] Frequently during this period the non-partisan *Daily Dispatch* expressed its confidence in a change of sentiment.[108] Even John B. Floyd, a member of the Breckinridge party and later an ardent secessionist, advised the cotton states to delay their action until the conservatism of the North could come to their rescue.[109] Many letters were received by Dabney from prominent religious leaders in the free states "giving the strongest assurance of moderate intentions on the part of all the better people, assuring me in the most solemn terms that the present congressmen from the Northern States do not represent the feelings of the people there."[110]

The economic strain in the North was apparently intense—banks suspended specie payment; and some expressed the fear that they would lose their Southern debts in case of secession. Consequently their hostility to the abolition leaders was evident. An anti-slavery convention in Boston was broken up and Wendell Phillips had to be protected by one thousand policemen.[111] In the city elections of New York and of several New England towns, the Republicans were either defeated or their majorities were reduced.[112] Several of their governors met in New York and decided to recommend the repeal of their personal liberty laws.[113]

In keeping with their appeal for "delay and moderation" the conservatives of Virginia offered various plans for obtaining redress. Some of these were fantastic such as that of John L. McCue whose plan provided for canceling all debts to Northern creditors as a means of bringing the people there to their "senses."[114] But the most widely advocated plans included a national convention, an assembly of representatives from all the Southern states, a border-states conference, and a state convention. The national* and state conventions were eventually held, and the border-states conference had been practically agreed to when the firing on Sumter occurred.[115] The idea of a Southern assembly was dropped entirely. In late November the secessionists supported this plan, but by the time the conservatives favored it the lower South had refused coöperation and had decided on separate state action.[116]

At the same time the conservatives were trying to check radicalism at home and in the lower South and working out plans of saving the Union, their press and leaders emphasized the disadvantages disunion would bring to Virginians. They appealed to the people's sentiment by recalling the "glories of the Union"—its history, "revered" institutions, and the prosperity and peace it had brought to all the states. Contrasted with these "blessings," disunion, they contended, would bring civil war and evils which would follow the "internecine" conflict.[117] They insisted that the cotton states would reopen the African slave trade as soon as they had created a Southern confederacy. This in turn would ruin the domestic slave trade, one of the state's largest businesses.[118] When the Charleston *Mercury* and Governor Gist urged the South Carolina legislature to tax the slaves brought in from the border states, the Virginia conservatives were indignant. The Richmond *Whig's* editor looked upon this as an attempt to force the border states to secede; so he labeled it "coercion,"[119] and the Charlottesville *Review* was for letting "force meet force."[120] Even the *Enquirer* and the *Examiner* had to admit that the "temper of the Charleston *Mercury* towards Virginia is doubtless bad" and that the message of the governor was "irritating."[121]

In this review of the discussion between the radicals and conservatives during the latter part of November, December, and until the seventh of January, it has been pointed out that the secessionists maintained that Virginia's interests bound her to the South; that Southern rights were not safe in a Union where the Republicans controlled; and that compromise and concessions were merely dreams. They would as a result withdraw from the Union as soon as possible. Their program, then, was aggressive and its acceptance by others depended on whether or not the course of events conformed to their predictions. The conservatives, on the other hand, favored delay and negotiations with the North. Their position would succeed only if compromise

---

*Peace Conference in Washington in February, 1861.

could be obtained. It is appropriate, therefore, to trace the course of events in Washington and in the lower South and the influence of these factors on the minds of Virginians.

Since there were many conservatives in Congress it was hoped by the border states that the troubles of the time could be allayed in a compromise similar to that of 1850. As a consequence their attention was turned to Washington when Congress convened in December. Buchanan's message was a disappointment to all parties of Virginia. The Staunton *Vindicator* thought the views expressed in this address and the President's policy throughout December banished "all hope of an enlightened patriotism";[122] while the Whig organ of the same town held that the chief executive would "have taken a more tenable and consistent position if he had maintained that as there is no such Constitutional right as secession," the government had the authority to coerce but it was not "expedient to exercise that right."[123] On the other hand, the secessionist *Examiner* stated that the President had mentioned the wrongs from which the South suffered, but had only offered the polls, and as a last resort, rebellion as a relief. While his intentions, this editor continued, were commendable he had really made matters worse.[124] Only Floyd of the Democratic leaders expressed his approval of the message, and he was in the cabinet.[125]

Virginians took an active part in the congressional discussion which followed. A. R. Boteler in the House introduced the resolutions providing for the Committee of Thirty-three, but gave his place on that committee to John S. Millson who, he felt, would exert more influence than he in effecting a settlement.[126] Representatives John T. Harris, William Smith, and T. S. Bocock urged Virginians to remain loyal to the Union, at least during the discussions of compromises in Congress.[127] More radical members, including Roger A. Pryor, S. F. Leake, and Senator Mason, had little hope that the efforts in Congress would produce security for their section.[128] A little later Mason did all he could to obstruct a settlement.[129] Senator Hunter, a moderate force in the eastern wing of the "Southern Rights" party, had advocated coöperation with the lower South as a means of obtaining concessions from the North. When this failed he continued in a more or less hopeless effort to work for redress.[130] On the Committee of Thirteen in the Senate he supported the Crittenden Compromise, but he would not go beyond that.[131] It was not their own congressmen, however, to whom Virginia conservatives looked for hope, but to Crittenden. Many wrote him letters of encouragement as he labored for a settlement.[132]

His proposal of extending the Missouri Compromise line to the Pacific was heartily approved in all sections of the state,[133] and enthusiastically worked for by Hunter and by most of the members in the House.[134]

This and other plans of meeting the crisis were referred to the Committee of Thirteen in the Senate and to the Committee of Thirty-three in the House. On the Senate committee were five Republicans, five Southerners, and three others friendly to the South.[135] The creation of this committee had been proposed in a resolution on December 6, but the Republicans of the Senate delayed its passage until the eighteenth. The committee's first session was two days later.[136] At the first meeting Jefferson Davis made a motion that no proposition was to be reported as adopted unless it were sustained by a majority of the Republican members.[137] The 36°30' division in Crittenden's plan was opposed by the five Republicans, and, because of their opposition, by Davis and Toombs.[138] The other six, including Hunter, voted in the affirmative.[139] On the second section which stated that Congress should not have the power to abolish slavery in the forts or the District of Columbia, the Republicans voted in the negative and the other members in the affirmative.[140] On all other clauses of the Crittenden proposal the vote was divided in the same way, the Republicans opposing every clause.[141] Consequently the committee reported to the Senate that it had been unable to "agree upon any general plan of adjustment."[142] A similiar story might be told for the House's Committee of Thirty-three. It was created by a vote of 145 to thirty-eight, the negative votes being cast by Republicans.[143] The Republican Speaker appointed Corwin, in whom the South had lost confidence, as chairman; and wherever possible members of their own party were placed on the committee. No Northern supporters of Douglas were included, only two Bell men were selected, and in the South the followers of Douglas were given preference over friends of Breckinridge.[144] Consequently, Southern congressmen either maintained that it was merely a scheme to gain time and to disorganize the South, or they accepted it as "another indication" that the party in control of the House would never accede to measures of conciliation.[145] The committee became a sort of graveyard for every proposal of compromise.[146] The Republican party was opposed to granting the demands of the South. Seward and Weed were willing to consent to some concessions on the territorial question,[147] but Lincoln refused these. He realized that this was the one plank in his platform which bound the radicals to his party and without their support it would crumble. To yield on this would have meant the loss of what they had gained in their fight for democracy and the hemming in of slavery. Lincoln was emphatic, therefore, in his refusal to accede to Weed's proposals made to him in Springfield. He wrote Trumbull on December 10, 1860: "Let there be no compromise on the question of *extending* slavery. If there be, all our labor is lost, and ere long must be done over again. . . . Stand firm. The tug has to come; and better now than any time thereafter."[148]

In place of concessions on this issue, Lincoln offered a constitutional amendment guaranteeing the permanency of slavery in the states. He also recommended that the free states "review" their personal liberty laws.[149] This did not satisfy the Southerners; consequently the Virginia secessionists made much of the Republican refusal to compromise. Congressman Pryor, in a public letter to his constituents, stated that he saw "among the Black Republicans, and a few persons of other parties, a spirit of sullen resolve to bring the issue to the arbitrament of the sword."[150] About two weeks later he wrote Lewis E. Harvie that the last hope was "extinguished to-day. Even Etheridge's compromise* [was] voted down by Black Republicans nearly unanimously."[151] Several radical editors of eastern Virginia considered this another proof that the dominant Northern party had no idea of compromise.[152] "Proposition after Proposition," one wrote, "has come from the Union men of the South, and the patriots of the North, who are powerless for good. Yet not one has been favorably entertained."[153]

While the congressional plans of compromise were meeting with little success, forces in the South were taking a course which served to hasten disunion. Upon the election of Lincoln the South Carolina legislature, which had remained in session after selecting electors, called a convention. On December 20 the convention adopted an ordinance of secession.

Most conservative Virginians had from the first condemned the attitude of South Carolina. Even before the Palmetto State had passed her ordinance some expressed the desire that she secede for the "Union would be rid of some pestiferous grumblers who like Lucifer, would become tired of the golden streets and adornments of Heaven itself."[154] The Staunton *Spectator* said that South Carolina was a "nuisance anyway";[155] and Botts did not feel that she was worth bringing back into the Union for she had been "disturbing the peace for the past thirty years."[156] At the state banquet for the presidential electors in early

---

*This compromise related to the return of fugitive slaves.

December, Marmaduke Johnson, the Whig elector from Richmond, declared that he would like to take South Carolina *"by the neck and throw her into the bottomless pit, never to be resurrected."*[157]

This hostility was increased when the Charleston *Mercury* and Governor Gist recommended a restriction on the importation of slaves from the border states,[158] and even more when South Carolina adopted the secession ordinance. In an open letter Wyndham Robertson said that he did not deny her right to secede but he did feel that her judgment was "wrong and ill-advised," for she should not break the contract with those of the Union who had been faithful and against whom she had no grievances.[159] Dabney wrote his mother on December 28 that the little "impudent vixen has gone beyond all patience. She is as great a pest as the abolitionists. And if I could have my way, they might whip her to her heart's content, so they would only do it by sea, and not pester us."[160] The Petersburg *Intelligencer* called the action "hasty and ill-advised" and unfair to the other slave states.[161]

The Virginia secessionists, on the other hand, rejoiced at the conduct of the Palmetto State. Demonstrations of approval were made at Norfolk, Portsmouth, and Richmond.[162] On the day the ordinance was adopted in Charleston the Richmond *Enquirer* reminded the conservatives that South Carolina had proposed a conference of the slave states after the Brown raid and Virginia had spurned the offer. Furthermore, it stated that, since the hour of consultation was over, their friends to the south were following the proper course in withdrawing without waiting for other states.[163] The South Carolina congressmen were requested to attend a dinner in their honor as they passed through Richmond on their way home, but most of them had already left when the invitation reached Washington.[164]

Regardless of the Virginians' attitude on the justice of South Carolina's conduct, secession itself forced many conservatives to realize that the disruption of the Union had become a reality, and that with the spread of the movement into the other cotton states this would be increased. The Petersburg *Intelligencer* said that South Carolina's action "undoubtedly increased the precariousness of our position."[165] The secessionists, therefore, advised Virginians that the question was not whether they liked the Union or disunion but whether they would join the lower South where there was a kindred civilization or the North where there was no protection for their economic and social institutions.

Other events which tended to further the secessionists' cause were those relating to the forts. At one time or another virtually all factions in Virginia expressed their intention to resist any form of Federal "coercion" in a seceded state.[166] In his regular message to Congress on December 3, Buchanan denied the right of secession but opposed "coercion." He did not mean that he would surrender Federal property such as forts in seceded states. In his Cabinet meetings this provoked heated discussions during the month of December. Cass, Holt, and Black continually urged Buchanan to reinforce the forts in the Charleston harbor; Cobb and Thompson opposed it; Toucey was non-committal; and Floyd disapproved reinforcement because it would excite South Carolina, although he favored retaining what the Federal Government held.[167]

There were three forts, Moultrie, Castle Pinckney, and Sumter, in the Charleston harbor. In early December only Moultrie was garrisoned by Federal troops. The other two controlled the harbor, and Sumter, being away from the mainland, could be defended from an inland attack. On December 11 Floyd, as Secretary of War, sent the assistant adjutant-general to Charleston to inform Major Anderson, commander at Moultrie, that the administration, desiring to avoid a conflict with South Carolina, did not wish to send reinforcement or to make any move which would produce anxiety in that state; but if Anderson were attacked or placed in a dangerous position he could take the necessary steps to defend and protect himself and men.[168] As soon as there was evidence of an attack, this message continued, Anderson was advised to occupy the forts which could easily be defended.[169] Later the Secretary of War wrote him to defend the forts to the "last extremity," but not to expose his men or himself to needless danger.[170] On December 26 the troops were moved from Moultrie to Sumter.[171] This occurred on the day that the South Carolina commissioners arrived in Washington to confer with the President about the Charleston forts. It put Buchanan in such an embarrassing position that he considered ordering Anderson back to Moultrie, thinking that such a step would increase the chances of the compromises then under consideration in the Senate Committee of Thirteen.[172] Floyd advised such a policy, and the South Carolina commissioners were insistent.[173] Three days before this Floyd had been asked by Buchanan to resign because of malfeasance in office. But he stayed on until December 29, when he used the crisis to justify his resignation even though Anderson had simply followed Floyd's instructions.[174] The excitement increased until the President apparently promised the South Carolina commissioners that he would give up Sumter if their governor would return Moultrie and Castle Pinckney to Anderson.[175] In accordance with this compromise he presented to his Cabinet a mild reply to the commissioners' demands. As a result Black threatened to resign, and so Buchanan agreed to follow a stronger policy directed by the Union members of his Cabinet.[176] Two days later orders to replenish the supplies at Sumter were issued and the *Brooklyn* was prepared for the mission. It was replaced by the merchant ship, *Star of the West,* which arrived in the Charleston harbor and was fired upon January 9.[177]

In Virginia there was great indignation at these proceedings, especially among the secessionists. Senator Hunter had acted as one of the meditators between the South Carolina commissioners and Buchanan. When the negotiations failed he advised the Palmetto State to destroy all the ships in the harbor.[178] The *Enquirer* accused the President of breaking his promise not to increase the supplies of the forts.[179] When the *Star of the West* was fired upon there was "clapping of hands in the galleries of the Virginia legislature and some on the floor."[180] A banquet was given to Floyd upon his return to Richmond, at which time ardent secession speeches were made.[181]

As a result of the agitation of the secessionists and the course of events in December and early January, the sentiment of Virginia had undergone a great change since early November. At the time of Lincoln's election only a few extremists dared advocate immediate secession, and not many others despaired of the Union or contemplated dissolution.[182] By January 7, when the legislature convened, the situation was different. In the western regions and in much of the Valley many still felt that there was no cause for alarm and determined to support the Union regardless of the lower South or the Republican rule. This view was expressed by a public gathering in Parkersburg where resolutions, denying that the legislature had the right to call a state convention to change the relations to the Union, were drawn up.[183] Public meetings in Marshall, Monongalia, Harrison, Ohio, Hancock, and Brook counties and in Wheeling city were held to show that the northwestern section of the state would not consider secession.[184] Waitman T. Willey, later United States Senator from West Virginia, respected in the eastern as well as in his own portion of the state, declared that he was for Virginia as a state but "if we are to be dragged into secession or disunion, become a mere outside appendage of a Southern Confederacy, defenceless and exposed as we must be by our geographical position, to all the wrong and contumely that may be heaped upon us, our oppression may became intolerable."[185] Despite several such statements from counties along the Ohio and Pennsylvania lines,[186] there were, on the other hand, some of that area who insisted that their section unite with eastern Virginians in the latter's "just demands" on the North.[187]

The people of the central and northern sections of the Valley advised against secession,[188] but they were more friendly than the northwestern part of the state to the Southern movement. At a public meeting in Jefferson County, resolutions censuring South Carolina and declaring that the election of Lincoln was not a just ground for secession were voted down; in their place, others favoring a state convention and an endorsement of the right to withdraw from the Union were adopted.[189] There were no Union meetings in Rockingham County because such gatherings might give encouragement to the "abolitionists."[190]

Although in other sections there were many people with views similar to those in these two divisions of the state, the reports from the southwest and from east of the Blue Ridge show a perceptible alteration in sentiment. The fact that the great number of county meetings, held throughout these latter districts and to a less degree in the Valley and northwestern section, advised the legislature to call a state convention indicates this change. One of the first and most widely circulated set of resolutions adopted at county meetings in this period was drawn up by J. J. Allen, justice of the Court of Appeals, for the Botetourt gathering in the southern part of the Valley. It was copied or used as a guide by other counties.[191] After reviewing the nature of the Union and justifying the right of secession, these resolutions called for state and Southern conventions as agencies for obtaining redress. If, however, such efforts should fail secession would be resorted to.[192] While the resolutions adopted in the counties east of the Blue Ridge varied in content from advocating immediate secession to expressions of attachment to the Union, the majority were for the former position,[193] or for withdrawing as soon as compromise proved impossible.[194] Many expressed the view that the latter condition had already come to pass. On December 27 at the county court session in Amelia County, resolutions illustrating this view were adopted.[195] They stated that when a meeting had been held a month earlier, it had adjourned to await the course of events; that since then, events had occurred which destroyed all hopes of compromise, for the Republicans had rejected every acceptable proposal and, in place of guarantees, had advocated additional "outrages on the south," such as the "extinction by amalgamation, massacre or the surrender of the present slaveholding states to the ex-

clusive occupation of the black race." Thus they favored leaving a
Union with the South's enemies at once.[196]

There are other evidences of this changing sentiment. Robert Ridgeway wrote Senator Crittenden on December 16:

> I assure you that the *immediate secession* is exceedingly strong in this state and
> will prove, I fear, irresistible, in the event of the secession of nearly all the Cot-
> ton States, unless timed and earnest efforts are made to change the current.
> Thousands of Bell men have joined the Seceders, and nearly all the Douglas men
> besides, and unless we can bring about a speedy reaction, I fear all will be lost,
> so far as Virginia is concerned.[197]

On December 28 Dabney wrote that he was "sick at heart and had little
hope" for the Union.[198] The ministers of the different churches in
Richmond were rather bold on January 4, the "National fast day," in
their declarations that unless adjustments were made secession would
be the only remedy. The sermons delivered on that date and the discussions on the street the next day indicated to a Petersburg newspaper
correspondent that the people of the state capital, while loving the
Union as "established by our fathers" expressed a "very firm purpose
not to keep up at the expense of principle, and through the forfeiture
of freedom."[199] One of these divines declared: *"Should the arbitrament
of battle be forced upon us, I would glory in lifting my voice at the
head of Virginia's columns in a triumph of Zion for the safety of our
families and our homes."*[200] When Botts criticized the sermon of
George W. Peterkin, an Episcopal minister, for his radical views on
that occasion Peterkin replied: "Until recently, my ardent desire has
been for the preservation of the Union. . . . My *affections* still cling
to the whole country; but I am free to say, that, with the best light I
have, my *understanding* leads me to the conclusion that *separation,* in
some mode or other, would be better."[201]

By January 7 several of the most important Douglas newspapers and
the independent *Daily Dispatch* were definitely in favor of "resistance
to Black Republican rule."[202] In an editorial one of the strongest of
these advised the Southern states to seize all forts within their borders
before March 4.[203] Even the Alexandria *Gazette* was afraid that secession was inevitable; so the "main thing now to be considered, is the
preservation of the public peace."[204] A letter to the *Daily Dispatch*
from Greenbrier County in the southwest stated that secession there
was on the increase in spite of the fact that many hated to be led by
South Carolina. Of the three papers in that county, this writer continued, one was for secession, one was against "coercion," and the third,

a Whig journal, "deprecated civil war."[205] The Richmond correspondent of the Wheeling *Intelligencer* declared that the general feeling there was that dissolution could not be avoided and Virginia must go along with the South.[206]

Even the Whigs were emphasizing the fact that they would favor dissolution if satisfactory concessions could not be secured. Robert E. Scott in a letter to the House Committee of Thirty-three said that there was a strong undercurrent of conservatism and attachment to the Union, but that, since Virginia's prosperity depended upon slavery, the North would have to repeal her personal liberty laws, permit the expansion of slavery into the territories, and guarantee the safety of this institution in the states and the District of Columbia, or Virginia would secede.[207] The Charlottesville *Review* contended that: "If the Northern people or rather the Republicans, will not concede *equality* to Virginia as a member of the Confederacy, we are for disunion—and shut our eyes to the consequences."[208] Other conservatives agreed with this position of the Whigs. J. B. Jeter on December 11 said that he believed that the time had come "when we must have an adjustment of our difficulties with the North or go out of the Union."[209] As early as December 5, Ruffin had estimated that "there are scarcely any expressed opinions which do not admit the necessity for this state going with the South, if separation takes place, & that result but few doubt now."[210] Writing from Baltimore, December 12, Sam Philson reported to J. S. Black that in his recent trip to the South he had "found Virginians in favor of secession as a last resort and unless their constitutional rights were left undisturbed, and guarantees given of cessation of hostility upon the part of the North, they would feel themselves bound to join in establishing a Southern Confederacy."[211] On January 19 the moderate *Daily Dispatch* asserted:

> From the tone of the newspapers, and correspondence from various sections of the state, we have every reason to believe that secession sentiment is strongly on the increase in Virginia. There seems, however, to be a general desire that every honorable and consistent effort at reconciliation and adjustment shall be resorted to, and a full, fair, and explicit demand of our rights be made, before the final step of disruption is taken. Many of the counties are adopting measures of defense with a determination to be prepared for any emergency.[212]

From this survey it may be concluded that the agitation of this period, aided by the course of events, had convinced many in the eastern and southwestern sections that ultimate secession was not only desirable, but necessary. In all regions, others who had formerly refused to consider such a radical step even probable—so sure were they that adjustments would be procured—were beginning to lose hope and were wondering whether secession would not be the only course to follow. They favored keeping it off, however, until every effort to gain redress in the Union had been made. Although the northwestern division and a few strong Union men and papers of all parts of the state refused to consider secession in any circumstances, the majority of the people, leaders, and press, it would seem, were for saving the Union "if they could." But if the final decision of remaining with the North alone or of going with the South had to be made their lot would be cast with the South.[213] What had been the view of only the eastern plain at the time of the election had become the position of most Virginians by January 7 when the legislature met. The ardent secessionists found that their task now was not so much to convert the moderates among the conservative parties to the view that Virginia's interests bound her to the lower South, as to show the impossibility of preserving the Union and the inevitableness of a Southern confederacy. The period of agitation, then, had carried Virginia a step nearer secession.

CHAPTER VIII

THE LEGISLATURE OF 1861 AND THE CALL OF
THE CONVENTION

BEFORE the election of Lincoln, Governor Letcher, in a letter to the president of the James River and Kanawha Canal Company, promised to call the General Assembly into extra session January 14, 1861, for the purpose of considering a French company's offer to purchase the canal.[1] On November 7, ninety-four members of the legislature petitioned him to convene the assembly the first Monday in December to meet the crisis which Lincoln's election had produced.[2] Letcher compromised by selecting January 7.[3]

The General Assembly was composed of members elected in the spring of 1859; consequently it was not qualified, as the Richmond *Whig* stated, to represent the sentiment of the people on the existing crisis.[4] Since sixty-two per cent of its members were Democrats[5] and most of those were of the Breckinridge wing, its radicalism was evident. Their leadership and party harmony, furthermore, were conducive to pushing through extreme measures. In the senate, B. B. Douglas of King William County, an able Hunter partisan, was the aggressive secessionist leader; and, in the house, Judge J. C. Rutherfoord of Goochland and O. M. Crutchfield of Spotsylvania marshaled these forces. The able James Barbour of the old Ritchie faction but a supporter of Breckinridge in the late election and Wyndham Robertson of the Whig party in the house, and A. H. H. Stuart in the senate led the forces which advocated delay. But judging from the measures passed and the rapidity with which they were put through, the secessionists controlled both bodies until the convention bill and the Peace Conference proposals came up.

Supporting the conservatives in the legislature was the popular Governor. After reminding the General Assembly of the gravity of the situation, he asserted that if his recommendations of the previous session had been enacted the new crisis would not have arisen. Believing that his former proposals were still wise, he repeated them. He urged that a convention of all the states be called, and, if after discussion it were seen that differences between the North and South were too great for adjustment, that convention should consider peaceful separation and the settlement of private property rights. He thought it "monstrous to see a government like ours destroyed, merely because men cannot agree about a domestic institution, which existed at the formation of the government." He bitterly assailed the governors of South Carolina and Mississippi for proposing the taxation of slaves brought in from the border states as a means of forcing those states to secession. This, he said, was as truly "coercion" on their part, as was the government's plan against the Palmetto State. Turning his attention to the Northern states, he indicted them for permitting the agitation which had brought on all the trouble. The South, he said, demanded the following guarantees from those states: first, they must repeal their personal liberty laws and fulfill their obligations under the fugitive slave law; second, they must agree to protect slavery in the District of Columbia; third, they must grant equality to the slave states in the territories; fourth, they must grant the right to transfer slaves from one state to another by water and by land; fifth, they must enact rigid laws against those who try to abolish slavery; and sixth, the Federal Government must not appoint to office in the slave states those hostile to slavery.[6]

The people of Virginia in their county meetings, he continued, had expressed a desire for a state convention, but his convictions led him to believe that this was neither necessary nor wise.[7] Instead, he favored sending a commission to the Northern states to beg them to repeal their personal liberty laws, and another to the Southern states to find on what grounds they would return to the Union. He affirmed the doctrine of secession and condemned "coercion." He recommended the division of the state into twelve rather than the existing five militia districts, and the adoption of a distinctive uniform for the different militia organizations.[8]

There was nothing new in this message. Governor Letcher had made similar recommendations at the time of the Brown raid the year before. The message showed how strongly attached to the Union he was. Such conservative papers as the *Virginia Free Press* thought it wise[9] but the moderate Staunton *Vindicator* felt that it failed to meet the demands of the time. The editor of the latter was especially antagonistic to sending a commission to the North to urge the repeal of the personal liberty laws because "Virginia cannot assume the position of mendicant for rights which she is entitled to under the Constitution." Moreover, he objected to a convention of all states, for without the seceded states the other slave states would be in the minority.[10] So displeased with the message were the members of the General Assembly that they showed "some hesitancy" in voting to print fifteen hundred copies, arguing that the Governor did not express their views.[11] Jones of Appomattox did not want any printed, because he thought the "time and the people were rife for secession."[12] A better indication of the legislators' reaction to his message is shown in their refusal to accept more than one of his major recommendations.*

Scarcely had the message been read before the radicals were at work. Mason and Floyd were at Richmond "propping up the weak-backed in the cause of secession, and 'seeing to things in particular.' "[13] The atmosphere of the capital was excited.[14] The Richmond correspondent of the Wheeling *Intelligencer* described this on January 8. "The war spirit is running mountain high and seems as if it would actually engulph the State into a civil war with the general government before the next thirty days."[15] On the next day the same correspondent wrote:

> The very air here is charged with electric thunders of war—on the street, at the capital, in the barroom, at the dinner table nothing is heard but resistance to the General Government, and sympathy with the cause of South Carolina. In the Legislature the great aim, even among most of its Western members, appears to be to hurry things *and precipitate* the crisis.[16]

Another correspondent from Richmond on January 9 gave a similar picture: "The air is rife with sensational rumors; the halls and galleries of the Legislature are crowded daily long before the hour of meeting," and spectators approved or disapproved "vociferously the speeches delivered."[17] A member of the legislature wrote a friend January 14: "There is a great and continued effort here to *hasten* the *impending* revolution—constant dispatches, sensational paragraphs, startling reports etc. are some of the means resorted to."[18]

In both houses resolutions against "coercion," a bill calling for a state convention, and measures reforming the militia were introduced the first day.[19] On the same day the resolution against "coercion" passed the house, but the senate delayed for several days.[20] For the sake of unanimity, care was taken to leave out of these resolutions the doctrine of secession. In the house only five out of 117 were against it, four of these being from the northwestern region and one from Norfolk County;[21] whereas in the senate only Caldwell, a Republican from Wheeling, voted against the measure, and three did not vote at all.[22]

This resolution may be taken as a fairly accurate expression of the opinion of Virginia at that time. Even Union-loving Whigs who denied

---

*They agreed to his recommendation that a national convention be called.

the right of secession and objected to South Carolina's seizure of the forts were not for permitting "coercion." On January 4 the Charlottesville *Review* stated that it was "among those who believed that . . . any resistance to the Federal authority [is] . . . rebellion," and that it hated South Carolina for precipitating affairs, but, since this issue had been made, the subjugation of any seceded state "is a blow at the entire South. . . . The naked fact is that at the South, upon any display of force, whether belonging to the political school of Mr. Calhoun or Mr. Webster, every sword will leap from its scabbard from the mouth of the Susquehanna to those of the Mississippi."[23]

Shortly after the passage of the resolution against "coercion," the legislature recognized the bond which bound Virginia to the South by agreeing that, if all efforts at redress failed, Virginia would go with the South.[24] This passed the House of Delegates by a vote of 108 to 0, and the senate by 37 to 0.[25] This was not a real test because the main purpose was to force the North to grant concessions and because many did not vote. Yet it does to a certain degree illustrate the loyalty of the legislature to the South.

In spite of these resolutions the attachment of the legislators to the Union was very strong. In conformity with this fact and with the demands in many public meetings, Governor Letcher's national conference was considered.[26] On the first day of the session a committee was appointed in each house to draw up a plan for such a convention. For several days in the following week the matter was debated. At the same time was proposed a resolution which provided that commissioners be sent to Buchanan and the seceded states, for the purpose of urging both to withhold any step leading to a conflict until after the Peace Conference was held. These two ideas, combined into one joint resolution, were adopted on January 19.[27] For the sake of unanimity, the secessionists were willing to give the conservatives another chance at reconstruction. The resolutions declared that, desiring to employ "every reasonable means to avert" a permanent dissolution, the General Assembly was inviting all states, slaveholding and non-slaveholding, "as are willing to unite with Virginia in an earnest effort to adjust the present unhappy controversies in the spirit in which the constitution was originally formed." The delegates from each state were to meet at Washington on February 4. John Tyler, W. C. Rives, John W. Brockenbrough, George W. Summers, and James A. Seddon were appointed to represent Virginia. The Crittenden Compromise was proposed as the basis of an adjustment in this conference; and the agreements of that body were to be submitted to Congress for ratification.[28]

The other part of the joint resolution provided for commissions to President Buchanan and to the seceded states to request that each "agree to abstain, pending the proceedings" of the Peace Conference "from any and all acts calculated to produce a collision of arms between the states and the government of the United States."[29] This part of the resolution could be carried out at once; so Ex-President John Tyler and Judge Robertson were appointed to visit Buchanan and the cotton states, respectively. Neither met with great success. Tyler had a conference with the President on January 24 and presented the resolutions of his state. The latter replied that although the request did not come within his jurisdiction, he would deliver a special message to Congress on the matter.[30] This he did on January 28 in such a manner as to satisfy Tyler himself, but both houses of Congress ignored the request.[31] Fortunately Buchanan had already practically agreed not to interfere with the forts.[32]

Two incidents connected with Tyler's visit to Washington show how sensitive Virginians were at this time. On January 25 there were rumors current in the South and Washington that the *Brooklyn* was sailing to relieve Sumter.[33] Judge Robertson, then at Montgomery, wired Tyler for information.[34] Buchanan let the ex-President know that no harm was intended, for before Tyler's arrival the *Brooklyn* had been ordered on an errand of "mercy and relief" and not to South Carolina.[35] The other incident was the rumor current on January 28, just before Tyler started home, about the guns at Fortress Monroe. The story was that the guns were being planted on the western side of the fort with "their muzzles turned landward and overlooking the country."[36] Tyler, being alarmed, wrote the President that "when Virginia is making every possible effort to redeem and save the Union, it is seemingly ungracious to have cannon leveled at her bosom."[37] An investigation by Secretary of War Holt showed the rumor to be without foundation.[38]

While Tyler was in Washington, Judge Robertson was in the South trying to gain a pledge to prevent hostilities during the Peace Conference and to get the Southern states to send delegates to that assembly. After he had stated his mission to the governor of South Carolina, Pickens replied that while utmost deference should be shown Virginia, his state was permanently out of the Union and the proposed plan called for restoration. Consequently he could not adhere to the resolutions.[39] As to the request that the Federal and the seceded governments abstain from conflict during the period of the Peace Conference, the

South Carolina governor said that the promises of United States were without value, and he cited the *Brooklyn* episode.[40] Robertson accepted the report and did not push the latter point, although he wrote Letcher that he felt that the Palmetto State would not disturb the peace.[41] This attitude of that state's executive made the Virginia conservatives indignant. The Petersburg *Express,* for instance, suggested that this little state "should be troubled with no more commissioners, but left 'to the grandeur of that amazing destiny which her ravished vision sees looming up in the future.' "[42]

From Charleston Robertson went to Montgomery where the Alabama governor promised to lay the resolutions before the legislature and to comply with the request relative to suspending hostilities.[43] The governors of Georgia, Louisiana, and Mississippi gave similar assurances and replies.[44] In his report Robertson was very careful to justify the states and to emphasize the desire of the lower South to have the Old Dominion join her. Instead of remaining neutral he even sided with South Carolina in the *Brooklyn* episode.[45]

In addition to the resolutions discussed so far in this chapter, the legislature made preparations for defense, and, most important of all its accomplishments, called a convention. Military reorganization had begun at the time of the John Brown raid.[46] Throughout the fall of 1860 there was a renewed campaign by conservatives as well as secessionists for military preparations.[47] Judge Burks, a conservative member of the House of Delegates from Bedford County, wrote Buford on January 20 that Virginia had "no means of defending herself—no guns, no army—," and the state would be exposed on her frontier if war should come. Therefore, he continued, even secessionists of the legislature realized that the state could not afford to secede until preparations had been made.[48] The Richmond *Whig* ridiculed the "precipitators" for desiring disunion without first putting the state in a defensive condition.[49] Several counties had not waited for the legislature, but had already appropriated from their own sources money to equip the local volunteer companies.[50] Essex, for instance, borrowed five thousand dollars from the *glebe* and poor fund.[51]

On January 19 the adjutant-general made a special report to the senate showing that only thirty of the ninety-two troops of cavalry of the state militia were armed, and that a similar situation existed in the infantry.[52] Even before receiving the report, the legislature was considering appropriating one million dollars for the purchase of arms and munitions, for the establishment of arsenals in different parts of the state and for the fortification of the rivers, coast, and harbors.[53] On January 28 and 29 this was agreed to by an overwhelming majority in both houses.[54] On January 25 an ordnance department was created.[55] Another act, passed six days prior to this date, gave the counties the privilege of borrowing money for defense purposes and of paying for these bonds by an increased tax rate.[56] Special acts permitting individual counties to borrow certain amounts, and others allowing the organization of particular militia companies were enacted.[57] Moreover, the legislature chartered a number of private factories, with capital stocks of from $150,000 to $1,300,000, for manufacturing arms and munitions.[58]

More important than these military measures and the one for which many urged the calling of the legislature was the convention bill. Virtually all sections and factions during the autumn had in county meetings expressed their desire for a convention. The petitioners were more numerous and urgent from east of the Blue Ridge than from other sections, but at least eight of those from the northern Valley and southwestern counties demanded the calling of such a constitutional body.[59] The Richmond *Whig,* the *Daily Dispatch,* and the Staunton *Vindicator,* as well as the secessionists' papers, endorsed the idea of a convention.[60] The Staunton *Spectator* and *Valley Democrat* thought it unwise, but acquiesced when they saw the force of the movement.[61] A few scattering Union meetings, like the one at Parkersburg, opposed the idea,[62] but in the main the northwestern section favored the covention, inasmuch as it might give them a means of gaining tax reform.[63] So strong was the sentiment throughout the state that Governor Letcher, although in opposition to the idea himself, admitted that the majority of the people had expressed their desire for one.[64]

In conformity to this popular demand, a bill providing for a state convention was introduced early in the session. Along with the "coercion" resolution this was pushed through without much debate but amid great excitement. The Richmond correspondent of the Staunton *Vindicator,* January 9, stated that the convention bill "is pressed with pertinacity and precipitancy that would have astonished the 'Fathers of the Republic.' "[65] Between Joseph Segar, an indepedent in politics and a conservative from the eastern coast, and those who favored immediate secession, a warm discussion arose on the rapidity with which the measure was put through the General Assembly. " 'For heaven's sake,' " Segar urged, " 'give us a little more time—one short day's time at least —to ponder over these great questions, the most important ever presented for the reflection of American freemen.' "[66] George Rives from

Prince George County replied that the only amendment that the bill needed was one to shorten the time of assembling; and J. L. Wilson of the eastern coast contended that " 'Delays were dangerous.' He was for 'action, . . . immediate and decisive.' 'I cannot,' he said, 'sing pæans to a Union . . . of wrong, of injustice, of insult, and of oppression.' "[67]

A feature of the bill which met opposition from the first was the provision for the convening of the convention without first permitting the people to vote on whether or not they wanted a convention. The Staunton *Spectator* and several western county meetings had urged that no convention should be called without first presenting the matter to a vote of the people.[68] In the legislature the devout Union men insisted that there had been no authority to call such a body without first presenting it to the electorate. No recent convention had been held in Virginia without first allowing a vote on calling it.[69] B. B. Douglas replied to these champions of delay that the hesitation of the General Assembly had already made the "Black Republicans jubilant."[70] Burks took a similar stand when he argued that the adding of this feature would cause the North to regard it as an act of timidity.[71] The *Enquirer* reminded the "delayers" that over 140 public meetings had expressed the desire for a convention, and that their proposal would simply cause delay.[72] The Staunton *Vindicator* thought it would defeat the purpose of the bill, merely to influence the North to grant concessions.[73] In the midst of this discussion came reports of the firing on the *Star of the West*. The news was received by the "clapping of hands" in the galleries and by some on the floor of the House of Delegates.[74] This incident probably influenced some to vote against submitting the question of "convention or no convention" to the electorate.[75] A more important reason for its defeat was the feeling that events were moving so rapidly that a situation necessitating a sudden change of course might arise, and the feeling that a prompt meeting of a state convention, called by an almost unanimous vote of the General Assembly, would influence the North to grant guarantees.[76]

The only other important controversy in connection with the passage of this bill was the question of referring the decision of the convention to the people before its ordinances became binding. The opponents of "reference" contended that delay would mean war, and that, if the convention found the course of events demanded immediate secession, the act should be operative at once in order to prevent Lincoln's applying "coercion" before ratification could be carried through.[77] Some radicals openly avowed that the time for separation had come, and objected to postponing it by accepting the "reference" provision. George Rives declared that his people were for "secession, disunion, war, anything you might call it, to assert and defend these rights. He had heard too much talk. He and his people were for action *now! now! !* . . . He would die before he would submit" to Lincoln.[78] In spite of the opposition to the clause, it was approved in the House of Delegates, where the real fight was, by a vote of seventy-seven to sixty-two.[79] The delegates from the Tidewater and the Piedmont were about evenly divided on this motion. The same was true of those of the Valley and southwestern counties; but those of the northwestern area were almost a unit for "reference."[80]

As passed January 14, this bill was a compromise. It was worded in such general terms that the non-slaveholding counties could interpret it so that the taxing of slaves at the same ratio of other property—a tax which the slave regions had always prevented—might be brought up.[81] The western Virginians had warned the eastern planters that they would propose this and equal representation in the senate, if the convention were called.[82] In order to gain the western support, the latter agreed to allow representation in the convention to be according to population rather than on the "mixed basis" as had been the case in the preceding ones.[83] The easterners had decided beforehand not to make an issue on this point.[84] The other concession to the non-slaveholding region was the "reference" clause. The passage of the bill itself was a concession to the planters. The act provided for the election of delegates on February 4 and the convocation of the convention on February 13.[85]

As soon as the bill was passed an exciting campaign for the election of delegates ensued.* The candidates in this campaign may be divided into three groups: the first of these was for remaining in the Union in all circumstances; the second was for gaining redress if possible and resorting to secession only as a last means; and the third was for immediate withdrawal. A few of the first group not only denied the right of secession, but also admitted the authority of the Federal Government to employ arms in enforcing its laws in a seceded state.[86] Most of the candidates in all factions, however, left the doctrines of secession and "coercion" out of their discussion. To the immediate secessionists, it was not necessary to argue the right of secession, for, if it were

---

*The passage of the convention bill practically completed the work of the legislature. It remained in session until April 4, but after the first of February its sessions were of no great consequence; therefore it will not be treated further.

illegal, revolution would be resorted to rather than continue under Republican rule; and to others it would be wiser to leave a discussion of this theory out of the campaign, since many of its supporters did not think the time "rife for exercising" it.[87] In the northwestern part of the state where the Union sentiment was strongest the secessionists did not have a chance. Consequently, the real contest there was between those who favored eventual withdrawal, if redress could not be gained, and the out and out Unionists. In Wheeling, Ohio, Harrison, and Monongalia, the successful candidates promised to vote against secession in all circumstances.[88] It was pointed out by the Union men there that secession at any time would expose that region to attack and destroy their trade.[89] The Wellsburg *Herald* demanded that every candidate answer whether he would vote for disunion "in any shape, or any pretext or in any contingency whatever."[90] In the Valley something of the same situation prevailed, although the middle group was more successful there. In the eastern and southwestern areas it was a contest between all three factions, with the Unionists having the smallest chances of success. In these the Union candidates emphasized the evils of secession, appealed to sentiment, tradition, and the flag.[91] The middle group emphasized the chances of gaining guarantees within the Union, but carefully explained that if no redress could be obtained it would go with the cotton states. B. J. Barbour, a candidate of this group in Orange County, said:

If you tell me that our Union is gone, I answer: 'no.' While Virginia remains firm, we still have the soul of the Union, though its body is 'curtailed of its fair proportions.' Without submission to the North or desertion of the South, Virginia has that moral position *within the Union* which will give her power to arbitrate between the sections.[92]

Its members believed the Crittenden Compromise and the Peace Conference would save the day,[93] and if these did not succeed, they would not secede until Lincoln had revealed aggression. But even these pledged themselves to vote for disunion in case of "coercion" or the final failure of redress.[94] They contended that there was no cause for precipitancy, and that such a momentous step as dissolution should be given serious consideration.[95]

The immediate secessionists rehearsed the old argument of Virginia's attachment to the lower South, the danger of Republican rule, and the futility of depending on redress in Congress.[96] As proof of the last contention, they stated that the legislatures of New York, Pennsylvania, Ohio, Maine, Wisconsin, and Michigan had just offered men and money

to "coerce" Virginia if she should secede.[97] On January 16 the Crittenden Compromise was defeated again in the Senate.[98] The permanency
of the Southern Confederacy, moreover, was declared to be a certainty.
Judge Robertson had been told very frankly by the cotton states that
they were out of the Union for good.[99] Since disunion was inevitable,
these radicals argued that delay would only result in war and afford
the Republicans an opportunity to "coerce" the South.[100]

In keeping with the position of the secessionists, ten of the Virginia
congressmen and senators drew up a joint letter to their constituents,
January 26, insisting that all hopes of redress were gone.[101] After reviewing the attempts and failures at compromise in Congress—failures
which were due to the Republicans, the address stated—they maintained that it was their duty to warn their constituents that it was useless to expect any measures of conciliation or adjustment from the
national legislative body. They were satisfied that the party in power
had designs "to coerce the Southern States"; and it was their "solemn
conviction" that "prompt and decided action, by the people of Virginia in Convention, will afford the surest means, under the providence
of God, of averting an impending civil war, and preserving the hope
of reconstructing a Union already dissolved."[102]

The Unionists and middle group were indignant at this method of
influencing the vote in Virginia. The Staunton *Vindicator* felt that
the address was unwise, for there was still hope of conciliation. Besides, it said, this would tend to excite feelings.[103] The Alexandria
Gazette saw no excuse for such an address.[104] And the *Valley Democrat*
advised the voters to "treat this manifesto as an arrogant and impudent
assumption of power on the part of the servants to dictate to the
masters."[105] This paper criticized the activity of the signers in Congress,
and said that the address was designed to embarrass the Peace Conference when it met.[106]

The Richmond *Enquirer*, as the organ of the immediate secessionists,
maintained that the "election of the submissionists to the State Convention" would permit "coercion." This in turn would "tend to open
a conflict between the State Government and a large minority, if not a
majority, of the citizens of the Commonwealth." Therefore, every
"patriotic duty and public security demands that the good citizens of
the State shall unite to secure the election of the delegates . . . pledged to
the policy of prompt resistance to abolition rule."[107] Its editorials were
continued in this strain until the final one on the day of the election
which summed up the case for the immediate secessionists.

Is there any man in this community who desires to place himself, his family and friends on a level with the negro? Is there a man who desires to destroy the property of his fellow-citizens—who seeks to degrade his State, and bring ruin and destruction to every branch of trade and industry? If so, let him this day vote for the submission ticket . . .; he will find himself bound hand and foot to the Northern Black Republican Confederacy, from which there can then be no other means of separation but through rivers of blood and carnage. On the contrary, if he desires to prevent these evils . . . if he seeks to bring peace to his now distracted country, and thereby furnish the means for a re-construction of our once glorious confederacy—let him vote for ROBERTSON, RANDOLPH, and STEGER, and against reference.[108]

On the question of "reference" only the "prompt actionists" recommended that it be voted down. The Staunton *Spectator* said little about the candidates and concentrated on gaining the approval of this mandate.[109] The Alexandria *Gazette* reminded the people that the convention would have "in its hands not only our federal relations, but our whole state organization."[110]

At some polling places on February 4 there was considerable agitation. The election in Richmond, where the contest was probably as intense as at any place, was the most exciting in the memory of the editor of the *Dispatch*. The city hall was crowded for the whole day and several fights occurred, although no serious damage was done. About midday a flag inscribed with an extract of one of Botts's speeches was raised by the "Southern Rights" party. Some of Botts's friends tore it down and called on him for a speech. This produced further commotion, but the mayor quieted everything.[111] In spite of the excitement the vote for the whole state was not particularly large.[112] Possibly this was due to the season of the year and to the snow which fell in various parts of the state.[113]

On the face of the returns it was an overwhelming victory for the cause of the Unionists. Certainly the immediate secessionists were defeated, for they had advocated secession and a defeat of the "reference" clause. They succeeded in electing about thirty of the 152 delegates,[114] and out of a total of 145,697 votes only 45,161 were cast against "reference."[115] Consequently, the conservative factions were jubilant, for they maintained that the large majority for "reference" showed their strength—a defeat for the secessionists of 55,000. Furthermore, it was held that, since all delegates who were not for immediate secession were Unionists, this gave them a total of about 120 out of 152.[116] A conservative from the western part of the state wrote Seward, February 6, "we have scarcely left a vestige of secession in western Virginia, and very little indeed in any part of the state. The success of the friends of the Union, has really astonished us all . . . not a single secessionist, or 'conditional Union' man, has been returned in Virginia west of the Blue Ridge. The Gulf Confederacy can count Virginia out of their little family arrangement—*she will never* join them. . . . The majority of the delegates elected will, I think, be found to be against secession without contingency or mental reservation."[117] At first the South and North interpreted the results to mean that Virginia would not withdraw. A Charleston, South Carolina, paper bemoaned the fact that the Old Dominion "would never secede now, and even though the convention should pass an ordinance of secession the people would vote it down."[118] The Northern papers construed the election to mean that Virginia would have nothing to do with a Southern confederacy.[119] A Washington dispatch stated that the election "is generally considered to have broken the back of secession."[120] The New York *Times,* acting as Seward's agent in behalf of reconciliation, declared, after hearing from the Tennessee and Virginia elections, that these returns made it necessary for the Republicans to adopt a more friendly attitude toward the border states.[121]

After the wane of the first enthusiasm and the positions of the delegates had been studied more carefully, it was found that the results were not as overwhelming for the Union as many supposed. The conservative Virginia papers saw this and reminded the North not to be deceived by the results, for the election only proved that the people were against "precipitate secession, and in favor of making every honorable effort to restore the Union."[122] The Staunton *Spectator* characterized the election as "an expression of moderation, of peace, of good will, of national unity, that must speak with a potential voice to the people of the free States, and by challenging their admiration and their sympathy extort from them willing terms of compromise."[123] The Richmond *Whig* reminded the North that it means that Virginia's connection with the Union would end "unless satisfactory and inviolable assurances are given that every constitutional right she has will be . . . respected."[124] James Barbour, one of the so-called Union delegates and the leader of the old Ritchie conservative wing of the Democratic party, wrote Seward, February 8, that the Democratic leaders of the South Carolina school

would have carried the recent election if we had not been able to hold out tolerable evidences that there was a hope of obtaining by radical appeals to the Northern people constitutional guaranties. . . . We had to place our men in the recent contest upon that ground, and concede that secession ought to follow the extinction of the hope. . . . I for one assumed that ground. . . . Upon that ground most of those called Union men prevailed. Men like Mr. Botts who took the unconditional Union ground went down generally. The most potent campaign power in this part of the state was the statement of Messrs. Douglas and Crittenden that an adjustment was to be expected.[125]

In this letter, Barbour also declared that these Union men would "shiver the bonds if their efforts to get guaranties" failed.[126] John Pendleton, another Union candidate, wrote Seward the same day and independently of Barbour, that if the Union party had "received a little more decisive encouragement from our Northern friends there is not a county in Virginia that would have elected a secessionist." "There will not be," he continued, "one man in it [the Convention] who is not for a final separation of the states, in double quick time—unless there is reason to hope for a perfectly full, final and unqualified surrender of the slavery question to those whom it concerns."[127] The Charlottesville *Review* took pains to show the free states that the terms "Conservative" and "Union" were not applied in the South as in the North. It continued:

In the Eastern part of the State (we cannot speak for the West) a man is ranked as a Conservative who plants himself on the amended Crittenden resolutions, and is willing to remain in the Union until he has exhausted all reasonable efforts to effect an adjustment on that basis. We understand by a 'Secessionist,' one who is for *precipitate* action—for seceding before the 4th of March, unless the question is settled by that time.[128]

Even the secessionists of Virginia interpreted the results so as to obtain comfort. The *Daily Dispatch,* which by February 4 was almost converted to this side, maintained that there was little difference between "Secessionists" and "Union men." The former, it said, were "warmer in their declarations" than the latter, and "more positive" in their specification of the time for definite action. The Unionists "favor a restoration of the Union, and do not limit themselves as to time; yet, they indicate very clearly that the troubles of the section must be settled . . . satisfactorily, and honorably to the South."[129] As proof of this the editor recalled that J. L. Marye, considered one of the strongest conservatives in the campaign, was anxious for Virginia to remain in the Union if practicable, but the "moment it becomes apparent that she cannot have a permanent guarantee of settlement she should withdraw," for her interests were with the South.[130] Edmund Ruffin, the ardent secessionist, wrote in his diary, February 8, that if the "black republican party" did not give any guarantees, there would be few delegates elected as "Union men" who would not be ready for secession.[131] A letter from Winchester to the *Enquirer,* February 5, stated that the only difference between the successful "Union candidates" and the defeated secessionists was that the former deemed it wise and prudent to afford more time for the growth of conciliatory sentiment in the North.[132] This paper also declared that the "prompt actionists," the "uncompromising, unconditional Secessionists, will number about thirty—the remaining delegates [except for the Botts type] are men who will promptly adopt a secession ordinance when satisfied that proper guarantees cannot and will not be given in the present Union."[133] Virginia congressmen, likewise, tried to convince the North that she had misinterpreted the meaning of the election.[134]

Some of this re-interpretation of the results was doubtless designed for effect on the free states, but there is little doubt that the term "Union" carried a different meaning in Virginia from what it did in the North. In the campaign for the election of delegates this contention was upheld. In Richmond, which was fairly representative of the country east of the Blue Ridge and the southwest, the successful conservatives, Marmaduke Johnson and William Macfarland, declared that if they could not gain protection for slavery they were for separation.[135] Some candidates refused to commit themselves, and in the eastern counties out and out Union men, such as W. C. Rives, J. M. Botts, and J. H. Gilmer, were invariably defeated.[136] This is not true of the northwest where the majority of the successful candidates pledged themselves against disunion in any circumstances.[137]

According to our earlier division, candidates were divided into the three groups—secessionists, moderates, and Unionists.[138] The party alignment will be analyzed more carefully later,[139] and so here it will be sufficient simply to state that there were about thirty in the first group, seventy in the second, and the remainder in the third.[140] In the main, the Piedmont and coastal sections elected the secessionists, although there were a few scattered ones from the southwestern counties. These three regions—especially the towns of each—aided by a few districts of the Valley, selected those of the middle group; and the northwestern people, assisted by the voters of the Valley and some inhabitants from various other parts of the state, elected the members of the third group.

If these facts are compared with the "reference" vote, it will be found that the districts most enthusiastic for secession were the Piedmont and Tidewater, although a few counties in these two sections were attached to the Union. The counties from Washington city to Fauquier, those from Danville to the Blue Ridge, and a few in the coastal plain voted for "reference," but some of these elected moderate candidates. At no time were there more than eleven representatives from the territory east of the Blue Ridge opposed to ultimate secession. With the exception of Shenandoah County, the northern part of the Valley voted against "reference," and its delegates were predominantly Unionists. In the southwest, four counties favored "reference," one was evenly divided, and five out of its twenty-two delegates were for immediate secession. This area elected only three unconditional Union men. From the northwest there were fewer than a dozen representatives of the middle group, possibly two secessionists; and the entire region was for "reference."

It would seem, then, that the state was still loyal to the Union, and in this election expressed her desire to preserve it, provided this could be done without interfering with what she considered her interests. Most people in all parts of Virginia, except the tobacco section of the Piedmont and the Essex district of the Tidewater, were for making other attempts at compromise. If eventually their efforts failed they would turn to the "dernier resort." It was up to the conservatives of the state to prevent such a crisis. Many, therefore, agreed with the Charlottesville *Review* that the election would show the North that Virginia really wished to save the Union, and as a means to this end they would champion coöperation. Since both sections of the country, it continued, wanted the same thing—the preservation of the Union—they would work in a friendly rather than antagonistic spirit. There was only one danger, it felt, and that was that South Carolina, in order to drag the border states out, might attack Sumter and call on these states for aid; but "so far as we are concerned they may cry till the crack of dawn" without Virginia's help.[141] It was in the light of this optimistic feeling among the conservatives that Seward made his compromise proposals to Congress, as well as to the border state conservative leaders, and that the Peace Conference at Washington began its sessions.

CHAPTER IX

SECESSION CONVENTION — PERIOD OF DELAY

THE Secession Convention which convened February 13 and passed an ordinance of secession on April 17 was divided into three more or less distinct periods.[1] The first extended from February 13 to the report of the Federal Relations Committee which was made on March 9, when the conservatives changed from a policy of inactivity to a definite plan of compromise. This period was characterized by delay. Beginning in early March, the second continued until early April when more or less definite information that Lincoln had decided to reinforce Sumter was received. It was distinguished by a play of parties, schemes of compromise by the conservatives, and agitation by the secessionists. The last period extended from early April until after actual secession was accomplished. It was characterized by a revolution and the breaking up of the conservative coalition.

The Convention was composed of 152 delegates proportioned according to population. Although not equal to the Constitutional Convention of 1829 in distinguished membership, it was probably above the average state assembly of this type. Among its members were an ex-President of the United States, two former Cabinet officers, one ex-Governor, two former lieutenant governors, three defeated gubernatorial candidates, and many former judges, legislators, and members of previous constitutional conventions.[2] It was not, however, a body of great political sagacity. Its membership was recruited largely from those who were active in the old Whig régime. Consequently the *Examiner* wrote, with some truth, that it was made up of "old fogies who had not represented Virginia in the past thirty years."[3] Of the 152 members about eighty-five had favored Bell, thirty-seven had voted for Douglas, and thirty had supported Breckinridge.[4] Of the Whig and Douglas leaders in the state probably the ablest were elected to the Convention, but the Breckinridge party, for many years in control of the state government, did not send its strongest men. Hunter, Mason, the congressmen, state judges, and most of the legislators were not candidates.

Most of the delegates were interested in politics; a few were men of business; several had had military training; and others were leading planters and lawyers.[5] There were some keen thinkers and able orators and debators.[6] Some were level-headed men who kept down the extremists on both sides.[7]

It is difficult to group the members of the Convention according to their Union and secession inclinations at the opening, because no vote giving a basis for judging them was taken until April 4, and even that was not entirely accurate.[8] The candidates' statements in the campaign and the views of contemporary writers indicate that there were three distinct groups, but each merged into the other. Those of the first, variously labeled by their contemporaries,* were the secessionists; those of the second, the moderates; and those of the third, the Unionists.** The secessionist party, recruited largely from the Breckinridge Democrats, was composed of about thirty members who were mainly from the Tidewater, Piedmont, and southwest.[9] Its members believed that the doctrine of secession was right; that Virginia's interests bound her to the lower South; and that she should follow the cotton states as soon as possible since they were permanently out of the Union. Some of them advocated waiting for the report of the Peace Conference in order to gain unanimity of sentiment.[10] Inasmuch as this party included less than one-fourth of the delegates, its leaders followed a course of agitation as a means of preparing the way for their ultimate goal. It was led by Harvie, an able and popular party and business man, who had been connected with the "Southern Rights" wing of the Democratic party since its formation in Virginia in 1844.[11] Associated with him in this leadership was Henry A. Wise, possessor of one of the most alert and penetrating minds in the Old Dominion.

The moderates were composed largely of the states' rights Whigs, the supporters of Douglas, and a few followers of Breckinridge. In the main this group accepted the doctrine of secession,[12] and admitted that the South had just cause for alarm, but favored using every means of gaining concessions before applying this ultimate right. It was never a united party and its strength varied at different times, probably numbering seventy on February 13.[13] Its members coöperated with the Unionists in the early part of the Convention under the leadership of R. Y. Conrad who held the two conservative factions together until the first week

---

*They were called "Prompt Actionists," "Pro-Southern Party," "States' Rights Party," "Secessionists," and "Fire Eaters."

**The press of the first group labeled these the "Submissionists." This term, however, was used so loosely that it often included those of the middle group.

in April. Assisting him were R. E. Scott of the old Whig party, James Barbour of the Breckinridge Democrats—until he went over to the secessionists in early March—and W. B. Preston of the states' rights Whigs. Their plans depended largely upon the trend of events and the chances of compromise. At first they looked to Seward and the Peace Conference for help; but when these failed they turned to a border-states convention which some of their members supported until the secession ordinance was passed.[14] This "party" gradually lost its members throughout March, and in early April it crumbled to pieces.[15]

The third group of the Convention, the Unionists, including about fifty delegates[16] was recruited from the old national Whigs and a few followers of Douglas. George W. Summers and A. H. H. Stuart were its leaders. Its strength lay among the Valley and the northwestern representatives, although some of its members were from elsewhere.[17] Most of this faction denied the right of secession, but opposed the enforcement of Federal laws in a seceded state, because to some this was considered unconstitutional and to others unwise.[18] Disunion, they said, would be possible only by revolution. They were willing to coöperate with the moderates in order to gain a compromise with the North, but they would oppose dissolution even though these efforts failed.

The Convention held its first session in the hall of the House of Delegates, February 13, but the next day it was transferred to Mechanics Institute where it continued to hold its meetings until its work was completed.[19] For president of this body Summers nominated John Janney of Loudoun, an honest and honored Whig of the Clay school; and the secessionists selected for their candidate W. V. Southall of Albemarle, a Whig of the moderate group.[20] Janney was elected by a vote of seventy to fifty-four.[21] This does not reveal the strength of the parties, for three of those opposing secession in April cast their ballots for Southall in this election, and twenty-eight failed to vote.[22]

Following Janney's brief and colorless address and the election of the minor officers of the Convention,[23] the president appointed members to the Federal Relations Committee which was created by a resolution of R. Y. Conrad.* Of the twenty-one on this committee, four were secessionists, ten were moderates, and seven were Unionists.[24] The selections were fairly representative of all sections and parties.[25] It was an able one,[26] and was well led by Conrad who proved to be a master at hold-

---

*The term "conservative" is used hereafter to refer to the members of the moderate and Unionist factions taken together.

ing his forces together, even after the excitement of early April produced a revolution in the state.[27]

As soon as this committee had been organized, it proceeded to consider the numerous resolutions pertaining to the main purposes of the Convention and the numerous petitions from the county meetings. It delayed its report, however, until March 9, partly because its task was great, but more because it wished to await the Peace Conference's report and Lincoln's inaugural address.[28] All factions in the committee and the Convention favored delay. The Unionists of the western counties felt that this would afford them an opportunity to bring up again the taxation question;[29] the moderates fully expected the Peace Conference or Seward to find a way to save the Union;[30] and the secessionists saw in delay further failures to compromise and a chance to agitate their cause.[31] Consequently, to satisfy their desires for delay throughout February and until March 9, the Convention was "entertained" with long-set speeches—a practice which diminished after the report of the committee, though it was not entirely abandoned.

Representatives of South Carolina, Georgia, and Mississippi appeared with their credentials. Out of courtesy they were asked to address the Convention. Fulton Anderson of Mississippi and H. L. Benning of Georgia spoke on February 18, and J. S. Preston of South Carolina followed the next day. The first two were expected to "supply the arguments" and Preston would "fire the Southern heart, stimulate their old pride, and arouse their old-time chivalry in behalf of a cause that appealed to them as Virginians in a peculiar manner."[32] In a rather perfunctory address, Anderson reviewed the hostility of the Republicans to slavery and to the South, declared that the Brown raid was only an example of what might be expected under Republican domination, and in closing urged Virginia to join the lower South so as to avert the dangers of war and cause the return of prosperity to the country.[33]

Benning in a very forceful and logical speech, considered by a Unionist delegate more eloquent and influential than the others,[34] explained at some length that Georgia had seceded because her institutions were unsafe in a union with the North where the sentiment in the free states was hostile. Separation, however, would cause the North to lose interest in slavery; consequently, it would be permanently safe in the Southern Confederacy. In a confident tone he reminded Virginia that she would find a union with the other slave states in keeping with her social, political, religious, and material interests. She would become the New England of the South with factories, cities, and trade. As a guarantee of this, the Southern Confederacy would promise at least a ten per cent tariff, or, if necessary, more. Furthermore, he denied the charge that there was danger of reopening the foreign slave trade and of thereby injuring the domestic slave trade of the border states.[35]

On the following day John S. Preston of South Carolina, a former Virginian and an effective orator, addressed the body. After the usual indictment of the free states for their "infringements" upon the Southern "rights," he defended South Carolina against the charge of "precipitancy." He maintained that reconstruction was impossible since the interests of the two sections were different—the North had the philosophic idea that numbers should control and that property did not count, a sort of socialism; while the South insisted that property in the form of slaves rather than mere numbers should count; and finally in a sophomoric peroration, he appealed to Virginia's pride. "Sir," he said,

whenever Virginia has a son beyond her borders, his voice is known, because he speaks in the ancient tongue of his mother. Mr. President, I, one of the humblest of these sons, have told my adopted brethren—I have promised them —that before the spring grass grows long enough to weave a chaplet of triumph, they will hear the stately tramp as a mighty host of men—a sound as if the armies of destiny were afloat—and they will see floating above that host a banner, whose whole history is one blaze of glory, and not one blot of shame; and coming up from that host, they will hear one voice . . .; the resounding echo of that voice which first thundered into the hearts of your god-like sires: 'Give me liberty, or give me death!' and on that banner will be written the unsullied name of Virginia. The world knows her history and knows no history above it in the niche of fame. And knowing it none dare doubt where Virginia will be found when her offspring, divine liberty, and justice call her to fight.[36]

The three speeches made a profound impression. According to Mc-Grew they caused some to go over to the secessionists.[37] Burks of the legislature considered Preston's address one of the finest he had ever heard,[38] according to the Charlottesville *Review* it "brought tears to the eyes of those most uncompromisingly opposed to the object of the mission."[39] John Goode tried to have ten thousand copies printed.[40] In this he failed, but he succeeded in getting 3,040 for distribution by the members of the Convention, despite the conservatives' control at that time.[41]

Throughout the period prior to the report of the Federal Relations Committee on March 9, and during the early hours of each session, the delegates introduced resolutions and followed them with long speeches. A review of these proposals and the debates provoked thereby will give an idea of what the members thought, or wished the people to think, were the remedies they would demand. Most of these related to the attachment of the Old Dominion to the lower South, "coercion," and the right of secession. Marr of Fauquier, a moderate, urged the Convention to declare itself in favor of preserving the Union, to refuse to allow the "coercion" of any slave state, and to preserve the Union under "honorable terms" if possible, if not, to consent to its division.[42] Another resolution stated that although there was no cause for secession, it was unwise for the Federal Government to employ force against those attempting disunion.[43] J. S. Carlile of the northwest declared in answer to these resolutions that no one favored "coercion"; that the government rested on individuals; and that it was not illegal to force an individual to live up to the law.[44] Such secessionists as E. T. Morris of Caroline offered resolutions which frankly called for immediate dissolution.[45] Others of this party were content to resolve that since Virginia was tied to the South she must join the cotton states when the issue came to the point of choosing between the two sections.[46] On the other hand, resolutions of Sharp, Wilson, and other Unionists declared that secession, whether constitutional or not, was suicidal, and therefore should not be resorted to.[47]

Most of these proposals were read and reported to the Federal Relations Committee, but some provoked heated debates when introduced. Woods from west of the Alleghanies aroused the old state sectional animosities by introducing a resolution which declared the "allegiance . . . [of] the citizens of Virginia . . . to the Federal Government . . . is subordinate to that due to Virginia, and may, therefore, be lawfully withdrawn by her whenever she may deem it her duty to do so," and if she exercised this authority her citizens would be bound in allegiance and obedience to her alone.[48] Wise and Neblett from the east thanked Woods for his western expression of loyalty to the eastern interests.[49] J. L. Hall, a moderate favoring secession, replied that only a few from this western territory were in favor of dissolution for the sake of slavery, but his people accepted the right itself.[50] Willey and Jackson, Unionists from the same section, declared that their constituents were not disloyal to the easterners, but were determined to keep Virginia in the Union unless some cause greater than the existing one arose.[51]

A few days later S. M. Moore, an able Unionist of Rockbridge who had already antagonized the secessionists of the galleries and city of Richmond,[52] introduced a resolution declaring that he would not favor a confederacy which did not prohibit a foreign slave trade. His resolutions also approved the Crittenden Compromise, and stated that if a settlement were impossible Virginia should join a border-states confederacy rather than a Southern one.[53] In his speech which followed, he brought down the wrath of the gallaries upon his head[54] by centering his attack on South Carolina and the Gulf states for having split the Democratic party—thereby making Lincoln's election possible—and for having deserted the other slave states by seceding without consulting them. The lower South, he maintained, was not concerned over fugitive slaves or other real grievances, but over free trade, the reopening of the African slave traffic, and direct taxes. If Virginia joined their confederacy, her slave trade would be ruined and her tax burden would be excessive. He denied that cotton was king, discredited the rumors of "coercion" by the Federal Government, and declared the doctrine of secession to be "the most absurd and ridiculous notion that was ever presented. . . . [The advocates] make government nothing but a rope of sand, and the most solemn compact that men can enter into is to be set aside by one of the parties to it."[55]

The young John Goode, Jr., of Bedford, to the great delight of the galleries,[56] came to the defense of the cotton states, and especially South Carolina, which, he said, was not too timid to stand for Southern rights when others were delaying. He denied Moore's contention that the domestic slave trade would be hampered in a Southern confederacy with the cotton states. As proof of this he cited the latter's constitution and the promises of the leaders from those states. Likewise, he referred to the Confederate laws on the tariff and taxation to show that free trade and direct taxes would not be resorted to there. Rather, he said, Virginia would be the manufacturing and shipping center in the Southern Confederacy.[57]

In the days following and until the report of the Federal Relations Committee on March 9, Moore's resolution, "coercion," and the right of secession came up constantly for further debate. The advisability of disunion was, in like manner, discussed with all the fervor characteristic of that age. It furnished the orators opportunities to make their "set" speeches and to "entertain" the large number of visitors. It also gave the committee more time to work out its program. J. W. Sheffey, a moderate from the southwest, centered his attack on "coercion." The right of secession he would not discuss, he said, since it was an object of so much disagreement and since the former was of more direct concern. If the principle of "coercion" were accepted and carried out it would mean centralization and eventual destruction of the states. In the records of the Federal Constitutional Convention of 1787, he stated Madison had made it clear that this idea was dropped.[58] George Baylor of the same party from the county of Augusta declared that secession was nothing more than revolution, and expressed his opposition to embracing it, but he pledged himself to oppose "coercion."[59] A Unionist, Osburn from near the Maryland line in the Valley, followed with the contention that secession was "contrary to and subversive of the fundamental principles" upon which the Constitution was formed; "wholly at variance with the legitimate objects of its creation, and can only be justified as a revolutionary means of obtaining redress when every peaceable, honorable and constitutional expedient has been exhausted and failed." But, he continued, it would be wise for the general government to waive the claims to collect taxes, and protect the Federal property during the period of adjustment.[60]

The most forceful of the prepared speeches in the Convention were probably those of W. T. Willey, representing the Unionist party, W. L. Goggin of the moderates, and George W. Randolph of the secessionists. Goggin spoke first on February 26 and 27. Although a moderate and later in favor of disunion, he denied the doctrine of secession and upheld the right of revolution. He quoted Madison to the effect that after all constitutional means had failed there remained one resort—" 'an appeal from the cancelled obligations of the Constitutional compact to original rights and the law of self-preservation. This is the *Ultima ratio* under all governments, whether consolidated, confederated, or a compound of both.' " Goggin did not object to the secessionists' taunt that this would make him a rebel, for Washington and others had been rebels; consequently, on this doctrine of revolutionary right he would defend Southern "honor, integrity, rights, and privileges." But if an attempt to use an army against Virginia under the guise of enforcing laws were made, the whole state would stand as one man. Turning to the merits of a Southern confederacy, he argued that cotton was not king; that England would use Indian cotton; that Virginia sold more tobacco to the North than to the South; and that the Old Dominion would not be contiguous to the lower South, since North Carolina, Kentucky, and Tennessee would not be likely to secede. He would favor, therefore, a border-states conference as a step toward gaining satisfaction within the Union, but, if this failed, eventual disunion as a final program.[61]

On March 4, leaving off the trappings of oratory so characteristic of that age, Willey stuck closely to reasoning. He was from near the

Pennsylvania line in northwestern Virginia, but he was respected by the planters of the east. He had been the Whig candidate for lieutenant governor in 1859, and was a devout Methodist and large property owner. In his speech he began by admitting that the South had grievances, but he was not in favor of breaking the Union to right them. The fault, he maintained, had not been with the Federal Government, but with the individual states of the North. He refuted the doctrine of secession by quoting Madison's letter which denied that the Virginia resolution of 1798 accepted that view, and another written in 1788 to Hamilton to the effect that the *" 'constitution requires an adoption in toto and forever.' "* The secession doctrine, he said, came into being at the Hartford Convention but gained little headway until the thirties. He quoted old resolutions of South Carolina and Mississippi to show that those states had not, until recently, accepted the doctrine.[62]

Following this line of argument, Willey analyzed and refuted the contentions of the secessionists. Separation from the Union, he held, would not stop the attacks made on slavery by the Northern press, scholars, and the pulpit; nor would it check the encouragement which that section gave fugitives. Instead, it would increase their migration since the slaves' absolute safety would be nearer their habitat, and there would be no law to bring them back. As for Southern rights in the territories, the Supreme Court had already guaranteed them. Like other Southerners, he felt that Lincoln's election by a sectional party was unfair, but he would not "give up the ghost" because of that. The Republican presidential candidate was elected by a minority and his hands would still be tied by a hostile Congress if the cotton states had not deserted the Union. The Senate and the Supreme Court, moreover, were there to check him. Then he turned to the secessionists' strongest argument that there was an "irrepressible conflict" between the North and the South; that their "social system, the system of civilization, of education and the interests of the people of the two sections are so diverse, that it will be impossible to construct a government that will harmonize them and enable them to live together in peace." Here his only reply was an appeal to sentiment—he pointed to the "glory" of the Union and the prosperity it had brought.[63]

Finally, he recounted the evils which dissolution would bring; namely, the danger of slaves on the border escaping would make Virginia a free state; the hostile sentiment of the world to slavery would work against the South; several confederacies would come from the acceptance of the secession theory; a costly war between the North and the South would at some time ensue, because of an inevitable hostile feeling between the sections; and secession would probably bring about a division of Virginia.[64]

Randolph, representing the secessionists, delayed his "set" speech until a later discussion on the Peace Conference report, March 23, 1861. Briefly he defended portions of this report, but most of his address was devoted to the relative merits of the Southern Confederacy and the Union to Virginia. In this connection he first compared the probable revenue policies of the North and the South. The former's interests, he said, demanded a high tariff, as was indicated by the recent discussion of the Morrill bill; whereas the Constitution of the Confederacy showed the South to be for a low tariff but not for free trade. The latter position would be strengthened when the border states joined, for their voting population was as large as that of the cotton states.[65]

In the second place, Randolph after a rather careful study of various reports maintained that Virginia would gain more in the way of market for her products through a union with the South than through one with the North. The three most important of the Old Dominion's agricultural products were wheat, tobacco, and livestock. According to the census of 1850, the most recent available report, his state had a wheat surplus above her seed, consumption, and exports of 5,036,595 bushels. After similar deductions, the North had a surplus of 3,043,-141 bushels, and the border states, exclusive of Virginia, plus the cotton states were deficient to the extent of about 7,500,000 bushels. Hence the competition in a union with the South would be less than one with the free states. Besides, the tariff policy of the latter would reduce the price of wheat. As proof of this, he reminded the Convention that from 1816 to 1824 when there was a moderate import duty, wheat sold for $6.19 a barrel; that from 1842 to 1846 when there was higher protection, it sold for $5.88; and that from 1846 to 1861 when there was a low tariff, it sold for $6.93. Similarly tobacco was protected by this same tariff policy, because seven-tenths of it was exported. He quoted statistics to show that when the tariff was low the price of tobacco was high, and *vice versa*. Moreover, a large proportion of Virginia's tobacco was consumed in the South, whereas the North used Connecticut tobacco. Here again the competition of the cotton states would be less than that of the free section, as was indicated by the fact that the former produced only 500,000 pounds of tobacco in 1849 as contrasted with Connecticut which alone grew seven million pounds.[66]

Randolph stated further that he did not have statistics on livestock but, since the North produced it in great quantities, Virginia would find it difficult to market her cattle and hogs in a confederacy with the free states.[67] He pointed out, too, that a similar situation prevailed regarding salt, coal, and iron, which were produced in moderately large quantities in Virginia.[68] He agreed with Hunter and Ruffin that his state would never become a manufacturing center as long as she had the competition of the North, but in a separate union with a low tariff her young industries would thrive, and the Old Dominion would become the New England of the South.[69]

While the members were "entertaining" the Convention and galleries with these prepared speeches and while the Federal Relations Committee was threshing out its recommendations, the Peace Conference made its report and Lincoln delivered his inaugural address. Until then the moderates expected to gain redress for Southern grievances, and thereby preserve the Union. In support of this expectation they had obtained Northern encouragement in several ways even before the Peace Conference. Their efforts in Congress throughout December and January have already been reviewed. In a less enthusiastic and at times despondent mood, these endeavors were continued by many after January. Millson, for instance, was active in the Committee of Thirty-three, trying to obtain through it a satisfactory compromise. Harris and Boteler were engaged in similar efforts in the House itself;[70] whereas Pryor, Garnett, Hunter, and Mason not only sounded despondent notes and urged secession, but, with the exception of Hunter, obstructed compromise.[71] The conservatives' hopes, however, were not in the congressmen, for few of these were moderates. Instead, it was the direct contacts with the conservative Republicans that gave them most hope. It was noted above how this Northern party blocked the Crittenden Compromise.[72] Nevertheless, as the dangers of war increased, there were indications of concessions from some of its leaders, and these signs gave the Virginia moderates encouragement.

In these contacts, Seward assumed the leadership of the conservative Republicans. Backed by the powerful New York *Times* under the editorship of Henry J. Raymond, he attempted in January to allay the fears of the border states in order to preserve the Union, or at least to prevent their joining the Confederacy until after the new administration had been installed.[73] As a forerunner of this policy he made a speech in the Senate, January 12, which won the respect and confidence of many moderates.[74] In this address he informed the South that she need not fear the Republican rule; that slavery in the states would be safe—as a guarantee of which he prepared a constitutional amendment to that effect; that the personal liberty laws of the free states would be repealed; and that there would be a national convention to settle all difficulties.[75] Within a week he opened negotiations with the leaders of the old-line Whigs of the border states, and again advised Lincoln to offer a Cabinet post to a conservative leader from this district.[76] In a letter to Lincoln, January 27, he wrote that the appeals of respected Whigs and Union men of the border states

for something of concession or compromise are very painful, since they say that without it their states all go with the tide, and your Administration must begin with the free states meeting all Southern states in a hostile Confederacy. . . . Disunion has been contemplated and discussed so long there that they have become frightfully familiar with it, and even such men as Mr. Scott and William C. Rives are so far disunionists as to think that they would have the right and be wise in going if we will not execute new guarantees.[77]

As a part of this program of checking the border states, Seward invited James Barbour, whom he had suggested for a Cabinet post and whom he called the " 'master-spirit of the Union Party' in Virginia," for an interview.[78] At the conference which followed Barbour told Seward rather bluntly that " 'nothing materially less than the Crittenden Compromise would allay it [excitement] in Virginia.' "[79] When he asked the Senator from New York for his support on the compromise, the latter replied: " 'I am of your opinion that nothing short of that will allay the excitement, and therefore I will favor it substantially.' "[80]

After the February elections in Tennessee and Virginia had been carried by the moderates—a fact with which the Seward assurances had much to do—[81] the New York *Times* declared:

We have no hesitation in saying that the result of these elections not only enables, but requires, the Republican Party to treat the whole question in a different spirit, and to tender to the Union party in the South every guarantee which justice can grant or ask, against any infringement of their rights, or any disturbance of their domestic peace.[82]

In accordance with these proposals, the editor of the New York *Times* shortly after this urged that the Republicans who desired to preserve the Union adopt an attitude of friendly benevolence towards the South. " 'Let the Southern people know,' he said, 'that we want peace instead of pressing the alternative of war.' "[83] At the same time many Virginia moderates wrote Seward of the conditions in their state, and pleaded with him to prevent any force bill passing Congress, lest all be lost.[84] One of these, Barbour, expressed great concern over the situation, but had hopes in Seward's mediation. He urged Seward to use the Peace Conference as a means of proposing a compromise, and offered to go to Washington, or to "do anything" to save the Union. He and his brother suggested that the New York Senator keep in touch with them through Congressmen J. T. Harris and J. S. Millson.[85] Millson wrote J. R. Kilby, a member of the Convention, February 11: "I know that the *most influential agencies* of the Republican party will be exerted to secure a *permanent & satisfactory* settlement of the sectional controversy. . . ." He was not speaking from conjecture, he stated, but "from instruction which assures me the efforts will be made, in good faith, to accomplish a final adjustment of the slavery quarrel."[86]

These activities of Seward and the assurances of other Northern conservatives continued to give the moderates hope. They listened to such prominent Republicans as E. W. Bates who promised that Lincoln was " 'as true a conservative national Whig as . . . (could) be found in Missouri, Virginia, or Tennessee,' " and if he were permitted to organize his government and thus satisfy party demands, he would adopt a conciliatory policy.[87] Later, when the congressional compromises were blocked by the Republicans in the committees, the moderates continued to feel that the conservative part of the North was friendly and powerful, and that if they could only get in touch with the people from there, their requests would be granted.[88] The encouragements gained from Seward's negotiations were at their height when the Peace Conference met. It was believed that the conservative Republicans would comply with the needs of the slave states, and that the Conference would be a success.[89]

The Peace Conference was called with the avowed motive of "employing every reasonable means to avert" a permanent dissolution,[90] and with the additional purpose of allowing time for a friendly reaction to develop in both sections of the country.[91] All states including the seceded ones were invited to send delegates. The six cotton states and Texas, Arkansas, Michigan, Wisconsin, Minnesota, California, and Oregon were not represented. This left only twenty-one of the thirty-four states in the Union to send representatives, and of these only fourteen had delegations present on the opening day.[92] Outside the border states there seems to have been little hope, and even in Virginia the secessionists and some of the moderates did not expect much success.[93] Since none of the seceded states coöperated, there was the feeling that whatever program was adopted the lower South would not agree to it.[94] With a few exceptions, the delegations, according to the conservative New York *Herald,* were products "of the grog-shop and other low influences which direct the politics of their respective states";[95] and according to the New York *Tribune* they belonged to the "beaten and broken down factions utterly rejected and thrust aside by the people, and without prestige or influence in nineteen of the most important states of the Union."[96]

The greatest reason for the failure of the Conference, however, was the feeling of Republicans that they had nothing to concede. Many of them went into the Conference with the purpose of preventing important concessions to the disgruntled Southerners. In an interview with Orville Browning, February 9, 1861, Lincoln agreed "that no good would come of the Peace Conference," and it would only increase the excitement when it failed. He felt that no concession by the free states, short of surrendering everything "worth preserving," would satisfy the South, and that Crittenden's resolutions should not be supported.[97] A little earlier on February 2, E. Peck of Illinois wrote Senator Trumbull that the peace commissioners from his state were appointed as a matter of political necessity, " 'because if we had not united to do so, some of our knock-kneed brethren would have united with the Democracy and would have given them sufficient strength' " to have the representatives appointed by the legislators instead of the Republican governor.[98] Michigan refused to send delegates. Being afraid that the Conference might agree on a compromise, Senator Chandler of that state wrote Governor Blair to send "stiff-backed men or none," who would vote against compromise. In a postscript he added, "without a little blood-letting this Union will not, in my estimation, be worth a rush."[99] On February 15 Senator Bingham also asked Blair to send delegates, for they would hold the balance of power.[100] In the sessions of the Conference, moreover, the Republicans offered most of the opposition to the compromise proposals.[101]

The first session of the body was held on February 4, at which time, Tyler was elected president. After he had delivered his address, a resolution committee, on which Seddon represented Virginia, was appointed.[102] This committee reported fifteen proposals less favorable to the South than the Crittenden Compromise. Consequently Seddon proposed the latter as a substitute, although even it did not go far enough for him.[103]

Many delegates from the border states went into the Conference with an earnest desire to bring about an acceptable settlement.[104] On the other hand radicals, such as Seddon of Virginia, L. M. Morrill of Maine, and David Wilmot of Pennsylvania, refused to consider the positions of their opponents.[105] After rather heated discussions, resolutions differing from the Crittenden plan in certain particulars were finally adopted.[106] Having completed its work, this body adjourned on February 28. Its president presented the recommendations to Congress with the request that they be approved and submitted to the states for ratification. Even before this report was presented, the Senate on February 27 appointed a committee of five to receive and report it for consideration next day.[107] Seward and Trumbull, the two Republicans on the committee, opposed the recommendations, but were not allowed to present a minority report; so Seward presented on the floor a substitute in favor of a national convention.[108] Hunter tried to amend the first section of the report of the Peace Conference so that it would conform to the Crittenden Compromise. He declared that the judicial claim of this provision was worse than the Wilmot Proviso.[109] Mason agreed with him.[110] The proposals of the report were voted down in the committee by a vote of seven to twenty-eight. Hunter and Mason opposed them.[111] In the House, Speaker Pennington withheld the proposals until March 1 when that body refused to suspend the rules in order to consider them.[112] In the subsequent discussions, Harris, Boteler, and Millson supported the proposals of the Peace Conference; and Bocock, Garnett, DeJarnette, Leake, and Pryor opposed them—the other seven Virginia congressmen were either absent or failed to vote.[113]

The failure of the Peace Conference strengthened the secessionists in Virginia by convincing them that reconciliation was an impossibility. They had predicted its failure from the first; and while it was in session the Confederate-states commissioners, Benning, Anderson, and Preston, had reminded Virginia of the impossibility of a compromise.[114] In his speech in Richmond after his return, Seddon proved to many the truth of this when he reminded them that the Republicans had frankly told them that they had no compromises to offer. This view, he said, was summarized before the Conference adjourned by David Wilmot who maintained that the government—even the Supreme Court—had been under the domination of the "Slave Power," and against this his party was resolutely set. Furthermore, he stated that it would not recognize slavery as property, and that it would not permit the expansion and extension of this institution into the common territory.[115]

Senators Hunter and Mason openly condemned the report and said
that it was another evidence of the Republicans' hostility to the Southern interests.[116] Upon his return to Richmond, John Tyler stated to a
gathering there: "I bring you . . . as the result of our mission, a poor,
rickety, and disconnected affair, not worthy of your acceptance."[117]
The moderate Staunton *Vindicator* pronounced the report an "emascu-
lation" of the Federal Constitution and a "defiant insult to and fraud
upon the South. We regard it as a significant verification of the fact
that the free States do not mean to make any concessions to the just
demands of Virginia and the South, but to seek by every agency to
seduce us into a fatal delay, and when too late for successful resistance,
to plant the iron heel of power upon us to compel submission to Black
Republican iniquity and outrage."[118] Even the Unionist Petersburg
Express was "so much disgusted and sickened with Black Republican
impertinences, insolence and meaneses, since the movement for a
compromise began, that we have arrived at the state of feeling in which
we are utterly indifferent about any further political connection with
such a graceless, miserable set of scamps" as the radical wing of the
Republicans.[119] The Petersburg *Daily Express,* formerly Unionist in
sympathy, added that this wing of the party in power had "pretty
essentially and effectually cured us of *unionism*. We have not another
word to say against secession."[120]

In the Secession Convention, the debate on Moore's resolution which
had been up for discussion for three days preceding the Peace commissioners' report[121] was dropped, and attention was turned to the
report when Sheffey introduced a resolution calling for an oral explanation from the Virginia representatives to the Washington meeting.
His proposal recommended also that Seddon, Rives, and Brockenbrough, who were not legally members of the Secession Convention, be
allowed the privilege of speaking in that body on the subject.[122] This
provoked great excitement among the conservatives for they did not
want Seddon to speak. If these were not allowed to appear, Summers,
the Unionist commissioner, would more than hold his own against
the venerable John Tyler, the secessionist commissioner. They were
afraid that Seddon would use this occasion "for firing the hearts" of
the people. W. C. Scott of Powhatan said that he did not object to
the commissioners appearing and answering questions to give information. If they came, however, they would appear not as witnesses but
as advocates to champion their cause.[123] Harvie, the secessionists'
leader, replied that his faction was in the minority, but that the majority

should realize that the interest of this body demanded that they obtain all possible evidence, whatever the character.[124] The conservatives offered a substitute motion allowing the delegates the privilege of sitting in the Convention, but requiring them to make their report in writing. This passed by a vote of seventy-one to fifty.[125]

In accordance with this resolution, three reports were made: one by Rives and Summers who endorsed the recommendations of the Peace Conference and expressed the belief that they would be acceptable to Congress; another by Tyler and Seddon who felt that the Southern "rights" were not protected by the recommendations, and that even this report would be defeated by Congress; and still another by Brockenbrough who expressed his disapproval of some of its features, but declared that he would have voted for it had the vote been taken on the whole rather than by items.[126]

Several times thereafter these reports came up for discussion. In a rather able five-hour speech on March 11, Summers defended his contention. In this he claimed that these recommendations of the Conference would safeguard the Southern rights, since they practically included the Crittenden proposals; and that not only was the rumor of congressional rejection untrue, but that the reaction of the feeling in the North[127] gave every indication that they would be adopted.[128] In reply Tyler denied that the recommendations embodied all the guarantees of the Crittenden plan. He also repeated the arguments of Mason and Hunter.[129] Before this discussion in the Convention had gone further, Conrad, the manager of the conservative forces, had the whole thing referred to the Federal Relations Committee where it died a natural death.[130]

The moderates began to waver as a result of the failure of the Peace Conference. They had put much faith in its success and realized that it was the last great hope of reconciliation. James Barbour, who had urged Seward to use this Conference as an agency for proposing guarantees,[131] in a speech in Culpeper shortly after the adjournment of the Conference labeled it a failure, and all other such attempts to gain concessions from the North useless.[132] Some time later R. E. Scott, another leader of this group, stated that its failure and the indifference of the Northern people to that fact "extinguished all hope of a settlement by the direct agency of those States, and I at once accepted the dissolution of the existing Union . . . as a necessity."[133]

Following close on the failure of the Peace Conference came Lincoln's inauguration. Many Virginia conservatives had been encouraged by friends in the free states, especially by Seward, to believe that the new President would be conciliatory in his policies.[134] J. M. Broadus of Alexandria, for instance, on February 26, 1861, in a letter to a friend, said, " 'that a Henry Clay Whig could not well be far wrong. . . . I also confess that he [Lincoln] is probably quite a rough . . . uncultured man . . . but if he will only listen to Seward he will put him through.' "[135] After an interview in Washington with Lincoln on February 25, Davidson wrote Letcher that the President would not only avoid "coercion" but would grant guarantees which would ensure Virginia's safety.[136]

Because of this hope the conservatives delayed their work until they had heard from the Peace Conference and Lincoln. They had expressed their hostility to any form of "coercoin" or force. Seward's representative in Virginia wrote him that the Whigs controlled the Convention, but that the younger element of this party would go over to the secessionists if a force bill passed Congress. If, however, Lincoln's inaugural address should be conservative and an extra session of Congress should be called by him " 'no *extreme* measure can pass here.' " If, on the other hand, Lincoln determined to use force, he would lose Virginia.[137] He pleaded with Seward to tone down the President's message and not to permit him to make "any more speeches" before his inauguration, for those made on his way to Washington had done his cause "no good in the border states."[138]

On March 4 the secessionist Richmond *Enquirer* appeared in mourning partly out of respect for George W. Hopkins, who had just died, but more because of the inauguration. It looked upon the inauguration as marking the day of Virginia's shame.[139] Edmund Ruffin was already on his way to South Carolina so that he would not be in the United States after a "Black Republican" had assumed power.[140] Most of the state, however, calmly awaited the message. The members of the Convention spent the day listening to Willey's strong Union speech.[141]

Although Lincoln's address was intended to give no offense,[142] it was far from what the conservatives of the border states had desired and expected as a result of Seward's promises. They interpreted his message to mean not only that he would employ "coercion," but also that a fugitive slave law guaranteeing the right of *habeas corpus* and jury trial to the fugitives would be passed; a citizen, even a negro, of one state should have the privileges of those of another; and every power not expressly granted or denied in the Constitution should be subject to the decision of the numerical majority.[143]

With few exceptions[144] all factions in Virginia disapproved the message. The secessionists declared that it inaugurated civil war and that it would soon force the border states out of the Union.[145] Accepting this view, the Richmond *Examiner* rejoiced because it would make Virginians see their "proper course."[146] In the same tone the *Enquirer* declared that "no action of our Convention can now maintain the peace. She [Virginia] *must fight!* The liberty of choice is yet hers .... To war! to arms! is now the cry."[147]

The moderates were equally as hostile to the "coercion" portions of the address. The Staunton *Vindicator* agreed with the Richmond *Whig* *"that it will be met by the stern resistance of an united South."*[148] "Our heart and hand and life and destiny," it continued, "are with the South."[149] Likewise the Fredericksburg *Herald* explained that, although there were differences as to the right of secession,[150] "we can scarcely believe there is a difference of opinion among the men of the South as to the right or expediency of coercion."[151] Many other moderate papers looked upon the President's address as an endorsement of "coercion" and expressed their disapproval of it in strong terms.[152] Those who admitted the existence of the right to enforce the laws felt that the exercise of that right, in the face of hostility of a whole people, was unwise.[153]

Despite their protest and disapprovals, few of these moderates advocated immediate secession as a remedy. Instead they were in favor of arming the state and calling a conference of the border states.[154] Some of this group, however, did go over to the radical camp.[155] The Pittsburgh *Post* for March 8 expressed the view that "in Virginia everywhere the inaugural seems to have created intense excitement, and has been received with universal dissatisfaction. Hundreds, hitherto for the Union, avowed boldly for revolution, if the Convention does not immediately pass the secession ordinance."[156] Several county meetings at the March court sessions drew up strong resolutions condemning the address and urging secession.[157] A correspondent of the New York *Times* stated on March 14 that undoubtedly the disunion sentiment in eastern Virginia and North Carolina was on the increase because of the inauguration.[158]

In the Convention the radicals tried to make the most of this wave of secession sentiment.[159] For a few days preceding Lincoln's inauguration, the tension connected with the debate on "coercion" resolutions which the President-elect provoked by his speeches en route to Washington had been strained. The galleries had been vociferous in their applause of the secessionists' remarks and discourteous to the Unionists.[160] The trouble began when Goggin, after a rather excited speech against Lincoln's "coercion" ideas, introduced resolutions calling for a border-states conference to check the President and to unite its members for secession if necessary. [161] Harvie, the leader of the secessionists, endorsed the sentiment in Goggin's resolutions, but asserted that a border-states conference was too slow and that he was for separate state action. He urged, therefore, that the Convention prepare to withstand the "coercion" policy of Lincoln.[162] W. D. Leake followed with a proposal for immediate secession.[163] In introducing these ideas, Harvie declared, "for the last twenty years she [Virginia] has been passing resolutions of resistance to the death, and, one by one her resolutions . . . have been disregarded."[164] Now that Congress, he continued, had refused the proposals of the Peace Conference which were not even "just to the South," and the new President had declared his intention to make war on the slave states, there was nothing except secession left to save the Old Dominion's honor.[165]

For a short time the secessionists had their way in the Convention. "We had a rough time of it," a moderate explained at the time, "some of our friends were considerably alarmed—the extremists were exultant —& matters did indeed look rather squally."[166] Several conservatives were called on to check the danger by making calming speeches. One of these, Dorman, reminded the Convention that to pass an ordinance of secession at this time would be foolish, for the people would certainly reject it, and the Convention would adjourn without having prepared to meet "coercion."[167] Following Dorman, Thomas Branch of Petersburg ridiculed the haste and excitement of Harvie and Leake. Furthermore, he stated, he found some rejoicing as they read Lincoln's address, but that he was not anxious for war.[168] Major Early attempted to finish the blow by procuring an adjournment before a vote could be taken.[169]

The night's rest, however, did not destroy the extremists' ardor. The next day they continued the discussion. Thomas Flournoy of Halifax, after reviewing Virginia's efforts to preserve peace, stated that while she was deliberating on a remedy for the crisis, Lincoln issued his address promising to enforce the laws in the seceded states. He recommended, therefore, that the Federal Relations Committee frame and report as soon as possible a pledge to resist the President's plan of "coercion."[170] Objecting in a rather fiery speech, John Goode maintained that adopting resolutions was all that the Convention had done "so far," and that the people's patience was exhausted even in Early's home county, Franklin.[171] Undeterred by Early's denial of this change of sentiment there, Goode proceeded to insist that Virginia's honor and safety demanded that she take her stand beside Jefferson Davis "the bright Paladin of the South."[172]

On the third day, March 7, John S. Carlile from the northwestern section of the state at last got the floor and denounced the secessionists. For the past week, he said, in the Convention and on the streets speeches had been made by "fire-eaters to fire the Southern heart. . . . It is resorted to day after day in this convention to effect, if possible, the purposes of gentlemen who seem to have a perfect contempt for the will of the people. . . . And the time has come when this firing process should be met and promptly met, and while I have a voice to raise or an arm to lift if no one else will meet it I will attempt it."[173] The whole purpose of the secessionists, he maintained, was not to prevent "coercion," but to use the excitement caused by the President's inaugural address to stir the delegates to radical steps.[174]

On March 9 the Federal Relations Committee made its report. As a result the Cox-Leake-Harvie resolutions which had provoked this heated debate was tabled by Cox's own motion.[175] The secessionists had lost and the conservatives were again in control.[176]

It is difficult to determine how much Lincoln's inauguration increased the disunion feeling in the Convention, for no test vote was taken at the time. The excitement certainly gave the conservatives a scare and made them hasten their program. Conrad stated, in a letter to his wife on March 6, that the "inaugural message came upon us like an earthquake, and threatened to overthrow all our . . . plans. Great prudence was necessary to counteract its effect, and prevent some hasty and dangerous action. The tone of the Convention is now fast coming back to its first condition. Still the folly of Lincoln's position has embarrassed and changed somewhat our movements."[177] Burks wrote Buford the same day: "Many members of the Convention heretofore hesitant are now out for resistance and an ordinance of secession."[178] According to Moore a "large number . . . who were elected as Union men, . . . cannot be relied on."[179]

After the excitement subsided the conservatives regained their control and directed affairs. By March 7 the editor of the *Enquirer* was despondent.[180] A rumor was soon current that Sumter would be evacuated,[181] and so the moderates were again confident. Moreover, since the Federal Relations Committee's report was at hand, there would be less time for debate and agitation of a general character and the moderates would have something definite to work on.

CHAPTER X

THE SECESSION CONVENTION — THE PLAY OF PARTIES

THE second period of the Convenion began with the report of the Federal Relations Committee on March 9, and continued into early April when it was learned that Lincoln planned to reënforce Sumter. In this period the conservatives pressed matters, and the secessionists championed delay and agitation. The former composed of Unionists and moderates were held together only by the hopes of compromise and the coöperation of the border states.

After the excitement following the Peace Conference's report and Lincoln's inauguration had subsided and after the conservatives felt secure again in their control, the Federal Relations Committee which had awaited these two events made its preliminary report on March 9, and the final one ten days later. The former was presented before the latter, so that the Convention might be occupied with a definite project, and thereby diminish the chances of agitation. Twelve of the twenty-one members endorsed the preliminary report, two opposed it, several were absent, and others made minority or individual recommendations.[1] Later, on March 19, the committee presented as a supplement a thirteenth amendment to the Constitution of the United States.[2] The first report was an explanation of the nature of the Union and a list of grievances of the South.[3] The supplementary one recommended that a series of guarantees similar to those in the Crittenden Compromise be incorporated into the thirteenth amendment.[4] A minority report by Wise recommended that several demands more drastic than those of the majority report be presented to the several states with the request that they be approved by October 1. While awaiting these approvals, he would strengthen the defenses of the state, request the Federal Government to withdraw from the forts of the seceded states, and reduce the forces in those of Virginia and Maryland. If these proposals were not accepted by the Northern states, he would join the South.[5] Harvie's report simply recommended that an ordinance of secession be passed and presented to the people for their approval or rejection.[6] James Barbour's plan stated that Virginia had done all she

179

could for redress and the time had come for the North to do some proposing. His plan called for the appointment of a committee to confer
with the Davis government on common defense.[7] Baldwin, the only
conservative to present an individual report, recommended the agreement of the Peace Conference and the coöperation in the "Frankfort
Border State Conference,"[8] but in order to keep the party together he
soon withdrew his proposal and supported the Conrad recommendations.[9]

After the report of this committee had been submitted, the conservatives abandoned their old policy of delay and pushed forward
matters in every way possible.[10] They had made their report as pro-
Southern as the Union men would permit in hope of retaining many
moderates who were threatening to break away.[11] Although the report did not specifically recognize the right of secession, it had "an
awful squinting toward the recognition" of this principle, as the Staunton *Spectator* disapprovingly stated.[12] The Staunton *Vindicator*, a recent convert for the secession cause, found it better than it had expected,
for it "so clearly" upheld this doctrine.[13] The Richmond *Whig*, on the
other hand, said that the clause which stated that a state might withdraw *"for just cause"* was simply the old doctrine of the right of revolution; otherwise the report would not have put the qualifying clause
"for just cause." If one party, it contended, interpreted the cause as just
and the other unjust, each would have the right to its views, and, if
neither would give in, war would be the only means of escape. If the
parties decided there was no just cause for withdrawal and gave the
Federal Government powers to prevent revolution, that agency could
carry this order out.[14] In opening the debate on this clause Conrad, the
chairman, tried to satisfy those of both views by striking a middle
course. He interpreted the contention of the report to be that of Washington in 1776 and that of the Declaration of Independence, but he did
not call it the right of revolution, for that implied revolt. Other states,
he continued, had the right to obtain redress from a seceded state for
any wrong inflicted on them by such a withdrawal.[15] The fact is, the
report was so worded as to avoid characterizing the right of withdrawal "whether it be revolutionary or constitutional—leaving to each
gentleman the pleasure of cherishing his own crochet, and traveling his
own road. But as to the result—the grand result—that each state has
the right of withdrawal—that commands the assent of the assembled
sovereignty of the state."[16] If there were any uncertainty on the
character of the withdrawal as outlined in this report, there was cer-

tainly no vagueness on "coercion" for it definitely condemned the use of force by the Federal Government for any purpose against a state.[17]

The rabid secessionists, such as the *Enquirer,* felt that the report was too "indefinite, incomplete, and imperfect," intended only to cause delay.[18] The *Examiner* maintained that it only showed that the Convention "determines to do nothing and calls on seventeen others to help it in that profitable occupation."[19] The Richmond *Whig,* however, assured the secessionists that if this last attempt failed its party would insist that New York, New Jersey, Pennsylvania, Ohio, Indiana, Illinois, and the border states join the South in a new union in which the obstreperous New England and Northwest would be allowed to drift their own way.[20]

The conservative forces knew that they could put their program through if all forms of "coercion" were withheld while their plans were being adopted. Consequently they urged Seward "to hold Lincoln in check," and, at the same time, they pushed their program through the Convention as rapidly as possible. In this first endeavor they received great encouragement. Even before the inauguration, certain Union men of Virginia had gathered from an interview with Lincoln that he would not use force in the seceded states, but his commitment was very vague;[21] whereas their contacts with Seward were more definite. From the first Seward had planned to take charge of the policies of the administration, and most Virginians looked upon him as the real leader and Lincoln as a mere figurehead.

Throughout most of March, Seward promised the Virginia conservatives that Sumter would not be reënforced. Lincoln was either ignorant of these promises, or acquiesced for the time being. Two days after the inauguration the Secretary of State sent a second messenger to Richmond with "positive assurances" that the new administration would make no attempt either to strengthen or hold Fort Sumter, but, in order to clear the way for a practical understanding of the border states, it would soon be evacuated.[22] On March 11 Lincoln assured Stephen A. Douglas that he intended the "forts to be evacuated as soon as possible and all his cabinet whom he has consulted are of the same mind except Blair."[23] About this time J. C. Welling, an editor of the *National Intelligencer,* upon the suggestion of Seward wrote Summers that for military reasons Sumter would be abandoned. This was common knowledge around Washington, and had the approval of Lincoln and Scott.[24] Stanton wrote Buchanan on March 14 that there was "no doubt of Sumter being evacuated."[25]

About the middle of the month, state newspapers were circulating the rumors of this change in policy relative to the forts.[26] Conservatives from other parts of the South as well as from Virginia were encoureged. John A. Campbell, justice of the United States Supreme Court from Alabama but at that time a resident of Washington, stated in a memorandum written on March 18, 1861, after an interview with Seward: "I feel perfect confidence in the fact that Fort Sumter will be evacuated in the next few days." As a result of this assurance, he asked the Southern commissioners to delay their negotiations with the administration until the effects of this new policy could be ascertained.[27] Hunter who assisted in these negotiations agreed to support the confirmation of Seward's nomination to the Cabinet on the condition that the report about this South Carolina fort be sent to Richmond.[28]

In the Virginia Convention these reports and rumors had a most desirable effect. Summers wrote Welling, March 19, that it had "acted like a charm—it gave us great strength. A reaction is now going on in the state. The outside pressure has greatly subsided. We are masters of our position here, and can maintain it if left alone," but if Sumter or the other forts are reënforced it would "ruin us."[29] The Enquirer reported on March 20 that "The smile of joy that wreathed the faces of the submissionists when it was announced that Fort Sumter was to be surrendered will be remembered. . . . It was talked of at the street corners, proclaimed in the Convention; they telegraphed it to their constituents."[30]

These reports, however, soon proved false. Seward had either acted without Lincoln's approval, or the administration changed its position. In Connecticut, Rhode Island, and Ohio, state and congressional elections were to take place in the latter part of March and early April. A fusion ticket of the old Whig party and the Democrats was gaining many Republicans; so to hold the conservative forces there required that no radical steps be taken.[31] By the latter part of March the conservatives of Virginia became uneasy. Rumors of contemplated relief spread. Even on March 19 after asking Welling what delayed the removal of Anderson, Summers inquired if there were "any truth in the suggestion that the thing is not to be done after all."[32] On the following day the Enquirer expressed its doubt on abandonment, because of the fact that the New York Times admitted that it had not even been considered by the President's Cabinet.[33] Radical Republican Senators and governors began to bring pressure on Lincoln.[34] On March 29 relief was definitely decided upon, but instructions for an expedition did not go out until later.[35] The conservatives of Virginia did not know definitely of this changed policy,[36] but the rumors increased their fears and strengthened the cause of the secessionists. On April 5 the Unionists probably learned of it through one of their own members, J. B. Baldwin, who had visited Lincoln the preceding day.*

Realizing that the success of their cause depended on prompt action, the conservatives hastened the discussion and adoption of the report of the committee. On March 15 they began the debate,[37] and on April 4 closed it.[38] Between these two dates they found it difficult to hold the moderates in line in the face of rather shrewd tactics by the secessionists and because of a growing sentiment in the state for dissolution. They resorted to nightly caucuses and instructed their members for the next day so as to keep them together.[39] To check the long-winded speeches of the radicals, Conrad in the face of hectic hostility had a resolution passed to close the debate in the committee of the whole as soon as the balloting commenced.[40] Under this system he hoped to complete their work by April 15, adjourn for a border-states conference, give the North an opportunity to reply to their demands, go into the congressional election in May with a strong Union ticket, and return for further deliberation in the fall.[41] By April 15 when Lincoln called for troops, they had practically accomplished the first part of their program.[42]

While the conservatives were trying to hasten matters, the leaders of the opposition who formerly clamored for prompt action now advocated delay and a full discussion.[43] This new policy would give them another opportunity to convert the people to their position, for the course of events and the changing sentiment in various parts of the state were on their side. They opposed closing the debate and made long speeches on the advantages of the Southern Confederacy.[44] They also delayed the proceedings by presenting resolutions from various public meetings to show the moderates how rapidly the secession sentiment was growing in all parts of the state.[45]

Aiding the secessionists of the Convention in their efforts at agitation were the aggressive and well-edited Richmond newspapers.[46] The *Daily Dispatch* with its eighteen thousand circulation, one of the largest in the entire South, the Richmond *Enquirer*, respected for its history and read because it alone carried the full reports of the debates, and the Richmond *Examiner*, now under the editorship of the interesting John M. Daniel, carried on in this period a relentless war. Even the Rich-

---

*This incident and the actual relief of Sumter are treated on pages 192-195.

mond *Whig* became lukewarm for the Union cause after the inauguration. Throughout March it advocated a border-states conference as a
step towards concerted secession after redress efforts had failed. On
March 29 its conservative editor was forced to resign because the
readers demanded that he support disunion.⁴⁷ To counteract this change
in the *Whig's* policy, several Union leaders proposed the establishment
of an organ in the state capital to take its place,⁴⁸ but for some reason
this was never carried out. Consequently, after March 29 the moderates, and even before that the Unionists, had no newspaper in Richmond to uphold their cause.

Of these Richmond papers the *Examiner* was the most forcefully
edited. The calm and cautious William Old had just been supplanted
as editor by Daniel, a sort of John Randolph in the use of invectives
and sarcasm.⁴⁹ As soon as he learned of South Carolina's secession he
left Sardinia, where he had been the American representative since
1853, and returned to the United States so that he might assist his
state to follow a similar course.⁵⁰ On his way he stopped by Washington for a few days to talk over matters with Mason, Seddon, Pryor, and
Hunter, who had long since pleaded with their state to withdraw.⁵¹ In
Italy, Daniel had been greatly impressed by the nationalistic movement under way there, and, upon his return to the editorship of this
paper on February 28, he began preaching the idea of a Southern
nationalism. Although many secessionists even in Virginia accepted
this interpretation, none expressed it more effectively than he. In a
leading editorial in early March he said: "The true cause of the approaching separation of this vast country into two parts is the fact that
it is inhabited by two peoples, two utterly distinct nations. . . . The
difference between Virginians and Yankees is a thousand times greater
than that which existed in '76 between Americans and English." In
addition to the differences in climate, laws, means of living, "etc.,"
which changed the colonists from Englishmen to Americans, the South
had as a foundation for all her social system, slavery. "It," he continued,

has become the basis of our lives in the South—It has developed peculiar . . .
faults, all of them the exact reverses of those created by the system of levelling
materialism and of numerical majorities which has attained in the North a logical perfection of application hitherto unknown and unheard of in any part of
the whole world. Under the operation of these causes, we repeat, the North and
South have come to be inhabited by two nations. They are different in everything
that can constitute difference in national character; in their sentiments toward
women, in their manners to each other, in their favorite foods, in their houses
and domestic arrangements, in their method of doing every species of business,

in their national aspirations, in all their tastes, in all their principles, in all their pride and in all their shame . . . and in addition to such dissimilarities as these, have long subsisted direct contradictions of interests so deep, so widespread, so complete that it is astonishing, not that they are now divided, but that [they are] . . . parts of one great country, rather than . . . two smaller nationalities, of minor importance in the eyes of mankind.[52]

This idea of Southern nationalism was at the heart of Daniel's campaign. It was a holy and inevitable war, one of those great national movements "in which individuals, senates, and rulers are only the chips and the straws that drift with the foam on the overflowing river."[53] The South was so different from the North that it was foolish and impossible for them to live together. Disruption was a fact, the old United States no longer existed, and Virginia should recognize this fact for she cannot "run with the hare and hold with the hounds."[54] He reviewed again the advantages which she would gain in a confederacy with the South, and insisted that slavery would be unsafe elsewhere.[55] In addition to the "nationalistic" editorials Daniel was unmerciful in his vituperative attacks on the conservative delegates. He characterized them as "old fogies," "conceited old ghosts who crawled from a hundred damp graves to manacle their State and to deliver her up as a hand-maid to the hideous Chimpanzee [Lincoln] from Illinois."[56] The delay of the Convention and the proposal of further conferences brought from him bitterness and ranting which satisfied the secessionists and increased his circulation. "Nothing since the fiddling of Nero, while Rome was blazing," he said, "furnishes a parallel to the Dead Sea of pointless, vapid, dull, tiresome, dreary rigamarole with which the Convention is delaying the country."[57]

How much influence the *Examiner* had in creating secession sentiment which in turn influenced the delegates is not easily determined. In an editorial of this paper near the close of the war, John Mitchell who succeeded Daniel contended that the latter had "contributed more to bring about [secession in Virginia] than any other single individual."[58] Certainly the circulation of his paper increased during this period.[59]

The other secession papers at Richmond were not so ably edited as the *Examiner*, but their circulation was larger. They reproduced the old arguments of the autumn,[60] and concentrated on showing that "coercion" was inevitable and that the secession feeling was growing, hoping, thereby, to convince the Convention that it no longer represented the sentiment of the people. As an aid to this they insisted that the people express their opinions in public meetings,[61] while they played up all changes of attitude among the leading people, the press, and especially reports of public gatherings.[62]

In their agitation these papers were assisted by local ones in various districts. Since the Democrats controlled most of the papers and since most of the leaders of that party had by this time become secessionists, it is safe to assume that the majority of the local papers were on their side. Taking their cue from the larger party organs, these district and county papers assisted in this campaign.[63]

Another method for keeping alive the excitement and for intimidating the members of the Convention was the frequent reports of threatened revolts in eastern Virginia.[64] Other radicals broke up Union meetings,[65] while some resorted to demonstration in the galleries and, at night, on the streets of Richmond.[66] Constant rumors, too, were being spread that many people out of disgust for the Convention's indefinite policy were leaving the state for the Southern Confederacy. Thirty of the "best families" of Amelia and one hundred from Mecklenburg were reported to be preparing to leave in the middle of March. Other threats of a similar character were constantly circulated.[67]

As a check on these activities, the conservative papers attacked such methods of frightening the members of the Convention. The Charlottesville *Review* took the *Examiner* to task by stating that "There is an intolerance and lawlessness about the whole movement that is absolutely appalling. We do honestly assure our friends among the Secessionists, that many who would be willing to go out of the Union, *fear a Southern Confederacy*" because it might be like the Jacobins.[68] Furthermore, they tried to show that the county meetings did not represent a change in sentiment. "A little knot of persons," the *Whig* explained, "about the court houses and crossroads of some of the counties commit a grievous mistake in imagining . . . that because *they* are in favor of immediate secession and revolution, therefore the whole people of the State are equally as run mad as themselves. . . ." The instructions, it continued, of these "packed one-sided meetings are great humbugs and worthy of but little respect."[69]

But even the moderate papers realized that, although the public meetings were not entirely representative, there was at this time a new attitude under way.[70] They shifted their position, therefore, to the old coöperationist argument urging a border-states conference and defense preparation before secession. The Alexandria *Gazette* claimed that the issue was not whether Virginia should join the North or the South but "shall we consult first with the Border *Southern* States, and endeavor, before we do anything else, to form with them a union of sentiment as to what we shall propose as *guarantees,* and effect a concert of action as to future proceedings, either in or out of the Union."[71] The Norfolk *Herald* declared: "Suppose the Border Conference movement brings no concession from the North. We will have done our duty by our sister Slave States. We will have consulted with them, and if separation must come, all will separate together. Co-operation is our policy."[72]

Another outside agency aiding the secessionists in the Convention at this time was the rapid change of sentiment which the secessionist press and Convention members took pains to play up. The reports from public meetings in March revealed a decided drift toward the secessionists' view in the Tidewater, Piedmont, and southwestern sections.[73] East of the Blue Ridge even the counties around Washington and the larger towns showed signs of weakening. Petersburg "went over" near the middle of March when Thomas Branch, its representative in the Convention, was instructed by a popular vote of 879 to 762 to support an ordinance of secession.[74] Marye of Fredericksburg who had been elected as a moderate was advised early in March by his constituents to vote for disunion.[75] In Portsmouth the conservative party's majority of 768 on February 4 was reduced to 206 in the latter part of March.[76] Before April 5 the Norfolk secessionists had gained the signatures of half the qualified voters to a petition instructing their delegates to vote to withdraw from the Union.[77] The Alexandria *Gazette* reluctantly stated on March 27 that "it is evident to all who observe, that in the upper end of Fauquier the sentiment of the people is gradually drifting towards a separation."[78]

West of the Blue Ridge the change was not so pronounced in all counties; but it was very evident in the southwest. At the end of the second week in April, the *Marion Visitor,* from the latter section, maintained that nearly all of the people there were for secession.[79] About the same time the Lynchburg *Republican* declared that Franklin County, just east of the Blue Ridge but within the southwestern section, had as many secession votes as conservative, although on February 4 Early had won by a majority of eleven hundred out of eighteen hundred votes cast.[80] Walter Preston of Washington County, a conservative Whig elector in 1860, shifted to the opposition before April 5,[81] and the Abingdon *Democrat* of the same county held that the "Union fever" there was "gradually, but surely dying out."[82]

In the Valley, Shenandoah County had become an ardent supporter of disunion. Rockingham is "coming around," and even "Augusta is changing," the *Enquirer* joyfully announced on March 23.[83] A similar change was evident in Botetourt.[84] One of the strongest indications of this difference in attitude in the Valley was the fact that the conservative Lexington *Valley Star* changed front in the latter part of March.[85] Next to the *Vindicator* it was the most influential Douglas paper in Virginia; besides, it had been the organ of Letcher who was tremendously popular in the western part of the state.* In announcing his change of view, the editor declared:

'As the readers of this paper are aware, we have been decided for maintaining the union of these States . . . and now, we think it is our duty to take a stand for Virginia. . . . The Old Dominion has done all that honor will allow to preserve the Old Union. Everything has failed, and the question now is shall we unite with the prosperous South—or shall we starve with the Black Republicans?'[86]

This reversal of attitude in the Rockbridge region is further illustrated by the case of Judge E. C. Burks. He went to Richmond as a member of the House of Delegates in January and kept the clerk of his county court posted on conditions there and his reaction to them during the weeks which followed. In January he was a moderate in favor of compromise, but, as efforts failed in Congress and in the Peace Conference, he wanted the state to make military preparations and to consult the border states for joint defense. In early March he supported the report of the Federal Relations Committee as a means of gaining those states, but by the middle of March he had lost all hope of any redress and urged immediate dissolution.[87] Only the northwestern section remained practically unchanged in its feeling toward the Union.[88]

While these outside agencies were conducting this campaign for secession, those of the same party within the Convention were maneuvering rather skillfully. Until early April, nearly all of them realized that immediate separation was an impossibility, and that the submission of an ordinance to the people at this time would be unwise. Instead, as Wise asserted, "We must train the popular mind and heart"—[89] in other words, agitate and delay. In keeping with this policy they insisted on reading and printing in full all the secession resolutions of public meetings.[90] Their ablest speakers delivered lengthy orations, in spite of the fact that the Federal Relations Committee had made its

---

*Letcher, of course, had nothing to do with this. He remained loyal to the Union until after the firing on Sumter.

report and advised prompt action.[91] Several days in succession the Convention's sessions were cut short because the speaker of the day was not well or forgot his notes.[92] L. S. Hall of Wetzel carried these tactics to extreme when he tried to substitute for the majority report the Confederate Constitution which Wise insisted should be read in its entirety. This consumed two hours. After this, Hall asked the committee of the whole to rise until the next day in order that he might have his notes. Upon its refusal to comply with this request, he asked permission to withdraw his resolutions so that he could bring them up the next day. This second request also met with a rebuff; whereupon, he tried to tire the committee out with other dilatory tactics. He questioned every ruling of the chairman, and at frequent intervals had some member of his party to repeat his request that the committee rise. Finally the committee did rise because there was not a quorum. Immediately in the Convention, the leader of the conservative forces made a motion that on the next day the debate on Hall's substitute be limited to fifteen minutes.[93] A few days later Conrad tried to diminish such policies of obstruction by closing all debates in the committee of the whole, except five-minute speeches to each member offering an amendment, and a similar period to the opposition, with the restriction that no one speak more than once on the same subject. This proposal almost provoked a riot in the hall. One of the secessionists begged Conrad to withdraw this motion, or "there would be at once a popular revolution raised in Richmond, which would involve the whole country."[94] This did not intimidate this conservative leader, but "one or two of our party began to quail." As a result the matter was delayed until the next day.[95] During the night, Harvie called a party conference which in turn agreed to support the measure, provided it were amended so as to go into effect on April 4 instead of April 2 and provided ten, rather than five, minutes were given to the one proposing an amendment.[96] Conrad accepted this alteration, and it was adopted in this form.[97]

The conservatives' strength was unstable during the period of agitation. The inaugural gave them great fear, but the promised evacuation of Sumter strengthened their ranks again.[98] After March 20 the coalition began to disintegrate. Conrad's letters reveal the truth of this. On March 15 he expected to complete the Convention's task by April 1.[99] Nine days later he was still holding his party together.[100] By March 29 he found it necessary to hold a caucus each night for three or four hours to drill them in his program, so that they might withstand the excitement which the disunionists were stirring up.[101] He appealed to the political ambitions of some by promising a Union party which would rule Virginia for years to come.[102] Despite his efforts, however, he was forced to admit that his party was gradually weakening.[103] In the face of this he remained hopeful that his program would succeed. His main fear was that the North would not grant his demands.[104]

The voting on the report of the Federal Relations Committee began on March 27 and proceeded slowly until April 4 when the debate was closed. After that the provisions of the report were adopted more rapidly. The votes taken in this period showed some weakening of party ranks. On February 4 there were probably not more than thirty secessionists, but by March 27 when Turner's substitute, which amounted to delayed secession, was considered, thirty-seven were on the affirmative side of his motion.[105] A few secessionists failed to support this measure, because they felt that it would delay dissolution longer than was wise.[106]

Something akin to a test vote on immediate secession occurred on April 4 when Harvie tried to substitute for the report of the Conrad committee a resolution presenting an ordinance of secession to the people in the May election for their approval or rejection.[107] This proposal brought great excitement. Goggin tried to amend it so that a border-states conference would be held preliminary to the execution of the ordinance.[108] Wise induced him, though, to withdraw this amendment so that a test vote on immediate secession might be obtained.[109] Wise explained that although he favored "fighting in the Union"[110] he would support Harvie's substitute because it might offer a way for reconstructing the Union.[111] Harvie's motion was lost by a vote of forty-five to eighty-eight.[112] Three on each side paired.[113] Fifteen were absent or failed to participate.[114] Some maintained that eight of those absent were in favor of the measure.[115] Moreover, several moderates who usually supported the secessionists voted in the negative.[116] In spite of these qualifications this vote was a sufficient test to show that, regardless of the gain of the disunionists, from fifteen to twenty recruits since the opening of the Convention, the conservatives still held control. That control depended on reconciliation, and, if it failed, on cooperation with the border states rather than an opposition to ultimate secession. Feeling confident of their strength, therefore, they pushed forward the adoption of their report; and the secessionists, somewhat despondent, looked to outside pressure to bring the Convention to "its senses."[117]

CHAPTER XI

SUMTER, "COERCION," AND REVOLUTION

E VER since the first session of the Convention, the hostility to "coercion" had been expressed in no uncertain terms by the moderates and secessionists, and to a certain extent by the Unionists. Even at the time of Lincoln's election, the first faction had promised the "Southern Rights" leaders its aid if the National Government should employ force against a state.[1] This pledge was constantly renewed with increased firmness. The legislature and Convention had adopted resolutions to that effect.[2] "Coercion," to the moderates, meant the use of force for collecting the revenue, enforcing the Federal laws, and retaining or repossessing the forts wherever the state as a political organization offered resistance.[3] Whether these representatives believed in the right of secession or not, they believed that "coercion" would bring about the subjugation of a state, and not only change the nature of the Union but destroy the South's social and economic system.[4] Furthermore, it would provoke a conflict in which Virginia would be forced to stand with the North or the South. Realizing this fact, some rabid secessionists asked the Southern Confederacy to precipitate matters in order to force the issue.[5] There is no evidence, however, that this attitude was subscribed to by many in Virginia, or that it influenced the Confederate government's policy.

The conservative leaders had been able to hold the support of the moderates largely because of Seward's promise that Sumter would not be reënforced. In the latter part of March and to a greater extent in early April,[6] these encouragements began to lose effect, and the fear that Lincoln planned to hold the forts increased. This uneasiness was illustrated by the reaction to the rumor that munitions were being removed from the Federal armory in Richmond to strengthen Fortress Monroe.[7] After an all-night session, as a result of this report, the legislature passed resolutions instructing the Governor to use the public guard for preventing the removal of these arms over Virginia soil, and to seize for state use any which might have been moved.[8] Later it was learned that the transfer of guns and munitions was simply

191

a fulfillment of an agreement made before Lincoln became President, and even the *Enquirer* was forced to admit that the alarm had been without just cause.[9] Because of the excitement which the incident provoked, the national administration countermanded the order.[10]

In the first few weeks of his term and while the office seekers were crowding the capital, Lincoln took no definite steps toward holding the forts. At one time, upon the recommendation of General Scott, the Cabinet favored abandoning Sumter as a military necessity,[11] and Seward continued to hold out hope to the border states. But by the latter part of March, after the appointments to Federal offices had been made, after local elections in several pivotal states had been held,[12] and after many radicals had brought pressure to bear,[13] Lincoln decided to send relief to Sumter. On March 29, at the close of the Cabinet meeting in which two members still recommended surrendering the forts and three insisted on holding them, Lincoln directed that an expedition be prepared to sail April 6.[14] The order for its departure was issued April 4.[15] In compliance with Seward's pledge to the Southern commissioners that he would give notice of any change of policy toward Sumter, the President, April 6, dispatched a messenger to Governor Pickens informing him that he was sending provisions only to the garrison, and that, if the expedition were not resisted, no attempt at this time to throw troops and munitions into the fort would be made.[16] This was delivered on April 8.[17] Rumors of the planned relief were current in Virginia as early as April 3.[18] Each succeeding day these were increased until eventual confirmation on the eighth.[19]

Before discussing the reaction of the Convention to these rumors and the event itself, the famous interview which John B. Baldwin had with the President on April 4 will be reviewed. The details of this incident are still uncertain, for there is no available record written at the time, and the testimonies of the parties involved were given after the Civil War when prejudices were strong and memories were weak.[20] According to Baldwin's story as related before the Joint Reconstruction Committee, February 10, 1866, and later included in a pamphlet written by himself, Lincoln and Seward, April 3, sent Allan B. Magruder, a conservative Virginian residing in Washington, to Richmond to request Summers or his representative of the "Union Party" to come to Washington for a conference. Feeling that he could not leave the Convention at that time, Summers sent Baldwin who arrived the next morning and around noon had a private conference with Lincoln. After telling Baldwin that he was probably too late, although he had come directly upon receiving the message, the President asked him why the Union leaders of Virginia did not adjourn their Convention since it was a "standing menace" to him. The Virginian replied that there was no cause for adjournment; that it was within the Unionists' control; and that if they gave in to this request the legislature was likely to call another one, which would be even more radical. He suggested that if Lincoln would uphold the hands of the conservatives by adopting a conciliatory policy, they would save the border states. In this connection he asked that the troops be withdrawn from the South Carolina and Florida forts. Lincoln admitted that from military necessity he might be forced to recall the troops from Sumter, but that his supporters would not allow him to abandon all forts in the seceded states. Thereupon Baldwin told the President that "if there is a gun fired at Sumter—I do not care on which side it is fired—the thing is gone. . . . Virginia herself, strong as the Union majority in the Convention is now will be out in forty-eight hours."[21]

John Minor Botts, on the contrary, maintained that in a conference with Lincoln, April 7, the President told him a different story. According to his account, Lincoln invited Summers or his representative a week rather than the day before Baldwin's arrival; hence the orders for the relief expedition had been issued before the interview occurred. For this reason the chief executive at the beginning expressed the fear that Baldwin was too late. Nevertheless he offered to recall the expedition if the Virginia conservatives, who had recently shown by a vote of ninety to forty-five that they were in control there, would adjourn *sine die* and go home. Baldwin became excited, and not only refused the offer but "hardly treated me [Lincoln] with civility." When Botts learned of this refusal, he offered to take the proposition to the Convention, but the Presidnt told him that it was too late. Thereupon, Botts went to Richmond and had an interview with Baldwin in the presence of John F. Lewis, a delegate who remained loyal to the Union throughout the war. At the Richmond conference, Botts demanded of Baldwin an explanation for not submitting Lincoln's offer to the Convention. According to Botts, Baldwin rushed off to Mechanics Institute without answering this question;[22] yet Baldwin, in his report, asserted that he did not take the matter to the Convention, because there was nothing to report.[23]

Baldwin's story was more exact in minute details than Botts's. The former contended that the interview was on the morning of the fourth,[24] and the latter held that it was on the fifth.[25] Here Baldwin was right and Botts was wrong.[26] Botts, furthermore, held that the fleet was ready to sail that afternoon,[27] when in fact it was not even ordered to leave until the sixth.[28] Botts was wrong again in his reference to a recent vote on secession in the Convention, for no ballot such as he described was taken there until the afternoon of April 4, and the interview was that morning.[29] In fact, it seems quite possible that Botts had the date of Baldwin's interview confused with his own conference with Lincoln, for, along with several other Union men from Virginia, he was in Washington as early as April 4.[30] At ten o'clock that night in a meeting with Bates and Seward, he proposed a plan for adjusting the differences between the sections. This met with such enthusiasm from these Cabinet officers that they induced him to present it to the President on April 6.[31] Botts's charge that Baldwin refused Lincoln's proposal in order to break up the Union is absurd in view of the fact that he voted against the ordinance of secession even after its passage was inevitable.[32] In fact his views were decidedly pro-Union throughout the entire period of the Convention.[33]

Despite the discrepancies in Botts's account and despite the fact that Baldwin's reputation for honesty was better than that of the former, there was possibly some truth in his main contention that Lincoln offered to surrender Sumter if the Unionists would adjourn the Convention. In his diary for October 22, 1861, John Hay, the President's secretary, stated that at Seward's the night before, Lincoln "spoke of a committee of Southern pseudo-unionists coming to him before Inauguration for guaranties, etc. He promised to evacuate Sumter if they would break up their convention, without any row or nonsense. They demurred. Subsequently he renewed [the] proposition to S— [Summers], but without any result."[34] Although there are other confirmations of the first offer,[35] there are none available on the second unless Botts's story be accepted as such. He did not state that the proposition was made to Baldwin, but to Summers.

About the time of this interview, Lincoln consulted several Virginians and it is possible that he said to someone else what he is supposed to have related to Baldwin. He seems to have worked out his relief program gradually.[36] In his testimony, Baldwin admitted that the President had suggested that military necessity might force him to give up Sumter. "It is probable," as Mr. Hall concludes, "that he stated to Baldwin partially and guardedly, and to Botts, more freely, the proposition which was to have been made."[37] Whether Lincoln made the offer to Baldwin, Botts, or someone else, it would not have been satisfactory to the Convention members at that time, for they demanded guarantees that would bring the cotton states back.

While Baldwin was in Washington, rumors were current that a relief expedition had been sent to the South Carolina fort. They increased each day and caused great alarm among the people around Richmond. Consequently, to allay their fears and to "remove the uncertainty" in the public's mind, W. P. Preston—from now on the leader of the moderates—after consulting several conservatives and secessionists, introduced three resolutions in the Convention. The first two of these in rather strong terms stated anew Virginia's hostility to "coercion," and the third provided for a committee of three to "respectfully ask" the President to "communicate to this Convention the policy which the authorities of the Federal Government intend to pursue in regard to the Confederate States."[38] In presenting these, Preston explained that he was not moved by excitement, newspapers or telegraphic reports, but that, since the new administration had been in office for over a month without disclosing its policy, he thought it time for the Convention to know before it completed its task.[39]

Speaking for the Unionists of the northwestern counties, Jackson opposed the resolutions not only because they were impolite to Lincoln, but also because the next move, in case of an unfavorable report, would be secession. He was willing to join a confederacy of the middle states but he could not agree to a union with the lower South, for it would break up "our markets, impoverish our people, destroy our domestic interests, . . . drench our houses in blood . . . exile us from our altars, and stultify ourselves in the sight of the whole world by admitting that which we know is not true, that there is any sufficient cause to break up their Union." He favored standing with eastern Virginians in order to gain their guarantees, but when the demands were to split the western section from its commerce and interests "we will take care of ourselves."[40]

Carlile suggested that a similar committee be sent to the Confederate states.[41] In reply to this sectional appeal, Montague called on the eastern delegates to stand by their interests.[42] Hot words passed until Willey, who was inclined to support the measure, said that such a reaction would do no good and that, in order not to make a mistake, time should be given to think over the matter.[43] Baldwin followed with a calming speech and delayed the balloting until the following Monday.[44]

By Monday, April 8, the situation in the Convention was rather tense.

Rumors of relief became more numerous. The empty seats in the hall were given to the spectators and the place was crowded.[45] The contest started over a motion to abandon the regular order of business—the report of the Federal Relations Committee—and to consider the Preston proposal.[46] This was carried by a narrow margin, sixty-seven to sixty-four. The Unionists assisted by a few moderates voted in the negative.[47] The main question was then taken up. Those in opposition argued that it would set a bad precedent to make such a demand on a President; that it would be only another attempt to "fire the heart" of the people; and it would accomplish no good, for Lincoln would refuse to furnish any information.[48] Most of the moderates refuted these contentions and added that they were skeptical of the President's employing force. This mission, they said, would allay the excitement and permit the continuation of their program; hence the Convention should know as soon as possible if he did intend to follow such a course.[49]

The secessionists were not enthusiastic in their support of the measure. Their leader, Harvie, who since the defeat of his plan for secession on April 4 had practically abandoned all hope of disunion by the Convention, declared that since his party had not cared whether or not the committee was sent he had not remained to vote on the sixth. Since then, however, he had decided to support the plan if it were made drastic enough, for some advised that it might result in the Convention taking a "decided step." He was not willing to send weak resolutions which would merely afford the President another opportunity to evade the issue.[50] Wise refused to endorse the idea because it was not "direct enough."[51] The secession press of Richmond was even more disgusted and hostile than these two leaders. The editor of the Richmond *Examiner* illustrated this view when he said, "God of our fathers, think of that! Virginia prostrating herself before an official brute of the school of John Brown, who has already initiated civil war, and asking him 'respectfully.' "[52]

The motion to approve the resolutions was finally adopted by a vote of sixty-three to fifty-seven. It was passed by the ever-increasing combination of moderates and secessionists, although some Unionists were on the affirmative side.[53] Preston from the moderates, Randolph from the secessionists, and Stuart from the Unionists were selected as commissioners. Conrad tried to prevent the choice of Randolph, but the moderates would not stand by him.[54]

The committee set out at once, but heavy rains turned them back each time until April 12 when they succeeded in reaching Washington.

The next day they had an interview with Lincoln who, expecting them, had written out a reply which he gave to them at the meeting.[55] In this he reminded them that in his inaugural address he had explained as plainly as he could his intended policy, and he regretted that they did not understand it. Nevertheless, he repeated his former pledge.[56] The conference with Lincoln occurred on the morning of the thirteenth, and the commissioners had already accepted Seward's invitation for dinner that evening. After receiving the answer of the President they broke the engagement "at the last minute" because they wished to reach Richmond on Sunday, the fourteenth.[57] On the fifteenth they made their report to the Convention.

During their absence events had moved rapidly. In the Convention the conservatives, refusing to believe that war was at hand, hastily pressed the report of the Federal Relations Committee, so that they might finish the work and call a border-states conference before it was too late.[58] The voting on this proceeded despite rumors and obstructions; consequently, by April 13 the preliminary part and the first section of the proposed thirteenth amendment had been adopted by the committee of the whole.[59] Carlile tried to change the eighth resolution on the right of withdrawal, so as to make it declare that the only way to disrupt the Union was through revolution. But for the sake of harmony, Conrad and others who denied the right of secession refused to support him.[60] At another time, Campbell Tarr offered a motion to strike out a clause which declared that if the non-slaveholding states refused to respond favorably to the committee's plan, Virginia would feel compelled to resume the power granted by her to the central government. This motion, however, was defeated by a combination of the moderates and secessionists.[61]

The secessionists, on the other hand, delayed the voting by offering "100's of meaningless propositions," by calling for the "ayes and noes" on unimportant items, and by reading telegrams and "war dispatches."[62] They concentrated their attack, in this period, on the border-states conference. At first they tried to kill the whole idea but were defeated by a safe margin.[63] Failing in this, Harvie and Wise tried to have the delegates to this conference elected by the people of the respective states rather than appointed by conventions.[64] A motion on this enabled Harvie to make one of his characteristically defiant speeches—an indication that the growing secession sentiment made him certain that the Convention did not represent the public attitude.[65] His motion was defeated by a vote of forty-four to seventy-six.[66]

In spite of these Union majorities, there was a decided weakening in the ranks of the conservatives as the reports of preparation for war increased and as the excitement of the streets was carried to the Convention hall.[67] Moderates like Dorman were convinced that civil war was at hand.[68] Each day many telegrams and reports were read, all of which the Unionists maintained were either entirely false or halftruths—after April 12 even they were forced to accept the news about Sumter.[69] On the morning after the firing on this fort, the conservatives retained their composure except for a short "flurry" when Hall of Wetzel proposed a vote on an ordinance of secession.[70] In the evening session feeling was not so easily controlled when a debate over South Carolina's conduct developed. John Goode warned the Unionists that "we of the East do not mean to be held in this Union by any power, within or without the State—out of it we intend to go."[71] Letcher sent in official telegrams from Governor Pickens which related the happenings in the Charleston harbor, but no action on these was taken at this time by the Convention. The next day they learned of Lincoln's proclamation calling for 75,000 troops.

After April 4 the secessionists realized that unless something happened to change her course, Virginia would not secede until the other border states did. In the Convention Harvie was despondent and the Richmond papers of this party had little hopes for independent state action.[72] Consequently, as was stated above, several extreme disunionists outside the Convention asked the cotton states to precipitate affairs.[73] Ruffin and Pryor, who had been "firing the Virginia heart" at county meetings ever since Lincoln's election, went to Charleston and John Tyler, Jr., to Montgomery to help carry out this plan.[74] In a speech at Charleston, April 10, Pryor urged the Southern Confederacy to fire on Sumter and he would assure them "that just so certain as to-morrow's sun will rise upon us, just so certain will Virginia be a member of the Southern Confederacy. We will put her in if you but strike a blow."[75]

The attack on the fort by the Confederate battalion began on April 12 and, possibly, Ruffin who was enrolled at that time in the "Palmetto Guards" fired the first shot.[76] The report of this cannonading reached Richmond that afternoon and by the next day the news of the surrender was generally known. It was received with greatest enthusiasm, and demonstrations followed in the state capital.[77] Many Union delegates of the Convention failed to be at their caucus that night, because it was unsafe for them to appear on the streets.[78] In other parts of eastern Virginia there were also ardent expressions of approval.[79]

The Preston committee with its unfavorable report returned to Richmond, April 14. This "sickened the heart" of Union men, such as Conrad, who felt that Lincoln's order to hold Sumter and his reply to the Virginia commission made civil war certain. He was afraid that the idea of a border-states conference would fail, and that within the next few days the state would withdraw independently.[80] Conrad and Dorman as representatives of the conservatives have left records revealing the conflict which went on in their minds during this period. Both of them came from the Valley; hence they were partly inclined to the western view and partly to the eastern. They were devoted to the Union and hated to see it broken up, but they loved their state more. Each was perplexed as to which course would prevent the division of the state. Dorman wrote Davidson, April 14, that eastern Virginia would not remain in the Union now, and that the Trans-Alleghany region would not go without consulting Kentucky and the other border states. This situation caused him and others to waver between immediate secession and a border-states conference as means of preventing civil war in eastern and western portions of the state.[81] He leaned toward the immediate secession alternative; yet Conrad still hoped to bring about coöperation.

The feeling east of the Blue Ridge for prompt separation from the Union was very strong before it was known that reënforcements had been sent to Charleston. The firing on Sumter and the President's reply to Virginia's commission had increased this; and all chances for conciliation and even coöperation were wiped out there and in some other sections the next day when it was learned that Lincoln had called for 75,000 troops to "coerce" the seceded states. Even Conrad felt that resistance should be made to the proclamation, and his only hesitancy in carrying this out was in deciding on the method best suited to meet the situation. His hope in coöperation was due partly to the feeling that the North would not back Lincoln. He could not conceive of it.[82]

After Lincoln's proclamation, moderates as well as secessionists, outside of the Convention, were ready for independent state action, for they felt that the "end was at hand." As soon as Mason who had been at his home near Winchester heard of the call for troops, he set out for Richmond because he was sure that Virginia would secede at once.[83] The *Whig* declared that this proclamation meant war, and so it advocated a levy "*en masse* of every man able to bear arms to fight to the death."[84] J. R. Anderson, head of the Tredegar Iron Works, assured his friends in South Carolina that "Virginia *must* follow now, and we believe she will."[85] Even the Union-loving Lynchburg *Virginian* maintained that "the last feather which breaks the camel's back has been applied."[86] and the Staunton *Spectator* predicted that "every man is ready to take up arms."[87] The call for troops caused Bristol and Rockbridge to change to secession, a complete reversal of their former position.[88] Governor Letcher, who had been so severely criticized by the secessionists for his loyalty to the Union, satisfied even the *Enquirer* in his stern refusal to comply with Lincoln's order for men from Virginia.[89]

In the state capital disunion sentiment was rampant. According to the *Daily Dispatch,* what the Convention did was of little consequence, for it was "powerless to control or shape or alter the great stream of events."[90] A newspaper reporter who was in Richmond on the fifteenth recorded in his copious diary that disunion sentiment there was at "white heat," business was suspended, and people roamed the streets.[91] A mob of 250 would have overthrown the Convention itself if Marshall Ambler, a secessionist delegate, had not held them in check.[92]

In the midst of the excitement the Convention reconvened on Monday, April 15. Many expected an ordinance of secession that day because the moderates had gone over in sufficient numbers to make it possible,[93] but the secessionists were not ready to take such a drastic step without almost unanimous support.[94] Consequently before the session opened, a committee from this party suggested to Conrad that it was willing to follow his leadership if he would agree to put aside the regular order of business and consider the recent course of events.[95] Conrad accepted the offer and asked Holcombe, a secessionist, to propose a secret session as soon as Preston's report had been made.[96]

At first Holcombe's motion met with opposition from several conservatives who had not been informed of its origin.[97] Conrad then called Summers to instruct him of the plan, but before they returned to the hall the body had adjourned. Although it was only noon,[98] this adjournment was satisfactory to all parties, because they wanted time to obtain official confirmation of Lincoln's proclamation.[99] The session, however, was long enough for Scott, the spokesman for the moderates, to propose the delay of secession until after the coöperation of the border states had been gained.[100] This brought to the front the alternative which bothered Dorman—[101] whether they should resort to immediate secession, or delay this act until after consultation with the slave states which were still in the Union. The fact that the ordinance was not passed until the seventeenth was due to the fight for Scott's motion, rather than to the lack of a majority for some kind of disunion. Moderates who had gone over to the secession side tried to keep this issue in the background in order that they might concentrate on immediate defense.[102]

The next morning the forces were more harmonious on Holcombe's resolution. As a result, the Convention went into secret session with almost unanimous approval. Soon Preston who assumed the leadership of the moderates introduced an ordinance to "repeal the ratification of the Constitution of the United States of America, by the State of Virginia and to resume all the rights and powers under said Constitution." This significant measure provided:

> The people of Virginia, in their ratification of the constitution of the United States of America, adopted by them in convention on the twenty-fifth day of June in the year of our Lord one thousand seven hundred and eighty-eight, having declared that the powers granted under the said constitution were derived from the people of the United States, and might be resumed whensoever the same should be perverted to their injury and oppression; and the Federal Government having perverted said powers not only to the injury of the people of Virginia, but to the oppression of the Southern slaveholding states:
>
> Now, therefore, we the people of Virginia do declare and ordain that the ordinance adopted by the people of this state in convention on the twenty-fifth day of June in the year of our Lord one thousand seven hundred and eighty-eight, whereby the constitution of the United States of America was ratified and all acts of the general assembly of the state ratifying or adopting amendments to said constitution, are hereby repealed and abrogated; that the union between Virginia and the other states under the constitution aforesaid is hereby dissolved, and that the state of Virginia is in the full possession and exercise of all the rights of sovereignty which belong and appertain to a free and independent state.
>
> And they do further declare that said constitution of the United States of America is no longer binding on any of the citizens of this state.[103]

Scott made one last endeavor to secure the passage of the plan which he proposed the day before by amending Preston's ordinance in such a way that the people would vote for secession or a border-states conference.[104] Before this amendment was acted upon the Convention adjourned again.[105] The secessionists were not ready to push matters, for their majority in favor of disunion was still small. Believing that the course of events would continue to increase their strength, they felt that they could afford to wait.[106]

The pressure from the outside continued to grow. There was much talk in the eastern counties, and especially at Richmond, of overthrowing the Convention and of obtaining the end by an extra-legal body. For some weeks individuals had threatened to follow this course.[107] On April 12 the Richmond *Examiner* asked if these were not times "when the outburst of revolution becomes the path of duty? . . . Shall tens of thousands of honest and valuable citizens be driven into exile, or shall the Convention be given notice to quit?"[108] As he approached Richmond from Washington, J. B. Jones on the tenth and eleventh heard the Convention and Letcher denounced on all hands. He was convinced that before many days the Convention would be disposed of by another assembly which would meet in the state capital on the eighteenth.[109]

In the latter part of March, four secessionists from the Convention, two from the House of Delegates, and three other prominent Democrats[110] sent out a call to selected men, mainly from the Tidewater and Piedmont, to meet them at Richmond on April 16 for the purpose of consulting "with the friends of Southern rights as to the course which Virginia should pursue in the present emergency."[111] Wise, the father of the idea, held that the main purpose in calling this assembly was to organize a "resistance party for the spring elections. Once organized we will be ready to concert action for any emergency, mild, middle, or extreme."[112] Many of the delegates to this assembly were on hand, April 15. Either these or some other radicals threatened to break up the Convention on that day, and were checked only by the most strenuous efforts of Ambler.[113] On the next day this "Spontaneous Southern Rights" assembly, as it was labeled, met behind closed doors in a hall near that of the legal one. The membership of the former included some of the ablest leaders of the state—some were in the regular Convention and went from one to the other at frequent intervals.[114] David Chalmers from the tobacco-growing county of Halifax was made president.

Many in this "Spontaneous Southern Rights" assembly wanted to overthrow the regular body, but the more conservative members led by P. H. Aylett, a descendant of Patrick Henry, persuaded them to allow the other body a little more time.[115] Constant reports brought from the Secession Convention convinced this extra-legal assembly that the conservatives in the former were weakening.[116] As a result of this it accepted the advice of Aylett.[117] A delegate reported that boats had been sunk in the channel at Norfolk to obstruct passage, and "some one who seemed to know something of the matter" announced that before another day elapsed Harper's Ferry would fall into their hands, all of which news was received with "wildest enthusiasm."[118] The next day constant reports of the proceedings in the Convention were made to the "Spontaneous Southern Rights" assembly, although the sessions of the former were supposed to be secret. Those who were members of both bodies went frequently from one to the other.[119] On the night of the sixteenth, the enthusiasm on the streets increased "in intensity" so that it became apparent "that if an ordinance of secession were passed by the new Convention, its validity would be recognized and acted upon by the majority of the people."[120]

In keeping with this revolutionary spirit which prevailed in the city on the sixteenth and seventeenth, Wise and other ardent disunionists vehemently addressed the regular Convention on the latter date. Although the proceedings of that session were secret and the debates have never been published, the subsequent reports of James C. McGrew and Waitman T. Willey, members of this body, and J. D. Imboden, a close friend of Wise but not a member of the Convention, give some idea of what happened.[121] According to these accounts, as Wise in the midst of great excitement rose to address the Convention, he drew "a pistol from his bosom laid it before him, and proceeded to harangue the body in the most violent and denunciatory manner."[122] He concluded by taking his watch from his pocket and "with glaring eyes and bated breath, declared that events were now transpiring which caused a hush to come over his soul. At such an hour, he said, Harper's Ferry and its armory were in possession of Virginia soldiers; at another period the Federal navy yard and property at Norfolk were seized by troops of the State."[123] He and others had taken this responsibility because the Governor was unwilling to act, and because they saw that this was the only guarantee to Virginia's safety, since war was inevitable.[124] According to Imboden, moderate members expressed their admiration for Wise's foresight, and the Unionists when they saw the response his speech met with in the Convention lost hope of averting the severance of the Union.[125] Lewis and Willey also maintained that this incident aided by the "Spontaneous Southern Rights" assembly was responsible for the passage of the ordinance of secession.[126]

There is contemporary evidence to support parts of this story. Certainly attacks on Harper's Ferry and the Gospert navy yard at Norfolk were planned without Letcher's approval.[127] It is also evident that Wise, independently of the Governor, issued orders and communicated directly with military officials.[128] Although the actual attack was instigated by Wise, it was completed under the orders and with the sanction of Letcher.[129] The effects of the incident on the Convention were probably overestimated by Imboden, Willey, and Lewis. This conclusion is borne out by the fact that Wise's political influence at the time was limited;[130] that the sentiment for secession had been steadily growing since the Peace Conference's report, and especially since the war rumors of early April and the firing on Sumter; that the vote of the eighth on Preston's resolutions showed that the majority would resist "coercion"; and that the feeling in the Convention on April 16, before Wise's speech, was already for disunion.[131] Possibly its only effect was to show to the Convention the trend of sentiment.

In the midst of the excitement brought on by Wise's remarks and the extra-legal assembly, Scott's amendment on the border-states conference[132] came up in the legal body and was defeated by a vote of sixty-four to seventy-nine.[133] This was the last stand of the coöperationists. Nine who later supported secession were still willing to join the Unionists in an effort to gain those states, and thereby prevent a division of Virginia.[134] Of these nine, five were from the southwestern counties, and the others were from east of the Blue Ridge. All the Unionists were on the affirmative side, for they realized that it was a matter of this conference or secession. With the defeat of Scott's amendment the way was clear for the passage on that day, April 17, of the ordinance of secession. This was approved by a vote of eighty-eight to fifty-five.[135]

In accordance with the provision of the legislative bill calling the Convention, this ordinance was presented to the people for ratification in their election of May 23.[136] As things turned out this endorsement proved a farce,[137] and, to all points and purposes, Virginia was out of the Union after April 17. Immediately thereafter the Convention proceeded to enroll and equip an army, to exercise the powers of a sovereign state, and to form a union with the Confederacy by an agreement of April 25.[138]

In the vote on the ordinance, as given above, one delegate, Benjamin Wilson who usually supported the moderates, was excused from voting, and eight were absent. Six of the eight later recorded their approval of the ordinance.[139] Judged on this basis, the vote was ninety-four to fifty-five; two were still absent and one did not vote. Nine of the fifty-five who were in the negative changed to the affirmative.[140] Out of those refusing to shift to the support of the measure, only twenty-two failed to sign it.[141] Many delegates later elected to the Convention were allowed to attach their names to the ordinance. As a result there were 143 signatures.[142]

In analyzing the votes on this ordinance, it must be realized that the final tabulation, which after all changes were made was 103 to forty-six, did not represent the real sentiment of this body on April 17. Some of the eighty-eight on the initial ballot, doubtless, supported secession in order to show the North that Virginia was a unit. Such a manifestation, they hoped, might force the free states to change their policy.[143] On the other hand, such members as R. Y. Conrad, who voted in the negative because he felt that coöperation was still possible, were inclined toward disunion as a last resort.[144] In its issue of April 19, the *Examiner* held that one-third of the fifty-five who had voted against secession were for delaying the measure until their slaveholding neighbors could be won, rather than for preserving the Union itself.[145] Even discounting the influence of the partisan motive in this estimate, other evidence seems to prove that this was partly true.[146]

Of the eighty-eight who voted for the ordinance, fifty-five were from east of the Blue Ridge, ten were from the central and northern parts of the Valley, eighteen were from the southwest, and five were from the northwest.* Twelve and two-thirds† votes were cast by delegates from the section which later became West Virginia. Of the fifty-five who voted in the negative, ten were from east of the Blue Ridge, seventeen were from the central and northern part of the Valley, three were from the southwest, and twenty-five were from the northwest. Those from east of the Blue Ridge and the southwest were in the main responsible for the passage of the ordinance. Of the forty-three and

---

*The vote according to sections was as follows:

	For Secession	Against Secession
Tidewater	23	6
Piedmont	32	4
Valley (north of James River)	10	17
Southwest (west of Blue Ridge and practically south of James and Kanawha rivers)	18	3
Northwest	5	25
West Virginia	12⅔	31
Virginia	75⅓	24

(This information was gathered from "Journal of Secret Sess.," *Journal of Sec. Conv.,* 10-11).

†This fractional division is due to the fact that McDowell, which was later included in West Virginia, was in the electoral district with Buchanan and Tazewell, which remained in Virginia. These three counties together elected two delegates to the Convention; consequently, McDowell's vote is estimated as two-thirds of that for the whole electoral district.

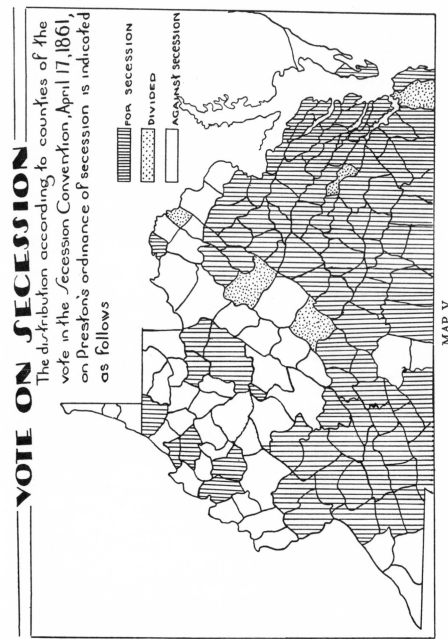

VOTE ON SECESSION

The distribution according to counties of the vote in the Secession Convention, April 17, 1861, on Preston's ordinance of secession is indicated as follows

FOR SECESSION

DIVIDED

AGAINST SECESSION

MAP V

two-thirds votes cast by those from the counties later organized into West Virginia, twelve and two-thirds were for secession and thirty-one were for the Union.[147]

A more detailed analysis of these votes will reveal some interesting facts. East of the Blue Ridge, the delegates voting in the negative were from Franklin and Henry counties which were on the edge of the tobacco belt in the southwestern Piedmont, Norfolk and Portsmouth in the southeast, Accomac on the Eastern Shore, Henrico in which Richmond was located, and Alexandria, Fairfax, and Loudoun which were near Washington city. The position of those from Franklin, Henry, and Henrico are not easily explained, for the neighboring counties supported secession. It is doubtful if the stand taken by these delegates represented the sentiment of their constituents.[148] The other Union votes from east of the Blue Ridge are more easily explained. Norfolk County was rapidly developing her truck farming, and the market for her products was in Northern cities. Along with Norfolk, Portsmouth and Accomac, in case of war, would be open to an attack from the United States navy. People from this section, moreover, were already dreaming that a great city would be built in their midst out of the trade from the Middle West and Europe.[149] Railroads and the James River and Kanawha Canal gave them grounds for their hope of trade with the West, and a steamship line recently organized offered prospects for trade with Europe.[150] If Virginia withdrew from the Union the Western trade would be lost. Likewise, the counties around Washington were connected with the free states in trade and interests.[151] But the thing that carried most weight in their decision was probably the fact that they would be the border counties and open to attack. There were also some farmers here from the North.[152]

The delegates from the southwest were almost as unanimous for secession as those from east of the Blue Ridge. The valleys there were fertile, slaves were numerous, the plantation system prevailed, and the Southern Methodists were strong.[153] This section's only railroad outlet was over the Virginia and Tennessee which ran from Bristol to Lynchburg and from there over the Southside Railroad to Richmond.[154] The James River and Kanawha Canal also extended into this section as far as Botetourt, and many expected it to be completed to the Kanawha River, thereby giving them another connection with the eastern part of the state.[155] There was little fear here of invasion, for its valleys extending northeast and southwest were protected by mountains on two sides and the distance from the border was too far to cause any great concern.

In the northern and central parts of the Valley and in the northwestern part of the state, however, the story was the reverse. Their delegates voted almost solidly against secession. In the former section, railroads, churches, and trade ties connected the people with Baltimore, Washington, and the North.[156] Some of the counties here were mountainous and without many slaves.[157] They, too, were open to attack. Like the Valley, only more so, the northwest was bound to the free states by economic ties. Throughout the period of the Convention their representatives had reminded the east of this fact.[158] Their products, grain, hay, cattle, hogs, oil, minerals, and wool, found their best market in the North, and their railroad and river systems gave them their most satisfactory connection with the free states.[159] Between northwestern and eastern Virginia there were few things in common. The newspapers, colleges, churches, and social and economic systems there were more akin to those of the free states than to those of the South.[160] "We are," as Robert Johnson of Clarksburg expressed it in a letter to Governor Letcher, May 9, 1861, "not slaveholders, many of us are of Northern birth, we read almost exclusively Northern newspapers and books, and listen to Northern preachers."[161] Coupled with these facts was the ever-present fear of invasion, which the Wheeling *Intelligencer* explained in one of its editorials as follows: "One glance at the map reveals our predicament. Here we are . . . wedged tightly . . . between two of the most powerful and one of the most warlike States of this Union, and utterly at the mercy of either."[162]

The people's response to the passage of the secession ordinance was in most sections in keeping with the votes of their respective delegates.[163] From east of the Blue Ridge, from a large part of the southwest, and, to a limited degree, from the northern and central parts of the Valley, enthusiastic endorsements were made by the press, individual leaders, and public meetings.[164] On Main Street in Richmond there was a great torchlight procession nearly a mile in length. Windows were illuminated and bonfires were prevalent.[165] Frederick A. Aikien, secretary of the "National Democratic Executive Committee" from Massachusetts, notified Benjamin F. Butler that he had just returned from a trip in Virginia and that

there is no reason in my judgment to doubt but that the secession of the state will be strongly sustained in the western counties. In the eastern it is not a debatable question. . . .

The sentiment of the people is that they are engaged in a just and righteous war for independence and the defense of their homes and firesides. In this they seem united and determined to fight.[166]

The Richmond *Whig* asserted that "Lincoln gives us no alternative, but to fight or run."[167] And according to Botts, Lincoln's proclamation calling for troops "almost entirely swept . . . the Union Party, and the Union feeling" out of existence. "You cannot meet with one man in a thousand who is not influenced with a *passion for war*."[168] Loudoun County, whose delegates in the Convention had voted against secession, favored defending the "Old State" now that she had broken relations with the North.[169]

In the southwest the response to Letcher's call for troops on the seventeenth was equal to that of the eastern counties. Before May 1 Washington County had organized six new volunteer companies of one hundred men each; its county court had subscribed fifteen thousand dollars for arms; and individuals had raised another fifteen thousand dollars to buy horses, saddles, and other necessary equipment.[170] By the same date three volunteer companies were to be mustered into service, and two others were in the process of formation in the neighboring county of Smythe.[171] Lee, Russell, Tazewell, Monroe, Wise, and Grayson were almost as active.[172] Even Wayne, Cabell, Logan, Fayette, and Greenbrier had companies for the Confederacy by this date, and probably would have furnished more had they been able to obtain arms.[173]

Before April 17 the northern and central parts of the Valley opposed secession. After the passage of the ordinance, however, their attachment to the state caused them to acquiesce. Augusta County, in the heart of this Union region, provided through its court on April 22 thirty thousand dollars for arming local volunteer companies to be used for the defense of Virginia.[174] Stuart, Baldwin, and Baylor, the three delegates from this county who had voted against the ordinance, after consulting their constituents accepted the decision of the majority, and advised ratification.[175] Baldwin declared that while many people did not believe in the right of secession, they did believe in the right of revolution, and so, in the face of Lincoln's "aggressive" policy "there are no union men in Virginia now."[176] Several former staunch Union members of the Convention from this section advocated the acceptance of secession rather than permit Lincoln's "despotism."[177]

In the northwestern section there was less support for the ordinance of secession at the time of its passage than in any other corresponding portion of the state; but even here sentiment was not entirely united. The expressions of opinion at the public meetings, by newspapers, and by individual leaders indicate that with few exceptions, the counties served by the Baltimore and Ohio Railroad and the Ohio River with its tributaries were strongly attached to the Union, even to the extent of desiring the disruption of the old state. At Grafton, where the two branches of this railroad—one to Parkersburg and the other to Wheeling—met, the few secession delegates who returned through there from Richmond had to hide in their train to escape mob violence. All arms coming into this town for the Virginia forces were seized and used by the Unionists.[178] A pro-Southern man traveling through Upshur, Harrison, Doddridge, and the neighboring counties of this part of the state reported that two-thirds of the people west of Barbour were for a separate state movement.[179] As soon as the ordinance was passed, large public meetings condemning the action of the Convention were held in Monongalia, Wetzel, Harrison, Preston, Marion, Tyler, Taylor, and Parkersburg in addition to the Panhandle.[180] The Panhandle, of course, was almost a unit against any form of disunion.[181]

In the rest of the northwest there was much more sympathy for disunion, possibly more because of the desire to keep the state intact than from an inclination to join the South. A letter from Roane County, May 16, explained that there "are a great many true Southern men here, who as soon as the election is over, will take decided stands in favor of Virginia and Southern independence."[182] Public mass meetings, although poorly attended, held in Jackson, Cabell, and Boone endorsed secession.[183] Samuel Peders, a Unionist, admitted in a letter of April 30 that there was in Parkersburg a *"very considerable minority* of as *rabbed secessionists* as could be *found* in *South Carolina."*[184] Phillippi in Barbour, which is Southern in sentiment even to this day, prevented delegates' passing through on their way to the Wheeling Convention.[185] The citizens of Kanawha County, the home of Summers, held a public gathering on April 19, accused Lincoln of forcing war on the South, and pledged themselves to support the Confederacy.[186] On May 6 another meeting in the same county asked the court to provide ten thousand dollars for defense against the President's "aggression."[187] Meetings in Fayette, Putnam, and Logan endorsed this position.[188] Pocahontas appropriated fifteen thousand dollars for the same purpose.[189]

A further evidence of this division of sentiment is found in the response of that region to the call for troops. M. B. Hogans, June 22, wrote Governor Pierpoint from Cincinnati that the people there were disappointed that only one regiment from "Western Virginia" had been formed and two were being organized when there should be twenty.[190] Even by early August the Wellsburg *Herald* pessimistically stated that "Western Virginia" had placed in the field only *"four, not entire,* regiments of soldiers, and one of these hails almost entirely from the abolitionized Panhandle. In a white population of over a quarter of a million, three thousand men to stand up for the Union is truely a heavy draft upon the patriotism of our section."[191] A correspondent of the Indianapolis *Journal* wrote a little later that he had found in his section only 150 men from Virginia. The rest were from Pennsylvania and Ohio.[192] During 1861, eight Federal regiments were organized in the counties which later were included in West Virginia, and of these only two were organized south of the Baltimore and Ohio Railroad. Of course the fact that they were formed north of this railroad does not mean that no troops were recruited from other sections, but it does indicate that these were the centers. Most of the Union troops were raised in the counties bordering on Maryland, Pennsylvania, and Ohio, and in the central part of what is today West Virginia.[193] The counties of the upper New River, Greenbrier Valley, valleys of the Southern Branch of the Potomac and Lower Shenandoah —now the eastern panhandle—on the other hand, furnished many to the Confederacy.[194] Every county south of the Baltimore and Ohio except Tucker, Braxton, and Wirt furnished from a fraction of a company to several to the Confederacy. The same was true in four counties north of that road.[195] In 1865, five thousand Confederate soldiers returning to the Kanawha district were paroled.[196]

The sentiment of the west, at the time that secession was adopted, was partly illustrated by the half-hearted way in which the separation of western Virginia from the east was entered into. This statement does not mean that all who opposed the movement were secessionists. Many, like Summers, remained loyal to Virginia even though they disapproved disunion.[197] The separate state movement was a part of a long, sectional rivalry,[198] but secession consummated the dream of many. The Panhandle and Baltimore and Ohio Railroad territories, especially, wanted to break with the planter control. Many of the old grievances were still alive—unfair taxation,[199] unequal representation in the senate, lack of state aid for internal improvements, and the refusal of the east to aid public education, despite the large appropriations to eastern colleges.[200] These differences, along with the danger of invasion from the North, were constantly referred to by the western delegates in the

Secession Convention.[201] Consequently when the ordinance was passed, Carlile supported by several others from his section began a movement for a division of the state. Between twelve and twenty of these met at the Powhatan Hotel in Richmond two days after the adoption of the ordinance and decided to leave the Convention, go home, and try to detect what the reaction there to separation would be. At the same time Carlile left for Washington to obtain Lincoln's assistance.[202] Governor Letcher allowed these men to leave Richmond without molestation.[203] Under the influence of these and such others as Pierpoint, Caldwell, and Campbell, county meetings were held and a division of the state was openly discussed.[204] The call for a convention to meet in Wheeling on March 13 for considering the "course for Western Virginia to follow" was issued April 27.[205] A public meeting which Carlile headed in Clarksburg on April 22 had suggested such a step.[206] The response to this invitation was half-hearted. Twenty-six of the fifty counties later included in West Virginia sent representatives,[207] but these twenty-six elected their delegates in an irregular manner. Some were selected at mass gatherings called by the leaders after only Union sympathizers had been notified. In Wood and two or three other counties, it was resolved that any good Union man who happened to be present could represent them.[208] Most of the delegates were from the Panhandle.[209]

The sessions of the Wheeling Convention, May 13-15, were little more than wrangles between Carlile who favored the formation of a separate state immediately, and Willey and Jackson who advised delay until after the ratification of the ordinance of secession.[210] The latter position prevailed and the convention adjourned without taking any important step.[211] Most of the Northern newspapers which sent correspondents to report the proceedings agreed that the Union sentiment in "this part of the state" was overestimated.[212] In the June session of this body, eighty-two delegates representing twenty-seven counties were present, but again the elections were irregular. Even in the election of October 21 the popular vote on the division of the state was very small in some counties.[213]

The vote throughout the state on the ratification of the ordinance of secession was a poor test of the disunion sentiment. As soon as the ordinance was adopted by the Convention, ratification was taken for granted.[214] Nevertheless, the secession press did not take any chances. It advocated a large affirmative vote for effect.[215] Hoping to check preparations for war in the North by showing them that the South was united, many formerly staunch Union men campaigned for ratification.[216] The soldiers voted in their camps, where a refusal to support the ordinance would have been considered treason. The balloting was *viva voce*. Intimidation was doubtless common throughout the state. In districts where the secessionists were in control, it was not safe to vote in the negative;[217] and in many northwestern counties where the Unionists dominated, it was probably hazardous to vote in the affirmative.[218] As a result of these practices, the counties were either solidly for or against the ordinance.[219] The total vote of the state was almost as large as in preceding elections, yet some districts cast more ballots than there were eligible voters.[220]

Thus, as a result of the ratification on May 23, Virginia, the leader of the border states, severed the bonds of the Union which her Revolutionary leaders had done so much to form. She took this step after great deliberation and hesitation, evidently with great concern and misgivings. For ten years her leaders, not so able as those of the earlier period, had been uncertain as to the road to follow. Instead of striking out on a bold course for Southern independence as Tucker and Ruffin advised, or of reading aright the trend of events and throwing herself on the side of a nationalistic program as Botts and Summers suggested, most of the leaders in power from 1847 to 1860 complacently and almost indifferently followed an uncertain course.

All the while, there were a few bold spirits who foresaw the inevitable and threw their influence and efforts on the side of the slave states' confederacy. In every conceivable manner they preached Southern unity and hostility to a continuation of the union with the North. In schools, in churches, in magazines, and in societies of various kinds they spread their ideas for Southern nationalism. They used to advantage each event that tended to support their contention. As the decade wore away, their efforts bore fruit, especially in connection with the Brown raid and the election of Lincoln. Finally, in the exciting months of late 1860 and early 1861 their ideas were brought to a test. As much as Virginians disliked to make a final decision, they were forced to take a stand with the North and her democratic system or the South and her aristocratic civilization. The Old Dominion accepted the latter, for the radicals had convinced the majority of her people that their interests were more closely connected with those of the South than with those of the North.

NOTES

CHAPTER I

SOCIAL AND ECONOMIC BACKGROUND

1. An illustration of this is given in a letter of C. C. Jones of Lenoir, North Carolina, to Z. B. Vance, February 4, 1861. Here he wrote: "After all the action of Virginia will decide the fate of North Carolina." Z. B. Vance Papers (in North Carolina Historical Commission, Raleigh, N. C.).

2. Charles H. Ambler, *Sectionalism in Virginia from 1776 to 1861* (Chicago, 1910), 1. Hereafter cited as Ambler, *Sect. in Va.*

3. A. O. Craven, *Soil Exhaustion as a Factor in the Agricultural History of Virginia and Maryland, 1606-1860* (Urbana, 1926), 25. Hereafter cited as Craven, *Soil Exhaustion.*

4. James C. McGregor, *The Disruption of Virginia* (New York, 1922), 2.

5. Ambler, *op. cit.,* 1-2.

6. It has been estimated that 50,000,000 tons of the most fertile soil of the upland South are still carried away annually by erosion. Craven, *Soil Exhaustion,* 17.

7. These counties were Culpeper, Fairfax, Fauquier, Loudoun, Orange, Prince William—about 600 square miles in all. *Report of the Commissioner of Agriculture for the year 1864* (Washington, 1865), 17.

8. *Ibid.,* 17.

9. Virgil A. Lewis, *West Virginia: Its History, Natural Resources, Industrial Enterprises, and Institutions* (Charleston, 1904), 3-4.

10. *Ibid.,* 4-5.

11. *Ibid.,* 6.

12. *Ibid.;* Ambler, *op. cit.,* 2.

13. Lewis, *op. cit.,* 4-5.

14. Such rivers as the Guandotte, Great and Little Kanawha, Big Sandy, Monongalia, and the Ohio are navigable. Ambler, *op. cit.,* 3.

15. Norfolk County alone produced $292,968 worth of trucking produce in 1860. *Report of Com. of Agric. for 1864,* 17. For the whole state the increase had been as follows: in 1840, $92.359; in 1850, $183.947, and in 1860, $589.467. Craven, *op. cit.,* 154.

16. Wealth, *Resources and Hopes of the State of Virginia* (Norfolk, 1857), 9.

17. Craven, *op. cit.,* 154.

18. F. L. Olmstead, *A Journey in Seaboard Slave States with Remarks on their Economics* (New York, 1863), 158.

19. *Report of Com. of Agric. for 1864,* 17-42. In 1860 only 12,727 bales of cotton were produced in Virginia, and 7,163 of these came from Essex and Southampton counties. *U. S. 8th Census,* vol. on agric., 154-156.

20. In 1860 Virginia produced 123,968,312 pounds of tobacco, an increase of 48,621,-195 pounds since 1840 and about twenty-eight per cent of the tobacco grown in the entire country in 1860. Albemarle, Amelia, Bedford, Brunswick, Campbell, Caroline, Charlotte, Chesterfield, Halifax, Hanover, Henrico, Henry, Louisa, Lunenburg, Mecklenburg, Nelson, Nottoway, Pittsylvania, Powhatan, and Prince Edward produced over 2,000,000 pounds each. *Ibid.*

21. Of the fifteen counties in Virginia which grew over 2,000,000 pounds of wheat each, six were from the Piedmont, three were from the Tidewater, six were from the Valley, and not one was from west of the Alleghanies. Of the thirty-six other counties which produced over 100,000 bushels each, seventeen were from the Piedmont, nine

were from the Tidewater, nine were from the Valley, and one was from west of the Alleghanies. *Ibid.*

22. *Ibid.*

23. *Ibid.*, vol. on agric., 243-245.

24. Of the 5,810 slaveholders having over twenty slaves each, 5,410 lived east of the Blue Ridge. *Ibid.*

25. W. F. Switzer, *Report on the Internal Commerce of the United States. Submitted December 20, 1886* (Washington, 1886), 189. Hereafter cited as Switzer.

26. In 1860 the assessed value of the real and personal property amounted to $635 per capita (slaves included) in the Piedmont and Tidewater as against $516 in the other portions of Virginia. *Doc. of Secession Conv.*, doc. 37.

27. A. O. Craven, *Edmund Ruffin, Southerner: a study in Secession* (New York, 1932), chapter III. Hereafter cited as Craven, *Ruffin*. *Cf.* also Craven, *Soil Exhaustion*, 135-161; *William and Mary Quarterly*, XIV, 193; Ambler, *Sect. in Va.*, 186-187.

Ruffin did not confine his agricultural crusade to eastern Virginia. In the period prior to 1860 his pamphlets and addresses had made him the outstanding authority on Southern agriculture. W. P. Cutler, "A Pioneer in Agricultural Science," *Year-book of the United States Department of Agriculture, 1895* (Washington, 1896), 493-502. This writer maintained that while Ruffin's greatest contribution was in the use of marl, his farm lectures, articles, and experiments also related to drainage, the use of root crops, methods of harvesting wheat, and the treatment of insects and pests.

28. Of the $1,326,249 worth of imports which came into the custom districts of Virginia in 1859-1860, $902,114 came through Richmond, $201,460 came through Norfolk and Portsmouth. The remainder came through Alexandria and Petersburg. Of $5,814,074 worth of exports, $5,079,750 went through Richmond, and $479,885 went through Norfolk and Portsmouth. Switzer, 120-123.

29. Richmond, $4,838,995; Petersburg $2,081,149; Lynchburg, $2,161,202; Danville, $1,031,340; Clarksville, $295,000. Total for Virginia $12,236,863. *U. S. 8th Census*, vol. on man., 604-634.

30. This includes the production in all sections of the state.

31 *U. S. 8th Census*, vol. on mfg., 604-634; Kathleen Bruce, *Virginia Iron Manufactures in the Slave Era* (New York, 1931), 179-180.

32. *U. S. 8th Census*, vol. of man., 604-634.

33. *Ibid.*, vol. on mortality and miscellaneous statistics, 327; W. F. Dunaway, *History of the James River and Kanawha Company* (New York, 1922), 160.

34. Sometimes the tobacco was rolled to market in hogsheads which were drawn by horses. In 1841 more than 110,140 tons of freight were hauled on the James River and Kanwha Canal. This increased to 244,273 in 1860. Dunaway, *op. cit.*, 168.

35. Its receipts in 1855 were about one-fourth of those of the James River and Kanawha Canal. *Wealth, Resources and Hopes of Virginia*, 24.

36. The Seaboard and Roanoke which ran from Weldon in North Carolina to Norfolk, eighty miles, connected the southeastern section of the state to Norfolk. Other roads connected Petersburg, Lynchburg, Charlottesville, and Alexandria (the present Southern Railroad), Gordonsville and Fredericksburg, Gordonsville and Richmond, Strassburg in the Valley and the Potomac at Quantico, and Alexandria and Harper's Ferry. *U. S. 8th Census*, vol. on mort. and misc. statistics, 327; Dunaway, *op. cit.*, 184.

37. Dunaway, *op. cit.*, 184.

38 C. H. Ambler, "The Cleavage Between Eastern and Western Virginia," *American Historical Review*, XV, 765-766. Hereafter cited as Ambler, "Cleavage."

39. *Report of the Com. of Agric.*, 28; *U. S. 8th Census*, vol. on agric., 154-165.

40. *Report of the Com. of Agric.*, 28.

41. Augusta with 171 out of 520 slaveholders led in the total number of slaveholders of more than ten slaves each to the county. In Clarke 124 out of the 674 farmers owned over ten slaves each. *U. S. 8th Census*, vol. on agric., 243-245.

42. *Ibid.*

43. *Cf. infra*, 12.

44. *U. S. 8th Census*, vol. on mort. and misc. statistics, 327.

45. Edmund Hungerford, *The Story of the Baltimore and Ohio Railroad, 1827-1927* (2 vols., New York, 1928), II, 113; W. F. Evans, *History of Berkeley County,*

West Virginia (Martinsburg, 1928), 88-89; Milton Reizenstein, *History of the Baltimore and Ohio Railroad* (Baltimore, 1897), 71.

46. *U. S. 8th Census,* vol. on agric., 243-245.

47. *Ibid.*

48. *Ibid.*

49. There were only 13,858 slaves in the region west of the Alleghanies in 1860. Greenbrier, Kanawha, Lee, Russell, and Tazewell had 7,948 or fifty-seven per cent of these. *Ibid.*

50. *Ibid.*

51. From 1800 to 1810 whites increased 35% and the slaves 40%. From 1830 to 1840 the whites increased 25% and the slaves 5%. From 1850 to 1860 the whites increased 19% and the slaves decreased 10%. J. M. Callahan, *History of West Virginia* (Chicago, 1923), I, 247. Hereafter cited as Callahan, *Hist. of W. Va.*

52. The counties along the Baltimore and Ohio which had increased in slavery were Ritchie, Doddridge, and Harrison. From 1850 to 1860 the slaves decreased in the northwest 19.6%, while in the southwest the increase was 14.5%. *U. S. 8th Census,* vol. on agric., 243-245.

53. *Ibid.,* vol. on man., 604-636.

54. *Ibid.;* Dunaway, *op. cit.,* 180. The Baltimore and Ohio Railroad hauled 427,793 tons of coal in 1860. Hungerford, *op. cit.,* I, 346.

55. *U. S. 8th Census,* vol. on man., 604-636.

56. *Kanawha Valley Star,* Sept. 13, Oct. 10, 1859. In 1854 over $1,000,000 worth of salt was produced in the Kanawha Valley. Dunaway, *op. cit.,* 180.

57. *U. S. 8th Census,* vol. on man., 624-625.

58. *Ibid.,* vol. on mort. and statistics, 327.

59. The Wheeling branch of the Baltimore and Ohio Railroad was finished in 1852, and the Parkersburg wing, the construction of which Wheeling bitterly opposed, was completed in 1857. The two branches connected at Grafton. In the first year of its operation, the Parkersburg wing received $248,000 worth of trade. The road brought relative prosperity to the northwestern counties and made them more independent of Richmond. Callahan, *Hist. of W. Va.,* I, 331; Hungerford, *op. cit.,* I, 293, 326; Reizenstein, *op. cit.,* 71.

60. Packets ran daily from the mouth of the Great Kanawha to Charleston after 1845. Callahan, *Hist. of W. Va.,* I, 234; McGregor, *Disruption of Va.,* 3-4.

61. Callahan, *Hist. of W. Va.,* I, 191.

62. *Ibid.,* I, 331.

63. *Kanwha Valley Star,* Apr. 2, 1860.

64. *Ibid.*

65. *Report of Com. of Agric. for 1864,* 20; Olmsted, *op. cit.,* 158.

66. McGregor, *op. cit.,* chapters IV-V.

67. *Ibid.,* 10.

68. Ambler, *Sect. in Va.,* 251.

69. *Ibid.* There were sufficient Germans in this section and the Valley to warrant the Constitutional Convention's (1850-1851) printing its documents in German.

70. *U. S. 8th Census,* vol. on pop., 523.

71. *Ibid.*

72. *Ibid.*

73. *Ibid.*

74. Ambler, "Cleavage," 768; C. G. Woodson, *The Disruption of Virginia* (Ph.D. Dissertation, Harvard University, 1912), 138-139.

75. Ambler, *Sect. in Va.,* 274; Callahan, *op. cit.,* I, 296.

76. Ambler, "Cleavage," 768.

77. McGregor, *op. cit.,* 16; Ambler, *Sect. in Va.,* 282.

78. *Ibid.,* 275.

79. McGregor, *op. cit.,* 16.

80. Of the 3,105 churches in Virginia in 1860, 1,403 were Methodist, 787 were Baptist, 290 Presbyterian. *U. S. 8th Census,* vol. on mort. and statistics, 477-485.

81. Ambler, *Sect. in Va.,* 287.

82. *Ibid.* The division of the churches is discussed on pages 79, 82.

83. *Cf.,* chapter XI.

84. *U. S. 8th Census,* vol. on agric., 247.

85. *Statistical View of the United States . . . Being a Compendium of the Seventh Census,* J. BeDow, ed. (Washington 1854), 85-86. Hereafter cited as DeBow's *Compendium. Cf.* also *U. S. 8th Census,* vol. on agric., 247.

86. Alabama's increase was from 32.7% in 1820 to 44.4% in 1850, and 45% in 1860. South Carolina's increase was from 51.4% in 1820 to 57.1% in 1860. Louisiana, Mississippi, and Georgia had about the same percentages of increase. DeBow's *Compendium,* 85-86; *U. S. 8th Census,* vol. on pop., iv, 604.

87. *Ibid.,* vol. on pop., 604; DeBow's *Compendium,* 85-86; *Documents of the Secession Convention, 1861,* doc. 37, p. 10.

88. *Ibid.;* DeBow's *Compendium,* 85-86.

89. *Cf. supra,* 5.

90. *Cf. supra,* 7, 8.

91. *Cf. infra,* chapter VI, note 123, for the counties included in the respective sections. In the northwestern counties there was a decline of 19.6%; the Shenandoah Valley and neighboring counties between the Alleghanies and the Blue Ridge as far south as the James declined 3.3%; the eastern plain increased 2.1%; the Piedmont increased 6.4%; and the southwest grew in the number of slaves 14.5%. *U. S. 8th Census,* vol. on agric., 243-245; DeBow's *Compendium,* 320-326.

92. Accomac —9.5%, Essex —17%, Mathews, —3%, New Kent —5%, Northumberland —8%, Southampton —6%. *U. S. 8th Census,* vol. on agric., 243-245; DeBow's *Compendium,* 320-326.

93. The percentage in the southwestern Piedmont varied from an increase of 7% in Campbell to 50% in Henry; but in the Warrenton section the decline was from a —5% in Prince William to a —12% in Fairfax.

94. Harrison, for instance, had 485 slaves in 1850 and 582 in 1860.

95. These counties had less than 200 slaves each.

96. With the exception of two counties—Jackson and Putnam every county in this section declined in slave population from 22% to 70% in this period, 1850-1860.

97. W. W. Sweet, *The Story of Religion in America* (New York, 1930), 19-23.

98. Craven, *Ruffin,* 123; W. S. Jenkins, *The Political Theories of the Slaveholders* (Ph.D. Dissertation, University of North Carolina, 1927), 23.

99. Ambler, *Sect. in Va.,* 188-190.

100. *Ibid.,* 196. There were exceptions to this. S. McDowell Moore of Rockbridge County said that slavery was the "heaviest calamity which has ever befallen any portion of the human race" and that it destroyed every semblance of virtue and morality. T. M. Whitfield, *Slavery Agitation in Virginia 1829-1832* (Baltimore, 1930), 76.

101. Ambler, *Sect. in Va.,* 196.

102. *Ibid.*

103. *Ibid.,* 192.

104. Charles H. Ambler, *Thomas Ritchie, a Study in Virginia Politics* (Richmond, 1913), 167. Hereafter cited as Ambler, *Ritchie.*

105. Ambler, *Sect. in Va.,* 196.

106. W. H. Collins, *The Domestic Slave Trade of the Southern States* (New York, 1904), 64-66. This author estimates that each year the border states sent south over 8,000 slaves for sale from 1850 to 1860. This yielded $17,200,000 profit.

107. Bruce, *op. cit.,* 234-235. Olmsted in his *Journey through the Seaboard Slave States,* 127, held that slaves were in great demand in the tobacco factories of Richmond and Petersburg, and that their masters were paid from $150 to $200, in addition to expenses, for each slave a year. Moreover, the slaves were given from five to twenty dollars as bonuses each month for extra productions.

108. Thomas C. Johnson, *The Life and Letters of Robert L. Dabney* (Richmond, 1903), 67. Hereafter cited as Johnson, *Life of Dabney.*

109. Roger A. Pryor, congressman from the Petersburg district, declared in a speech in the House of Representatives, 1859, that, as a result of the 1832 debate in the Virginia legislature, citizens of the slaveholding communities were driven "by the apparent insecurity of the system, to explore its foundations. . . . In controversion of traditional ideas, it was discovered and demonstrated that Negro slavery, instead of

being an accidental evil . . . is an institution which exists in virtue of the most essential human interests and the highest sanction of the moral law." *Remarks Delivered in the House of Representatives and Senate of the United States on the Announcement of the Death of Honorable William O. Goode* (Washington, 1860), 16 pp. *Cf.* also Craven, *Ruffin,* 128.

110. Ambler, *Sect in Va.,* 269.

111. *Ibid.,* 308. In 1857 the grand jury of Harrison County indicted Horace Greeley for sending the New York *Tribune* into Virginia. In 1856 in Wood County, W. E. Stevenson, later governor of West Virginia, was indicted for circulating Helper's *Impending Crisis.* Callahan, *op. cit.,* I, 248.

112. Ambler, *Sect. in Va.,* 311.

113. D. S. Freeman, *Attitude of Political Parties of Virginia on Slavery and Secession,* MS. (in possession of Mr. Freeman), 5-6. Hereafter cited as Freeman, *Attitude.*

114. *Cf.* Carlile's speech in the Convention, Mar. 7, 1861; Richmond *Enquirer,* Mar. 11, 1861. Hereafter cited as Rich. *Enq.* W. T. Willey agreed with the position of Carlile in a speech in the Convention, March 4, 1861. Rich. *Enq.,* Mar. 6, 1861.

115. W. T. Willey Papers (in the possession of Miss Lilly Hagan, Morgantown, West Virginia). *Cf.* also *Object of the War: Speech of Hon. W. T. Willey, of Virginia in the Senate December 19 and 20, 1861* (Washington, no date), 9-12.

116. Richmond *Whig,* July 8, 1859. Hereafter cited as Rich. *Whig.* Ambler, *Sect. in Va.,* 308.

117. Letter of D. H. Conrad to P. R. Fenall, Jan. 8, 1851 (in Virginia Collection at University of Virginia).

118. J. D. Davidson Papers (in McCormick Agricultural Library, Chicago).

119. Ambler, *Sect. in Va.,* 233.

120. Freeman, *Attitude,* 6.

121. Letter of Hunter to Calhoun, June 16, 1843. *Correspondence of John C. Calhoun,* J. Franklin·Jameson, ed., American Historical Association *Annual Report* for 1899 (Washington, 1900), II, 865.

122. Letter of Hunter to Calhoun, Feb. 7, 1844, *ibid.,* 928.

123. Ambler, *Sect. in Va.,* 234.

124. Ambler, *Ritchie,* 253.

125. Freeman, *Attitude,* 7.

126. *Ibid.,* 9.

127. *Ibid.,* 15.

128. *Ibid.,* 9.

129. In 1843 the Whigs elected six of the fifteen congressmen; two years later they returned only one; in 1847 they regained the old six. Ambler, *Sect. in Va.,* 236; Rich. *Whig,* Nov. 28, 1848.

130. Ambler, *Sect. in Va.,* 235.

131. For the historical and traditional causes of sectionalism within the state see Ambler, *Sect. in Va.,* and McGregor, *Disruption of Va.*

132. *U. S. 8th Census,* vol. on agric., 154-165.

133. W. L. Goggin in the Secession Convention, February 26, 1861, explained the significance of this trade. Rich. *Enq.,* Feb. 28, 1861.

134. W. E. Dodd, *The Cotton Kingdom* (New Haven, 1921), 38.

135. *Ibid.,* 40.

136. *Cf.* chapter IV.

137. *U. S. 8th Census,* vol. on agric., 186-189.

138. *Ibid.,* vol. on agric., 189.

139. *Ibid.,* vol. on agric., 186-189.

140. R. R. Russell, *Economic Aspects of Southern Sectionalism, 1840-1861* (Urbana, Illinois, 1924), 277. Hereafter cited as Russell, *Econ. Aspects.*

CHAPTER II
VIRGINIA AND THE COMPROMISE OF 1850

1. *Debates and Proceedings of the Convention of Virginia in 1788* (Second edition, Richmond, 1805), 469.

2. Nicholas in this ratification convention said: "If thirteen individuals are about to make a contract, and one agrees to it, but at the same time declares that he understands its meaning . . . to be . . ., that it is not to be construed so as to impose any supplementary condition upon him, and that he is to be exonerated from it, whensoever any such imposition shall be attempted—I ask whether in this case these conditions on which he assented to it, would not be binding on the other twelve?" *Ibid.*, 447.

3. *The Resolutions of Virginia and Kentucky, Penned by Madison and Jefferson, in Relation to the Alien and Sedition Laws* (Richmond, 1826), 18.

4. W. E. Dodd, "John Taylor, of Caroline, Prophet of Secession," John Branch Historical *Papers*, II, 224. Hereafter cited as Dodd, "John Taylor of Caroline."

5. *Ibid.*

6. Ambler, *Ritchie*, 62.

7. In this editorial he said: " 'No man, no association of men, no State. or set of States, has a right to withdraw itself from this Union of its own account . . . The majority of States which formed the Union must consent to the withdrawal of any one branch of it. Until that consent has been obtained any attempt to dissolve the Union or distract the efficacy of its constitutional law is treason—treason to all interests and purposes.' " Quoted in Alexandria *Gazette,* Nov. 15, 1860.

8. Ambler, *Ritchie,* 62.

9. Dodd, "John Taylor of Caroline," 241.

10. John Taylor, *New Views of the Constitution of the United States* (Washington, 1823).

11. "Spencer Roane Reprint from Richmond *Enquirer* by Hampden," in Randolph-Macon Historical *Papers,* I, 325.

12. E. J. Smith, "Spencer Roane," Randolph-Macon Historical *Papers,* II, 25.

13. *Ibid.*, 26, 29; Dodd, "John Taylor of Caroline," 243-250.

14. H. V. Ames, *State Documents on Federal Relations: The States and the United States* (Philadelphia, 1906), 104.

15. A. C. Gordon, *William Fitzhugh Gordon, a Virginian of the Old School* (New York, 1909), 127.

16. *Ibid.*

17. *Ibid.*, 126.

18. *Ibid.*, 130-131.

19. Ames, *op. cit.*, 141-142.

20. Gordon, *op. cit.*, 133.

21. Ames, *op. cit.*, 141-142.

22. *Ibid.*, 157.

23. Ambler, *Sect. in Va.*, 202.

24. Gordon, *op. cit.*, 128.

25. C. H. Ambler, *The Life and Diary of John Floyd, Governor of Virginia, an Apostle of Secession, and the Father of the Oregon Country* (Richmond, 1918), 179. Hereafter cited as Ambler, *Diary of Floyd.*

26. *Ibid.*, 202.

27. *Ibid.*

28. *Ibid.*, 203.

29. *Ibid.*, 206-207.

30. Letter of B. W. Leigh while in Columbia, Mar. 12, 1833, to Governor John Floyd, Richard K. Cralle Papers (in Library of Congress).

31. Ambler, *Sect. in Va.*, 212-214.

32. *Ibid.*, 215; cf. Littleton W. Tazewell, *A Review of the Proclamation of President Jackson of the 10th of December, 1832* (Norfolk, 1888), 112 pp.

33. Rich. *Enq.*, July 25, 1851, quoting its own editorial of Dec. 31, 1832.

34. Resolutions of Jan. 26, 1833, Ames, *op. cit.*, 53-56.

35. Van Buren Papers (in Lib. of Cong.).

36. Tyler's *Quarterly*, I, 276-279.

37. A. C. Cole, *The Whig Party in the South* (Washington, 1913), 121. The Richmond *Whig* said: "Like the Trojan horse, this fatal gift of Mexican territory is fraught with danger and death." Apr. 14, 1847.

38. Rich. *Whig*, Jan. 21, 25, 28, Feb. 1, 8, 15, 1848.

39. *Ibid.*, Aug. 25, 1848.

40. Philip May Hamer, *The Secession Movement in South Carolina, 1847-1852* (Allentown, Pa., 1918), 3.

41. *Cf. infra*, 24.

42. Craven, *Ruffin*, 102.

43. M. J. White, *The Secession Movement in the United States, 1847-1852* (New Orleans, 1916), 8.

44. Rich. *Whig*, Jan. 18, 1847.

45. *Ibid.*, Feb. 18, 1847.

46. Rich. *Enq.*, Jan. 12, 1847.

47. *Ibid.*, Jan. 10, 20, Feb. 8, 16, 18, 1847.

48. *Cf. infra*, 23.

49. Rich. *Enq.*, Feb. 18, 1847.

50. Hamer, *op. cit.*, 5, 16; White, *op. cit.*, 10.

51. *Acts of the General Assembly of Virginia, 1846-1847* (Richmond, 1847), 236.

52. This was true in South Carolina, Alabama, and Florida. White, *op. cit.*, 10.

53. *Ibid.*, 18.

54. Rich. *Whig*, Jan. 2, 1849: "We are on the defensive, and we are in the right. Let us not forfeit this impregnable position by gasconading."

55. Rich. *Enq.*, Apr. 17, Aug. 21, 26, Oct. 15, 27, 1847.

56. *Ibid.*, Jan. 4, 1848. The Norfolk *Argus* (Dem.) stated this was but a step toward the destruction of slavery and Southern civilization. Quoted in Rich. *Enq.*, Dec. 8, 1848. The *Enquirer*, Dec. 22, 1848, said that the North depended on the South, and so, if the latter would let the former know that the continuation of the Wilmot Proviso agitation would mean disunion, she would come to terms.

57. Most of the eastern counties, southwest section, northern Valley, and a few counties of the Kanawha district, *cf.* Rich. *Enq.*, Jan. 25 to Mar. 3, 1848.

58. *Ibid.*, Mar. 7, 1848.

59. Rich. *Whig*, Nov. 24, 1848 quotes Richmond *Times*.

60. *Ibid.*

61. U. B. Phillips, *The Life of Robert Toombs* (New York, 1913), 60; Rich. *Whig*, Dec. 5, 1848.

62. On Dec. 5, 1848, the *Whig* said: "Of all the States in the Union, it appears to us; that none would suffer more than South Carolina from a dissolution. On the contrary, if she were drifted a thousand leagues out to sea, . . . the Union would never miss her, so far as the loss of any advantage from her presence would go." Her leaders "are eternally endeavoring" to find some new ground of quarrel with the general government.

63. "If the spirit which dictated it [Gott's resolution to abolish slave trade in D. of C.] be not rebuked by the good sense and patriotism of the Northern people, and if this or other kindred measures, involving . . . degradation of her honor and equality, be carried out by Congress—then, as an inevitable consequence all fraternity must be at an end." Rich. *Enq.*, Dec. 25, 1848.

64. W. B. Preston tried to allay the feeling by introducing in the House of Representatives a bill creating California, New Mexico, and Utah into one state, and allowing the people in those territories to give the North what she had hoped for in the Wilmot Proviso. *Congressional Globe*, 30 Cong., 2 sess., 477.

65. Rich. *Whig*, Dec. 5, 1848.

66. Rich. *Enq.*, Dec. 25, 1848.

67. Quoted in Rich. *Enq.*, Dec. 29, 1848.

68. *Ibid.*

69. Rich. *Enq.*, Jan. 2, 1849.

70. White, *op. cit.*, 129.

71. Rich. *Enq.*, Jan. 26, 1849.

72. *Ibid.*, Dec. 29, 1848.

73. *Ibid.*, Jan. 2, 1849.

74. *Ibid.*

75. *Ibid.*, Jan. 5, 1849.

76. Rich *Whig,* Jan. 2, 1849.
77. Quoted in Rich. *Enq.,* Jan. 9, 1849.
78. Quoted in *Ibid.*
79. Quoted in *Ibid.*
80. *Acts of General Assembly of Virginia 1848-9* (Richmond, 1849), 257-258.
81. Rich. *Enq.,* Jan. 12, 1849.
82. *Ibid.*
83. *Ibid.*
84. *Ibid.,* Jan. 16, 1849.
85. *Ibid.,* Jan. 19, 1849.
86. *Ibid.* In reply to this the *Enquirer* explained that bad roads had prevented the people from expressing their views in the county meetings.
87. White, *op. cit.,* 34.
88. The Parkersburg *Gazette,* February 10, 1849, expressed the northwestern disapproval by referring to them as "certain gaseous resolutions . . . having an awful squinting toward final disunion."
89. Rich. *Enq.,* April 3, 1849.
90. *Ibid.,* February 27, 1849.
91. Ibid.
92. *Ibid.,* Apr. 3, 1849.
93. *Ibid.*
94. *Ibid.,* May 4, 15, 1849.
95. *Ibid.,* May 15, 1849.
96. *Ibid.,* May 18, 1849.
97. Senator Hunter's speech, *Cong. Globe,* 30 Cong., 2 sess., 440.
98. Senator Mason's speech, *ibid.,* appendix, 309.
99. *Correspondence of Calhoun,* 1200-1201.
100. J. F. Rhodes, *The History of the United States from the Compromise of 1850* (7 vols., New York, 1893-1906), I, 109.
101. *Ibid.,* 110.
102. Rich. *Enq.,* Oct. 19, 1849; T. S. Bocock, congressman from Virginia, made the same objection in Congress February 26, 1849. *Cf. Cong. Globe,* 30 Cong., 2 sess., appendix, 180-181.
103. Rich. *Whig,* Nov. 27, 1849.
104. Quoted in Rich. *Enq.,* Nov. 20, 1849.
105. *Ibid.*
106. *Ibid.,* Nov. 30, 1849.
107. Rhodes, *op. cit.,* I, 119.
108. Cole, *Whig Party in South,* 152-153.
109. Phillips, *Toombs,* 66.
110. Rich. *Enq.,* Dec. 14, 1849. T. S. Haymond, a Whig of the northwest, voted for Winthrop on many of the sixty-three ballots. Jeremiah Morton, the other Whig congressman from Virginia, voted with Toombs and Stephens for Whigs such as Morehead of Kentucky who had not favored the Proviso. *Cong. Globe,* 31 Cong., 1 sess., *passim.*
111. *Ibid.,* 26-27; Phillips, *Toombs,* 66.
112. *Ibid. Cong. Globe,* 31 Cong., 1 sess., 26-27.
113. Rich. *Whig,* Dec. 21, 1849.
114. *Cf. supra,* 23-24.
115. Farror Newberry, "The Nashville Convention and Southern Sentiment of 1850," *South Atlantic Quarterly,* XI, 261-262.
116. White, *op. cit.,* 65.
117. Rich. *Enq.,* Oct. 16, 1849.
118. *Ibid.,* Dec. 28, 1849. Compare these figures with ones given below.
119. *Cf. infra,* 70-71, for Ruffin's view.
120. H. D. Foster, "Webster's Seventh of March Speech and the Secession Movement, 1850," *American Historical Review,* XXVII, 251.
121. Hammond to Tucker, Jan. 20, 1849, Tucker Papers (in possession of Mr. George P. Coleman, Williamsburg, Va.).

122. Letters of Tucker to Hammond, Dec. 4, 27, 1849, Hammond Papers (in Lib. of Cong.); W. P. Trent, *William Gilmore Simms* (Boston and New York, 1892), 177-183.

123. *Correspondence of Calhoun*, 778.

124. Rich. *Enq.*, Jan. 4, 1850.

125. *Ibid.*, Jan. 15, 1850.

126. *Ibid.*, Feb. 1, 1850.

127. *Ibid.*, Jan. 15, 1850.

128. *Acts of the General Assembly of Virginia for 1849-50*, 233-234.

129. Cole, *Whig Party in South*, 161; Rich. *Enq.*, Feb. 19, 1850.

130. *Ibid.*

131. The majority on the fifth resolution, which was the smallest majority, was 77 out of 117 votes. *Ibid.*, Feb. 8, 19, 1850.

132. *Ibid.*, Feb. 19, 1850.

133. *Ibid.*, Jan. 8, 1850.

134. *Ibid.*, Jan. 29, 1850.

135. Rich. *Whig*, Jan. 4, 1850. The *Kanawha Republican* held a similar view. It felt that the problems before Congress were not within the jurisdiction of the states; that no good had ever come to the state from all the resolutions on Federal relations since 1798; and that the legislature could spend its time more profitably on economic development of the state. *Kanawha Republican*, Feb. 13, 1850.

136. Quoted in Rich. *Whig*, Jan. 25, 1850.

137. Rich. *Whig*, Feb. 1, 5, 1850.

138. The northwestern section had been very unfavorably inclined. Congressman T. H. Hammond in his speech on the Compromise in the House of Representatives said that his people were already "labelling it the Hartford Convention No. 2 . . . The Northwest are as one man against it [The Nashville Convention]." *Cong. Globe*, 31 Cong., 1 sess., appendix 599. The influential Wheeling *Gazette*, which later became the *Intelligencer*, at first considered it a disunion movement; but by February 16 it was satisfied that there would be no excuse for sending delegates, since Congress had practically dropped the Wilmot Proviso. Wheeling, *Gazette*, Feb. 3, 13, 16, Mar. 12, 1850.

139. *Republican Vindicator* (Staunton, Va.), Jan. 28, Feb. 18, 1850.

140. Ambler, *Ritchie*, 280.

141. *Ibid.*, 280-281.

142. Tucker Papers.

143. Hammond Papers; Rich. *Whig*, Apr. 9, 1850.

144. *Ibid.*

145. Rich. *Enq.*, Mar. 19, 1850.

146. *Acts of the General Assembly for 1849-50*, 234.

147. Halifax, Mecklenburg, Gloucester, Rich. *Enq.*, Mar. 8, 1850.

148. Rich. *Enq.*, Mar. 26, Apr. 2, 5, 9, 12, 16, 19, 23, 26, 30, 1850; Rich. *Whig*, May 10, 17, 31, 1850.

149. The following counties and towns sent representatives to these district conferences: Northumberland, Lancaster, Williamsburg, New Kent, Brunswick, Greensville, Madison, Amherst, Westmoreland, Caroline, Essex, King William, Princess Anne, Louisa, Hanover, Appomattox, Campbell, Elizabeth City, King George, Richmond County, King and Queen, Jefferson.

150. This was true of Sussex, Appomattox, King George, Rich. *Enq.*, Apr. 16, 1850.

151. *Ibid.*

152. Rich. Whig, Mar. 8, 1850; *Daily Wheeling Gazette*, Mar. 12, 1850.

153. Rich. *Enq.*, Apr. 30, 1850.

154. Rich. *Whig*, May 10, 17, 1850.

155. *Ibid.*, Apr. 16, 1850; D. T. Herndon, "Nashville Convention of 1850," *Transactions of the Alabama Historical Society* (1904), V, 215.

156. *Correspondence of Robert M. T. Hunter, 1826-76*, C. H. Ambler, ed., American Historical Association *Annual Report* for 1916 (Washington, 1918), II, 109-113. Hereafter cited as *Hunter's Correspondence*.

157. This was true of W. F. Gordon, S. F. Leake, J. M. Mason, M. R. H. Garnett, R. M. T. Hunter, H. A. Wise, J. A. Seddon, P. H. Aylett, R. M. K. Meade. *Cf.*

district and county meetings as reported by Rich. *Enq.*, May 10-31, 1850, and the Rich. *Whig*, May 10-31, 1850.

158. Rich. *Whig*, May 4, 1850.

159. *Ibid.*, May 10, 1850.

160. *Ibid.*

161. *Ibid.*

162. *Ibid.*, Rich. *Enq.*, Apr. 2, 12, 1850.

163. *Hunter's Correspondence*, 113.

164. Rich. *Whig*, May 17, 1850.

165. In the eighth district conference at Tappahannock, May 10, five counties were represented. Two of these had three representatives together, and Willoughby Newton and W. P. Taylor were elected to go to Nashville. Garnett was elected alternate. Resolutions were adopted instructing the delegates not to attend if the difficulties were settled by Congress before June 3. The fourth district conference met at Farmville in Prince Edward County, May 10. It selected W. C. Flournoy and J. T. Thornton as delegates, and R. H. Glass and J. R. McDearman as alternates. On May 17, the sixth district conference met at Richmond with twenty-four delegates from five counties present. James Lyons and R. G. Scott were selected to go to Nashville. The Portsmouth congressional district conference selected Henry A. Wise. Rich. *Whig*, May 17, 24, 1850.

166. Herndon, *loc. cit.*, 215.

167. B. H. Wise, *The Life of Henry A. Wise of Virginia, 1806-1876* (New York), 1899), 162-3. Hereafter cited as Wise, *Wise*.

168. Rich. *Whig*, May 31, 1850.

169. Born and reared in the states' rights atmosphere of William and Mary College, Tucker had travelled little beyond the border of Virginia except for a sojourn in Missouri, 1815-1830. From 1834 to 1851 he taught law at William and Mary. In 1835 his *Partisan Leader,* a novel urging disunion, was published. Soon this was followed by two other novels and several scholarly treatises on legal subjects. As early as 1833 he was advocating secession. Throughout 1848-1850 he carried on a continuous correspondence with South Carolina leaders urging secession. *Cf.* Maude H. Woodfin, "Nathaniel Beverly Tucker," Richmond College Historical *Papers*, II, 9-42; Lyon G. Tyler, *An Address Delivered at V. P. I. on April 25, 1913 . . . on Edmund Ruffin* (Roanoke, 1913). Hereafter cited as Tyler, *Address on Ruffin. Cf. infra*, 67-69; Hammond Papers; Tucker Papers.

170. Ambler, *Sect. in Va.*, 188-190; *Hunter's Correspondence*, 114; *Encyclopedia of Virginia Biography*, L. G. Tyler, ed., III.

171. *The Southern Quarterly Review*, XVIII (old series), 216-23.

172. White, *op. cit.*, 69-70; *Herndon, loc. cit.*, 225.

173. *Ibid.*, 225; *The Southern Quarterly Review*, XVIII (old series), 216-23.

174. *Ibid.*, 216-217.

175. *Southern Convention—Remarks of the Honorable Beverly Tucker of Richmond* (published by Celin, Baptist and Nowlan, 11th St., no date), 10.

176. *Ibid.*, 13-16.

177. Rich. *Enq.*, June 14, 18, 21, 25, 1850.

178. *Ibid.*, June 21, 1850.

179. *Ibid.*, June 18, 1850.

180. *Ibid.*, June 25, 1850.

181. Rich. *Whig*, July 26, 1850.

182. *Ibid.*, July 30, 1850.

183. *Cf. supra*, 22. 24-27.

184. Rich. *Enq.*, Feb. 5, 1850.

185. Quoted in Rich. *Enq.*, Feb. 8, 1850.

186. Richmond *Times* and Fredericksburg *News*, quoted in Rich. *Enq.*, Feb. 8, 12, 1850.

187. Rich *Whig*, Feb. 1, 1850.

188. Rich. *Enq.*, Feb. 8, 1850.

189. *Cf. supra*, 31-32.

190. Rhodes, *op. cit.*, I, 135.

191. *Hunter's Correspondence,* 109. The Richmond *Compiler* characterized Webster's speech as "more than great, it is sublime." Quoted in Wheeling *Gazette,* Mar. 18, 1850.

192. Ambler, *Ritchie,* 280.

193. *Ibid.,* 280-282.

194. Rhodes, *op. cit.,* I, 171.

195. *Ibid.,* I, 175. In February and June Southern Whigs tried to convince Taylor that the safety of the Union demanded that he weaken on these, but he angrily replied that he would use force to preserve the Union if necessary. Phillips, *Toombs,* 68.

196. Rich *Whig,* June 21, 1850.

197. L. G. Tyler, *Letters and Times of the Tylers* (3 vols., Richmond, 1884-1896), II, 484-488.

198. Albemarle, Hanover, and Shenandoah are typical. Rich. *Enq.,* June 7; Rich. *Whig,* Aug. 6, 1850.

199. *Cong. Globe,* 31 Cong., 1 sess., 1555, 1573, 1830.

200. *Ibid.,* 1589, 1660.

201. *Ibid.,* 1578.

202. Hunter explained this protest as follows: "We protest against the admission of California, because it would seem to imply, . . . that the object of excluding slavery was so high and important as to justify a departure from the principle and good policy, and even a violation of the Constitution, and we say that the principle thus adopted is one which, if persisted in would lead to the destruction of this Confederacy." Rich. *Enq.,* Aug. 23, 1830.

203. *Cong. Globe,* 31 Cong., 1 sess., 1772.

204. *Ibid.,* 1764, 1776.

205. *Ibid.,* 1776.

206. *Ibid.,* 1764.

207. *Cf.* map in Garrison, *Westward Extension,* 328.

208. Rich. *Enq.,* Oct. 15, 1850.

209. He stated that the Texas boundary bill was a gain for the South "in removing the anti-slavery restriction from all the territory north of 36° 30′ over which it previously extended by the resolution of Texas annexation. The California bill is properly condemned—but that act should not be made the cause of dissolving the Union—a step which, without affording redress to the South will cause the institutions of the only Republic in the world to go down in blood. . . ." Rich. *Enq.,* Oct. 15, 1850.

210. Rich. *Whig,* Oct. 15, 1850.

211. *Ibid.,* Jan. 28, 1851.

212. Meetings in Chesterfield, Richmond city, and Charlotte, Rich. *Whig,* Feb. 7, 14, 1851.

213. *Ibid.,* Sept. 30, 1851.

214. *Cf. infra,* 42-45.

215. Rich. *Enq.,* Sept. 10, 1850.

216. *Ibid.,* Nov. 12, 1850.

217. Rich. *Whig,* Dec. 10, 1850; *The Democratic Banner* (Fairmont), Dec. 21, 1850.

218. Rich. *Whig,* Jan. 21, 1851.

219. *Ibid.,* Jan. 28, 1851.

220. *Public Life and Diplomatic Correspondence of James M. Mason,* by his daughter (Roanoke, 1903), 84-5. Hereafter cited as *Public Life of Mason.*

221. *Cf. infra.* 62.

222. *Origin and Objects of the Slaveholders Conspiracy against Democratic Principles as well as against the National Union* (no place, no date), 16 pp. Edmund Ruffin held a similar view. Craven, *Ruffin,* 116. *Cf.* also Tucker to Hammond, Sept. 21, 1850, Hammond Papers.

223. Seddon wrote to Hunter, January 18, 1852: "The Compromise, curse on it, both in inception and accomplishment is perilous ground to every true Southern man." *Hunter's Correspondence,* 132. Cralle in 1857 wrote Hunter that "after the base calculating treason of 1850, I gave up all hopes that the Southern States could ever secure an acre of the public domain over which to extend their institution." *Hunter's Correspondene,* 243.

224. Several cases of the rescue of fugitive slaves in the North occurred in 1851. *Cf.* T. C. Smith, *Parties and Slavery 1850-59* (New York, 1907), 23-25.

225. *Acts of General Assembly of Virginia for 1850-51,* 201.

226. Rich. *Enq.,* Dec. 22, 1848.

227. Some conservatives voted for the reëlection of Mason, the author of the fugitive slave law, because they believed that his election would convince the North that Virginia intended to stand by this law. *The Democratic Banner* quoted in Petersburg *Gazette,* Oct. 5, 1850.

228. *Southern Literary Messenger,* XVI, 697.

229. Rich. *Whig,* Oct. 18, 1850.

230. *Ibid.,* Mar. 4, 1851.

231. Parkersburg *Gazette,* Nov. 2, 1850.

232. Rich. *Enq.,* Nov. 12, 1850.

233. *Ibid.,* Feb. 1, 1850.

234. *Ibid.,* Feb. 15, 1850.

235. *Ibid.,* Mar. 15, 1850.

236. *Governor's Message and Annual Reports of the Public Officers of the State* (Richmond, 1850), doc. I, 24.

237. Rich. *Enq.,* June 28, 1850; Cole, *Whig Party in South,* 208. On June 28, 1850, before the compromise measures had passed Congress, the Richmond *Enquirer* suggested that true safety of the South lay in the development of her resources. The Richmond *Republican* (Whig) declared: "The true policy of the South is to stop *talking* and resort to *acting.* Let the puffing of locomotives, the busy murmur of factories, and the splashing of steam paddles be our eloquence. By that policy we shall be able ere long to assert our rights and to prove that right is might."

238. Rich. *Whig,* Nov. 26, 1850. A Southern Rights Association was also organized at the University of Virginia in 1850. P. A. Bruce, *History of University of Virginia* (5 vols., New York, 1920), III, 258.

239. Rich. *Whig,* Nov. 26, 1850.

240. Rich. *Enq.,* Dec. 31, 1850, Jan. 3, 1851.

241. *The Proceedings and Address of the Central Southern Rights Association of Virginia to the Citizens of Virginia adopted January 10, 1851* (Richmond, 1851), 13 pp; Herbert Wender, *Southern Commercial Convention, 1837-1859* (Baltimore, 1930), 89-91).

242. *Ibid.*

243. *Cf. infra,* 93-94.

244. Arthur C. Cole, "The South and the Right of Secession in the Early Fifties," *Miss. Val. Hist. Review,* I, 376-399.

245. *Ibid.,* I, 376.

246. Rich. *Enq.,* Nov. 19, 1850.

247. Rich. *Whig,* Nov. 22, 1850.

248. Rich. *Enq.,* Nov. 26, 1850.

249. Rich. *Whig,* Nov. 29, 1850.

250. Rich. *Enq.,* July 25, 1851.

251. Rich. *Whig,* Mar. 18, 1851.

252. *Cf.* chapter X.

253. Rich. *Whig,* Mar. 25, Apr. 25, 1851. On June 20 this paper argued that the states, whether sovereign or not before 1788, in the Federal Constitution made a compact which bound them to each other. "They have reserved no right of disobeying their own compact: how, then, can they have any legal or constitutional right to cancel it altogether, at their separate pleasure?"

254. *Ibid.,* July 29, 1851.

255. *Ibid.*

256. *Ibid.,* Aug. 19, Oct. 3, 1851.

257. *Ibid.,* Aug. 19, 1851.

258. Rich. *Enq.,* Sept. 26, Oct. 3, 1851.

259. Rich. *Whig,* Sept. 26, 1851.

260. *Ibid.,* Oct. 28, 1851.

261. *Ibid.*

262. *Ibid.; cf. infra,* 48.
263. Cole, *Whig Party in South,* 205.
264. Rich. *Whig,* Nov. 18, 1851.
265. *The Tribune Almanac and Political Register for 1856* (New York, 1856), 51.
266. Freeman, *Attitude,* 19.
267. *Cf. infra,* 49.

CHAPTER III

PARTY POLITICS, 1851-1859

1. Freeman, *Attitude,* 10.
2. This constitutional convention extended suffrage, made the basis of representation in the House of Delegates according to population, and provided for popular election of governor, judges, and other state officers. Wise, *Wise,* 151; F. M. Green, *Constitutional Development in the South Atlantic States, 1776-1860, A Study in the Evolution of Democracy* (Chapel Hill, N. C., 1930), 287-297.
3. *Hunter's Correspondence,* 124.
4. *Ibid.,* 131.
5. Wise, *Wise,* 145-146.
6. Freeman, *Attitude,* 12.
7. *Ibid.*
8. Ambler, *Sect. in Va.,* 303.
9. James P. Hambleton, *A Biographical Sketch of Henry A. Wise with a History of the Political Campaign in Virginia in 1855* (Richmond, 1856), 7-27.
10. Freeman, *Attitude,* 13.
11. *Ibid.,* 14.
12. Hambleton, *op. cit.,* 33-4.
13. Callahan, *Hist. of W. Va.,* I, 331.
14. *Ibid.*
15. Freeman, *opt. cit.,* 15.
16. Rich. *Enq.,* Apr. 21, 1848, quoted in D. S. Freeman, *History of Secession of Virginia, 1846-1860,* MS. (in possession of Mr. Freeman), 237. Hereafter cited as Freeman, *Notes, 1846-1860.*
17. Cole, *Whig Party in South,* 133.
18. *Cf. supra,* 45.
19. Freeman, *Attitude,* 15.
20. Rich. *Whig,* Feb. 14, 1854; J. M. Botts, *The Great Rebellion: Its Secret History, Rise, Progress, and Disastrous Failure* (New York, 1866), 156-157. Hereafter cited as Botts, *Great Rebellion.*
21. S. L. Steward to W. M. Burwell, Nov. 13, 1854. William M. Burwell Papers, 1851-1863 (in Lib. of Cong.).
22. W. C. Rives to Burwell, Nov. 12, 1854, Burwell Papers.
23. In its editorial of Aug. 12, 1851, the Rich. *Whig* stated: "Establish the right of Peaceful Secession and the Federal Government's duty to yield to it, and everybody knows that South Carolina secedes tomorrow."
24. Rich. *Whig,* Nov. 3, 1850.
25. *Hunter's Correspondence,* 137; Ambler, *Sect. in Va.,* 302.
26. *Ibid.,* 303.
27. Freeman, *Attitude,* 10.
28. Rhodes, *op. cit.,* I, 425.
29. *Ibid.,* I, 433, 439.
30. Quoted in Rich. *Whig,* Jan. 31, 1854.
31. Quoted in Freeman's *Notes, 1849-60,* 357.
32. Parkersburg *Gazette,* Mar. 4, 1854.
33. Some Whig papers were active for the bill after January 23. Rich. *Enq.,* Feb. 7, 1854.
34. Rich. *Whig,* Feb. 6, 1854; Rich. *Enq.,* Feb. 7, 1854.
35. John M. Botts, the nationalist, reminded the South that by the Kansas-Nebraska bill she was throwing "wide open the whole question of slavery, to unsettle all that

has been done to produce harmony between the North and South for the last thirty years. . . ." Botts, *Great Rebellion*, 156-157. The Parkersburg *Gazette*, March 4 and June 3, took the same stand.

36. Cf. Rich. *Enq.*, and Rich. *Whig*, *passim*, 1848-1850.

37. *Ibid., passim.*

38. Petersburg *Intelligencer*, quoted in Rich. *Enq.*, Jan. 24, 1854; Rich. *Whig*, Feb. 10, 1854.

39. Rich. *Enq.*, Jan. 27, 1854.

40. Freeman, *Attitude*, 2.

41. On March 10, the Richmond *Enquirer* said that the climate would prevent slavery going into Kansas, but that the South was supporting the measure "solely for the reason that it would vindicate the equality and sovereignty of the States." The same view was expressed by Tyler in his *Letters and Times of Tyler*, II, 510. Cf. Richmond *Whig*, Feb. 10, 1854.

42. Rich. *Enq.*, Mar. 3, 1854.

43. Quoted in Rich. *Whig*, Mar. 31, 1854.

44. Rich. *Whig*, May 30, June 6, 1856; *cf.* also Mason's speech in Senate and Bocock's in House, *Cong. Globe*, 34 Cong., 1 sess., appendix, 818-22.

45. Rich. *Whig*, Mar. 1, 1856.

46. Ambler, *Sect. in Va.*, 306; *Official Proceeding of the National Democratic Convention held at Cincinnati June 2-6, 1856.*

47. Freeman, *Attitude*, 22-23.

48. *Letter of Fayette McMullen to the 13th Congressional District of Virginia* (no place, April 8, 1858), 7 pp.

49. *Speech of R. M. T. Hunter of Virginia before the Democratic Mass Meeting of Poughkeepsie on October 1, 1856* (New York, 1856), 14 pp.

50. *Proceedings of the Merchants' Great Democratic Meeting at the New York Exchange October 2, 1856 with the Speech of Governor Floyd* (printed by John F. Trow), 32 pages.

51. *North Carolina Standard*, Nov. 28, 1856.

52. Tyler, *Letters and Times of Tylers*, II, 531.

53. *Ibid.*, II, 533.

54. Wise, *Wise*, 209.

55. *Ibid.*, 210.

56. *Public Life of Mason*, 117.

57. *Complete Works of Abraham Lincoln*, J. G. Nicolay and John Hay, eds., (10 vols., New York, 1890), II, 300. Hereafter cited as Nicolay and Hay.

58. Gov. H. V. Johnson of Georgia declined Wise's invitation on the ground that he had no authority to act, and that Georgia had stated her position in the "Georgia Platform" in 1850. Until Congress passed laws violating this platform he would take no action. "From the Autobiography of H. V. Johnson, 1856-1867," *American Historical Review*, XXX, 312.

59. Wise, *Wise*, 210.

60. Rich. *Whig*, Nov. 7, 1856.

61. In a speech in October, Garnett tried to show that the sectional differences between the North and South from early times had developed two civilizations which both sections wished to extend. These two civilizations would provoke conflicts as long as they were under one government. Rich. *Whig*, Oct. 28, 1856.

62. Cf. Hunter's, Floyd's, and McMullin's speeches, *supra*, 52, and a letter of Lewis Webb of Richmond to J. D. Davidson, Oct. 10, 1856, Davidson Papers. Some did not think that it would bring secession. Davidson wrote a "New York friend," October 17, that the talk of disunion in the South was among the politicians, but that the people would have none of it. Davidson Papers.

63. *The Western Herald* of the northwest on February 18, 1856, in connection with the contest for Speaker said that the election of a black Republican would jeopardize the Union. The *Kanawha Valley Star*, October 14, 1856, asserted that the election of Fremont would grant the North privileges which were denied the South and would give cause for secession.

64. Rich. *Whig*, July 4, 1856.

65. *Ibid.*, Aug. 8, 1856.
66. *Ibid.*, Aug. 12, 1856.
67. *Ibid.*, June 24, 1856.
68. Tyler, *Life and Letters of Tyler,* II, 532.
69. H. A. Wise to Robert Cooke, Nov. 26, 1856, MS. (in Library of Universiity of Virginia).
70. Rich. *Enq.*, Jan. 6, 1857.
71. Freeman, *Attitude*, 24.
72. *Ibid.*
73. *Ibid.*
74. Smith, *Parties and Slavery*, 211.
75. Richmond *South,* June 30, 1857.
76. Wise had refused a post in Buchanan's Cabinet, but he had been influential in making J. B. Floyd, Secretary of War. Wise to Cooke, Nov. 26, 1856; Letcher to Dorman, Dec. 10, 1856, Davidson, Papers.
77. Quoted in Rich. *South,* July 23, Aug. 11, 1857.
78. Rich. *South,* July 23, Aug. 11, 1857.
79. Quoted in Rich. *South,* Aug. 26. 1857.
80. Letter of Lewis E. Harvie to Hunter, Sept. 4, 1857, *Hunter's Correspondence,* 221. Compare also William Old's letter to Hunter August 15, 1857, *ibid.*, 217.
81. *Ibid.*, 218.
82. *Ibid.*, 217.
83. E. T. Montague to Hunter, Sept. 14, 1857, *Hunter's Correspondence,* 226.
84. William Old's letter to Hunter, Aug. 15, 1857, *Hunter's Correspondence,* 117.
85. Letcher to Dorman, Dec. 21, 1856, Davidson Papers.
86. *Cf. infra,* 62-63.
87. Freeman, *Attitude,* 25.
88. *Ibid.*, 26.
89. Smith, *Parties and Slavery,* 217-18.
90. Freeman, *Attitude,* 27. Compare also Wise's letters to Tammany Hall and the Philadelphia anti-Lecompton meetings. Rich. *South,* Jan. 11, 1858, and pamphlet; *Letter of Governor Wise to the Philadelphia anti-Lecompton Meeting, Feb. 6, 1858.*
91. *American Union,* Feb. 5, 1858.
92. Rich. *South,* Apr. 23, 1858.
93. On August 13, 27, 31, 1858, the Richmond *South* rejoiced that the Kansas question was over. It said that the object of the South was to gain a principle; it never hoped to make the region one of slavery.
94. Rich. *South,* Aug. 13, 27, 1858.
95. Ambler, *Sect. in Va.,* 320.
96. Rich. *South,* June 18, 1858.
97. *Ibid.;* letter of R. B. Moorman to Davidson, Aug. 12, 1858, Davidson Papers.
98. *To the People of Virginia! John Letcher and his Antecedents, Read and Circulate* (printed by Whig Book and Job Office, Richmond. 1859).
99. Letter of Letcher, June 25, 1858, Rich. *South,* June 29, 1858.
100. Letcher's memory was not entirely correct here. On July 20, 1852, he wrote Davidson: "I have no fancy for buying and selling that sort of property—never wishing to own more . . . than were absolutely necessary for the convenience of my family." Davidson Papers.
101. Rich. *South,* June 29, 1858.
102. *Ibid.*
103. *Ibid.*, June 24, 1858. R. B. Moorman wrote Davidson August 12, 1858, that the accusation against Letcher was "absurd." Davidson Papers.
104. Rich. *Enq.*, Nov. 23, 1858.
105. *Ibid.*, Nov. 26, 1858.
106. General W. H. Richardson, November 18, 1858, wrote Davidson that he was afraid the nomination would be stolen, that Judge Brockenbrough was an eastern man by birth and proclivities and a near relative of W. F. Ritchie. He expressed his fear of the old influence of Ritchie's family and its desire to control the executive. He

doubted if Brockenbrough were the primary mover; instead, he thought it was Faulkner. Davidson Papers.

107. Rich. *Enq.*, Dec. 10, 1858.

108. Even Harvie opposed the nomination. *Ibid.*

109. *Ibid.*

110. *Ibid.*

111. *Ibid.*

112. *Ibid.*

113. *Ibid.*

114. *Ibid.*

115. *Ibid.*

116. The center of the organization was in Augusta County. Rich. *Whig,* May 20, 1856.

117. The Alexandria *Gazette* advised Southern congressmen not to debate with abolitionists on slavery, so that they would die out for lack of fuel. Quoted in the Rich. *Whig,* Dec. 19, 1856.

118. Freeman, *Attitude,* 34.

119. Rich. *Whig,* Feb. 15, 1859.

120. *Ibid.*

121. R. T. Daniel of the Whig "Central Committee" to Willey, Mar. 21, 1859, Willey Papers; Rich. *Whig,* Mar. 15, Apr. 21, 1859.

122. Letters of F. H. Pierpoint and R. T. Daniel to Willey, Mar. 16, 21, 28, 1859, Willey Papers.

123. Letter of T. J. Evans, Apr. 4, 1859, Willey Papers.

124. Letter of R. A. Worrell to Willey, Mar. 19, 1859, Willey Papers.

125. Ambler, *Sect. in Va.,* 323.

126. *Ibid.*

127. On February 22, 1859, the *Enquirer* stated: "We hope that every man may take warning from Mr. Letcher's folly, and that Mr. Goggin may teach wisdom to the rising generation of young Democrats, by inflicting on Mr. Letcher no little amount of public punishment during his canvass." *Cf.* also Wheeling *Intelligencer,* May 25, 1859. Thomas J. Evans of the "Central Committee" wrote Willey April 16: "The *Wise Democrats* don't care a straw for Letcher's election. In truth they had rather see him defeated." Willey Papers.

128. A. H. H. Stuart wrote: "I regard the present contest as but the initiative step to the great struggle of 1860." Rich. *Whig,* Mar. 11, 1859. *Cf.* Willey's *Journal,* 76, MS., Willey Papers.

129. Rich. *Whig,* Feb. 5, 11, 13, 22, Apr. 12, 1859; Rich. *Enq.,* June 14, 1859.

130. Rich *Whig,* June 7, 1859. The New York *Herald* made the same analysis. Quoted in Wheeling *Intelligencer,* June 13, 1859.

131. *Kanawha Valley Star,* June 21, 1859.

132. Ambler, in his *Sect. in Va.,* 525-6, and McGregor, in his *Disruption of Virginia,* 98-9, agree that Letcher was elected because of his former anti-slavery views and that his strength in the east was small for the same reason.

133. *The Tribune Almanac* (1860), 51.

134. *Ibid.*

135. *Ibid.*

136. *Ibid.*

137. *Blue Ridge Republican,* quoted in *Kanawha Valley Star,* June 28, 1859.

138. *Ibid.*

139. *Ibid.*

140. William Old took charge in April, 1859.

141. On August 31, 1858, this paper said that not only had the anti-slavery feeling in the South gone but the anti-slavery movement of the North "seems to be on the ebb. The Supreme Court has become the champion of state's rights and slavery."

142. The Rich. *South,* July 31, 1858.

143. Salutation of Old, quoted in Richmond *Enquirer,* Apr. 15, 1859.

144. Rich. *Enq.,* Nov. 12, Dec. 10, 1858.

145. Wise, *Wise,* 27; Freeman, *Attitude,* 30.

146. *Ibid.,* 31.
147. *Ibid.*
148. Rich. *Enq.,* June 21, 1859.
149. Freeman, *Attitude,* 30.
150. Rich. *Enq.,* June 17, 1859.
151. *Ibid.*
152. Rich. *Enq.,* July 4, 1859; Rich. *Whig,* June 25, July 12, 1859.
153. Rich. *Enq.,* July 19, 1859.
154. *Ibid.*
155. Freeman, *Attitude,* 31.
156. *Cf.* western papers cited in Richmond *Whig,* July 12, 1859.
157. Rich. *Whig,* July 12, gives evidence that Petersburg *Press* and Lynchburg *Republican* in the east were for Douglas. The Staunton *Vindicator* of the Valley was of the same view.
158. Rich. *Enq.,* Aug. 30, 1859; Freeman, *Attitude, 32.*
159. *Ibid.*
160. Letter of Robert Tyler to John Tyler, July 13, 1859, John Tyler Papers (in Lib. of Cong.). *Cf. infra,* 105.
161. Rich. *Whig,* Mar. 11, Apr. 12, May 6, Sept. 20.
162. Washington Hunt had written Wyndham Robertson, January 5, 1859 to this effect. Craven, *Ruffin,* 167.
163. Rich. Whig, July 8, 1859. A little later it stated that there was no territory left to invoke the slavery questions; that the subjects under dispute were abstractions; that the controversy in regard to forming new states of Texas could not rise for this was already settled; that no one would think of taking slaves into New Mexico, Utah, Nebraska, Washington, or the Dakotas; and that the only possible chance of controversy was in the Indian Territory and that would not come up any time soon. Rich. *Whig,* Aug. 5, 1859.
164. *Ibid.* W. C. Rives, the Alexandria *Gazette,* and Lynchburg *Virginian* were of the same opinion. Cf. Rich. *Whig,* July 8, 12, 1859; Rich. *Enq.,* Oct. 4, 1859.
165. Rich. *Whig,* Sept. 2, 1859.
166. *Ibid.,* June 25, July 1, 1859.
167. *Ibid.,* July 15, 1859.
168. *Ibid.,* Oct. 4, 11, 1859.
169. *Ibid.,* Sept. 30, 1859.

CHAPTER IV

SECESSIONISTS AND SOUTHERN NATIONALISM, 1850-1860.

1. *Cf. supra,* 31-35.
2. *Cf. supra,* 53-54.
3. Quoted in Freeman, *Notes, 1846-60,* 557.
4. Rich. *South,* July 21, 31, Aug. 7, 12, 1858.
5. *Cf. supra,* chapter III.
6. *The Union, Past and Future, How it works, and How to Save it,* by a "Citizen of Virginia" (Washington, 1850), 30 pp.
7. Foster, *loc. cit.,* 251.
8. *The Union, Past and Future, 29.*
9. *Origin and Objects of the Slaveholders' Conspiracy,* 10.
10. H. Findley, "Nathaniel Beverly Tucker," *Library of Southern Literature,* XII, 5501. *Cf. supra,* n. 169, chapter II.
11. Letters in J. H. Hammond Papers and Tucker Papers.
12. Hammond to Tucker, Jan. 20, 1849, Tucker Papers.
13. Woodfin, "Nathaniel Beverly Tucker," Richmond College Historical *Papers,* II, 31.
14. Nathaniel Beverly Tucker, *The Partisan Leader, reprint from first print of 1836 when published under the name of Edmund William Sidney and printed by Duff Green with the eroneous date of 1856* (New York, 1861). Hereafter cited as Tucker, *Partisan Leader.*

15. Tucker, *Partisan Leader*.
16. Trent, *Simms, passim*.
17. *Ibid.*, 177; Tucker Papers.
18. Dec. 4, 1849, Hammond Papers; Trent, *op. cit.*, 177.
19. *Cf.* letters to Hammond, Dec. through Apr., 1849-1850, Hammond Papers.
20. He suggested that Hammond and Tucker write for the Virginia and South Carolina papers under a common name, "C." Letter to Hammond, Feb. 8, 1850, Hammond Papers.
21. Letters to Hammond, Apr.-Aug., Hammond Papers.
22. *Cf. supra*, 34-35.
23. *Cf. supra*, 36.
24. Trent, *op. cit.*, 183-184.
25. Hammond Papers.
26. Craven, *Ruffin*, chapter III.
27. *Ibid.*, 107-110.
28. Tyler, *Address on Ruffin*, 7.
29. Craven, *Ruffin*, 110-111.
30. Tyler, *Address on Ruffin*, 8; *William and Mary Quarterly*, XIV, 193.
31. Rich. *South*, July 31, 1858.
32. Tyler, *Address on Ruffin*, 8.
33. *Ibid.*; Craven, *Ruffin*, 178-179.
34. Tyler, *Address on Ruffin*, 8-9.
35. Craven, *Ruffin*, 130.
36. H. Ellis, "Influence of Industrial and Educational Leaders on the Secession of Virginia," *South Atlantic Quarterly*, IX, 374; Craven, *Ruffin*, 155.
37. Edmund Ruffin, *Anticipations of the Future to Serve as Lessons for the Present Time* (Richmond, 1860). Hereafter cited as Ruffin, *Anticipations of the Future*.
38. "Address of Professor Washington of William and Mary," *DeBow's Review*, XVIII, 454-455; A. T. Bledsoe, *An Essay on Liberty and Slavery* (Philadelphia, 1856); W. A. Smith, *Lectures on the Philosophy and Practices of Slavery* (Nashville, 1856); *Address of T. S. Flournoy Delivered at the 2nd Annual Exhibition of the Union Agricultural Society of Virginia and North Carolina the 25th of October, 1855* (Petersburg, 1855), 24 pp; "Speech of Newton to the Literary Society of Virginia Military Institute," Rich. *South*, July 10, 1858; *Address of Hon. A. H. H. Stuart before the Central Agricultural Society of Virginia at Richmond, October 28, 1859* (no date, no place), 16 pp.; J. P. Holcombe, *An Address Delivered before the Seventh Annual Meeting of the Virginia Agricultural Society, November 4, 1858* (Richmond 1858), 21 pp; Craven, *Ruffin, passim;* and various articles by Ruffin and Fitzhugh in *DeBow's Review* for 1850-1860. *Cf.* also Jenkins, *Political Theories of Slaveholders*.
39. George Fitzhugh, "Reaction and the Administration," *DeBow's Review*, XXV, 414-416; W. Newton, "An Address at V. M. I.," *North Carolina Standard*, July 21, 1858; *Southern Literary Messenger*, XVII, 133-142; Craven, *Ruffin*, 44.
40. Rich. *South*, Dec. 1, 1857.
41. Along with several other Virginians, Fitzhugh maintained that the North with all her "isms" would eventually destroy "liberty." In an article for April, 1857, he said that the abolitionists were working for a social revolution. First they would destroy slavery, then government, religion, and private property. *DeBow's Review*, XXII, 419-461. After lecturing in Boston he wrote a friend: "I do not believe there is a Liberty man in the North who is not a socialist." Moncure D. Conway, *Autobiography and Experiences* (2 vols., Boston and New York, 1904), I, 225. *Cf.* Newton's "Address at V. M. I.," Rich. *South*, July 10, 1858; Jenkins, *Political Theories of Slaveholders*, 188-196; Fitzhugh, "Southern Thoughts," *DeBow's Review*, XXIII, 337-349, 449-462.
42. Fitzhugh, "The Conservative Principle or Social Evils and Their Remedies," *DeBow's Review*, XXII, 419-461.
43. *Ibid,* 423, 251. *Cf.* other articles of Fitzhugh's in *DeBow's Review*, XXII-XXIX, and G. Fitzhugh, *Cannibals All! or, Slaves Without Masters* (Richmond, 1857).

44. "The Great Issue: Our Relations to It," by "Bland," *Southern Literary Messenger,* XXXII, 166.

45. *Ibid.*

46. In this connection Newton stated in 1858: "A majority inflamed by fanaticism and the lust of dominion, will never surrender their power to the appeals of reason or patriotism, however urgent.

"Disguise it as we may, the time is fast approaching when there will be no alternative but separation from the North, or tame submission to uncontrolled despotism." *N. C. Standard,* July 21, 1858. *Cf.* also editorials in Rich. *South,* Apr. 21, May 1, Aug. 31, Dec. 18, 1857.

47. Ruffin, *Anticipations of the Future, passim.*

48. *Ibid.,* 353.

49. *Ibid.,* 416.

50. *Southern Quarterly Review,* XVIII, 221.

51. Ruffin, *Anticipations of the Future,* 387.

52. In the latter statement Garnett was not entirely correct. From 1789 to 1860, $45,129,951 were spent by the Federal Government for lighthouses, fortifications, internal improvements, nautical services, and hospitals in the North; and $42,266,731 in the South. J. G. Van Deusen, *Economic Bases of Disunion in South Carolina* (New York, 1928), 334-341.

53. *N. C. Standard,* July 21, 1858. The same argument was resorted to by the secessionists in the 1860-61 crisis. *Cf.* chapters VII, IX.

54. Letter on "Crisis," Nov. 24, 1860, in *DeBow's Review,* XXX, 115.

55. Russell, *Econ. Aspects,* 274.

56. *Ibid.,* 275.

57. In an article in *DeBow's Review,* April, 1858, on "Democracy *vs.* Monarchy," R. H. G. [lass] asserted: "The North would have too much sense not to know that she would have everything to lose and nothing to gain by a war upon the South. She could not hope to conquer us and force upon us again the Union; and if she were to succeed in such an impossible undertaking, her object would be defeated, because we would no longer be a *free* but a *subjugated* people." XXIV, 317.

58. Ruffin, *Anticipations of the Future,* 356.

59. *Southern Quarterly Review,* XVIII, 218. The Richmond *South* sounded a similar note in its issues of February 4 and March 18, 1858.

60. Letter of Beverly Tucker to St. George Tucker, Mar. 25, 1850, *William and Mary Quarterly,* XVIII, 45.

61. *So. Quart. Rev.* XVIII, 218-220.

62. John Tyler to Robert Tyler, Apr. 17, 1850, Tyler, *Letters and Times of the Tylers,* II, 483. For an analysis of the "cotton is king" thesis see Frank L. Owsley, *King Cotton Diplomacy: Foreign Relations of the Confederate States of America* (Chicago, 1931), chapter I.

63. Ruffin, *Anticipations of the Future,* 355-389.

64. Rich. *South,* July 10, 1858.

65. *Cf.* U. B. Phillips, "The Literary Movement for Secession," *Studies in Southern History and Politics, Inscribed to William Archibald Dunning* (New York, 1914), 31-60; Phillips, *Life of Toombs;* E. A. Pollard, *The Lost Cause: A New Southern History of the War of the Confederacy* (New York, 1868); Craven, *Ruffin;* N. W. Stephenson, *Abraham Lincoln and the Union* (New Haven, 1920), 1-19.

66. Edward Krehbiel, "Nationalism," American Historical Association *Annual Report* for 1915 (Washington, 1916), 219-222.

67. Craven, *Ruffin,* 101-102; Phillips, "Literary Movement for Secession," 35-36.

68. In January, 1861, he stated in a speech in Congress that the "cause of the present crisis is . . . the domination of one section over another differing in character, institutions and race." Wheeling *Intelligencer,* Jan. 17, 1861.

69. Rich. *South,* June 9, 1857. *Cf.* "Disfederation of the States," *Southern Literary Messenger,* XXXII, 118-129.

70. "The Difference of Race Between the Northern and Southern People," *Southern Literary Messenger,* XXX, 401-409; "A Contest for the Supremacy of Race, as Be-

tween the Saxon Puritan of the North, and the Norman of the South," *Southern Literary Messenger,* XXXIII, 19-27.

71. "Northern Mind and Character," *Southern Literary Messenger,* XXXI, 343-349.

72. "Monarchy *vs.* Democracy," by "R. H. G.," *DeBow's Review,* XXIV, 314-315.

73. Phillips, "Literary Movement for Secession," 57; Craven, *Ruffin,* chapter IV.

74. Barbarossa [John Scott], *The Lost Principle or the Sectional Equilibrium* (Richmond, 1860); Phillips, "Literary Movement for Secession," 57. During the period of the Secession Convention the idea of a Southern nationality was frequently referred to. *Cf. infra,* 184-185. A. H. H. Stuart held the same view in his *The Recent Revolution: Its Causes and its Consequences* . . . (Richmond, 1866), 6-15. *Cf.* also Pollard, *The Lost Cause,* 46-47.

75. *Cf.* chapters VII and X. *Cf.* "The Great Issues: Our Relations to it," by "Bland," *Southern Literary Messenger,* XXXII, 161-188.

76. *Southern Literary Messenger,* XXV, 21-94.

77. Rich. *Whig,* Oct. 1, 1847.

78. Wender, *op. cit.,* 92.

79. Rich. *Whig,* Mar. 17, 1854.

80. *DeBow's Review,* XVI, 551.

81. *Cf.* Rich. *South,* Feb. 10, 1858, and the Rich. *Whig,* Dec. 16, 1856. Resolutions similar to the ones just quoted were introduced by R. G. Keen of Virginia at the Savannah Commercial Convention, 1856.

82. Ambler, *Sect. in Va.,* 279. This sectional pride along with the economic prosperity of the period caused tremendous expansion in the higher educational system of the state. From 1850 to 1860 the number of colleges in Virginia more than doubled; the student enrollment increased from 1,343 to 2,824; and the annual income of these institutions grew from $159,760 to $246,940. This was the largest number of colleges, teachers employed, students, and annual income of any other state in the Union in 1860. DeBow's *Compendium of 1850,* 141; *U. S. 8th Census,* vol. on mort. and misc. statistics, 505.

83. Ambler, *Sect. in Va.,* 279; *Kanawha Valley Star,* July 12, 1859.

84. *Ibid.*

85. Bledsoe had the reputation of interspersing his lectures on calculus with discussions of states' rights. Holcombe "with copious learning, cogent arguments, and persuasive eloquence" advocated the same idea in his law lectures. He became an avowed leader of secession in 1860-1861. It is interesting that the students who were sons of conservative parents, such as Davidson, should have supported secession shortly before South Carolina passed her ordinance. Letter of Chas. A. Davidson to his father, November 23, 1860, Davidson Papers. H. A. Herbert, *Grandfather's Talk about his Life under two Flags,* MS. (in possession of K. C. Frazer, Chapel Hill, N. C.); W. F. Dunaway, *Reminiscences of a Rebel* (New York, 1913), 10; Bruce, *Hist. of Univ. of Va., 1819-1919,* III, 262.

86. J. W. Morgan, "Our School Books," *DeBow's Review,* XXVIII, 434-440; Rich. *South,* July 24, 1857. The *Kanawha Valley Star,* Dec. 9, 1856, stated that Northerners found it almost impossible to obtain places to teach in eastern Virginia, although ten years prior to this nearly all public school teachers were from the free states.

87. *Cf. supra,* 9, 11.

88. *Cf. supra,* 9.

89. *Southern Literary Messenger,* XXIII, 387.

90. J. L. King, *Dr. George William Bagby, A Study of Virginian Literature, 1850-1880* (New York, 1927), 42. Hereafter cited as King, *Bagby.*

91. He tried, in fact, to give it a national character. Northern writers were asked to contribute to its columns. Soon, however, the sectional feeling and lack of funds caused him to depend largely on Southern writers. J. R. Miller, *John R. Thompson: His Place in Southern Life and Literature. A Critical Biography,* MS. (Ph.D. Dissertation at the University of Virginia, 1930), 105, 146.

92. King, *Bagby,* 42.

93. Letter of J. R. Thompson to G. F. Holmes, Aug. 24, 1852, Holmes Papers (in Lib. of Cong.); G. F. Fitzhugh, "Southern Thoughts," *DeBow's Review,* XXIII, 337-349, 449-462; "The Duty of Southern Authors" by "W. R. A.," *Southern Liter-*

ary Messenger, XXIII, 241-247; "An Enquiry into the Present State of Southern Literature," *Southern Literary Messenger*, XXIII, 387-391; Miller, *op. cit.*, 146; letter of Thompson to P. P. Cooke, Sept. 12, 1852, MS., Cooke Papers.

94. King, *Bagby*, 89.
95. Rich. *Whig*, Dec. 16, 1856.
96. *Kanawha Valley Star*, Feb. 6, 1860.
97. King, *Bagby*, 38-39.
98. *Ibid.*, 50.
99. B. F. Riley, *A History of the Baptists of the Southern States East of the Mississippi* (Philadelphia, 1898), 199-214.
100. See an account of the disturbances on the Eastern Shore of Virginia, Rich. *Whig*, Apr. 15, 1847; J. N. Norwood, *The Schism in the Methodist Episcopal Church, 1844: A Study of Slavery and Ecclesiastical Politics* (Alfred, N. Y., 1923), 126-176.
101. *Cf. supra*, 11.
102. C. B. Swaney, *Episcopal Methodism and Slavery with Sidelight on Ecclesiastical Politics* (Boston, 1926), 204.
103. Richmond *Christian Advocate*, Jan. 25, 1855.
104. Swaney, *op. cit.*, 245.
105. Ambler, "Cleavage," 769.
106. Ambler, *Sect. in Va.*, 292.
107. *Kanawha Valley Star*, Oct. 3, 1859.
108. Swaney, *op. cit.*, 212.
109. *Ibid.*, 215.
110. *Ibid.*, 230-231.
111. *Ibid.*, 222.
112. *Ibid.*, 230.
113. *Ibid.*, 231.
114. *Ibid.*, 245.
115. One paper stated that the Northern Methodist church was "an abolitionist, anti-slavery, anti-southern, anti-Virginian institution." Ambler, "Cleavage," 770.
116. Morgantown *American Union*, Nov. 13, 1857.
117. *Cf.* Rich. *South*, May 14, 1857; Ambler, *Sect. in Va.*, 296; Sweet, *Methodist Church and Civil War*, 29.
118. *Ibid.*, 26; *Central Presbyterian* (Richmond), June 18, 1859.
119. Rich. *Whig*, July 4, 1856.
120. Rich. *South*, Aug. 31, 1857.
121. Johnson, *Life and Letters of Dabney*, 285; Rich. *South*, Aug. 31, 1857.
122. Bishop Gordon Battelle, one of the ablest Northern Methodist preachers in northwestern Virginia, was influential in the convention which created West Virginia in 1861. Ambler, *Sect. in Va.*, 299; Swaney, *op. cit.*, 303.
123. Russell, *Econ. Aspects*, 15-93; Wender, *So. Com. Conv.*, 1-88.
124. Russell, *op. cit.*, 153.
125. *Cf. supra*, 41; Wender, *op. cit.*, 89-91.
126. *Cf. supra*, 41.
127. Ambler, "Cleavage," 771.
128. *DeBow's Review*, XXVI, 661-662.
129. Rich. *Whig*, Nov. 14, 1856.
130. *Cf. infra*, 94.
131. Russell, *Econ. Aspects*, 15-32; Wender, *So. Com. Conv.*, 10. According to Wender, there were three periods of the Southern Commercial Conventions: the first, which covered the years 1837 to 1839, discussed direct trade with Europe; the second, which included the sessions of the forties, considered railroad and other internal improvement projects; and the third, 1852-1860, concentrated on sectional problems.
132. Russell, *op. cit.*, 12-32.
133. *Ibid.*, 122-141.
134. *Ibid.*
135. *Ibid.*, 139-141.
136. *Ibid.*, 140.
137. In the Savannah Convention, Gholson of Virginia argued that this attempt to

reopen the African slave trade was harmful to the South, for it would turn the whole civilized world against her. The convention agreed that the time was not ripe for recommending such a plan. Again in the Montgomery Convention when the "Southern Rights" men were in control, this subject was brought up. Ruffin, Pryor, and Preston of Virginia opposed the plan. Pryor and Ruffin told the cotton states that this discussion would tend to break down the unity of the South, for the border states would never support the reopening of the slave trade. Preston reminded the convention that this debate would lose friends in the North. Finally, when Yancey intimated that Virginia opposed the measure because of self-interest, Ruffin replied that his state did not breed slaves to sell; that ninety-nine out of every thousand owners desired to retain their slaves; and that those who sold theirs did so under necessity. The Richmond *Examiner* which took up the fight wondered if a union with the Northern states would not be better than one with the cotton states, if the latter were to reopen the slave trade. When the next convention met at Vicksburg, Virginia had no representatives; consequently, the resolution passed. Wender, *So. Com. Conv.*, 177-197, 214-228, 234; Craven, *Ruffin*, 161; W. E. B. DuBois, *The Suppression of the African Slave Trade to the United States of America, 1638-1870* (New York, 1904), 169-173.

138. Rich. *Whig*, Dec. 16, 1856.
139. *DeBow's Review*, XXIV, 425.
140. Rich. *South*, May 24, 1858.
141. *DeBow's Review*, XXV, 250.
142. The direct trade project was realized in 1859. Freeman, *Attitude*, 49.
143. Russell, *Econ. Aspects*, 144-150. From 1852 to 1859 the Richmond newspapers were full of articles relating to the new attitude of Southern people toward Southern manufacturers. At the agricultural fair held at Richmond in 1853, the mechanics had an exhibit which great crowds visited. The editor of the *Daily Dispatch* wrote: "Every Virginian who loves his own state and desires the prosperity of the South must feel proud of the effort being made by our mechanics to establish their independence of the North, and to build up a great manufacturing and mechanical community in the metropolis of the Old Dominion." This exhibit was repeated each year thereafter. Anderson at the Tredegar Iron Works made capital of this growing interest in Southern manufactures. He built locomotives, sugar mills, railroad rails, and sold them to the cotton states. He advertised his wares as "Southern products" and worked native white labor under the tutelage of Northern artisans. Bar, sheet, and railroad iron production increased one hundred and ninety-four per cent from 1850 to 1860 in Virginia. Similar increases were made in other fields; consequently by 1860 the state manufactured $39,-000,000 worth of products as contrasted with $29,705,387 in 1850. Bruce, *Va. Iron Manufactures*, 276, 280, 312, 317-319, 322-323; *U. S. 8th Census*, vol. on man., 604-634.

CHAPTER V

THE JOHN BROWN RAID

1. Ruffin said that he "knew of 'no candidate for office who . . . (did) not think he would be received by such avowal' [talk of secession], no publisher or press that would dare to support it. . . . He could count 'scarcely a dozen men in Virginia who . . . (would) now even speak openly, much less act, in defense of the South to the extent that was avowed very generally a year or two ago.' " Craven, *Ruffin*, 168.
2. O. G. Villard, *John Brown, 1800-1859, A Biography Fifty Years After* (Boston, 1911), 426. Hereafter cited as Villard, *Brown*.
3. *Report of the Joint Committee of the General Assembly of Virginia on the Harper's Ferry Outrages, January 26, 1860*, 5.
4. Villard, *Brown*, 523. Albert H. Wilson of Brighton, New York, in a letter to the mayor of Charlestown revealed a plot for rescue. *Cf.* MSS. in Colonial Dame Case, Virginia State Library. Several letters of similar character are in this collection. Wise wrote a friend, who lived near Charlestown, in the latter part of November that he had the "clearest evidence of a wide spread conspiracy—to seize hostages—and preserve the *hero* of Kansas." C. H. Conrad Papers (in Lib. of Cong.).
5. The Rich. *Whig*, Nov. 22, 1859, stated that "the condition of affairs in the

neighborhood of Harper's Ferry and Charlestown is of the most deplorable character." D. H. Conrad in a letter written from Martinsburg, near Charlestown, November 29, stated that he could not leave home because of the excitement caused by the raid. D. H. Conrad Papers.

6. Wise took possession of the Baltimore and Ohio trains coming into Harper's Ferry and Charlestown for December 1, 2, 3; he prevailed on Buchanan to keep 264 marines on hand until Brown's execution; he induced Maryland to guard her borders to prevent rescue; and he kept 1,000 of the Virginia militia on hand. Villard, *Brown,* 523; *Executive Letter Book, 1856-1860.* MS. (in Va. State Lib.), 327.

7. After receiving the report of the raid, Ruffin wrote in his *Diary* that he considered the incident the work of abolitionists, and that it would start a general slave insurrection. "I earnestly hope," he continued, "that such may be the truth of the case. Such a practical exercise of abolition principles is needed to stir the sluggish blood of the South." Ruffin's *Diary,* Oct. 19, 1859.

8. *Cf.* letter of Seddon to Hunter, Dec. 26, 1859, *Hunter's Correspondence,* 281; Wheeling *Intelligencer,* Oct. 19, 1859.

9. Freeman, *Attitude,* 575.

10. *Knawha Valley Star,* Nov. 28, 1859.

11. Letter of Seddon to Hunter, Dec. 26, 1859, *Hunter's Correspondence,* 281; Wheeling *Intelligencer,* Oct. 28, 1859.

12. In December, 1856, these rumors were more numerous than during any other period of the fifties. *Cf.* Rich. *Whig,* Dec. 16, 26, 30, 1856, Jan. 6, 1857.

13. Craven, *Ruffin,* 180-181.

14. Rich. *Whig,* Oct. 25, 1859.

15. Freeman, *Attitude,* 42; *Report of Joint Committee on Brown Raid.* 6.

16. Rich. *Enq.,* Oct. 21, 1859.

17. Rich. *Whig,* Oct. 21, 1859.

18. Quoted in *ibid.*

19. Villard, *Brown,* 559-560.

20. Nicolay and Hay, II, 211.

21. Ruffin's *Diary,* Nov. 10, 1859.

22. *Ibid.*

23. *Report of Joint Committee on Brown Raid,* 6.

24. Rich. *Whig,* Oct. 21, 1859.

25. *Ibid.,* Oct. 21, 1859, *et seq.*

26. *Ibid.,* Nov. 1, 11, 1859.

27. *Ibid.*

28. *Hunter's Correspondence,* 281. Mason tried to do the same thing in his report to the Senate, Nicolay and Hay, II, 210.

29. Rich. *Enq.,* Nov. 8, 1859.

30. The *Enquirer,* November 25, 1859, said: "The Northern States have permitted the sympathizers to plot and plan similar expeditions, and their press has been teeming with abuse and villification. The New York *Herald* . . . seems about to surrender to the demands of fanaticism that rages around it."

31. *Ibid.,* Nov. 11, 1859.

32. *Ibid.,* Dec. 2, 1859.

33. Rich. *Whig,* Dec. 9, 1859.

34. *Cf. supra,* 86.

35. Portsmouth *Transcript,* quoted in Rich. *Whig,* Nov. 22, 1859; *Kanawha Valley Star,* Dec. 5, 1859.

36. Tyler, *Letters and Times of Tyler,* II, 555.

37. Rich. *Whig,* Nov. 22, 1859.

38. On December 7, 1859, the Richmond *Whig* said: "Not a county paper reaches us which does not contain resolutions passed by the best citizens of some county. . . . Not a section, scarcely a town or village, is unrepresented—and everywhere the resolutions breathe precisely the same spirit. Never since the days of the Revolution, has there been such a popular upheaval."

39. Among the counties appointing such committees were: Hanover, Louisa, Caroline, Spottsylvania, Greenbrier, Page, Orange, Brunswick, King William, Clarke,

Nelson—all except Greenbrier from east of the Alleghanies. Rich. *Enq.*, Nov. 25; Rich. *Whig*, Nov. 29, Dec. 2, 6, 1859. Mass meetings in Kanawha County on December 19, Cabell County on December 12, and Putnam County on December 26 did not go so far as to appoint such committees, but they adopted resolutions to the effect that abolitionists would not be tolerated in their respective counties. *Kanawha Valley Star,* Dec. 26, 1859, and Jan. 13, 1860.

40. Rich. *Whig*, Dec. 6, 1859, and Jan. 13, 1860.
41. *Kanawha Valley Star*, Nov. 28, 1859.
42. Rich. *Whig*, Dec. 6, 1859.
43. *Ibid.*, Dec. 2, 1859.
44. *Ibid.*, Dec. 6, 1859.
45. *Ibid.*, Dec. 2, 6, 1859; Rich. *Enq.*, Nov. 25, 1859.
46. *Ibid.*, Oct. 25, 1859.
47. Rich. *Whig,* Nov. 22, 1859.
48. *Hunter's Correspondence*, 275. J. D. Davidson a conservative friend of Letcher's expressed a similar view in a letter to Bacon and Baskerville of Richmond, December 19, 1859. Davidson, Papers.
49. *DeBow's Review*, XXVIII, 174-175.
50. F. E. Chadwick, *Causes of the Civil War 1859-1861* (New York, 1906), 90.
51. *Cf. supra*, 65.
52. The *Whig* advised Americans not to vote for Democrats or Republicans unless forced to, and in that case to vote for a Democrat. Rich. *Whig*, Dec. 2, 1859.
53. *Cong. Globe*, 36 Cong., 1 sess., appendix, Apr. 5, 1860; Chadwick, *op. cit.*, 105.
54. *Ibid.*, 92-3; Hammond to Lieber, Apr. 19, 1860, Merritt, *Hammond*, 467.
55. *Cong. Globe*, 36 Cong., 1 sess., appendix, Apr. 5, 1860; Chadwick, *op. cit.*, 105.
56. *Cong. Globe*, 36 Cong., 1 sess., 44.
57. *U. S. Senate Reports*, 36 Cong., 1 sess., no. 278; Nicolay and Hay, II, 210.
58. Crittenden Papers (in Lib. of Cong.). J. D. Davidson wrote Bacon and Baskerville, December 16, 1859: "The present Congress in its discussion is doing nothing but exciting each other's hatred of the one to the other and through themselves this animosity is extended to their constituency, and thus the North and the South are rapidly growing in that knowledge which teaches them to hate each other." Davidson Papers.
59. Freeman, *Attitude*, 47.
60. *Ibid.*
61. *Document No. XXXIX. Communication from the Governor of Virginia enclosing letters from the Governor of Iowa responsible to a requisition from the State relative to Barclay Coppac* (no place, 1860), 6.
62. *North Carolina Standard*, Dec. 10, 1859.
63. *Ibid.*
64. Ruffin's *Diary*, Jan. 14, 1860.
65. *Report of Joint Committee on Brown Raid*, 24.
66. Ruffin's *Diary*, Nov. 27, Dec. 8, 1859.
67. Rich. *Enq.*, Dec. 6, 1859.
68. *Cf. supra*, 82-83.
69. *Cf. supra*, 41.
70. *Cf. supra*, 82-83.
71. Ruffin's *Diary*, Nov. 2, 1859.
72. Richmond *Whig*, for December 16, 1859, January 3, 1860, gave accounts of the organization of Southern Rights Associations in numerous counties.
73. *Ibid.*, Nov. 18, 1859.
74. *Ibid.*
75. *Ibid.*, Nov. 25, 1859.
76. Rich. *Enq.*, Dec. 9, 1859.
77. *Cf.* resolutions of Southern Rights Associations in early part of Dec., Rich. *Enq.*, Dec. 23, 1859.
78. Rich. *Whig*, Nov. 22, 1859.
79. *Ibid.*, Nov. 29, 1859.
80. *Ibid.*, Dec. 16, 1859; *Kanawha Valley Star*, Feb. 6, 1860; *North Carolina Standard*, Dec. 14, 1859.

81. Rich. *Enq.*, Dec. 20, 1859.
82. Rich. *Whig*, Jan. 10, 1860.
83. Rich. *Enq.*, Dec. 2, 1859.
84. *Ibid.* When the legislature voted $500,000 for defense purposes, a Massachusetts firm offered a low bid but the local Tredegar Iron Works was given the main contract because it was a Southern concern. Bruce, *Va. Iron Manufactures*, 328-329.
85. Freeman, *Attitude*, 48.
86. Rich. *Enq.*, Dec. 26, 1859.
87. Freeman, *Attitude*, 49; N. Y. *Herald*, Nov. 28, 1860.
88. Rich. *Whig*, Nov. 25, 1859.
89. *Ibid.*, Dec. 23, 1859.
90. *Ibid.*, Jan. 6, 1860.
91. *Ibid.*
92. The New York *Herald* for January 6 stated that "A. T. Stewart and Co. have had to discharge 50 clerks since January 1 in consequence of the great falling off in their Southern trade, occasioned by the indignation of merchants below Mason and Dixon's line at recent incendiary proceedings at the North. We are told, also, that over one hundred firms of lesser note have been compelled to curtail their establishments and their expenses from the same cause." Rich. *Whig*, Jan. 10, 1860.
93. Pittsburgh *Post*, Feb. 12, 1860.
94. *Speech of Wyndham Robertson . . . on the state of the Country, delivered in the House of Delegates on the 5th and 6th of March, 1860* (Richmond, 1860), 3-19.
95. Rich. *Whig*, Mar. 30, 1860.
96. On November 22, 1859, the Richmond *Whig* stated: "In all directions—in almost every county and neighborhood of the State—volunteer companies are being organized with great rapidity." The Richmond *Whig* and the *Enquirer* from November 1, 1859, to early February, 1860, were full of reports of military activities of these volunteer companies.
97. Rich. *Whig*, Nov. 22, 1859.
98. *Ibid.*, Nov. 25, 1859.
99. *Ibid.*; Rich. *Enq.*, Dec. 2, 1859.
100. Freeman, *Attitude*, 52.
101. *Cf. supra*, 92.
102. *Acts of the General Assembly of the State of Virginia, passed in 1859-1860*, 126-127.
103. *Ibid.*, 104-105.
104. Freeman, *Attitude*, 53; Ambler, *Sect. in Va.*, 329.
105. Ruffin's *Diary*, Oct. 19, 1859; cf. supra, 70.
106. Craven, *Ruffin*, 172, 179.
107. Ruffin's *Diary*, Dec. 8, 1859.
108. Craven, *Ruffin*, 172-177.
109. *Cf.* Ruffin's *Diary*, Jan. 13, 1860. Ruffin admitted to Memminger that he (Ruffin) had little influence. A reading of his diary for 1859-1861 will show the truth of this admission.
110. *Cf. infra*, 98, for the *Whig's* and *Enquirer's* estimates of this sentiment.
111. E. B. Prettyman, "John Letcher," John Branch Historical *Papers*, III, 336.
112. H. D. Capers, *The Life and Times of C. G. Memminger* (Richmond, 1893), 242.
113. *Ibid.*
114. Dumond, *Sec. Mov't.*, 29.
115. Rich. *Enq.*, Dec. 6, 1859; Rich. *Whig*, Dec. 2, 6, 1859.
116. *Hunter's Correspondence*, 285-286.
117. Capers, *Life and Times of Memminger*, 273-278.
118. *Cf.* Rich. *Whig*, Dec. 26, 1859, Jan. 8, 10, 12, 13, 1860. In a letter to his Whig friends in the legislature, January 17, 1860, Botts declared that it was absurd to blame the Republican party for the Brown raid. The *Past, the Present, and the Future of our Country. Interesting and Important Correspondence between Opposition Members of the Legislature of Virginia and Hon. John Minor Botts, January 17, 1860* (Washington, 1860), 16 pp. The Wheeling *Intelligencer* expressed this view on October 28, 1859.

119. Rich. *Whig,* Jan. 10, 13, 24, 1860.

120. *Ibid.,* Jan. 13, 1860; Rich. *Daily Dispatch,* Jan. 9, 1860. Hereafter cited as *Daily Dispatch.*

121. Rich. *Enq.,* Jan. 19, 20, 28, 30, 1860.

122. *Ibid.,* Feb. 1, 1860.

123. One of the leaders, James A. Seddon, told Ruffin, January 14, that he was afraid the South Carolina proposal would fail, and that the agitation of disunion in connection with it would be dangerous to Hunter's candidacy. Ruffin's *Diary,* Jan. 14, 1860. William Old, editor of the *Examiner,* advised Hunter that "independent state action" for gaining redress is "essential to our success at Charleston." *Hunter's Correspondence,* 286.

124. *Ibid.*

125. McGregor, *Disruption of Virginia,* 91.

126. Crittenden Papers.

127. C. G. Memminger Papers (in Lib. of Cong.).

128. Rich. *Whig,* Jan. 27, 31, 1860. Mississippi had recommended a Southern convention. Barbour held that Virginia should defend herself without the aid of other slave states.

129. Rich. *Whig,* Jan. 27, 1860.

130. *Ibid.,* Feb. 3, 1860.

131. Staunton *Vindicator,* Feb. 10, 1860.

132. *Kanawha Valley Star,* Feb. 13, 1860.

133. McGregor, *op. cit.,* 94.

134. Capers, *Life and Times of Memminger,* 280-281.

135. Rich. *Whig,* Mar. 9, 1860.

136. *Ibid.*

137. *Acts of the General Assembly of the State of Virginia passed in 1859-1860.* 707-708.

138. McGregor, *op. cit.,* 92.

139. *Speech of John C. Rutherfoord, of Goochland, in the House of Delegates of Virginia, 21 February, 1860, in favor of the proposed conference of Southern States* (Richmond, 1860), 11-12.

140. *Ibid.,* 17.

141. Rich. *Enq.,* Dec. 26, 1859.

142. *Ibid.*

143. Rich. *Whig,* Nov. 4, 1859.

144. *Daily Dispatch,* Jan. 19, 1860.

145. Craven, *Ruffin,* 182.

146. J. D. Davidson to Bacon and Baskerville. Davidson Papers.

147. Cf. Freeman, *Attitude,* 49-50; Dumond, *Sec. Mov't.,* 26.

148. As proof of this contention Mr. Freeman cites the unpublished *Memoirs of W. B. Freeman,* 48, and personal letters written in 1908 to Mr. Douglas Freeman by General T. T. Munford, Col. W. H. Stewart, Hon. Maryus Jones, and Rev. W. E. Wiatt who lived in different parts of the state. Freeman, *Attitude,* 50.

149. Cf. *supra,* 63-64.

150. Cf. *supra,* 64-65.

151. Rich. *Whig,* Dec. *passim,* 1859.

152. *Ibid.,* Dec. 2, 1859.

153. Freeman, *Attitude,* 55.

154. W. C. Rives to J. J. Crittenden, Jan. 9, 1860, Crittenden Papers.

155. A. H. H. Stuart to J. J. Crittenden, Jan. 22, 1860, Crittenden Papers.

156. Rich. *Whig,* Feb. 28, 1860.

157. *Hunter's Correspondence,* 278-279.

158. Cf. accounts of his speeches in *North Carolina Standard,* Dec. 10, 1859; Rich. *Enq.,* Oct. 25, 1859; *Hunter's Correspondence,* 281-282; Wheeling *Intelligencer,* Oct. 28, 1859; Bate's *Diary,* Nov. 23, 1859, MS. (in Lib. of Cong.); Ruffin's *Diary,* Feb. 23, 1860.

159. Cf. *infra,* 104.

CHAPTER VI

THE PRESIDENTIAL ELECTION OF 1860

1. Letter of F. W. Coleman to Hunter, Dec. 22, 1859, *Hunter's Correspondence,* 280.

2. *Ibid.,* 278, 280.

3. McGregor, *Disruption of Virginia,* 89-90.

4. *Ibid.;* Freeman, *Attitude,* 65.

5. McGregor, *Disruption of Virginia,* 90.

6. L. E. Harvie to Hunter, Jan. 24, 1860, *Hunter's Correspondence,* 289.

7. Letter of R. H. Coleman to Hunter, Feb. 22, 1860, *ibid.,* 295-297; John Goode, *Recollections of a Life Time* (New York, 1906), 35.

8. *Hunter's Correspondence,* 301. Letter of William Dillard, one of the Virginia delegates at Charleston, Rich. *Enq.,* July 25, 1860.

9. Freeman, *Attitude,* 56.

10. Letters of Old and Letcher to Hunter, Apr. 5, 6, 1860, *Hunter's Correspondence,* 314-318.

11. Old to Hunter, Apr. 5, 1860, *ibid.,* 315.

12. Freeman, *Attitude,* 56.

13. *Hunter's Correspondence,* 315.

14. Eighteen delegates were for Hunter, four for Douglas, and the other three had not committed themselves. Rich. *Enq.,* Apr. 19, 1860.

15. *Hunter's Correspondence,* 309-313.

16. *Ibid.,* 309.

17. *Ibid.,* 313. The New York delegation favored Hunter as a second choice. Statement of a member of the Virginia delegation at Charleston, Rich. *Enq.,* May 24, 1860.

18. One of the Pennsylvania delegates wrote him as late as June 8 that if he would support the tariff Pennsylvania would go for him. *Hunter's Correspondence,* 333.

19. *Ibid.,* 315-316.

20. *Ibid.*

21. Open letter of C. W. Russell, chairman of the delegation from Virginia, Rich. *Exam.,* June 2, 1860; *Hunter's Correspondence,* 325-326; Freeman, *Attitude,* 56-59; Open letter of S. M. Yost and S. H. Moffett, two delegates to the Charleston Convention, published in the Rich. *Enq.,* July 23, 1860.

22. "Journal of the Debates of the Virginia Delegation at Charleston," Rich., *Exam.,* Aug. 15, 16, 1860.

23. *Ioid.,* Aug. 15, 1860. Open letter of S. M. Yost and S. H. Moffett, members of Charleston Convention from Virginia, Rich. *Enq.,* July 23, 1860.

24. R. H. Glass, S. H. Moffett, and S. M. Yost, three Douglas delegates, explained later that they opposed the resolutions because the conference would result in the South's taking a position which would split the party. Moreover, they said, the conference would adopt resolutions which were contrary to the state convention's resolutions. *Ibid.,* July 23, 1860.

25. Rich. *Exam.,* Aug. 16, 1860.

26. Rich. *Enq.,* July 23, 1860; Rich. *Exam.,* Aug. 15, 16, 1860.

27. M. Halstead, *Caucuses of 1860, A History of the National Political Conventions of the Current Presidential Campaign* (Columbus, 1860), 67.

28. C. W. Russell, chairman of the Virginia delegation at Charleston, to Hunter, May 13, 1860, *Hunter's Correspondence,* 325-326.

29. The Tennessee Resolutions provided: "First, That all citizens of the United States have an equal right to settle with their property in the Territories, and that under the decision of the Supreme Court, which we recognize as the correct exposition of the Constitution, neither their rights of person or property can be destroyed or impaired by the Congressional or Territorial legislation. Second, That two-thirds of all the electorial votes of the United States shall be required to make a nomination." Rich. *Exam.,* May 3, 1960. Miers W. Fisher, a supporter of Wise and an ultra-Southerner, withdrew with the delegates from the cotton states. *Official Proceedings of the Democratic National Convention Held in 1860, at Charleston and Baltimore* (Cleveland, 1860), 67.

30. *Ibid.*, 73.
31. Dumond, *Sec. Mov't.*, 61-62.
32. *Ibid.*, 67-80.
33. *Ibid.*, 74.
34. Rich. *Enq.*, June 5, 1860.
35. *Ibid.*, May 8, 1860; the Danville *Appeal* and the Madison County *American Eagle*, quoted in the Rich. *Enq.*, May 8, 1860.
36. These two papers are quoted in Rich. *Whig*, May 11, 1860. *Cf.* also *Weston Herald*, May 21, 1860.
37. May 10, 1860, Davidson Papers.
38. Winchester *Virginian, Jefferson Advocate,* quoted in the Rich. *Exam.*, May 10, 1860. The Morgan County *Constitution* in the Shenandoah Mountain region said: "We confess our inability to see what good the Southern delegates, who seceded from the Convention, expected to accomplish for the South by their conduct. The proceedings show, and we have been informed by one of the Virginia delegates of the truth, that they would have had the Cincinnati Platform *pure upon the subject of slavery.* No more could be asked than this. As regards the nomination of Mr. Douglas, the ballots—after the Convention was deserted by most of the Southern delegates opposed to his nomination—clearly demonstrated the impossibility of his being nominated. Besides this, the two-thirds rule was adopted, giving ample assurance that Mr. Douglas could not be nominated. Hence there was no just ground for complaint here." Quoted in Rich. *Enq.*, May 24, 1860; *cf.* also *The Daily Union,* May 14, 15, 1860.
39. In this effort the *Examiner* was supported by the Charlottesville *Jeffersonian,* Bedford *Democrat,* Loudoun *Mirror,* Salem *Register,* Harrisonburg *Democrat,* and Norfolk *Argus.* Quoted in Rich. *Exam.*, May 8, 10, 18, 1860.
40. Rich. *Enq.*, May 25, 29, June 15, 1860; Rich. *Exam.*, May 12, 25, 29, 1860.
41. Northampton, Northumberland, Goochland, Harrison, Elizabeth City, Barbour, Monongalia, Buckingham, Rich. *Enq.*, May 18, 22, 23, 28, 1860; Rich. *Exam.*, May 23, 1860.
42. Rich. *Exam.*, June 17, 19, 1860. Of course the changed policy of the lower South made this convention unimportant. *Cf.* Dumond, *Sec. Mov't.*, 75.
43. Rich. *Enq.*, May 28, 1860.
44. Rich. *Exam.*, June 2, 1860.
45. Letter to Hunter, June 4, 1860, *Hunter's Correspondence,* 332.
46. On May 16, 1860, the Richmond *Enquirer* said: "No argument, however plausible, no appeals however urgent, and no considerations of party policy however serious, will induce the abandonment of the right of protection by the Southern States. Defeat may come, disunion may follow, but sustained by the Supreme Court in the Constitutionality of the doctrine of protection, the Southern States are free from the moral blame that may attach. . . . [The] Southern States would indeed be recreant to themselves did they submit to the degrading humiliation, of a denial of equal protection."
47. Quoted in Rich. *Exam.*, June 2, 5, 1860.
48. Hunter's friends found it wise to follow a middle of the road policy partly because of northwestern Virginia. C. W. Russell of Wheeling wrote Hunter May 13, 1860, that most Democrats of his section of the state were for Douglas, because they felt that only he could defeat the Republican candidate. *Hunter's Correspondence,* 326.
49. *Ibid.*, 325.
50. Rich. *Exam.*, May 2, 3, 10, 25, 29, 30, June 7, 18, 20, 1860.
51. *Ibid.*, May 21, 1860; Rich. *Enq.*, May 21, 1860.
52. Letters of Russell and Letcher to Hunter, May 19, 24, 29, June 4, 1860, *Hunter's Correspondence,* 328-332.
53. The *Enquirer,* June 12, specifically endorsed the *Examiner's* contention on the readmission of the secession delegates at Baltimore.
54. Rich. *Exam.*, June 18, 1860.
55. *Ibid.*, June 20, 1860.
56. *To the Democracy of the United States—A Letter of the Democratic National Executive Committee July 18, 1860, on the Seceders at Different Conventions* (Baltimore, n. d.), 11. Hereafter cited as *To the Dem. of U. S.*

57. Dumond, *Sec. Mov't.*, 89.

58. *To the Dem. of U. S.*, 11; Freeman, *Attitude*, 62.

59. Letters of W. G. Brown, S. M. Yost, and S. H. Moffett, Douglas delegates from Virginia, Rich. *Enq.*, July 14, 23, 1860.

60. Freeman, *Attitude*, 61-62.

61. Rich. *Enq.*, July 25, 1861.

62. Russell withdrew Hunter's name in order that harmony might prevail. Rich. *Exam.*, June 25, 1860; Halstead, *op. cit.*, 224.

63. One-half of the Virginia delegates were for Botts. Rich. *Exam.*, May 5, 1860; Horace Greeley and J. E. Cleveland, *A Political Textbook for 1860* (New York, 1860), 29.

64. Dumond, *Sec. Mov't.*, 92.

65. Greely, *op. cit.*, 29; Cole, *Whig Party in South*, 338.

66. Only nine of the sixteen members were present. Rich. *Exam.*, July 14, 1860.

67. *Ibid.*

68. Rich. *Enq.*, July 7, 1860.

69. *Ibid.*, July 10, 1860.

70. *Ibid.*, July 17, 1860.

71. *Ibid.*, Aug. 21, 1860.

72. Rich. *Whig*, Aug. 21, 1860.

73. *Ibid.*

74. *Ibid.;* Rich. *Enq.*, Aug. 21, 1860.

75. Rich. *Whig*, Aug. 21, 1860; Rich. *Enq.*, Aug. 21, 1860.

76. Rich. *Whig*, Aug. 21, 1860. In the Charlottesville convention, Willoughby Newton objected to attempts at compromise with the followers of Douglas. "We are here," he said, "to make a stand for the South, or we are here for nothing." Rich. *Whig*, Aug. 21, 1860.

77. Rich. *Enq.*, Sept. 26, 1860.

78. *Ibid.*

79. *Ibid.*

80. Rich. *Exam.*, Oct. 10, 1860.

81. In a letter to a fellow Whig August 23, 1860, A. H. H. Stuart said that Douglas's and Breckinridge's supporters in Virginia had rather vote for Bell than for the rival Democratic candidate. John Bell Papers (in Lib. of Cong.).

82. After Douglas's Norfolk speech J. L. Wilson, a Douglas elector for Virginia, went over to Breckinridge. Rich. *Enq.*, Oct. 3, 1860. *Cf.* also "A Protest" of the citizens of the Southern states at White Sulphur Springs to Douglas's Norfolk speech. Rich. *Enq.*, Sept. 10, 1860. In this speech, Aug. 25, Douglas said, "I think the President, whoever he may be, should treat all attempts to break up the Union by resistance to laws, as Old Hickory treated the nullifiers in 1832." Nicolay and Hay, II, 283.

83. Lynchburg *Republican,* quoted in Rich. *Enq.*, for Sept. 6, 1860. *Cf.* also *Daily Dispatch,* June 29, 1860.

84. Rich. *Enq.*, Aug. 29, 1860.

85. Letter of A. H. H. Stuart to Blanton Duncan, Aug. 23, 1860, John Bell Papers.

86. *Ibid.*

87. *Ibid.*

88. Rich. *Whig, passim;* Alex. *Gazette, passim.*

89. Rich. *Whig,* June 26, July 3, 27, Sept. 4, 11, 1860.

90. *Ibid.*, Sept. 11, 1860.

91. *Ibid.*, Aug. 28, Nov. 6, 1860. *Cf.* also *Speech of Hon. John Minor Botts at Holcombe Hall in Lynchburg, Virginia, on October 18, 1860,* 23 pp.

92. *The Conspiracy to Break up the Union, the Plot, Its Development, Breckinridge and Lane the Candidates of a Disunion Party* (Washington, 1860), 16 pp.

93. Rich. *Whig,* Oct. 19, 1860.

94. On November 3 and 5, before the election on November 6, the *Enquirer* made frantic appeals for the Democrats to go to the polls and vote for Breckinridge in order to save the Union.

95. *Ibid.*, Nov. 3, 5, Sept. 27, 1860; *cf.* also Wise's speech at Norfolk, Sept. 27, in

the *Enq.*, Oct. 12; Lynchburg *Republican* quoted in the Rich. *Enq.*, Sept. 6, 1860; Rich. *Exam.*, Oct. 26, 1860.

96. Chadwick, *Causes of the Civil War*, 126.

97. Cf. *supra*, 52-54.

98. On July 10 the *Enquirer* said: "Upon the accession of Lincoln to power we would apprehend no direct act of violence against negro property, but by the use of federal office, contracts, power and patronage, the building up in every Southern State of a Black Republican party, the ally and stipendiary of Northern fanaticism, to become in a few short years the open advocates of abolition, the confiscation of negro property by emancipation sudden or gradual, and eventually the ruin of every Southern State by the destruction of negro labor."

99. *Ibid.*, Oct. 12, 1860.

100. Ruffin's *Diary*, Aug. 25, Oct. 12, 1860. Tyler's letter from "Trans-Alleghany" in the Richmond *Enquirer*, October 6, 1860, stated that the North and South were so different they might as well separate "now" regardless of the election's outcome.

101. Staunton *Vindicator* (Douglas), Oct. 5, 1860; letter of J. H. Cox of Chesterfield, a member of the Douglas Democratic State Executive Committee, Rich. *Enq.*, Oct. 12, 1860; Rich. *Whig*, Oct. 12, 19, 1860; Ambler, *Sect. in Va.*, 332.

102. *Daily Dispatch*, Aug. 7, 8, 29, 1860.

103. Jer. S. Black Papers (in Lib. of Cong.).

104. Rich. *Whig*, Sept. 21, 28, 1860.

105. Rich. *Enq.*, Oct. 15, 1860.

106. *Ibid.*, Oct. 16, 1860. J. D. Imboden of Staunton suggested a similar idea in a letter to Davidson, July 31, 1860. Davidson Papers.

107. Rich. *Enq.*, Nov. 1, 1860.

108. McGregor, *Disruption of Virginia*, 96.

109. Rich. *Whig*, Oct. 19, 1860. This first appeared in the *Daily Whig* for Oct. 18, 1860.

110. Rich. *Enq.*, Oct. 19, 1860.

111. *Ibid.*, Oct. 23, 1860.

112. *Ibid.*, Oct. 22, 1860.

113. Rich. *Whig*, Nov. 2, 1860.

114. Rich. *Exam.*, Oct. 25, 1860.

115. *Ibid.*, Oct. 31, 1860.

116. Bell received 74,681; Breckinridge 74,323; Douglas 16,290; and Lincoln 1,929. *The Tribune Almanac* (1861), 50-51.

117. *Ibid.*

118. *Ibid.*

119. *Ibid.; cf.* map on page 116.

120. *Tribune Almanac* (1861), 50-51.

121. *Ibid.*

122. Rhodes, II, 502; Chadwick, *Causes of the Civil War*, 133.

123. The following counties and towns were included in the Tidewater: Accomac, Alexandria, Caroline, Charles City, Chesterfield, Elizabeth City, Essex, Fairfax, Gloucester, Greensville, Hanover, Henrico Isle of Wight, James City, Nansemond, New Kent, Norfolk city; Norfolk County, Northampton, Northumberland, Portsmouth, Prince George, Prince William, Princess Anne, Richmond city, Richmond County, Southampton, Spotsylvania, Stafford, Surry, Sussex, Warwick, Westmoreland, Williamsburg, and York.

The Piedmont included: Albemarle, Amelia, Amherst, Appomattox, Bedford, Brunswick, Buckingham, Campbell, Charlotte, Culpeper, Cumberland, Dinwiddie, Fauquier, Fluvanna, Franklin, Goochland, Greene, Halifax, Henry, Loudoun, Louisa, Lunenburg, Madison, Mecklenburg, Nelson, Nottoway, Orange, Patrick, Petersburg, Pittsylvania, Powhatan, Prince Edward, and Rappahannock.

The Valley as used in this and other analyses included: Alleghany, Augusta, Bath, Berkeley, Botetourt, Clarke, Craig, Frederick, Hampshire, Hardy, Highland, Jefferson, Morgan, Page, Pendleton, Rockbridge, Rockingham, Roanoke, Shenandoah, and Warren.

The southwest as used in this and other analyses included: Boone, Buchanan, Carroll, Fayette, Floyd, Giles, Grayson, Greenbrier, Lee, Logan, McDowell, Mercer, Monroe, Montgomery, Pulaski, Raleigh, Russell, Scott, Smythe, Tazewell, Washington, Wise, Wyoming, and Wythe.

The northwest included: Barbour, Braxton, Brooke, Cabell, Calhoun, Clay, Doddridge, Gilmer, Hancock, Harrison, Jackson, Kanawha, Lewis, Marion, Marshall, Mason, Monongalia, Nicholas, Ohio, Pleasants, Pocahontas, Preston, Wayne, Webster, Wetzel, Wirt, and Wood.

124. *Cf.* chapters VII-XI.
125. *Cf.* tables I and II, 117.
126. *Cf.* table II, 117.
127. *Tribune Almanac* (1861), 50-51.
128. *Ibid.*
129. *Cf. infra*, 159.
130. *Tribune Almanac* (1861), 50-51.
131. According to Dr. Ambler regularity had become a habit in the western part of Virginia in its long fight with the "Opposition" or Whig party. The only question was "'what is the Democratic ticket?'" The Breckinridge ticket carried the name of "'Jeffersonian Democracy'" and that name counted for much. Besides, Breckinridge had always been popular there. Ambler, "Cleavage," 778.
132. In the Valley where the leaders—Yost, Moffett, George Baylor, J. A. and M. G. Harman, and Governor Letcher—and the newspapers—the Lexington *Star*, the Staunton *Vindicator*, Charlestown *Spirit of Jefferson,* the Rockingham *Register*, the Harrisonburg *Register,* and the Harrisonburg *Democrat*—were active for Douglas, he polled more votes than he did in any other part of the state. Being on the borders of Ohio and Pennsylvania, Cabell and Monongalia counties had access to and contact with papers from Douglas regions. Moreover, in Monongalia Marshall Dent and his paper were influential supporters for Douglas. Ohio County, in which Wheeling is located, was probably influenced to give Douglas a large vote by the activities of Sherrard Clemens and C. D. Hubbard. In Petersburg Thomas Branch, a popular leader, was active for Douglas. In Richmond the *Index* was active. In Jefferson County A. M. Barbour and the Charlestown *Spirit of Jefferson* were engaged in trying to carry their region for Douglas.
133. R. H. Glass was a good illustration of this class. *Cf. supra*, 110.
134. Ambler, *Sect. in Va.*, 331.
135. See statements of Yost, Moffett, and Brown in Rich. *Enq.*, July 14 and 23, 1860.
136. *Cf.* Table I, 117; and 132 of chapter VI.
137. *Cf. supra*, 111.
138. Rich. *Enq.*, July 14, 1860.
139. Ambler, *Sect. in Va.*, 334; Wheeling *Intelligencer,* May 3, 1860.
140. *Ibid.*, May 12, Nov. 3, 12, 1860.
141. *Ibid.*, May 17, 1860.
142. Ambler, *Sect. in Va.*, 335.

CHAPTER VII

PERIOD OF AGITATION

1. N. Y. *Herald,* Nov. 9, 1860.
2. *Cf. supra*, 114, 115; Ruffin's *Diary*, Nov. 11, 1860.
3. Petersburg *Intelligencer* (Bell), quoted in Rich. *Daily Exam.*, Nov. 10, 1860.
4. Lynchburg *Virginian* (Bell), quoted in Rich. *Whig*, Nov. 16, 1860; Alexandria *Gazette*, Nov. 14; Staunton *Vindicator* (Doug.), Nov. 9; Staunton *Spectator* (Bell), Nov. 13; Greenbrier *Independent*, quoted in Staunton *Spectator*, Nov. 20, 1860.
5. Rockingham *Register* (Doug.), quoted in Alex. *Gazette*, Nov. 13.
6. Charlottesville *Review*, Nov. 23.
7. Charlestown *Free Press* (Bell), Nov. 22; Fredericksburg *Recorder* (Doug.), quoted in *Daily Dispatch*, Nov. 12; Staunton *Spectator*, Nov. 13; Rich. *Whig*, Nov. 9.
8. Rich. *Whig*, Nov. 13. The Lynchburg *Virginian* (Bell) declared: "So long as

the bones of Washington, Jefferson, Henry, Madison and their illustrious compatriots
. . . mingle with her soil, Virginia will be true to her ancient tradition and to their
memories." Quoted in Alex. *Gazette*, Nov. 29.

9. Quoted in Staunton *Spectator*, Nov. 20; *cf.* also Alex. *Gazette*, Nov. 14, and
Staunton *Spectator*, Nov. 27.

10. Alex. *Gazette*, Nov. 15.

11. The Shenandoah *Spirit of Democracy* said that it was opposed to going into
any Southern confederacy as a result of Lincoln's election. Quoted in Alex. *Gazette*,
Nov. 15.

12. There were several western Breckinridge papers which favored ultimate secession. Among these were the Charlestown *Democrat*, Barbour *Jeffersonian*, and the
Winchester *Virginian*.

13. *Cf. supra*, 113-114.

14. Most of the other "Southern Rights" papers favored coöperating with the lower
South to gain redress within the Union.

15. Rich. *Enq.*, Nov. 10, 19. The Norfolk *Southern Argus* (Breck.), November
3, stated that it was not alarmed from fear of immediate injury to slavery and to the
South, but "we know . . . that all these things [coercion, emancipation, sanction of
raids similar to Brown's] are in the logical development of the theory that slavery
is an evil and a crime; that after the proclaiming of the idea, the next step in its
triumphant march is its acceptance by a political majority, and its instalment as the
ruling policy of a federal administration. . . ." In the eastern plain the Richmond
Examiner, Portsmouth *Transcript*, Madison *Eagle*, Petersburg *Bulletin*, and the
Lynchburg *Republican* expressed similar views. In the Valley the Charlestown *Democrat*, Clark County *Journal*, and the Winchester *Virginian* held the same position.

16. Quoted in Charlottesville *Review*, Nov. 16.

17. *Ibid.*

18. Quoted in *Daily Dispatch*, Nov. 12; Alex. *Sentinel*, quoted in Rich. *Exam.*,
Nov. 13.

19. Rich. *Exam.*, Nov. 8, 10; Winchester *Virginian*, Nov. 21.

20. Lynchburg *Rep.*, quoted in Rich. *Enq.*, Nov. 13; Rich. *Exam.*, Nov. 8.

21. Winchester *Virginian*, Nov. 21.

22. Quoted in *Daily Dispatch*, Nov. 12. The Portsmouth *Transcript* accepted the
same position on the security of the South under Lincoln that the Charlottesville
Review did. *Cf. supra*, 120.

23. Quoted in *Daily Dispatch*, Nov. 12.

24. Ruffin's *Diary*, Nov. 11.

25. Alex. *Gazette*, Nov. 8.

26. Tyler, *Life and Times*, II, 575.

27. *Public Life of Mason*, 156; *Hunter's Correspondence*, 337.

28. Virginia *Sentinel*, Nov. 28.

29. "Narrative and Letter of William Henry Trescot Concerning the Negotiations
between South Carolina and President Buchanan in December, 1860," *American Historical Review*, XIII, 532.

30. McGregor, *Disruption of Va.*, 100.

31. Botts, *Great Rebellion*, 230-232.

32. McGregor, *op. cit.*, 101.

33. Wheeling *Intelligencer*, Nov. 16.

34. J. M. Hagan, *Formation of West Virginia from the Territory of Virginia.*
(Reprint from vol. I of *Reports of West Virginia Supreme Court.* Charleston, 1927),
37. Hereafter cited as Hagan, *Formation of W. Va.*

35. *Ibid.*, 38.

36. V. A. Lewis, *How West Virginia was Made* (Charleston, 1909), 26.

37. Similar resolutions were adopted in Monongalia, Ohio, Marshall, Hancock,
and Wood counties and in Wheeling city. Wheeling *Intelligencer*, Nov. 16, 28; Lewis,
How W. Va. was Made, 24-26; Hagan, *op. cit.*, 37-38.

38. Rich. *Daily Exam.*, Nov. 16.

39. J. L. Peyton, *History of Augusta County, Virginia* (Staunton, 1882), 227-9.

40. McGregor, *op. cit.*, 96.

41. Dorman to Letcher, Nov. 18, 1860. Davidson Papers.

42. *Cf.* resolutions of Gloucester and Louisa counties. *Daily Rich. Enq.,* Nov. 16. 19.

43. *Daily Rich. Enq.,* Nov. 16; Rich. *Whig,* Nov. 27 for resolutions of Louisa and Nelson counties.

44. Greene, Fluvanna, Henrico, King George, and Pittsylvania counties urged this view. Rich. *Exam.,* Nov. 15.

45. McGregor, *op. cit.,* 102.

46. Freeman, *Attitude,* 67.

47. *Cf.* speech of Governor William Smith in Fauquier meeting Nov. 26. Rich. *Enq.,* Dec. 4.

48. As early as November 15, pressure had been brought to bear on Governor Letcher to force him to call the legislature into special session in December. Wheeling *Intelligencer,* Nov. 16.

49. A. Robertson, *Life and Letters of John Albert Broadus* (Philadelphia, 1901), 179.

50. Rich. *Whig,* Nov. 13; Staunton *Spectator,* Nov. 13; Alex. *Gazette,* Nov. 19; and Charlottesville *Review,* Nov. 9, 16.

51. Norfolk *Southern Argus,* Nov. 16, 21; Winchester *Virginian,* Nov. 21.

52. Rich. *Whig,* Dec. 11.

53. Rich. *Enq.,* Nov. 15.

54. The sarcastic Yost, editor of the Staunton *Vindicator* (Douglas), took these leaders to task in a stinging editorial, entitled, " 'Where are our Statesmen?' " Only Letcher, he said, had offered a suggestion to meet the crisis. Hunter, who because of his prestige should point the way, is " 'fearful that he may not strike the current, [and so] awaits the development by which our country may be saved from impending ruins.' " Mason, he continued, was " 'too dull to emit anything original, and too soporific to play the part of an ingenuous plagarist, amuses himself . . . bedizening milk punch and apple toddy, while the very citadel of liberty is tumbling. Wise, that intellectual comet of the age . . . ventures no further than to organize his minute men,' " and the congressmen " 'are apathetic and indifferent.' " Quoted in New York *Herald,* Nov. 29, and Rich. *Whig,* Nov. 30.

55. *Cf. supra,* 69-71.

56. Ruffin's *Diary,* Oct. 12, 1860.

57. *Ibid.,* Nov. 6, 7.

58. *Ibid.,* Nov. 16; Rich. *Enq.,* Nov. 17.

59. Ruffin's *Diary,* Nov. 8; Rich. *Enq.,* Nov. 17.

60. In his *Diary,* November 26, he stated that upon returning to Richmond he was received very warmly, but that only a few men, such as Harvie, Morton, and Old, were interested in his efforts.

61. *Cf. supra,* 56.

62. The Norfolk *Herald* (Bell) pronounced this "one of the boldest and most startling schemes ever devised at any period in our history." The Richmond *Whig* called it a "revolution." But Edmund Ruffin felt that it was only a device for enabling Wise to go with the Union or secession forces according to which was in the lead. Rich. *Whig,* Nov. 6, 2; Ruffin's *Diary,* Nov. 11.

63. Alex. *Gazette,* Nov. 8; Rich. *Whig,* Nov. 2; Rich. *Enq.,* Dec. 20.

64. Hampshire County in the Alleghanies was the only one outside the Tidewater. N. Y. *Herald,* Nov. 12; Rich. *Enq.,* Dec. 8.

65. Rich *Enq.,* Dec. 20.

66. *Ibid.*

67. Wise, *Wise,* 267-8; Rich. Enq., Nov. 30, Dec. 15.

68. *Cf. infra,* 190, 203.

69. The *Enquirer* had the largest circulation of any paper in the state except the *Daily Dispatch,* which was a non-partisan penny sheet. *Cf.* Rich. *Enq.,* Apr. 22, 1859.

70. Rich. *Enq.,* Dec. 3, 4, 6, 24; *Daily Dispatch,* Jan. 14.

71. The nine leaders were R. M. T. Hunter, J. M. Mason, John B. Floyd, Robert E. Scott, George W. Summers, Joseph Christian, George W. Brent, General William H. Harman, and Henry L. Hopkins. Summers, Christian, and Scott were Whigs. Hunter, Mason, and Floyd were supporters of Breckinridge. Brent, Harman, and

Hopkins voted for Douglas. Summers and Christian did not reply. Rich. *Enq.,* Nov. 30.

72. Rich. *Exam.,* Nov. 15, 23; Rich. *Enq.,* Nov. 22; Alex. *Sentinel,* Dec. 13; R. A. Pryor to W. J. Cheatham, Rich. *Enq.,* Dec. 24. This emphasis of the common interest with the lower South was constantly made. *Cf.* letter of Mason to his sister, Nov. 29, *Pub. Life of Mason,* 160; Rich. *Exam.,* Nov. 23; Winchester *Virginian,* Nov. 21; Bagby in *Southern Lit. Messenger,* XXXII, 71. Even conservatives admitted the common bonds with the lower South. *Cf.* Staunton *Vindicator,* Dec. 7; Rich. Whig, Dec. 11; J. R. Anderson, head of the Tredegar Iron Works, Bruce, *Va. Iron Manufacturers,* 335; *Daily Dispatch,* Jan. 22.

73. Rich. *Exam.,* Nov. 23; Rich. *Enq.,* Nov. 22.

74. Rich. *Exam.,* Nov. 23, Dec. 10; *Daily Dispatch,* Dec. 14.

75. Rich. *Whig,* Nov. 23.

76. Rich. *Exam.,* Dec. 10.

77. Dumond, *Sec. Mov't.,* 134-135.

78. *Cf.* A. C. Cole, "Lincoln's Election an Immediate Menace to Slavery in the States?" *Amer. Hist. Rev.,* XXXVI, 740-767; J. G. deR. Hamilton, "Lincoln's Election an Immediate Menace to Slavery in the States?" *Amer. Hist. 'Rev.,* XXXVII, 700-711. Mr. Cole holds the view that Lincoln's election was not a menace to slavery in the States; while Mr. Hamilton takes the opposite position. *Cf.* also Craven, *Edmund Ruffin,* 209-212, and Drumond, *Sec. Mov't.,* 150-168.

79. Rich. *Exam.,* Dec. 8, 19. Even Samuel J. Tilden said that the Republican rule would " 'be in substance the government of one people by another' " and a shock to the Southern social order which would bring " 'a pervading sense of danger to the life of every human being and to the honor of every woman.' " Craven, *Ruffin,* 209.

80. Rich. *Exam.,* Nov. 23, 27; Rich. *Enq.,* Nov. 23, Dec. 13, 18; *Pub. Life of Mason,* 160; *Hunter's Correspondence,* 337-338; *Four Essays on the Right Propriety of Secession by Southern States,* by "Virginian" (n. p., 1861), 3-10.

81. U. B. Phillips, "The Central Theme of Southern History," *Amer. Hist. Rev.,* XXXIV, 30-40; *Speech of Hon. R. M. T. Hunter of Virginia, before the Democratic Mass Meeting, at Poughkeepsie, October 1, 1856* (New York, 1856), 7.

82. Charlottesville *Review,* Nov. 30; Rich. *Whig,* Dec. 18; *Daily Dispatch,* Dec. 19.

83. Rich. *Exam.,* Dec. 20.

84. *Hunter's Correspondence,* 338.

85. *Cf. infra,* 132-134.

86. Rich. *Enq.,* Dec. 24.

87. Winchester *Virginian,* Nov. 21; Rich. *Enq.,* Dec. 21.

88. *Pub. Life of Mason,* 160.

89. Pryor's letter in Rich. *Enq.,* Dec. 24, 29.

90. *Ibid.,* Dec. 4.

91. *Four Essays,* by "Virginian," 3-14; Rich. *Enq.,* Dec. 31; *Pub. Life of Mason,* 185-186; Pryor's resolutions at Petersburg public meeting, Rich. *Enq.,* Dec. 3. Some of the editors of the secession papers thought that the right of secession was of little importance, for revolution could be resorted to if necessary. *Cf.* Rich. *Exam.,* Dec. 13.

92. *Cf.* Rich. *Exam.,* Dec. 29, Jan. 1.

93. *Ibid.,* Jan. 1.

94. A correspondent of the New York *Herald* said that the people of Virginia seemed to feel that union with the lower South would increase manufacturing and commerce, because of patriotic pride. As proof of this, he pointed to the growth since the Brown raid. The *Virginia Dare,* a steamship which had recently made its maiden voyage from Europe to Norfolk, marked the establishment of the first direct line to Virginia from Europe—a project which had been discussed at the commercial conventions for years, but which had only been realized as a result of the Brown raid. N. Y. *Herald,* Dec. 22, 1860. In his public letter on the crisis, December 10, Hunter reviewed the arguments of Newton and others of the period before 1860 (*cf. supra,* 73-74) to show that Virginia would take the place of New England as the manufacturing center in the Southern Confederacy. *Hunter's Correspondence,* 347-348.

95. McGregor, *Disruption of Va.,* 103.

96. *Virginia Free Press,* Nov. 15, 22; Charlottesville *Review,* Nov. 23; Staunton

Spectator, Dec. 11 and Jan. 8; Botts, *Great Rebellion*, 232; Views expressed by J. J. Jackson and W. R. Staples at the banquet of Bell electors in Richmond, Rich. *Whig*, Dec. 11.

97. Cf. *infra*, 134-135.

98. Rich. *Whig*, Nov. 30, Dec. 14, 18.

99. *Ibid.*, Dec. 14.

100. *Ibid.*, cf. also letters of John Grome of Richmond and Robert Ridgeway to J. J. Crittenden, Dec. 8 and 16, for similar recommendations. Crittenden Papers.

101. Rich. *Whig*, Dec. 14.

102. L. J. Peyton, *Memoirs of William Madison Peyton of Roanoke* (London, 1873), 246-268; Rich. *Whig*, Dec. 21, 30.

103. Rich. *Enq.*, Nov. 29. Granville Parker, a native of Massachusetts who lived in western Virginia, wrote several friends in the former state urging the repeal of the personal liberty laws. Granville Parker, *The Formation of the State of West Virginia and other Incidents of the Late Civil War* (Wellsburg, 1875), 8-25.

104. Rich. *Whig*, Dec. 11, 14, and Jan. 4.

105. Johnson, *Life of Dabney*, 214.

106. Wyndham Robertson of Richmond kept in close touch with Northern leaders who encouraged him to believe that Lincoln would do the South no harm. Edward M. Bates wrote him that Lincoln was "'as true a conservative national Whig as . . . (could) be found in Missouri, Virginia, or Tennessee,' that he would 'endeavor to restore peace and harmony,' and avoid 'all those exciting subjects which . . . (had) so mischieviously agitated the country' for the past few years." Craven, *Ruffin*, 200-201.

107. Charlottesville *Review*, Nov. 30; cf. Rich. *Whig*, Dec. 18, for similar policy.

108. *Daily Dispatch*, Dec. 15, 19.

109. Rich. *Enq.*, Dec. 6.

110. Johnson, *Life of Dabney*, 214.

111. Rhodes, *Hist. of U. S.*, III, 171.

112. *Ibid.*

113. *Ibid.*

114. Rich. *Whig*, Nov. 30.

115. Cf. *infra*, 197.

116. Cf. *supra*, 127.

117. *Va. Free Press*, quoted in Rich. *Whig*, Dec. 18; Brent in Rich. *Enq.*, Dec. 4; Shenandoah *Spirit of Dem.*, quoted in Staunton *Vindicator*, Nov. 23.

118. The Staunton *Spectator*, November 20, Staunton *Vindicator*, November 30, Charlottesville *Review*, November 30 and Rich. *Whig*, January 4, maintained that the main purpose of the lower South was to reopen the slave trade. The British consul in Charleston was informed by Rhett that the slave trade would be reopened. *Amer. Hist. Rev.*, XVIII, 785-6. The discussions in the commercial conventions in the late fifties would indicate that many in the cotton states wanted to reopen the slave trade. Wender, *So. Com. Conv.*, 172-234. In order to gain the border states and to retain the respect of the rest of the world, however, the leaders of the Southern Confederacy were very careful to include a clause in their constitution prohibiting the slave trade.

119. Rich. *Whig*, Dec. 14.

120. Quoted in Alex. *Gazette*, Dec. 17.

121. Rich. *Exam.*, Dec. 25; Rich. *Enq.*, Dec. 20.

122. Staunton *Vindicator*, Jan. 4.

123. Staunton *Spectator*, Dec. 11.

124. Rich. *Daily Exam.*, Dec. 8.

125. J. S. Black, *The Last Days of Buchanan's Administration*, MS. Black Papers (in Lib. of Cong.), 1.

126. Charlottesville *Review*, Dec. 7.

127. Staunton *Vindicator*, Dec. 7.

128. On December 10, 1860, Mason explained in the Senate, for the benefit of his constituents, that he was voting to refer the parts of the President's message on the crisis to a committee, not because he thought their consideration important, but as a matter of routine and he did not want them to expect any good from it. Then he explained that the evil was "not the failure to execute this fugitive slave law; it is not

the passage of these personal liberty bills, as they are called, in various States; it is a social war . . . a war of sentiment, of opinion; a war by one form of society against another form of society." *Cong. Globe*, 36 Cong. 2 sess., 35; *The War of the Rebellion: A Compilation of the Official Records of the Union and Confederate Armies* (70 vols., Washington, 1880-1901), ser. I, vol. LI, pt. II, pp. 3, 5. Hereafter cited as *Official Records*.

129. Cf. *infra*, 168.
130. *Hunter's Correspondence*, 337-350; Rich. *Enq.*, Dec. 17.
131. *Hunter's Correspondence*, 337-350.
132. John Grome of Richmond, Robert Ridgway (editor of the Whig), and C. W. Anderson from the Shenandoah Valley wrote him December 8, 16, and 31, respectively. Andrews wrote that the hopes of the "republic center upon you perhaps more than upon any other *one* man at this time. . . . Do not despair, but lift up ye voice upon every available occasion in debate, and implore ye South to hold off, before they commit themselves irrevocably." Crittenden Papers.
133. Crittenden's proposals were as follows:
(1) Constitutional amendments providing:
(a) Slavery should be prohibited in the territory north of 36°30′, but south of that line it would be permitted. Congress and the territorial governments should protect slavery in the latter region.
(b) Congress could not abolish slavery where it existed.
(c) Congress could not abolish slavery in District of Columbia without compensation and the consent of the people of Maryland and Virginia.
(d) Congress should not interfere with the domestic slave trade.
(e) These guarantees should be irrepealable.
(2) A stricter fugitive slave law and the repeal of the personal liberty laws by the free states. L. E. Chittenden, *Report of the Washington Peace Conference* (New York, 1864), 421-424.
134. Seward wrote Lincoln, December 26, that "nothing could *certainly* restrain them [the border states] but the adoption of Mr. Crittenden's Compromise." Nicolay and Hay, III, 263.
135. Seward, Wade, Collamer of New Hampshire, Doolittle of Wisconsin, and Grimes of Iowa were the Republicans from the Northwest and New England. Toombs and Davis were the Democrats from the lower South. Powell and Crittenden of Kentucky and Hunter of Virginia were Whigs and Democrats from the border states. Douglas, Rice of Minnesota, and Bigler of Pennsylvania were the Northerners friendly to the South.
136. Dumond, *Sec. Mov't.*, 158.
137. "Journal of the Committee of Thirteen," 36 Cong., 2 sess., 2.
138. *Ibid.*, 4.
139. *Ibid.*
140. *Ibid.*, 5.
141. *Ibid.*, 6-19.
142. *Ibid.*, 1.
143. Dumond, *op. cit.*, 156.
144. *Ibid.*
145. *Ibid.*, 157.
146. *Ibid.*
147. Rhodes, *Hist. of U. S.*, III, 159-160.
148. Similar letters were written to Seward, Weed, and Kellogg of Illinois. Horace White, *The Life of Lyman Trumbull* (Boston, 1913), 111; Nicolay and Hay, III, 252-254, 259, 260.
149. White, *op. cit.*, 112.
150. Rich. *Exam.*, Dec. 25; Rich. *Enq.*, Dec. 24.
151. *Official Records*, ser. I, vol. LI, pt. II, p. 3.
152. *Democratic Recorder*, Jan. 1, 1861; Rich. *Enq.*, Dec. 25.
153. *Democratic Recorder*, Jan. 1, 1861.
154. *Virginia Free Press*, Nov. 15, 1860.
155. Staunton *Spectator*, Nov. 27.

156. Botts, *Great Rebellion,* 234; Rich. *Whig,* Dec. 11.
157. Virginia *Sentinel,* Dec. 13.
158. *Cf. supra,* 131.
159. Rich. *Whig,* Dec. 21.
160. Johnson, *Life of Dabney,* 215. The Staunton *Vindicator,* January 4, 1861, referred to South Carolina's secession as that of a "school boy in the dumps."
161. Quoted in *Daily Dispatch,* Dec. 24.
162. Rhodes, *op. cit.,* III, 206.
163. Rich. *Enq.,* Dec. 20.
164. *Ibid.,* Dec. 27.
165. Quoted in *Daily Dispatch,* Dec. 24. J. B. Jeter, a Baptist minister of Richmond, wrote, December 11, that the "precipitate action of South Carolina and the cotton states will change our situation." Robertson, *Life and Letters J. A. Broadus,* 179.
166. *Cf. infra,* 144. *Cf.* also Alex. *Gazette,* Jan. 8, 1861; *Daily Dispatch,* Dec. 24; Rich. *Whig,* Nov. 30, W. R. Staples, a Bell elector in 1860, declared that the conservatives should proclaim the fact that Virginia would not permit the coercion of South Carolina. Similar views were expressed by other speakers at the Bell electors' banquet. Rich. *Whig,* Dec. 11. The Richmond *Examiner,* November 16, reminded the North that the majority of the supporters of Bell and Douglas did not hold that states should not resist the Federal Government. *Cf.* also *Virginia Sentinel,* Jan. 23, 1861.
167. Letter of J. S. Black to Charles R. Buchalew, Jan. 28, 1861, Black Papers; W. S. Crawford, *The Genesis of the Civil War. The Story of Sumter, 1860-1861* (New York, 1887), 26. Hereafter cited as Crawford, *Genesis.*
168. *Official Records,* ser. I, vol. I, pp. 89-90; Crawford, *Genesis,* 73.
169. *Ibid.*
170. *Official Records,* ser. I, vol. I, pp. 103.
171. Rhodes, *op. cit.,* III, 217.
172. James Buchanan, *The Administration on the Eve of Rebellion. A History of Four Years before the War* (London, 1865), 181.
173. *Ibid.*
174. *Ibid.,* 185; letter of Black to Buckalew, Jan. 28, 1861, Black Papers.
175. Crawford, *Genesis,* 159; "Diary of a Public Man, Unpublished Passages of the Secret History of the American Civil War," *North Amer. Rev.,* CXXIX, 126-127. Hereafter cited as "Diary of Pub. Man"; "Narrative and Letters of W. Henry Trescot," *Amer. Hist. Rev.,* XIII, 543-545.
176. Black, *The Last Days of Buchanan's Admin.,* MS., Black Papers.
177. Nicolay and Hay, III, 95, 99.
178. Crawford, *Genesis,* 149, 159.
179. Rich. *Enq.,* Dec. 31.
180. Letter of E. C. Burks, Jan. 11, 1861, "The Change of Secession Sentiment in Virginia in 1861," (Letters of Judge E. C. Burks and Bishop Otey from November 23, 1860 to August 22, 1861) *Amer. Hist. Rev.,* XXXI, 83. Hereafter cited as "Change of Sec. Sent." *Virginia Sentinel,* Jan. 23, 1861.
181. *Daily Dispatch,* Jan. 14.
182. *Cf. supra,* 120-123.
183. *Daily Dispatch,* Jan. 5; Wheeling *Intelligencer,* Jan. 4.
184. *Ibid.,* Dec. 1, 7, 25, and Jan. 1, 4; Lewis, *How W. Va. Was Made,* 8-27; McGregor, *op. cit.,* 68-74, 84-86.
185. Alex. *Gazette,* Jan. 8.
186. *Cf.* extracts from Wellsburg *Herald* and Morgantown *Star* in Wheeling *Intelligencer,* Dec. 1, 25. The *Star* stated that "not 1,000 out of 12,000 in its district were for secession"; McGregor, *op. cit.,* 80-85.
187. *Cf.* statements of Wheeling *Union* (Breck.), Congressman A. G. Jenkins, and C. W. Russell, in Alex. *Gazette,* Dec. 31, Jan. 1, 8.
188. I. W. Paine of Lexington, Virginia, wrote Crittenden, January 5, 1861: "We are all for the Union in this part of Va. at least nearly all." Crittenden Papers.
189. Rich. *Enq.,* Dec. 25.

190. *Daily Dispatch,* Dec. 21.

191. *Cf.* resolutions of Giles, Pulaski, and Craig counties in Rich. *Enq.,* Dec. 18, 25, Jan. 11.

192. *Daily Dispatch,* Dec. 19; Rich. *Enq.,* Dec. 17.

193. Resolutions adopted in Accomac, Amelia, Charles City, Dinwiddie, Gloucester, King and Queen, Lancaster, Louisa, and Orange counties. Rich. *Enq.,* Dec. 18, 25, 28, Jan. 3, 16, Feb. 4.

194. Resolutions adopted in Bedford, Caroline, Chesterfield, Culpeper, Fauquier, Halifax, Hanover, King George, Mathews, New Kent, Northampton, Northumberland, Richmond city, Surry, and Sussex. Rich. *Enq.,* Dec. 13, 14, 21, 25, 31; Rich. *Whig,* Dec. 4, 14.

195. Rich. *Enq.,* Jan. 3.

196. *Ibid.*

197. Crittenden Papers.

198. Johnson, *Life of Dabney,* 214-215.

199. L. C. Bell, *The Old Free State, A Contribution to the History of Lunenburg County and Southside Virginia* (2 vols., Richmond, 1927), I, 562.

200. *Daily Dispatch,* Jan. 7; New York *Times,* Jan. 5. Another of these ministers said: *"Horrible as war is, there is one alternative which is worse, a surrender of inalienable rights and principles." Daily Dispatch,* Jan. 7.

201. R. E. L. Strider, *The Life and Works of George William Peterkin* (Philadelphia, 1919), 24.

202. These were the Staunton *Vindicator,* Rockingham *Register,* and *Spirit of Jefferson.*

203. Staunton *Vindicator,* Jan. 4.

204. Alex. *Gazette,* Jan. 7, 12. In early December a letter from near Danville stated: "Every body seems to think the Union is dissolved and war will be, if it had not already been declared. Consequently we are preparing for the worst." *Daily Dispatch,* Dec. 10, quoted in Freeman, *Notes,* I, 22.

205. *Daily Dispatch,* Jan. 22.

206. Wheeling *Intelligencer,* Jan. 15.

207. *Daily Dispatch,* Jan. 22.

208. Charlottesville *Review,* Jan. 25.

209. Robertson, *Life of Broadus,* 179.

210. Ruffin's *Diary,* Dec. 5.

211. Black Papers. August Belmont wrote Seward on January 17, 1861, that it was his "intimate conviction based upon information from the most conservative men in the border States, that nothing can prevent Virginia, Tennessee, North Carolina, and Kentucky from joining the movement of the cotton States, unless compromise measures, based upon the propositions of Senator Crittenden, can be carried by a sufficient majority through Congress to insure their embodiment in the Constitution." *Letters, Speeches, and Addresses of August Belmont* (privately printed, 1890), 46.

212. Quoted in Freeman's *Notes, 1861,* 102-103.

213. On January 21, 1861, the General Assembly of Virginia adopted the following resolution by a vote of twenty-six to seven in the senate and one hundred and eight to nothing in the House of Delegates: "Resolved by the General Assembly of Virginia, that if all efforts to reconcile the unhappy differences existing between the two sections of the country shall prove to be abortive, then in the opinion of the General Assembly, every consideration of honor and interests demands that Virginia shall unite her destiny with the slave-holding states of the South." *Acts of the Virginia Assembly* (1861), 377; *Journal of the House of Delegates* (1861), extra sess.; Rich. *Enq.,* Jan. 21, 1861.

CHAPTER VIII

THE LEGISLATURE OF 1861 AND THE CALL OF THE CONVENTION

1. Letter of Letcher to T. H. Ellis, Sept. 14, 1860, published in *Daily Dispatch,* Sept. 18.

2. Executive Papers of John Letcher (1860), MS. (in Va. State Lib.)

3. Executive Minute Book of 1859-1860, Nov. 7, 1860, MS. (in Va. State Lib.).

4. Rich. *Whig*, Sept. 18, 1860.

5. *Ibid.*, Nov. 29, 1859.

6. *Journal of House of Delegates* (1861), ex. sess., doc. 1, pp. vi-xxxvi.

7. J. P. Davidson, a close friend of Letcher, advised the latter in a letter of January 3 not to be too conservative in his message and to be quiet on the call of a state convention, or he would antagonize public sentiment. Davidson Papers.

8. *Journal of House of Delegates* (1861), ex. sess., doc. 1, pp. vi-xxxvi.

9. *Virginia Free Press*, Jan. 10. J. B. Dorman, a friend from Lexington, wrote Letcher on January 13 that the people of Rockbridge were delighted with the message. Davidson Papers.

10. Staunton *Vindicator*, Jan. 11.

11. *Daily Dispatch*, Jan. 8, quoted in Freeman's *Notes, 1861*, I, 16.

12. *Ibid.*

13. Wheeling *Intelligencer*, Jan. 11.

14. *Ibid.*

15. *Ibid.*

16. *Ibid.*, Jan. 14; *cf.* also letter to *Intelligencer*, Jan. 15.

17. Staunton *Vindicator*, Jan. 11.

18. "Change of Sec. Sent.," 85.

19. *Journal of House of Del.* (1861), ex. sess., 4, 9; *Journal of Senate of Virginia*, (1861); ex. sess., 49-50.

20. *Journal of House of Del.* (1861), ex. sess., 10; *Daily Dispatch*, Jan. 8; *Journal of Senate* (1861), ex. sess., 52.

21. *Journal of House of Del.* (1861), ex. sess., 10.

22. *Journal of Senate* (1861), ex. sess., 52.

23. Charlottesville *Review*, Jan. 4.

24. *Acts of the Va. Assembly* (1861), ex. sess.

25. The real test in the senate was on the motion to suspend the rules in order to consider the resolution. On this motion the vote was 26 to 7. Carraway of Norfolk, Carter of Loudoun, Wickham of Hanover, Marshall of Fauquier—all Whigs and all from east of the Blue Ridge—French of Mercer, Strickland of Augusta, and Newman of Jackson—all from west of the Blue Ridge—voted in the negative. *Journal of the Senate* (1861), ex. sess., 88; Rich. *Enq.*, Jan. 21.

26. James Barbour was the author of the plan. At the same time, he was in communication with Seward with a view to perfecting a compromise between the North and the South. Alex. *Gazette*, Jan. 25; Fred. Bancroft, *Life of Seward*, II, 32.

27. *Acts of Va. Assembly* (1861), ex. sess., 337-339.

28. *Ibid.*

29. *Ibid.*, 339.

30. Letter of Tyler to Letcher, Jan. 31, 1861. *Journal of Senate* (1861), ex. sess. doc. 13, pp. 5-6.

31. Tyler, *Letters and Times*, II, 589-590; P. G. Auchampaugh, *James Buchanan and his Cabinet on the Eve of Rebellion* (Lancaster, 1926), 185.

32. As a concession to the Union members of his Cabinet, Buchanan had sent the *Star of the West* to Sumter on January 5. It was fired upon January 9. Soon, thereafter, when Governor Pickens and Major Anderson failed to agree on the difficulties in the Charleston harbor each sent a representative to Buchanan—Lieutenant Hall representing Anderson, and Colonel Hayne representing Pickens. These agents arrived in Washington, January 13. Upon arrival, Hayne wished to demand the surrender of Sumter, but six Southern Senators urged him to withhold his demands until they could act together. These Senators then proposed to Buchanan and Pickens that the existing status in the Charleston harbor be maintained until the new confederacy could "devise a wise, just, and peaceable solution of existing difficulties." Buchanan refused to agree officially to the plan, but he let the Senators know that there was no necessity for reënforcements immediately. He also notified Anderson to employ utmost care in order to prevent a collision. He prevented the landing of troops at Fort Pickens from the *Brooklyn*. The Southern Senators considered this evidence that Buchanan would maintain peace until after the Peace Conference of February 8. The Southern Con-

federacy was formed and the control of the South Carolina forts passed into the hands of men more conservative than Pickens. *Cf.* Dumond, *Sec. Mov't.*, 176-178, 233-238; Rhodes, *Hist. of U. S.*, III, 245-249, 281; Nicolay and Hay, III, 153-180; *Official Records*, ser. I, vol I, 253-254.

33. *Cf.* letters of Tyler to Governor Letcher, Jan. 27, 1861, and Leonard Lamb to Letcher, Jan. 29, 1861, Miscellaneous Letters and Papers of Governor Letcher, Jan. to March, MS. (in Va. State Lib.).

34. *Journal of the Senate* (1861), ex. sess., doc. 13, pp. 6-7.

35. *Ibid.; Daily Dispatch,* Feb. 2, 1861; Freeman's *Notes, 1861,* 149-150; Tyler, *Letters and Times of the Tylers,* II, 587.

36. *Journal of Senate* (1861), ex. sess., doc. 13, p. 13; Tyler, *Life and Letters of the Tylers,* II, 590; letter of Tyler to Letcher, Jan. 27, 1861. Miscellaneous Letters and Papers, 1861 (in Va. State Lib.).

37. *Journal of Senate,* (1861), ex. sess., doc. 13, p. 13; letter of Buchanan to Holt, January 30, 1861, MS., Joseph Holt Papers (in Lib. of Con.).

38. *Official Records,* ser. I, vol. LI, pt. I, p. 315; letter of Buchanan to Holt, Jan. 30, 1861, Joseph Holt Papers.

39. *Daily Dispatch,* Jan. 29; "Report of Judge Robertson," quoted in Freeman's *Notes, 1861,* 186.

40. *Cf.* n. 32 of chapter VII.

41. *Journal of Va. Senate* (1861), ex. sess., doc. 18, p. 5.

42. Quoted in N. Y. *Times,* Feb. 1.

43. *Journal of Senate* (1861), ex. sess., doc. 25, p. 5.

44. *Ibid.,* docs. 18 and 25.

45. *Ibid.,* doc. 13, p. 7.

46. *Cf. supra,* 95-96.

47. *Cf.* Rich. *Enq.,* Nov. 24, Dec. 19, 1860; Wheeling *Union,* quoted in Rich. *Enq.,* Jan. 4, 1861.

48. "Change of Sec. Sent.," 87.

49. Rich. *Whig,* Jan. 15, 1861.

50. By January 29 Amelia, Appomattox, Caroline, Charlotte, Culpeper, Essex, Gloucester, Halifax, Henrico, Isle of Wight, King and Queen, Mecklenburg, Northampton, Orange, and Prince Edward had appropriated from $6,000 to $10,000 each, making a total of $57,500. Rich. *Enq.,* Jan. 21; Rich. *Whig,* Jan. 8, 15, 18, 29, 1861.

51. *Daily Dispatch,* Jan. 28, quoted in Freeman's *Notes, 1861,* 127.

52. *Journal of Senate* (1861), ex. sess., doc. 6.

53. *Acts of Va. Gen. Ass.* (1861), ex. sess., 28.

54. *Journal of House of Del.* (1861), ex. sess., 92.

55. *Acts of Va. Gen. Ass.* (1861), ex. sess., 27.

56. *Ibid.,* 35.

57. *Ibid.,* 246-249.

58. The charters read "from $50,000 to $500,000 each." *Ibid.,* 273-274.

59. Accomac, Bedford, Caroline, Charles City, Culpeper, Cumberland, Fauquier, Gloucester, Halifax, Hanover, King and Queen, Lancaster, Louisa, Mathews, Northumberland, Orange, Petersburg, Pittsylvania, Surry, and Sussex from east of the Blue Ridge, and Botetourt, Craig, Floyd, Frederick, Giles, Jefferson, Pulaski, and Rockbridge from the Valley and the southwest drew up such resolutions.

60. Rich. *Whig,* Jan. 4; Rich. *Enq.,* Jan. 5; Staunton, *Vindicator,* Dec. 7, 1860.

61. Staunton *Spectator,* Dec. 4, Jan. 8.

62. *Daily Dispatch,* Jan. 5.

63. Morgantown *Star,* quoted in Wheeling *Intelligencer,* Jan. 14.

64. *Journal of House of Del.* (1861), ex. sess., doc., 19.

65. Staunton *Vindicator,* Jan. 11.

66. Granville Hall, *The Rending of Virginia. A History* (Chicago, 1902), 122. Hereafter cited as Hall, *Rending of Va.*

67. *Ibid.,* 122-123.

68. Staunton *Spectator,* Nov. 27, 1860; Staunton *Vindicator,* Jan. 11.

69. This was true of the conventions of 1829-1830 and 1850-1851. *Cf.* McGregor, *Disruption of Va.,* 110.

70. *Daily Dispatch,* Jan. 14, in Freeman's *Notes, 1861,* 46.
71. "Change of Sec. Sent," 84.
72. Rich. *Enq.,* Jan. 10.
73. Staunton *Vindicator,* Jan. 11.
74. "Change of Sec. Sent.," 83-84; Pittsburgh *Post,* Jan. 12.
75. Rich. *Enq.,* Jan. 10.
76. *Cf.* the account of the debate in the two houses reported in the Rich. *Enq.,* Jan. 10, 1861, and in the *Daily Dispatch,* Jan. 12.
77. Rich. *Enq.,* Jan. 11, 14; *Daily Dispatch,* Jan. 12; Rich. *Exam.,* Jan. 15.
78. Rich. *Enq.,* Jan. 14.
79. *Journals of House of Del.* (1861), ex. sess., 21.
80. *Ibid.*
81. The bill provided that the convention "adopt such measures as they may deem expedient for the welfare of the commonwealth." *Acts of General Assembly of Va.* (1861), 26.
82. Alex. *Gazette,* Dec. 25; Wheeling *Intelligencer,* Jan. 14, 15. These threats were carried out in the convention. *Cf. infra,* note 199 of chapter XI.
83. The apportionment was the same as that of the House of Delegates, a total of 152 members. *Acts of Gen. Ass.* (1861), 25.
84. Letter of Burks to Buford, Jan. 7, 1861, "Change of Sec. Sent.," 83.
85. *Acts of Gen. Ass.* (1861), 24-26.
86. Wheeling *Intelligencer,* Jan. 18, 19; Rich. *Whig,* Jan. 28; Lewis, *How West Va. Was Made,* 28.
87. *Daily Dispatch,* Jan. 26; Rich. *Enq.,* Jan. 28.
88. Wheeling *Intelligencer,* Jan. 19, 21, 22, 24. In a letter to Willey, February 4, 1861, C. D. Hubbard of Wheeling said that he promised, in the campaign, not to sign an ordinance of secession, but his opponent had refused to pledge himself because it would injure his influence in the Convention. Hubbard was elected. Willey Papers.
89. In a letter to Letcher, Robert Johnston of Clarksburg said that it should be "recollected that our intercourse is almost entirely with the west and north, we have none with the eastern and central portions of Virginia." Miscellaneous Letters and Papers, 1861 (in Va. State Lib.).
90. Quoted in Wheeling *Intelligencer,* Jan. 19.
91. *Daily Dispatch,* Feb. 2, 1861, in Freeman's *Notes, 1861,* 156-158.
92. Charlottesville *Review,* Feb. 8. *Cf.* statement of similar candidates in Rich. *Enq.,* Jan. 26.
93. *Cf.* cards of R. T. Daniel, G. W. Richardson, James Barbour, William Macfarland, and W. C. Wickham announcing their candidacies. Rich. *Whig,* Jan. 18, 29, Feb. 1.
94. *Ibid.*
95. Alex. *Gazette,* Feb. 2.
96. Rich. *Enq.,* Feb. 4, 6.
97. *Ibid.,* Jan. 17; Dumond, *op. cit.,* 207-230.
98. *Ibid.,* 232.
99. Rich. *Enq.,* Jan. 25, 29.
100. *Ibid.,* Jan. 31, Feb. 4.
101. William Smith was sick but later admitted that he agreed with its sentiments. J. T. Harris, John S. Millson, Sherrard Clemens, and A. R. Boteler refused to sign. It was drafted by M. R. H. Garnett and J. M. Mason. *Pub. Life of Mason,* 176-178; N. Y. *Times,* Feb., 1861.
102. Rich. *Enq.,* Jan. 25; *Pub. Life of Mason,* 176-178.
103. Staunton *Vindicator,* Feb. 1, 1861.
104. Alex. *Gazette,* Feb. 2.
105. *Ibid.,* Feb. 8.
106. *Ibid.*
107. Rich. *Enq.,* Jan. 29.
108. *Ibid.,* Feb. 4.
109. Quoted in Alex. *Gazette,* Feb. 2.
110. *Ibid.*

111. *Daily Dispatch*, Feb. 5, quoted in Freeman's *Notes, 1861,* 166-167.

112. The total vote was 145,697. In the presidential election of 1860, the vote was 167,223. About 148,655 were cast in the Letcher-Goggin contest of 1859. *Tribune Almanac* (1860). In Richmond 512 less votes were cast than in 1860.

113. Snow fell in Mecklenburg and Montgomery counties and in Petersburg and Richmond cities. *Daily Dispatch,* Feb. 5.

114. *Cf. infra,* 159.

115. *Documents of the Secession Convention,* no. 9. The returns were not complete.

116. Staunton *Spectator,* Feb. 12; Charlottesville *Review,* Feb. 15.

117. Bancroft, *Life of Seward,* II, 533.

118. McGregor, *Disruption of Va.,* 116.

119. A New York *Tribune* correspondent, February 19, 1861, said: "As to Virginia seceding, that need not be thought of in any event. There are one hundred and twenty men in the Convention who will vote to remain with the North, thirty-two who prefer the Southern Confederacy—There is no event that could induce this Convention to secede, unless it were some foolish effort of Congress to abolish slavery, which nobody expects." Quoted in Rich. *Exam.,* Feb. 28. *Cf.* also Pittsburgh *Evening Chronicle,* Feb. 7.

120. N. Y. *Times,* Feb. 6.

121. *Ibid.,* Feb. 12.

122. Alex. *Gazette,* Feb. 8.

123. Staunton *Spectator,* Feb. 12.

124. Quoted in N. Y. *Times,* Feb. 11; Rich. *Whig,* Feb. 8.

125. Bancroft, *Life of Seward,* II, 534-535; letter of Burks to Buford, Feb. 3, 1861; "Change of Sec. Sent.," 89-90.

126. Bancroft, *op. cit.,* II, 534-535.

127. *Ibid.,* II, 534. Seward wrote Lincoln, January 27, 1861: "The appeals from the Union men in the border States for something of concession or compromise are very painful, since they say that without it their States must all go with the tide." Nicolay and Hay, III, 365.

128. Charlottesville *Review,* Feb. 8.

129. *Daily Dispatch,* Feb. 6, quoted in Freeman's *Notes, 1861,* 170.

130. *Ibid.*

131. Ruffin's *Diary,* Feb. 8.

132. Quoted in Rich. *Enq.,* Feb. 8.

133. *Ibid.,* Feb. 6.

134. *Cf.* McGregor, *op. cit.,* 119.

135. *Daily Dispatch,* Jan. 26, quoted in Freeman's *Notes 1861,* 124.

136. Rich. *Enq.,* Feb. 8; McGregor, *op. cit.,* 114.

137. *Cf. supra,* 151.

138. *Cf. supra,* 150.

139. *Cf. infra,* 159-160.

140. *Cf. infra,* 159-160.

141. Charlottesville *Review,* Feb. 8. The Pittsburgh *Post,* February 12, reminded the free states that Virginia "had placed herself as a barrier state to the further progress of disunion until it can be decided whether compromise is possible."

CHAPTER IX

SECESSION OF CONVENTION — PERIOD OF DELAY

1. Mr. Freeman makes practically the same division in his *Attitude,* 76.

2. Tyler was the ex-President; Stuart and Preston were former Cabinet officers; Wise was the ex-Governor; R. L. Montague and William McComas were former lieutenant governors; J. S. Carlile, W. G. Brown, Sherrard Clemens, W. M. Tredway, Jeremiah Morton, S. M. Moore, T. F. Goode, T. S. Flournoy, W. L. Goggin, Stuart, Wise, and Preston had served in Congress; and twenty-one had been members of the Convention of 1850-1851.

3. Rich. *Exam.,* Feb. 28.

4. Staunton *Vindicator,* Mar. 1; N. Y. *Tribune,* Feb. 19; Rich. *Exam.,* Feb. 28; Hall, *Rending of Va,* 142; W. A. Willey, *An Inside View of the Formation of the State of West Virginia* (Wheeling, 1901), 27.

5. C. D. Hubbard, James McGrew, William Macfarland, Lewis E. Harvie, and William T. Sutherland were business leaders; G. W. Richardson, James Barbour, A. M. Barbour, J. R. Chambliss, G. W. Randolph, A. T. Caperton, and J. B. Baldwin were men of military experience.

6. Among these were J. T. Thornton, J. P. Holcombe, R. E. Scott, H. A. Wise, W. B. Preston, G. W. Summers, J. B. Baldwin, R. Y. Conrad, A. H. H. Stuart, James Marshall, R. L. Montague, G. W. Randolph, J. C. Bruce, and W. T. Wiley. *Cf.* John Goode, "The Virginia Secession Convention of 1861," *The Conservative Review,* III, 83.

7. Summers, Stuart, R. Y. Conrad, Bruce, J. Barbour, and Goggin were the most successful of these.

8. *Cf. infra,* 190.

9. Rich. *Enq.,* Feb. 6; Freeman in his *Attitude,* 72; Goode, *loc. cit.,* 81.

10. *Ibid.*

11. *Hunter's Correspondence,* 8.

12. W. L. Goggin, R. E. Scott, and others refused to accept this doctrine.

13. Goode, *loc. cit.,* 81.

14. *Cf. infra,* 204.

15. *Cf.* chapter XI.

16. Goode, *loc. cit.,* 81.

17. Such outstanding members as Custic, Delaney, Early, Fugate, Holladay, Janney, Patrick, Wilson were from elsewhere.

18. *Cf. supra,* 150-151.

19. *Journal of the Acts and Proceedings of a General Convention of the State of Virginia Assembled at Richmond on February . . . 13, 1861* (Richmond, 1861), 3. Hereafter cited as *Journal of Sec. Conv.*

20. *Ibid.*

21. *Ibid.,* 7.

22. *Ibid.,* 7, 31-33.

23. J. L. Eubanks of Richmond was elected secretary.

24. Harvie, Montague, Williams, and Wise were secessionists; James Barbour, Blow, Bruce, Boyd, Johnston, Macfarland, Rives, Preston, R. E. Scott, and Southall were moderates; and Baldwin, Conrad, Jackson, McComas, Moore, Price, and Willey were Unionists.

25. Fourteen of these had voted for Bell, two for Douglas, and four for Breckinridge. Territorially the distribution was as follows: five from the Tidewater; five from the Piedmont; five from the Valley north of Roanoke; three from the southwest; and three from north of the Kanawha and west of the Alleghanies. Ten were from east of the Blue Ridge; eleven were from west of it; four were from the counties which later were included in West Virginia; and seventeen were from the region which is included in present Virginia. Mr. McGregor in his *Disruption of Virginia,* 128, says that ten of the committee were known to be secessionists. If he means that ten believed in the right of secession his estimate is rather small, but if he means that this number favored immediate secession his figures are rather high. On Harvie's motion, April 4, only five voted for secession. *Cf. Journal of Sec. Conv.,* 31-33. He states, furthermore, that there were only four delegates from west of the Alleghanies, "and none of these held very decided Union views." Jackson, Johnston, McComas, Price, and Willey were from that section. All of these except Johnston voted against secession, April 17. Although these men were not as aggressive as Carlile in the movement for a division of the state, it seems to me that Willey, McComas, and Jackson were very decided in their Union views. *Cf.* chapter XI.

26. The Charlottesville *Review,* February 22, stated that it was "as able as ever sat in Virginia."

27. *Cf.* chapter XI.

28. *Cf. infra,* 168.

29. Hall, *Rending of Va.,* 154.

30. J. B. Dorman, a moderate from Rockbridge, to J. D. Davidson, Feb. 14, 1861,

Davidson Papers; R. Y. Conrad to his wife, Mar. 2, 1861, Conrad Papers (in Va. State Lib.).

31. *Cf. infra*, 172-173.

32. Willey, *Inside View*, 39.

33. *Addresses Delivered before the Virginia State Convention by the Honorable Fulton Anderson . . .*, 5-19. Hereafter cited as *Addresses Delivered before the Va. State Conv.*

34. Hall, *Rending of Va.*, 520.

35. *Addresses Delivered before the Va. Conv.*, 21-24.

36. *Ibid.*, 43-64.

37. Hall, *Rending of Va.*, 520.

38. Letter of Burks to Buford, Feb. 21, 1861, "Change of Sec. Sent.," 90.

39. Charlottesville *Review*, Feb. 22. A correspondent in Richmond wrote the Pittsburgh *Post* that Preston's speech was "pronounced the greatest oratorical effort ever made here." Pittsburgh *Post*, Feb. 20.

40. *Journal of Sec. Conv.*, 80.

41. *Addresses Delivered before the Va. Conv. . . . .* , 3; *Journal of Sec. Conv.*, 80.

42. *Ibid.*, 45. Other anti-coercion resolutions were introduced by Leake, Flournoy, Richardson, Fisher, and Tredway. *Ibid.*, 46, 63.

43. *Ibid.*, 51.

44. *Ibid.*, 45.

45. *Ibid.*, 53.

46. Turner of Jackson and Whitfield of the Isle of Wight introduced resolutions to this effect. *Ibid.*, 51, 63.

47. *Ibid.*, 64.

48. *Ibid.*, 62.

49. "Proceedings and Debates of the Convention for Feb. 21," as printed in the Rich. *Enq.*, Feb. 22. Hereafter cited as "Proceedings," Rich. *Enq.*

50. *Ibid.*

51. *Ibid.* This sectionalism flared up many times thereafter.

52. McGregor, *op. cit.*, 134.

53. "Proceedings of Feb. 25," Rich. *Enq.*, Feb. 26.

54. That night an indignation meeting of 2,000 was held and many fiery speeches were made. They passed Moore's hotel and several groans came from the crowd. The crowd would have burned him in effigy if John Goode had not checked them. *Daily Dispatch*, Feb. 26; Charlottesville *Review*, Mar. 1.

55. "Proceedings of Feb. 25," Rich. *Enq.*, Feb. 26; *Substance of a Speech Delivered by S. McD. Moore, of Rockbridge in the Convention of Virginia on his Resolution on Federal Relations, on 24th of February, 1861* (Richmond, 1861), 24 pp.

56. The president of the Convention ordered that the galleries be cleared. "Proceedings of Feb. 25," Rich. *Enq.*, Feb. 26.

57. "Proceedings of Feb. 25," Rich. *Enq.*, Feb. 26, 28.

58. "Proceedings of Feb. 27," Rich. *Enq.*, Feb. 28.

59. "Proceedings of Mar. 1," Rich. *Enq.*, Mar. 2.

60. "Proceedings of Mar. 6," Rich. *Enq.*, Mar. 7.

61. *Speech of William L. Goggin, of Bedford, on Federal Relations, in the Convention of Virginia, on the 26th and 27th February, 1861* (Richmond, 1861), 31 pp.; "Proceedings of Feb. 26 and 27," Rich. *Enq.*, Feb. 28.

62. "Proceedings of Mar. 4," Rich. *Enq.*, Mar. 6.

63. "Proceedings of Mar. 5," Rich. *Enq.*, Mar. 6.

64. *Ibid.*

65. "Proceedings of Mar. 23," Rich. *Enq.*, Apr. 8, extra edition.

66. *Ibid.*, Apr. 8.

67. *Ibid.*

68. *Ibid.*

69. *Ibid.*

70. Rich. *Whig*, Jan. 29; *Speech of Hon. John T. Harris of Virginia, in Favor of Conciliation and the Union Delivered in the House of Representatives, February 8, 1861, on the Report of the Committee of 33* (printed by Towers, n.d.) 8 pp.

71. *Cong. Globe*, 36 Cong., 2 sess. 328-329, 332, 495; Rich. *Exam.*, Mar. 12, Wheeling *Intelligencer*, Jan. 17; N. Y. *Times*, Jan. 12, 14, 17, Feb. 1; Pittsburgh *Post*, Jan. 12; Henry Dering to Willey, Mar. 13, 1861, Willey Papers.

72. *Cf. supra*, 133-134.

73. Henry R. Dwire, "The New York Times and the Attempt to avert the Civil War," *South Atlantic Quarterly*, II, 273-280. August Belmont wrote Seward, January 17, that if something were not done the border states would certainly withdraw. *Letters, Speeches, and Addresses of Belmont*, 46.

74. Burks to Buford, Jan. 15, "Change of Sec. Sent.," 85. The Richmond *Whig*, January 18, felt, however, that in spite of the moderate tone of the speech, it was "empty rhetoric and stale platitude when it [the country] asked for substantial guarantees of adjustment, peace and concord."

75. N. Y. *Times*, Jan. 14.

76. Bancroft, *op. cit.*, II, 19. On December 25, Seward had suggested J. A. Gilmer of North Carolina and R. E. Scott of Virginia for posts in the Cabinet. Gilmer went to Springfield to see Lincoln and Seward interviewed Scott, but both Southerners were afraid of sentiment at home. *Diary of Ed. Bates*, Dec. 31, 1860; Nicolay and Hay, III, 350, 362-364.

77. Nicolay and Hay, III, 365; Bancroft, *op. cit.*, II, 30-31.

78. *Ibid.*, II, 31.

79. *Ibid.*, II, 32.

80. *Ibid.*

81. The conservative papers of Richmond and Petersburg carried notices from Douglas, Boteler, Crittenden, and Harris to counteract the address of the ten Virginia congressmen. Rich. *Whig*, Jan. 29, Feb. 1, 5.

82. N. Y. *Times*, Feb. 12.

83. Dwire, *loc. cit.*, 274; N. Y. *Times*, Feb. 11, 12, 19.

84. Letters to this effect were written to Seward by W. D. Moss, John Pendleton, James Barbour, and Sherrard Clemens. Bancroft, *op. cit.*, II, 533-537.

85. *Ibid.*, II, 534-536, 537.

86. John S. Millson to J. R. Kilby, Feb. 11, 1861, MS. Millson Papers (in Lib. of Cong.); *cf.* Charles Davidson to J. D. Davidson, Feb. 6. Davidson Papers.

87. General Winfield Scott wrote, February 19, that within a month after March 4 Lincoln would support as conciliatory a compromise as Crittenden's. Washington Hunt, Samuel Tilden, and R. B. Custis made similar promises. Craven, *Ruffin*, 200-201, 221-222.

88. Conrad to his wife, Mar. 13; Davidson to Letcher, Mar. 2.

89. *Ibid.*

90. *Acts of Gen. Ass.* (1861), ex. sess., 338.

91. Dumond, *op. cit.*, 241.

92. Chittenden, *Proceedings of Washington Peace Conf.*, 12.

93. A pamphleteer of eastern Virginia argued that the conduct of the chairman of the Committee of Thirty-three, that the course pursued by the Republicans in Congress, and that the delay of the Northern states to appoint delegates to the Peace Conference proved that they were using that body to gain time. *The Peace Convention at Washington, and the Virginia Convention at Richmond*, by "Westmoreland" (n.p., 1861), 18 pp.

94. The New York *Times*, February 4, 1861, said that until the lower South was represented, a proposal from the North would be a moral defeat.

95. Quoted in Rich. *Enq.*, Feb. 9.

96. Quoted in Rich. *Enq.*, Feb. 9. There were some distinguished members, such as Wilmot, Tyler, J. M. Morehead of Kentucky, James Guthrie, Chase, and Reverdy Johnson. Virginia's delegation was of average ability.

97. *The Diary of Orville Hickinson Browning*, T. C. Pease and James G. Randall, eds. *(Collection* of Illinois State Historical Library, Springfield, 1925), I, 453.

98. Mary Scrughman, *The Peaceable Americans of 1860-1861; A Study in Public Opinion* (Columbia University *Studies*, XCVI, No. 3, New York, 1921), 480.

99. W. C. Harris, *Public Life of Zachariah Chandler, 1851-1875* (Lansing, 1917), 53-54.

100. *Ibid.*, 54.

101. On every important amendment or resolution offering concessions to the South, Iowa and all the New England states, except Rhode Island, voted in the negative; the other Republican stronghold, the Northwest, was not represented. Even the Franklin amendment, which denied the right of a state to absolve its citizens from their allegiance to the government of the United States, would have been pushed through by the Republicans had they not been afraid of the effect—this would have split the conference on an issue which many would have interpreted as coercion. Dumond, *op. cit.*, 250-252; Chittenden, *op. cit.*, 448.

102. *Ibid.*, 22.

103. *Ibid.*, 43-45, 47-52.

104. Of these, Rives and Summers from Virginia denied the right of secession, and insisted that their state had not demanded the Crittenden Compromise as the only plan she would accept. Instead, she would agree to something else. Both of these men supported all the proposals of the committee on resolutions. *Cf.* Chittenden, *op. cit.*, 136-141, for the able and conciliatory speech of Rives, and pages 150-154 in the same reference for a similar speech of Summers. Their votes on the various proposals are given on pages 439-446 of Chittenden.

105. Seddon, in a long speech on February 18, made a savage attack on the Republicans. Morrill asked him if Virginia's proposals were an ultimatum, and if she would stand by the National Government while these proposals were being ratified. Seddon answered in the affirmative to the first of these questions, and in the negative to the second. The extreme views of Morrill and Wilmot were given in their speeches on February 19. Chittenden, *op. cit.*, 91-98, 147-148.

106. (1) The Peace Conference subjected slaveholding rights in the territories south of 36°30′ to judicial review, while the Crittenden Compromise made no such restriction.

(2) It forbade the acquisition of territory without the approval of a majority of Senators from each section. The Crittenden plan was silent on this.

(3) The foreign slave trade prohibited for all times. Crittenden said nothing about this in his proposals.

(4) The Crittenden plan provided for the restriction of negro franchise and for the colonization of free negroes in Africa. The Peace Conference omitted these.

(5) The Crittenden Compromise recommended that Congress request the free states to repeal their personal liberty laws, and that the 1850 fugitive slave law be strengthened. The Peace Conference was silent on these.

There were seven sections to the final report of the Conference. Of these the Virginians voted for the second which related to the acquisition of territory by the approval of Senators from both sections, for the third which pertained to the permanency of slavery in the states and Federal posts, and for the fourth which related to the enforcement of the fugitive slave law. On the first relative to the 36°30′, the fifth which pertained to the foreign slave trade, the sixth which included these guarantees in irrepealable amendments, and the seventh which required that the Federal Government pay for fugitive slaves, Virginians voted in the negative, except for Summers and Rives who supported all these measures. Later Brockenbrough said that he would have suppported the report as a whole, and Tyler, judging from his remarks near the end of the Conference, would have done likewise. This left only Seddon of the Virginia delegation as an opponent of the report as a whole. Chittenden, *op. cit.*, 421-425, 441-443, 451, 472-473.

107. Crittenden, Bigler, Thompson, Seward, and Trumbull were on this committee. Chittenden, *op. cit.*, 474-475.

108. *Ibid.*, 447, 481.

109. *Ibid.*, 490.

110. *Ibid.*, 506-513.

111. *Ibid.*, 571.

112. *Ibid.*, 576, 580.

113. *Ibid.*, 581-583.

114. *Cf. supra*, 161-162. Thomas R. R. Cobb of Georgia wrote his wife, February 7, 1861, that he felt certain that if the Peace Conference failed Virginia would secede.

"The Correspondence of Thomas Reade Roates Cobb, 1860-1862," *Publications* of the Southern Historical Association, XI, 165-166.

115. Rich. *Exam.,* Apr. 3.
116. Chittenden, *op. cit.,* 490, 506-513
117. Rich. *Exam.,* Mar. 1.
118. Staunton *Vindicator,* Mar. 8.
119. Quoted in *Daily Dispatch,* March 2.
120. Quoted in Bell, *Old Free State,* I, 573.
121. *Cf. supra,* 163-165.
122. "Proceedings of Mar. 1," Rich. *Enq.,* Mar. 2.
123. *Ibid.*
124. *Ibid.,* Mar. 4.
125. *Journal of Sec. Conv.,* 72-74.
126. "Proceedings of Mar. 6," Rich. *Enq.,* March 7.
127. At this time Seward and Lincoln were following a "hands off" policy regarding the forts. Summers was negotiating with the former. *Cf. infra,* 181-182.
128. *Speech of George W. Summers on Federal Relations in the Virginia Convention, delivered March 11, 1861* (printed by Whig Book and Job Office, Richmond, 1861), 29 pp. Rives agreed with Summers that the recommendations would be accepted by the North. As proof of this he cited the assurances which he had from leaders in Pennsylvania, Rhode Island, Illinois, Ohio, and others. *Speech of Honorable William C. Rives on the Proceedings of the Peace Conference and the States of the Union, delivered in Richmond, March 8, 1861* (printed by Whig Book and Job Office, Richmond, 1861), 24 pp. Similar views were expressed in the Charlottesville *Review,* March 15, 1861, in the Richmond *Whig,* March 5, 1861, and by J. D. Davidson in a letter to Governor Letcher, March 2, 1861. Davidson Papers.
129. "Proceedings of Mar. 14," Rich. *Enq.,* Mar. 29.
130. "Proceedings of Mar. 14," Rich. *Enq.,* Mar. 15.
131. *Cf. supra,* 170.
132. N. Y. *Times,* Mar. 23.
133. R. E. Scott, "Robert Eden Scott," *Bulletins* of Fauquier Historical Society (Richmond, 1921), 1st ser., 88.
134. *Cf. supra,* 169-170.
135. Robertson, *Broadus,* 183.
136. Davidson to Letcher, Mar. 2, Davidson Papers.
137. Bancroft, *op. cit.,* II, 536-537, 540
138. *Ibid.,* II, 540-541. This representative was F. W. Lander. In this letter he expressed the views of the conservatives and secessionists of Virginia. The *Daily Dispatch,* February 25, contended that Lincoln's speeches on his way to Washington and the radical statements of Thaddeus Stevens in Congress were designed by the Republican party to aid in the seizure of Southern forts. Likewise the Charlottesville *Review,* February 22, expressed its disgust at the President-elect's statements that " 'no one is hurt.' " It had no patience with his " 'nonsense' " and wished that Seward had charge. *Cf.* also letter of J. M. Hagan to W. T. Willey, Feb. 21, 1861. Willey Papers.
139. Rich. *Enq.,* Mar. 4.
140. Ruffin's *Diary,* Mar. 2.
141. "Proceedings of Mar. 4," Rich. *Enq.,* Mar. 6.
142. Seward's alterations in the address were intended to placate the border states. Many Republicans felt that the message was conciliatory. "Diary of a Public Man," *North Amer. Rev.,* CXXIX, 480; N. Y. *Times,* Mar. 6, 1861.
143. Dumond, *op. cit.,* 260-262; Rich. *Exam.,* Mar. 8.
144. J. D. Davidson wrote Dorman, March 6: "His avowed determinations [to collect revenue and seize the forts] are so much qualified by his *buts* & his *ifs* & his *unlesses* etc., that his inaugural amounts in part to a message against coercion." His party obligations, Davidson continued, forced him to make some show. Davidson Papers. Henry Dering wrote Willey on March 12 that the people of Morgantown found the message better than they expected. Willey Papers. The Wellsburg *Herald* and the Wheeling *Intelligencer* maintained that this address would strengthen the Union men in the South, Wheeling *Intelligencer,* Mar. 6, 9.

145. *Cf. Daily Dispatch,* Mar. 5, and 7, for expressions of this view from the Wheeling *Union,* Bedford *Sentinel,* Danville *Register,* and Charlottesville *Jeffersonian.* Mason considered it a declaration of war. N. Y. *Times,* Mar. 8, 1861.

146. Rich. *Exam.,* Mar. 8.

147. Rich. *Enq.,* Mar. 5.

148. Staunton *Vindicator,* Mar. 8.

149. *Ibid.*

150. This paper opposed the doctrine of secession.

151. Quoted in *Daily Dispatch,* Mar. 7.

152. These included Norfolk *Herald,* Fredericksburg *News,* Petersburg *Intelligencer,* and Petersburg *Express. Cf.* quotations from these papers in the *Daily Dispatch,* Mar. 7. Rich. *Enq.,* Mar. 8; Va. *Sentinel,* Mar. 7; Alex. *Gazette,* Mar. 7.

153. The Staunton *Spectator,* March 12, 1861, and the Lynchburg *Virginian* (quoted in Alexandria *Gazette,* March 7) were of this opinion.

154. Charlottesville *Review,* Mar. 8.

155. *Daily Dispatch,* Mar. 12. Congressman Boteler was of the same opinion. Charlottesville *Review,* May 17, 1861. J. D. Davidson who felt that Lincoln's address did not involve "coercion" wrote Governor Letcher, March 9, "I find some wavering here amongst Conservatives since the Inaugural." Davidson Papers.

156. Pittsburgh *Post,* Mar. 8.

157. Barbour, Botetourt, Caroline, Fredericksburg, Giles, Halifax, Petersburg, Pulaski, and Smythe drew up such resolutions. Rich. *Enq.,* Mar. 13.

158. N. Y. *Times,* Mar. 16.

159. Letcher wrote Davidson, March 9: "The disunionists were wild with joy, and declared if the Convention did not pass an ordinance of secession at once the state would be disgraced." Davidson Papers.

160. *Cf. supra,* 163. For treatment of Moore, and McGregor, *op. cit.,* 139, for treatment of Carlile. Moore to Davidson, Mar. 10, Davidson Papers.

161. "Proceedings of Mar. 5," Rich. *Enq.,* Mar. 6.

162. *Ibid.*

163. *Ibid.*

164. *Ibid.*

165. *Ibid.*

166. J. B. Dorman to Davidson, Mar. 8, 1861; Letcher to Davidson, Mar. 9, 1861. Davidson Papers; Conrad to his wife, Mar. 6, Conrad Papers.

167. "Proceedings of Mar. 5," Rich. *Enq.,* Mar. 6; Dorman to Davidson, Mar. 8, Davidson Papers.

168. "Proceedings of Mar. 5," Rich. *Enq.,* Mar. 6, 7; Dorman to Davidson, Mar. 8, Davidson Papers.

169. *Ibid.,* Mar. 8, Davidson Papers.

170. "Proceedings of Mar. 6," Rich. *Enq.,* Mar. 7.

171. *Ibid.*

172. Goode's advice was from letters of Early's defeated opponents. Early had won, on February 4, 1,060 votes and his opponent 213. *Ibid.*

173. "Proceedings of Mar. 7," Rich *Enq.,* Mar. 11; McGregor, *op. cit.,* 139.

174. "Proceedings of Mar. 7," Rich. *Enq.,* Mar. 11. Conrad in a letter to his wife, March 6, made a similar complaint against the secessionists. Conrad Papers.

175. "Proceedings of Mar. 9," Rich. *Enq.,* Mar. 11.

176. Conrad to his wife, Mar. 6, Conrad Papers; Dorman to Davidson, Mar. 8, Davidson Papers.

177. Conrad Papers.

178. Burks to Buford, Mar. 7, "Change of Sec. Sent.," 92.

179. Moore to Davidson, Mar. 10, Davidson Papers.

180. Rich. Enq., Mar. 7, 1861.

181. *Cf. infra,* 182.

CHAPTER X

THE SECESSION CONVENTION: THE PLAY OF PARTIES

1. *Journal of Sec. Conv.,* appendix.
2. *Ibid.*
3. It included the following:

(1) When the U. S. Constitution was adopted several states were "independent sovereignties."

(2) Since African slavery existed in 1787 and since it had become a vital part of the states wherein it existed, interference with it by the general government or other states "is contrary to the constitution."

(3) The formation of sectional parties was contrary to the principle on which the Federal system rested.

(4) The territories of the United States constituted a trust to be administered by the general government; consequently, there should be a division of territory if differences were not otherwise settled.

(5) When a state seceded, the Federal forts, arsenals, etc., became hers, and they should not be used by the Federal Government for intimidating that state.

(6) "We hope" that the Union will be preserved.

(7) The Federal and state governments should enforce the fugitive slave law, and advise the repeal of the personal liberty laws in order to remove the existing causes of complaint.

(8) The people of the several states had the right, for just cause, to withdraw from an association under the Federal government with the people of other states.

(Nine and ten are omitted because they are repetitions of others.)

(11) A national convention should be called, and if the principles herein stated were not guaranteed to the South, Virginia would feel it necessary to resume her old rights as an independent sovereignty.

(12) Virginia would wait a reasonable time for an answer to these demands, but in the meantime she would be opposed to the collecting of duties by the Federal Government, the recapturing of public property, and the reënforcements of the forts in the seceded states.

(13) The commencement of hostility by the Federal Government against the Southern Confederacy pending these negotiations would be considered as an unfriendly act against Virginia.

(14) A border-states conference of delegates from Delaware, Maryland, Virginia, North Carolina, Tennessee, Kentucky, Missouri, and Arkansas would be called to meet in Frankfort, Kentucky, the latter part of May "to consult together and concert such measures for their final action as the honor, the interests, and the safety of the people thereof may demand."

"Partial Report from Committee on Federal Relations, printed Mar. 9, 1861," *Journal of Sec. Conv.,* appendix.

4. "Report of the Committee on Federal Relations Proposing Amendments to the Constitution of the United States," *Journal of Sec. Conv.,* appendix.

5. "Substitute for the Report of the Committee on Federal Relations, presented by Mr. Wise, March 9, 1861," *Journal of Sec. Conv.,* appendix.

6. "Harvie's Substitute," *Journal of Sec. Conv.,* appendix.

7. "Barbour's Substitute," *Journal of Sec. Conv.,* appendix.

8. "Baldwin's Substitute," *Journal of Sec. Conv.,* appendix.

9. Conrad wrote his wife March 24. "Some days ago I thought he [Baldwin] would give us some trouble for he submitted a separate report." Conrad Papers.

10. Conrad's letters to wife, Mar.. 13, 15, 24. Conrad Papers.

11. *Ibid.,* Mar. 13, 1861.

12. Staunton *Spectator.* Mar. 19, 1861.

13. Staunton *Vindicator,* Mar. 15.

14. Rich. *Whig,* Mar. 26, 1861.

15. "Proceedings of Mar. 15," Rich *Enq.,* Mar. 16.

16. Rich. *Whig,* Apr. 9.

17. *Cf.* note 3 of chapter X; "Proceedings of Mar. 15," Rich. *Enq.*, Mar. 16.
18. Rich. *Enq.*, Mar. 18.
19. Rich. *Exam.*, Mar. 12.
20. Quoted in the N. Y. *Times,* Mar. 30, 1861. This plan was frequently recommended.
21. Letter of C. S. Morehead to J. J. Crittenden, Feb. 23, 1862, Crittenden Papers; J. D. Davidson to Letcher, Mar. 2, 1861, and Davidson to Dorman Mar. 6, 1861, Davidson Papers. Congressman Millson, on a visit to Richmond about the time of the inauguration, told Dorman that Lincoln would do nothing more about the forts; that he would not reënforce them or repossess them; but that he would let well enough alone for the time being. Dorman to Davidson, Mar. 8, 1861. Davidson Papers.
22. "Diary of a Public Man," *North Amer. Review,* CXXIX, 487-489.
23. *Ibid.,* 493; W. L. Hall, "Lincoln's Interview with John B. Baldwin," *So. Atl. Quart.,* XIII, 263. Hereafter cited as Hall, "Lincoln's Interview with Baldwin."
24. J. C. Welling, "The Proposed Evacuation of Fort Sumter," *The Nation,* XXIX, 384.
25. "A Page of Political Correspondence: Unpublished Letter of' Mr. Stanton to Mr. Buchanan," *No. Amer. Rev.,* CXXIX, 474.
26. Rich. *Enq.,* Mar. 15, 20; Rich. *Whig,* Mar. 15.
27. Papers of John A. Campbell (in Confederate Museum, Richmond).
28. "Diary of a Public Man," *No. Amer. Rev.,* CXXIX, 490.
29. Welling, *loc. cit.,* 384.
30. Rich *Enq.,* Mar. 20.
31. Scrugham, *Peaceable Americans,* 509.
32. Weling, *loc. cit.,* 384.
33. Rich *Enq.,* Mar. 20.
34. Hall, "Lincoln's Interview with Baldwin," 263.
35. *Ibid.,* 264.
36. Seward continued to give promises as late as April 4. Memorandum of Campbell, Campbell Papers.
37. "Proceedings of Mar. 5," Rich. *Enq.,* Mar. 16, 1861.
38. "Proceedings of Apr. 4," Rich. *Enq.,* Apr. 6, 1861.
39. Conrad to his wife Mar. 29, 1861, Conrad Papers.
40. *Ibid.*
41. Welling, *loc. cit.,* 384; Conrad to his wife Mar. 30, Conrad Papers.
42. *Cf. infra,* 197.
43. Wise wrote Andrew Hunter, April 2, 1861: "If the people were ready I am ready to-day to go out of this house of bondage with the North. . . . But it is folly to tender naked secession to Va. and risk final defeat forever. We must train the popular head and heart." Mass. His. Soc. *Publications* (Dec. 1912 - Jan. 1913), 248.
44. Conrad to his wife Mar. 24, 26, Apr. 6. Conrad Papers.
45. *Ibid.,* Rich. *Whig,* Mar. 19, 29.
46. A correspondent of the Alexandria *Gazette* stated that "Millions of copies of sensation and often incendiary papers have been scattered through our State." The conservative papers did not circulate the speeches of the Union men. Alexandria *Gazette,* Mar. 12, 1861.
47. Letters of Dorman to Davidson, Mar. 28, 31, and Moore to Davidson Mar. 29, Davidson Papers; *Virginia Free Press,* Apr. 4; Staunton *Vindicator,* Apr. 5.
48. F. H. Pierpoint to Willey, Apr. 3, Willey Papers.
49. F. S. Daniel, Richmond *Examiner During the War* (New York, 1868), 230.
50. *Ibid.*
51. *Ibid.*
52. Rich. *Exam.,* Mar. 14.
53. *Ibid.,* Apr. 11.
54. *Ibid.,* Mar. 15, Apr. 2, 11.
55. *Ibid.*
56. *Ibid.,* Mar. 22.
57. *Ibid.* The most famous article of this character in his paper was the Gli Animali Parlanti written by a young member of the staff, and published in the issue of

March 19. In this the writer characterized the Convention as a great assembly of animals of different kinds.

58. Emeline L. Stearns, *John M. Daniel and the Confederacy,* MS. (M.A. Thesis, University of Chicago, 1928), 30.

59. *Ibid.*

60. *Cf.* chapter VII.

61. Rich. *Enq.,* Mar. 7; Rich. *Exam.,* Mar. 26; Moore to Davidson Mar. 10, 1861. Davidson Papers.

62. Rich. *Enq.,* Mar. 15, 16, 21, 22, 23, 25, 28.

63. The most important of these district papers were: Alexandria *Sentinel,* Lynchburg *Republican,* Staunton *Vindicator,* and the Charlottesville *Jeffersonian.*

64. *Cf. infra,* 202; Hall, *Rending of Va.,* 161.

65. Alex. *Gazette,* Mar. 12, 1861.

66. Marshall M. Dent, a Union delegate from Morgantown, wrote in his paper, the *Virginia Star:* "Your readers cannot imagine the state of things here from the reports of the Convention in the newspapers. Every means is used to intimidate the members of this Convention. Meetings are held nightly. Bands are hired who parade the streets followed by a motley crew of free negroes, boys and mad cops, who go around to the different hotels calling upon the well known Secessionists for speeches . . . and every Union man is denounced as an abolitionist! The members from the Northwest are compelled to daily hear citizens of Richmond, who are allowed privileged seats, point them out with the remark that 'there is where the abolitionists sit.'" Quoted in the Rich. *Enq.,* Mar. 26, 1861. *Cf. Infra,* 202, for attempted revolts. Conrad mentions the demonstrations of "the mobs" in his letters to his wife Mar. 6, 13, 29, 1861. Conrad Papers.

67. Rich. *Enq.,* Feb. 28, Mar. 18; *Daily Dispatch,* Feb. 22, 26; Rich. *Whig,* Apr. 2; J. D. Imboden to J. R. Kilby, Feb. 25 (in Lib. of Cong.).

68. Charlottesville *Review,* Mar. 15. Conrad in his letters to his wife, March 6, 13, 29, constantly complained of this intimidation. Conrad Papers.

69. Rich. *Whig,* Mar. 15.

70. *Cf., infra,* 202.

71. Alex. *Gazette,* Mar. 30.

72. Quoted in Alex. *Gazette,* Apr. 5.

73. At this time forty county meetings in these sections drew up resolutions to this effect. "Proceedings of Mar. 5-31," Rich. *Enq.,* Mar. 6 to Mar. 13.

74. Alex. *Gazette,* Mar. 16.

75. "Proceedings of Mar. 9," Rich. *Enq.,* Mar. 12.

76. Rich. *Enq.,* Apr. 11.

77. *Ibid.,* Apr. 5.

78. Alex. *Gazette,* Mar. 27; Bell, *Old Free State,* I, 573.

79. Quoted in Rich. *Exam.,* Apr. 12.

80. *Ibid.,* Apr. 13.

81. *Ibid.*

82. *Ibid.*

83. Rich. *Enq.,* Mar. 23; Staunton *Vindicator,* Apr. 5; Davidson to Letcher, Mar. 9, Davidson Papers.

84. F. Woltz to Davidson, Mar. 25, Davidson Papers.

85. Rich. *Whig,* Apr. 2.

86. *Ibid.,* Alexandria *Sentinel,* Apr. 1.

87. "Change of Sec. Sent," 82-101.

88. Henry Dering of Morgantown wrote Willey, March 12, that eight-tenths of "our people" would vote against any ordinance of secession. *Cf.* letters of S. D. Dawson, Mar. 25, J. D. Byrne, Mar. 12, and Henry Dering, Mar. 26, to Willey, Willey Papers.; McGregor, *Disruption of Virginia,* 69-71.

89. Wheeling *Intelligencer,* Mar. 9; Wise to Hunter, Apr. 2, 1861, Mass. Hist. Soc. *Publications* (Dec. 1912-1913), 248.

90. *Cf.* "Proceedings for Mar.," Rich. *Enq.,* Mar. 8 to Apr. 13, 1861.

91. *Cf.* "Proceedings of Mar. 27, 28, 30," Rich. *Enq.,* April 1, 2, 8, 27,

92. On March 15, for instance, Randolph had the floor, but at 1:45 he asked for

adjournment. He made the same request the next day. These requests were granted him as a matter of courtesy, because he did not have his notes on one day, and he was ill the other day. "Proceedings of Mar. 15, 16," Rich. *Enq.*, Mar. 20.

93. "Proceedings of Mar. 26," Rich. *Enq.*, Mar. 28; S. M. Moore to Davidson, Mar. 29, Davidson Papers.

94. Conrad to his wife, Mar. 29, Conrad Papers.

95. *Ibid.*

96. "Proceedings of Mar. 30," Rich. *Enq.*, Apr. 2.

97. *Ibid.*

98. *Cf. supra*, 181-182.

99. Conrad to his wife Mar. 15. Conrad Papers.

100. *Ibid.*, Mar. 24.

101. *Ibid.*, Mar. 29; *cf.* Dorman to Davidson, Mar. 28, Davidson Papers.

102. Conrad to his wife, Apr. 2. Conrad Papers.

103. *Ibid.*, Mar. 30.

104. *Ibid.*, Apr. 3.

105. "Proceedings of Mar. 27," Rich. *Enq.*, Mar. 30.

106. *Ibid.*, Apr. 8.

107. "Proceedings of Apr. 4," Rich. *Enq.*, extra edition, Apr. 8.

108. *Ibid.*, Apr. 8.

109. *Ibid.*

110. *Cf. supra*, 125.

111. "Proceedings of Apr. 4," Rich. *Enq.*, Apr. 8.

112. "Journal of Committee of Whole," *Jour. of Sec. Conv.*, 31-33.

113. "Proceedings of Apr. 4," Rich. *Enq.*, Apr. 8.

114. "Com. of Whole," *Jour. of Sec. Conv.*, 33.

115. Rich. *Exam.*, Apr. 9.

116. "Com. of Whole," *Jour. of Sec. Conv.*, 33.

117. Rich. *Exam.*, Apr. 5.

CHAPTER XI

SUMTER, "COERCION," AND REVOLUTION

1. *Cf. supra*, 120.

2. *Cf. supra*, 144-145, 180-181.

3. "Report of Federal Relations Committee," *Jour. of Sec. Conv.*, appendix.

4. Rich. *Whig*, Mar. 8; Alex. *Gazette*, Jan. 12.

5. Pryor and Ruffin made speeches in Charleston urging the seizure of Sumter in order to provoke a conflict, and to force Virginia to secede. Pryor, *Reminiscences*, 120; Rich. *Enq.*, Nov. 20, 1860; *cf.* also L. Q. Washington's letters to Confederate Secretary of War, Mar. 5, *Official Records*, ser. I, vol. I, p. 263.

6. Rich. *Enq.*, Apr. 3, 5, 6.

7. *Ibid.*, Apr. 1.

8. *Acts of Gen. Ass.* (1861), 339-340.

9. Rich. *Enq.*, Apr. 8.

10. *Ibid.*, Apr. 1.

11. *Diary* of Bates, Mar. 9.

12. *Cf. supra*, 182.

13. *Cf. supra*, 182.

14. *Diary* of Bates, Mar. 29; Hall, "Lincoln's Interview with Baldwin," 263-264.

15. *Ibid.*, 269.

16. *Diary* of Bates, Apr. 8; "A Notice of Lincoln's Relief of Sumter to Pickens," MS. Samuel W. Crawford Papers (in Lib. of Cong.).

17. *Diary* of Bates, Apr. 8.

18. Rich. *Enq.*, Apr. 3.

19. *Ibid.*, Apr. 9; Conrad to his wife, Apr. 10, Conrad Papers; *Daily Dispatch*, Apr. 8, 9.

20. The most important pamphlets and magazine articles on this incident are: W. L.

Hall, "Lincoln's Interview with John B. Baldwin," *South Atlantic Quarterly*, XIII, 260-269; J. B. Baldwin, *Enterview between President Lincoln and John B. Baldwin, April 4, 1861* (Staunton, 1866), 28 pp.; J. M. Botts, *The Great Rebellion* (New York, 1866); *Report of Joint Committee on Reconstruction at the First Session, Thirty-ninth Congress*, Part II; Allan B. Magruder, "A Piece of Secret History: President Lincoln and the Virginia Convention of 1861," *Atlantic Monthly*, XXXV, 438-445.

21. *Report of Com. on Recon.*, 102-107; Baldwin, *Enterview between Lincoln and Baldwin*, 3-9. This story of Baldwin's was substantiated by letters of Summers, Janney, Stewart, Price, Whitehead, Judge Thomas, and Magruder. All of these were Union men, and one, Summers, remained loyal during the war. *Ibid.*, 1, 22-29.

22. "Testimonies of Botts and Lewis," *Report of Com. on Recon.*, 114-117, 69-73; Botts, *Great Rebellion*, 194-202.

23. Baldwin, *op. cit.*, 6.

24. *Report of Com. on Recon.*, 102.

25. *Ibid.*, 114.

26. "The Proceedings of April 4 and 5," Rich. *Enquirer*, April 6, show that Baldwin did not participate in the affairs of the Convention during the fourth, and until four in the afternoon of the fifth. The Washington correspondent of the Alexandria *Gazette* wrote on April 4 that Botts, Segar, and Baldwin were in Washington. Alex. *Gazette*, Apr. 5. Baldwin spoke in Alexandria on the night of April 4. *Diary* of Cornelius Walker, MS. (in Confederate Museum); Alex. *Gazette*, Apr. 5.

27. *Report of Com. on Recon.*, 114.

28. *Cf. supra*, 192.

29. *Cf. supra*, 190.

30. Alex. *Gazette*, Apr. 5.

31. *Ibid.*, Apr. 5, 6, 9; Rich. *Enq.*, Apr. 8, 10.

32. "Jour. of Secret Sess.," *Jour. of Sec. Conv.*, 10-11.

33. He tried to tone down the Preston resolution (*cf. infra*, 195) to prevent insulting Lincoln. "Proceedings of April 6," Rich. *Enq.*, Apr. 10.

34. *Letters of John Hay and Extracts from Diary*, Clara S. Hay, ed. (Washington, 1908), I, 47.

35. R. H. Lutz, "Rudolf Schleiden and the Visit to Richmond, Apr. 25, 1861," Amer. Hist. Asso. *Annual Report* for 1915, 211; Rich. *Enq.*, Mar. 16; C. S. Morehead to Crittenden, Feb. 23, 1862, Crittenden Papers.

36. *Cf. supra*, 182-183.

37. Hall, "Lincoln's Interview with Baldwin." Conrad wrote his wife April 6: "We hear directly from several gentlemen who have within a day or two called on Mr. Lincoln, that he really does not know his own mind." Conrad Papers.

38. *Journal of Sec. Conv.*, 137.

39. "Proceedings of Apr. 6," Rich. *Enq.*, Apr. 10.

40. *Ibid.*

41. *Ibid.*

42. *Ibid.*

43. *Ibid.*

44. *Ibid.*

45. "Proceedings of Apr. 8," Rich. *Enq.*, Apr. 11.

46. *Ibid.*

47. *Ibid.*

48. *Ibid.*, Apr. 11, 12.

49. *Ibid.*

50. *Ibid.*

51. *Ibid.*, Apr. 12.

52. Rich. *Exam.*, Apr. 11; *cf. Daily Dispatch*, Apr. 9.

53. *Journal of Sec. Conv.*, 143-144.

54. "Proceedings of Apr. 8," Rich. *Enq.*, Apr. 12.

55. Preston's report to the Convention in "Proceedings of Apr. 15," Rich. *Enq.*, Apr. 17.

56. He promised to use the powers confided in him by the Constitution "to hold, occupy and possess the property and places belonging to the Government, and to collect

the duties and imposts; but beyond what is necessary for these objects there will be no invasion, no using of force against or among the people anywhere. . . .

"But if, as now appears to be true, . . . an unprovoked assault has been made upon Fort Sumter, I shall hold myself at liberty to repossess, if I can, like places which had been seized before the Government was devolved upon me.

"And in any event, I shall, to the best of my ability, repel force by force." *Ibid.*

57. Gideon Welles to his wife, Apr. 14, 1861, Welles Papers (in Lib. of Cong.).

58. Conrad to his wife, Apr. 11, 12, 13, 14. Conrad Papers.

59. *Ibid.,* Apr. 12, 13; "Proceedings of Apr. 13," Rich *Enq.,* Apr. 24.

60. "Proceedings of Apr. 6," Rich. *Enq.,* Apr. 10.

61. The vote was 37 to 81. "Com. of Whole," *Journal of Sec. Conv.,* 76-77.

62. Conrad to his wife, Apr. 12, 13, Conrad Papers.

63. "Com. of Whole," *Journal of Sec. Conv.,* 98-99.

64. "Proceedings of Apr. 12," Rich. *Enq.,* Apr. 22.

65. "Sir," he said, "I defy the majority of this Convention . . . in the name of an overwhelming majority of the people of Virginia, to go before the people, not only upon the question of a severance of the State from the Federal Union, but upon the issue whether you or we represent them in this Convention." *Ibid.*

66. *Ibid.*

67. Dorman to Davidson, Apr. 9, 12, Davidson Papers; Conrad to his wife, Apr. 10, Conrad Papers.

68. Dorman to Davidson, Apr. 9, Davidson Papers.

69. Conrad to his wife, Apr. 10-13. Conrad Papers.

70. "Proceedings of Apr. 13," Rich. *Enq.,* Apr. 23.

71. *Ibid.,* Apr. 24.

72. *Cf. supra,* 196.

73. *Cf.,* 191.

74. Ruffin's *Diary,* Mar. 2; Pryor, *op. cit.,* 120; Hall, *Rending of Va.,* 191.

75. N. Y. *Tribune,* April 15. Ruffin and L. Q. Washington had made such statements earlier. *Cf. supra,* 191. Mrs. Pryor in her *Reminiscences,* 120, held that her husband went to Charleston and made this speech upon the recommendation of the secessionist party in Virginia. There seems to be no evidence to that effect other than her statement, which was made many years after the event. There is no proof that the Confederate policy was influenced by this assurance from Pryor.

76. Ruffin's *Diary,* Apr. 12; Pryor, *op. cit.,* 121; Henry G. Ellis, "Edmund Ruffin: His Life and Times," John Branch Historical *Papers,* III, 121-122.

77. J. H. Baughman in a letter, April 14, described the Richmond demonstration as follows: "When the news of the surrender of Fort Sumter arrived here yesterday evening the people seemed to be perfectly frantic with delight, I never in all my life witnessed such excitement, . . . the people met in procession, marched to the Capitol and the Fayette Artillery fired 100 Guns in honor of the victory. After firing the procession marched to the Governor's house and Letcher made a few remarks, which the people did not consider quite strong enough for secession, and he was hissed and groaned. After leaving the Governor's the procession went to the Capitol where it was proposed that the Confederate flag be raised—in place of the flag of the Federal government and for about 3 hours the Southern flag was left floating in the breeze . . . business was almost entirely suspended yesterday evening, everybody is in favor of secession, that is all Richmond is, with a very few exceptions." D. S. Freeman, *A Calendar of Confederate Papers* (Richmond, 1908), 185. *Cf.* also W. S. White, "A Diary of the War, or What I saw of it," *Contributions to a History of the Richmond Howitzer Battalion* (Richmond, 1883), 89-90; Conrad to his wife, Apr. 14, Conrad Papers.

78. *Ibid.*

79. In Lynchburg one hundred guns were fired in honor of the "victory." The Norfolk *Argus* declared: "Our hearts are with our brothers at Charleston, and our earnest prayers are for their victory over the abolitionists." And the Alexandria *Sentinel,* April 13, urged the people to "meet and declare and *resolve* that Virginia ought not, must not, can not, and *shall* not be held" longer.

80. Conrad to his wife, Apr. 14, Conrad Papers.

81. Dorman to Davidson, Apr. 12, 14, Davidson Papers; Conrad to his wife, Apr. 12, 14, Conrad Papers.

82. Conrad to his wife, Apr. 14, 15, 16, Conrad Papers.

83. *Public Life of Mason,* 191.

84. Rich. *Whig,* Apr. 17.

85. Bruce, *Va. Iron Manufactures,* 343.

86. Quoted in *Daily Dispatch,* Apr. 16.

87. Staunton *Spectator,* Apr. 16. The Norfolk *Herald* and Alexandria *Gazette* were also of this view. Alex. *Gazette,* Apr. 16, 19.

88. *Daily Dispatch,* Apr. 17; Davidson to Dorman, Apr. 17, Davidson Papers.

89. Rich. *Enq.,* Apr. 18.

90. *Daily Dispatch,* Apr. 15. The Richmond *Examiner,* April 15, carried the same type of editorial.

91. J. B. Jones, *A Rebel War Clerk's Diary, at the Confederate States Capital* (2 vols., Philadelphia, 1866), I, 20. Hereafter cited as Jones, *Rebel Clerk's Diary.*

92. Conrad to his wife, Apr. 15, Conrad Papers.

93. *Ibid.,* Apr. 14, 15; Ruffin's *Diary,* Apr. 15.

94. Conrad to his wife, Apr. 15, Conrad Papers.

95. *Ibid.*

96. *Ibid.*

97. *Ibid.*

98. *Ibid.*

99. *Ibid.*

100. "Proceedings of Apr. 15," Rich. *Enq.,* Apr. 17.

101. *Cf. supra,* 199.

102. This was the view of Preston, Branch, and W. C. Scott.

103. "Journal of Secret Sess.," *Journal of Sec. Conv.,* 3.

104. *Ibid.,* 3-4.

105. *Ibid.,* 4.

106. The favorable response of the North to Lincoln's call for troops and the growing pressure within the state for secession had much weight in increasing this majority. Dorman to Davidson, Apr. 16, Davidson Papers.

107. *Daily Dispatch,* Mar. 13; Staunton *Vindicator,* Mar. 22.

108. Rich. *Exam.,* Apr. 12.

109. Jones, *op. cit.,* I, 15-16.

110. Samuel Woods, Henry A. Wise, J. R. Chambliss, and J. W. Sheffey from the Convention; C. F. Collier and J. T. Anderson from the House of Delegates; and J. A. Harman, T. J. Randolph, and William F. Gordon. Alex. *Gazette,* Apr. 1, 1861.

111. *Ibid;* Charlottesville *Review,* Apr. 5.

112. Letter of Wise to Andrew Hunter, Apr. 2, 1861, in Mass. His. Soc. *Publications* (Jan. 1913), 248.

113. *Cf. supra,* 200.

114. It included such leaders as P. H. Aylett, John Rutherfoord, W. W. Crump, H. A. Claiborne, David Chalmers, G. W. Randolph, J. W. Sheffey, J. A. Seddon, Willoughby Newton, H. A. Wise, G. W. Bagby, John Robertson, J. R. Tucker, J. M. Mason, and the editors of the *Enquirer* and the *Examiner.* Rich. *Enq.,* Apr. 18.

115. Jones, *op. cit.,* I, 20-21.

116. In his diary for Apr. 16, Jones stated: "But it was evident that the Unionists were shaking in their shoes, and they certainly begged one—just one—day's delay." *Ibid.*

117. *Ibid.*

118. *Ibid.,* I, 21.

119. *Ibid.,* I, 22.

120. *Ibid.,* I, 21. On April 16 Dorman wrote Davidson: "One thing is certain unless a Secession Ordinance is submitted that by another day *there will be an open revolution in Eastern Va. This I know.*" Davidson Papers.

121. Hall, *Rending of Va.,* 183, 525-526; J. M. Hagan, *Sketch of the Election and Formation of the State of West Virginia from the Territory of Virginia* (Charleston, W. Va.), 1927, 28; Callahan, *Hist. of Va.,* I, 339-342.

122. Hall, *Rending of Va.*, 183; Hagan, *op. cit.*, 28; Callahan, *op. cit.*, I, 339. Imboden did not relate this part of the story. Wise, *Wise*, 277-278.

123. Hall, *Rending of Va.*, 183; Hagan, *op. cit.*, 28; Callahan, *op. cit.*, I, 339; Wise, *Wise*, 278-279.

124. Hall, *Rending of Va.*, 183; Hagan, *op. cit.*, 28.

125. Wise, *Wise*, 278.

126. Hall, *Rending of Va.*, 162, 183.

127. Jones, *op. cit.*, I, 20-21.

128. Telegrams to and from Governor Pickens, Apr. 17. Thomas J. Corfew of Norfolk to W. H. Parker in care of Wise, Apr. 17. A. M. Barbour to Wise Apr. 17. MS. Executive Papers of John Letcher (in Va. State Lib.).

129. Gov. Letcher's proclamation of Apr. 24. MS. Executive Papers of John Letcher (in Va. State Lib.).

130. *Cf.* chapter VI.

131. *Cf. supra*, 198-199.

132. *Cf. supra*, 201.

133. "Journal of Secret Sess.," *Journal of Sec. Conv.*, 8.

134. These included Aston of Russell, Campbell of Washington, Critcher of Westmoreland, French of Mercer, Gillespie of Fayette, Johnston of Lee, R. E. Scott of Fauquier, W. C. Scott of Powhatan, and Whitfield of Isle of Wight.

135. "Journal of Secret Sess.," *Journal of Sec. Conv.*, 10-11.

136. *Cf. infra*, 212-213.

137. *Cf. infra*, 212-213.

138. McGregor, *op. cit.*, 177-178.

139. Those absent were A. M. Barbour, Grant, A. Hall, Kilby McNeill, Marr, Maslin, and Saunders. Of these eight, all except Maslin and Saunders endorsed the ordinance.

140. These included Baylor, Berlin, C. B. Conrad, Fugate, Gray, Hammond, Haymond, Nelson, and Wickham. Rich. *Enq.*, June 18, 186.

141. *Journal of Sec. Conv.*, 240-241.

142. *Cf.* Copy of ordinance of secession in the Virginia State Library.

143. Dorman to Davidson, Apr. 16, Davidson Papers; Stuart to Willey, May 15, Willey Papers.

144. Conrad to his wife, Apr. 16, Conrad Papers; Dorman to Davidson, Apr. 16, Davidson Papers.

145. Rich. *Exam.*, Apr. 19.

146. *Cf. infra*, 208-209.

147. Three (two Unionist and one moderate) of the forty-three and two-thirds were absent, and one did not vote.

148. One of the two delegates from Franklin did not vote because of sickness. Public meetings in this county and Henrico expressed strong sentiment for secession. Rich. *Exam.*, Apr. 13.

149. *Cf. supra*, 82-84.

150. *Cf.* chapter I.

151. *Cf. supra*, 6.

152. *Cf. supra*, 5.

153. *Cf. supra*, 7, 9, 11.

154. *Cf.* map, frontispiece.

155. *Cf.* chapter I.

156. The upper part of this territory had railroad connections with Richmond and there were a few secession votes from this portion of the Valley. The only railroad of the Shenandoah Valley was the Baltimore and Ohio.

157. Alleghany, Bath, Hampshire, Hardy, Highland, and Pendleton had few slaves, and their delegates voted against secession. Shenandoah County had few slaves, but its delegates voted for secession.

158. Even after secession was accomplished, western leaders reminded the Governor of these facts. Letters from James L. Powell of Roane, May 17, Thomas Mathews of Fayette, April 30, James Hutchinson from the Ohio River district, May 1, and "Ro." Johnson of Clarksburg, May 9, to Letcher. Misc. Letters and Papers (in Va. State Lib.).

159. *Cf. supra*, 7-8.

160. *Cf.* chapter I. Alfred Caldwell, editor of the influential Wheeling *Intelligencer*, wrote Gideon Welles, March 30, that western Virginia "has no trade with Eastern Virginia, no homogenity of opinion, interest or sentiment, either political or social, and . . . the two portions are separated . . . by both moral and physical mountains." Gideon Welles Papers (in Lib. of Cong.).

161. Misc. Letters and Papers (in Va. State Lib.).

162. Wheeling *Intelligencer*, April 20.

163. On May 23 the ordinance was ratified by an estimated vote of 128,884 to 32,134. Rich. *Enq.*, June 20, 1861; Hall, *Rending of Va.*, 189.

164. Miscellaneous Letters and Papers (in Va. State Lib.); *Daily Dispatch*, Apr. 17, 18, 19.

165. Rich. *Enq.*, Apr. 20; Conrad to his wife, Apr. 20, Conrad Papers.

166. Aiken to Butler, Apr. 14, 1861 (This date is an error. The internal evidence shows that it was written between April 17 and May 23), Benj. F. Butler Papers (in Lib. of Cong.).

167. Rich. *Whig*, Apr. 18.

168. Botts, *Great Rebellion*, 257; Rich. *Exam.*, Apr. 26.

169. Alex. *Gazette*, Apr. 22.

170. These sums were as large as those appropriated by eastern counties. Rich. *Exam.*, Apr. 24-26, May 4.

171. *Ibid.*, May 4.

172. *Ibid.*, Apr. 24-26, May 4; Rich. *Enq.*, Apr. 26, May 4.

173. Letters of M. J. Ferguson and J. J. McGinnis to Governor Letcher, Apr. 30, May 1. Misc. Letters and Papers (in Va. State Lib.).

174. Rich. *Exam.*, Apr. 24.

175. Staunton *Vindicator*, May 17.

176. *Ibid.*

177. In a letter to Willey, May 15, Stuart wrote that he shared fully in the former's indignation at the way the secessionists carried "us out of the Union, & into the Southern Confederacy, in the most precipitate manner." But there was nothing left, he said, but to unite with the radicals in order to check Lincoln. Logan Osburn of Jefferson County and James Marshall from the same section showed in their letters to Willey that they agreed with Stuart. Willey Papers. A. S. Gray from Rockingham campaigned for ratification. Exec. Papers of John Letcher (in Va. State Lib.).

178. Letter of J. W. Ramsay from Grafton to Governor Letcher, May 5, 1861, Misc. Letters and Papers (in Va. State Lib.).

179. William Ewing to H. A. Wise, May 7, Misc. Letters and Papers (in Va. State Lib.).

180. Wheeling *Intelligencer*, Apr. 23, 24, 25; Alex. *Gazette*, Apr. 27; Lewis, *How W. Va. Was Made*, 32-34.

181. Dr. George W. Bruce of Marshall County wrote his brother in Winchester, May 14: "We have . . . but a very few who stand out for the State in this trying time. I am sorry to say it, but Marshall County I fear will give the largest . . . vote in proportion to her population of any county of the State. . . . There are but a handful of Secessionists in . . . two towns . . . and but a very few more in the county." Misc. Letters and Papers (in Va. State Lib.). James Drummond wrote Willey, April 17, from Morgantown that the Union sentiment there was as strong as before Sumter was fired upon. Willey Papers.

182. J. L. Powell to Letcher, May 16, Misc. Letters and Papers (in Va. State Lib.).

183. *Kanawha Valley Star*, Apr. 23, 30.

184. Willey Papers.

185. Callahan, *Hist. of W. Va.*, I, 343.

186. *Kanawha Valley Star.* Apr. 23.

187. *Ibid.*, May 7.

188. *Ibid.*, Apr. 30, May 7, 14.

189. Misc. Letters and Papers (in Va. State Lib.).

190. Exec. Papers of Pierpoint (in Va. State Lib.).

191. Wheeling *Intelligencer*, Aug. 5.

192. McGregor, *Disruption of Va.,* 245.

193. *Third Biennial Report* of the Department of Archives and History of the State of West Virginia, V. A. Lewis ed. (Charleston, 1911), 208-210.

194. *Ibid.,* 223.

195. *Ibid.*

196. *Ibid.,* 224

197. Letters of Summers and Jackson to Willey, Willey Papers; letters of Summers to Letcher, May 7, 22, Exec. Papers of John Letcher (in Va. State Lib.); Southern Hist. Soc. *Papers,* I, 456-458.

198. *Cf.* Ambler, *Sect. in Va.,* and McGregor, *op. cit.*

199. Since 1850 slaves over twelve years old had been taxed at the regular property rate provided that no slave were assessed at more than $300. The non-slaveholding section of Virginia wanted to assess and tax slaves as other property. As was stated above (p. 150) many of the west agreed to calling the Convention in order that they might gain this reform. Several resolutions to this effect were introduced in the Convention. *Cf. Journal of Sec. Conv.,* 74, 88, 106. The eastern part of the state, of course, tried to keep this issue down. On April 26, however, the Convention granted the western demands with the hope of retaining the loyalty of the west, and as a means of obtaining revenue to prosecute the war. Rich. *Exam.,* May 17, 1861.

200. *Cf. supra,* 9, 11.

201. *Cf. supra,* 178, 195.

202. Hall, *Rending of Va.,* 528, 532; Lewis, *How W. Va. Was Made,* 30; McGregor, *op. cit.,* 183.

203. Hall *Rending of Va.,* 545; McGregor, *op. cit.,* 183.

204. Wheeling *Intelligencer,* Apr. 23-25; Lewis, *How W. Va. Was Made,* 32-34.

205. McGregor, *op. cit.,* 187.

206. *Ibid.,* 186.

207. Lewis, *How W. Va. Was Made,* 34; McGregor, *op. cit.,* 192-193.

208. Lewis, *How W. Va. Was Made,* 34.

209. *Ibid.,* 45.

210. "Proceedings of the Wheeling Convention for May 13, 14," in *ibid.,* 45-57.

211. *Ibid.,* 63.

212. The N. Y. *Times,* N. Y. *Herald,* Pittsburgh *Chronicle,* Pittsburgh *Dispatch,* Chicago *Press,* Chicago *Tribune,* one Cleveland, and two Cincinnati papers had correspondents who expressed this view. McGregor, *op. cit.,* 199.

213. Putnam, which cast 806 votes on February 4, had only 209 on October 21. Others were as follows: Cabell 900 in Feb. and 200 in Oct.; Clay 243 in Feb. and 96 in Oct.; Raleigh 489 in Feb. and 32 in Oct.; Harrison 2,216 in Feb. and 1,150 in Oct.; Marion 2,199 in Feb. and 798 in Oct.; Monongalia 2,028 in Feb. and 1,609 in Oct.; Upshur 1,000 in Feb. and 614 in Oct.; Randolph 656 in Feb. and 173 in Oct. In the October 21 election 18,408 votes were cast in favor of a division of the state, and 781 against it. This section normally cast 47,000 votes. *Tribune Almanac* (1861); McGregor, *op. cit.,* 255.

214. The Richmond *Whig* stated April 23: "The ordinance of secession will be submitted as a matter of course to the vote of the people. But it will be a mere formality." *Cf.* also Rich. *Enq.,* Apr. 19 and Rich. *Exam.,* Apr. 26. Between April 17 and May 23 Senator Hunter, in a reply to a Richmond lady who expressed her fear that ratification would fail, declared: "'My dear lady . . . you may place your little hand against Niagara with more certainty of staying the torrent, than you can oppose this movement.'" Pryor, *Reminiscences,* 124.

215. *Daily Dispatch,* May 21, 22; Rich. *Exam.,* May 17.

216. Letters of Stuart and Marshall to Willey, May 11, 15, Willey Papers.

217. Robert Hogar, a delegate of the Wheeling Convention, asserted that in his county of Boone, south of the Great Kanawha River, it was given out before May 23 by the secessionists that any man who voted in the negative would be hanged immediately. Hall, *Rending of Va.,* 285. It was reported that troops went about in groups of ten and twenty in Grafton and warned the people that if they did not vote for secession the town would be put in ashes. Letter of John Smith (apparently a fictitious name) to Letcher, May 21, Misc. Letters and Papers (in Va. State Lib.).

218. Letters of J. Huddleson from near the Pennsylvania line to a friend of Letcher, May 13, and of R. McConikay from Kanawha County (but reporting conditions in Wood County), May 23, to Letcher, Misc. Letters and Papers, and Exec. Papers of John Letcher, 1861 (in Va. State Lib.).

219. *Cf.* report of vote by counties in Rich. *Enq.,* June 20, 1861.

220. Compare the vote on ratification with those in the elections of 1856, 1859, and 1860 as given in the *Tribune Almanacs.*

BIBLIOGRAPHY

PRIMARY MATERIALS

I. Official Publications: State and Federal

Acts of the General Assembly of Virginia, 1847-1861. Richmond, published annually and biennially.

Addresses delivered before the Virginia State Convention by Hon. Fulton Anderson, Commissioner from Mississippi, Hon. Henry L. Benning, Commissioner from Georgia, and Hon. John S. Preston, Commissioner from South Carolina, February, 1861. Richmond, 1861.

The Congressional Globe, 1847-1861. Washington, 1847-1862.

Debates and Proceedings of the Convention of Virginia, convened at Richmond, on Monday the Second Day of June, 1788, for the Purpose of Deliberating on the Constitution Recommended by the Grand Federal Convention. Second edition, Richmond, 1805.

Documents of the Virginia Convention of 1861 (several documents relating to the Secession Convention bound into a single volume). •

Documents of Virginia, 1861-1862. Richmond, 1862 (Virginia State Library).

The Eighth Census of the United States, 1860. Washington, 1864.

The Governor's Messages and Annual Reports of Public Officers of the State of Virginia, 1847-1861. Richmond, 1848-1862.

Journal, Acts and Proceedings of the General Convention of the State of Virginia, Assembled at Richmond, on Monday, the Fourteenth Day of October, Eighteen Hundred and Fifty. Richmond, 1850.

Journal of the Acts and Proceedings of a General Convention of the State of Virginia Assembled at Richmond, on Wednesday, the thirteenth day of February, eighteen hundred and sixty-one, together with an appendix which includes the Journal of the Proceedings of the Committee of the Whole. A Portion of the Journal of the Secret Session of the Convention, and The Ordinances and Report of the Committee on Federal Relations and the Adjourned Convention. Richmond, 1861.

Journal of the House of Delegates of the State of Virginia for the Extra Session, 1861. Richmond, 1861.

Journal of the Senate of the Commonwealth of Virginia: Begun and Held at the Capitol in the City of Richmond January 7, 1861, Extra Session. (Includes 32 documents). Richmond, 1861.

Report of the Commissioner of Agriculture for the year 1864. Washington, 1865.

Report of the Committee of Thirteen, Appointed by order of the Senate on the Twentieth Day of December, 1860 . . . , Second Session of the Thirty-sixth Congress. Washington, 1861.

Report of the Joint Committee of the General Assembly of Virginia on the Harper's Ferry Outrages. Richmond, 1860.

Report of the Joint Committee on Reconstruction at the First Session of the Thirty-ninth Congress. Washington, 1866.

Statistical View of the United States . . .; Being a Compendium of the Seventh Census . . ., J. D. B. DeBow, Compiler. Washington, 1854.

Switzer, William F., *Report of the Internal Commerce of the United States Submitted December 20, 1886.* Washington, 1886.

Yearbook of the United States Department of Agriculture, 1895. Washington, 1896.

United States Senate Reports, 36 Cong., 1 sess., report 278. Washington, 1860.

The War of the Rebellion: A Compilation, of the Official Records of the Union and Confederate Armies. 70 vols., Washington, 1880-1901.

II. Collections of Sources

Ames, H. V., *State Documents on Federal Relation: The States and the United States.* Philadelphia, 1906.

American Annual Cyclopedia and Register of Important Events, I-II. New York, 1862.

Chittenden, L. E., *A Report of the Debates and Proceedings in the Secret Sessions of the Conference Convention for proposing Amendments to the Constitution of the United States held at Washington, D. C., in February, 1861.* New York, 1864.

DeBow, J. D. B., *The Industrial Resources, Statistics, etc., of the United States and more particularly of the Southern and Western States.* 3 yols., New York, 1854.

Greeley, Horace, and Cleveland, John F., *A Political Textbook for 1860: Comprising a brief view of Presidential Nominations and Elections.* New York, 1860.

Freeman, D. S., *A Calendar of Confederate Publications.* Richmond, 1908.

Freeman, D. S., *History of Secession in Virginia, 1846-1861, being the notes collected from newspapers, journals, and private papers.* MS. 2 vols. (in possession of Mr. Freeman, Richmond, Virginia).

Halstead, M., *Caucuses of 1860. A History of the National Political Conventions of the Current Presidential Campaign.* Columbus, 1850.

Lewis, Virgil, *How West Virginia was made. Proceedings of the First Convention of the People of Northwestern Virginia at Wheeling May 13, 14, and 15, 1861, and the Journal of the Second Convention of the People of Northwestern Virginia at Wheeling. . . .* Charleston, W. Va., 1909.

McPherson, Edward, *The Political History of the United States of America, during the Great Rebellion. . . .* Second edition, Washington, 1865.

Moore, Frank, *The Rebellion Record: A Diary of American Events, with Documents, Narratives, Illustrative Incidents, Poetry, etc.* 11 vols., New York, 1861-1868.

Nicolay, John G., and Hay, John, *Abraham Lincoln, A History.* 10 vols., New York, 1890.

The Tribune Almanac and Political Register, 1856-1862. New York, 1856-1862.

III. Contemporary Newspapers and Periodicals

The Alexandria Gazette and Virginia Advertiser, 1860-1861; *Virginia Sentinel* (Alexandria), 1860-1861; *The American Union* (Morgantown, W. Va.), 1855-1859; *Charleston Courier*, 1860-1861; *Virginia Free Press and Family Journal* (Charlestown), 1860-1861; *Jeffersonian Republican* (Charlottesville), 1861; *The Review* (Charlottesville), 1860-1861; *Cincinnati Dispatch*, 1849-1850; *The Democratic Banner* (Fairmount, W. Va.), 1850; *DeBow's Commercial Review of the Southern and Western States.* 38 vols., New Orleans, 1846-1870; *Democratic Recorder* (Fredericksburg), 1861; *Kanawha Valley Star* (Charleston, W. Va.), 1855-1861; *Kanawha Republican* (Charleston, W. Va.), 1847-1850; *The New York Herald*, 1860; *The New York Times*, 1860-1861; *Southern Argus* (Norfolk), 1860; *The Parkersburg Gazette and Western Virginia Courier*, 1849-1854; *The Daily Express* (Petersburg), 1860; *The Virginia Index* (Petersburg), 1860; *The Pittsburgh Evening Chronicle*, 1861; *The Pittsburgh Post*, 1860-1861; *North Carolina Standard* (Raleigh, N. C.), 1856-1860; *Richmond Christian Advocate*, 1853-1860; *Daily Dispatch* (Richmond), 1860-1861; *Richmond Enquirer* (daily and semi-weekly), 1847-1861; *Richmond Examiner* (daily and semi-weekly), 1860-1861; *The South* (Richmond), 1857-1858; *Richmond Whig and Public Advertiser*, 1848-1861; *Richmond Daily Whig*, 1846-1847; *Southern Literary Messenger.* 36 vols., Richmond, 1834-1864; *Southern Quarterly Review.* 26 vols., Charleston, 1842-1856; *The Staunton Spectator and General Advertiser*, 1846-1861; *The Staunton Vindicator*, 1846-1861; *The Weston Herald*, 1856-1860; *The Daily Intelligencer* (Wheeling), 1849-1851, 1859-1861; *Winchester Virginian*, 1860.

IV. Contemporary Pamphlets, Addresses, and Speeches

Baldwin, John B., *Enterview between President Lincoln and Col. John B. Baldwin, April 4, 1861. Statements and Evidence.* Staunton, Va., 1866.

Letters, Speeches, and Addresses of August Belmont. Privately printed, 1890.

Botts, John Minor, *The Past, the Present, and the Future of Our Country. Interesting and Important Correspondence between Opposition Members of the Legislature of Virginia and Hon. John Minor Botts, January 17, 1860.* Washington, 1860.

Botts, J. M., *Speech of John Minor Botts at a dinner at Powhatan Court House, Virginia, January 15, 1850.* N. d., n. p.

Carlile, John S., *Remarks at the Mass Convention at Indianapolis, July 30, 1862.* Washington, 1862.

A collection of forty-five bound volumes of miscellaneous pamphlets in the Virginia State Library, including the following pamphlets:

Speech of Hon. John M. Botts at Holcombe Hall in Lynchburg, Virginia, on Thursday Evening, October 18, 1860. N. p., 1860. Pamphlet 48, IV.

Origin and Objects of the Slaveholders' Conspiracy against Democratic Principles as well as against the National Union, Illustrated in the Speeches of Andrew Jackson Hamilton . . . including a letter of M. R. H. Garnett written to William H. Trescott May 3, 1851. N. d., n. p. Pamphlet 72, IX.

The Democracy of the United States. Baltimore, 1860. Pamphlet 26, X.

The Conspiracy to Break up the Union. The Plot and Its Development. Breckinridge and Lane the Candidates of a Disunion Party. Washington, 1860. Pamphlet 30, X.

Democratic Expositor and National Crisis. N. p., 1860. Pamphlet 52, X.

Speech of John C. Rutherfoord, of Goochland, in the House of Delegates of Virginia. 21, February, 1860, in favor of the proposed Conference of Southern States. Richmond, 1860. Pamphlet 49, X.

Official Proceedings of the Democratic National Convention, held in 1860, at Charleston and Baltimore. Cleveland, 1860. Pamphlet 15, XIII.

Remarks delivered in the House of Representatives and Senate of the United States, on the announcement of the death of William O. Goode, late a member of the House of Representatives in the 35th Congress. Washington, 1860. Pamphlet 37, XVI.

Speech of H. W. T. Willey of Virginia on the Objects of the War, in the Senate, December 19 and 20, 1861. 1862. Pamphlet 29, XIX.

Proceedings of the Democratic National Convention held in Baltimore, June 1-5, 1852. Washington, 1852. Pamphlet 11, XX.

Official Proceedings of the National Democratic Convention held in Cincinnati, June 2-6, 1856. Cincinnati, 1856. Pamphlet 26, XX.

Letter of Governor Wise to the New York Tammany Society and Reviews of Wise's letter. N. d., n. p. Pamphlet 2, XX.

Document number XXXIX. Communication from the Governor of Virginia enclosing letters from the Governor of Iowa responsible to a requisition from this State relative to Barclay Coppac. N. p., 1860. Pamphlet 3, XXVII.

The Address of Southern Delegates in Congress to their Constituents. N. p., n. d. Pamphlet 12, XXVIII.

Document number XXVIII. Communication from Citizens of Philadelphia tendering a banner to Virginia. N. p., 1860. Pamphlet 29, XXIX.

Review of the Letter of Hon. A. H. Stephens by a Virginian, Reprint from the Virginia *Sentinel,* June 8, 1860. N. p., 1860. Pamphlet 33, XXIX.

To the People of Virginia! John Letcher and his Antecedents. Read and Circulate. Richmond, 1859. Pamphlet 3, XXXVII.

Two Great Evils of Virginia and their one Common Remedy, an address to Members of the General Assembly of Virginia, written Sept. 17, 1859, signed "Calx." N. p., 1859. Pamphlet 25, XXXVIII.

Speech of Hon. John M. Botts delivered before the Order of the United Americans in the Academy of Music, city of New York, February 22, 1859. N. p., 1859. Pamphlet 9, XXXIX.

Proceedings of the Merchants' Great Domestic Meeting at the New York Exchange, October 2, 1856, with the speech of Governor Floyd. New York, 1856. Pamphlet 11, XXXIX.

Letters to the Richmond Enquirer, 1858, relative to Douglas' Freeport Doctrine, signed "Virginius." N. p., 1858. Pamphlet 4, XLI.

Letter of John H. Gilmer to the People of Virginia, from the Virginia *Index,* Aug.

11, 1860. N. p., 1860. Pamphlet 14, XLII.

Speech of John M. Botts on the Political Issues of the Day, delivered at the African Church in Richmond, Aug. 8, 1856. N. p., 1856. Pamphlet 16, XLIII.

Flournoy, Thos. S., *An Address delivered at the 2nd Annual Exhibition of the Union Agricultural Society of Virginia and North Carolina on the 25th of October, 1855.* Petersburg, 1855.

[Garnett, M. R. H.], *The Union, Past and Future. How it Works, and how to save it,* by a "citizen of Virginia." Washington, 1850.

Gilmer, John H., *The State Convention—A Letter to Messrs. J. R. Humphreys, Higgins, and others, written from Richmond, January 19, 1861.* Richmond, 1861.

Goggin, W. L., *Speech on Federal Relations in the Convention of Virginia, on the 26th and 27th February, 1861.* Richmond, 1861.

Goode, William O., *Speech in the Virginia General Assembly of 1831-1832.* Richmond, 1832.

Holcombe, J. P., *The Election of a Black Republican President an overt act of Aggression on the Rights of Property in Slaves: The South urges to adopt Concerted Action for Future Safety. A Speech before the People of Albemarle on the 2nd day of June, 1860.* Richmond, 1860.

Hunter, R. M. T., *Speech before the Democratic Mass Meeting at Poughkeepsie, on October 1, 1856.* New York, 1856.

[Lyons, James], *Four Essays on the Rights and Propriety of Secession by Southern States,* "by a member of the bar of Richmond." Richmond, 1861.

McDowell, James, *Speech in Legislature of Virginia in the session of 1831-1832.* Richmond, 1832.

McMullen, Fayette, *Letter to the People of the 13th Congressional District of Virginia.* N. p., 1856.

Mitchell, Arthur, *A Word of Scripture to the North and South. A Sermon delivered at the Third Presbyterian Church, Richmond, Virginia, on Sunday, December 30th, 1860.* Richmond, 1861.

The Proceedings and Address of the Central Southern Rights Association of Virginia to the Citizens of Virginia adopted January 10, 1851. Richmond, 1851.

Richardson, George W., *Speech in the Committee of the Whole on the Report of the Committee on Federal Relations, in the Convention of Virginia, April 4, 1861.* Richmond, 1862.

Rives, William C., *Speech on the Proceedings of the Peace Conference and on the State of the Union, delivered in Richmond, Virginia, March 8, 1861.* Richmond, 1861.

Robertson, Wyndham, *Speech on the State of the Country, delivered in the House of Delegates on the 5th and 6th of March, 1860.* Richmond, 1860.

The Ruffner Pamphlet. Address to the People of West Virginia, delivered at Lexington, Virginia, in 1847, showing that slavery is injurious to the public welfare, etc., "by a slave holder of West Virginia." Wheeling, 1862.

Ryland, R., *The American Union. An Address, delivered before the Alumni Association of the Columbian College, D. C., June 23, 1857.* Richmond, 1857.

Segar, Joseph, *Letter to a friend in Virginia, in Vindication of his course in Declining to Follow his State into Secession.* Washington, 1862.

————————, *Speech on the Wilmot Proviso delivered in the House of Delegates, January 19, 1849.* Richmond, 1849.

Summers, George W., *Speech on Federal Relations in the Virginia Convention, delivered March 11, 1861.* Richmond, 1861.

State Secrets for the People—The Private Letters of Lieutenant-General Scott, and the reply of Ex-President Buchanan. New York, 1862.

Stuart, A. H. H., *Address before the Central Agricultural Society of Virginia, at Richmond, October 28, 1859, on the Importance of Diversified Employments—Harmony of Interests, Northern and Southern.* N. p., n. d.

Thompson, George W., *Secession is Revolution; the Dangers of the South; The Barrier States, their Position, Character and Duty; the Constitutional Democracy, in a Discourse delivered at Wheeling, Virginia, December 1, 1860.* Wheeling, 1861.

Tucker, Beverly, *Remarks at the Southern Convention.* N. d., n. p.

Virginia Pamphlets, 1 vol. (Duke University).

Carlile, John S., *Speech in the Virginia State Convention delivered Thursday, March 7, 1861.* Richmond, 1861.
Harris, J. T., *Speech in favor of Conciliation of the Union, delivered in the House of Representatives, February 6, 1861, on the report of the Committee of Thirty-three.* Washington, 1861.
Moore, S. M., *Substance of a Speech delivered by S. McD. Moore, of Rockbridge, in the Convention of Virginia, on his resolutions on Federal Relations, on the 24th of February, 1861.* Richmond, 1861.
Read, Rev. C. H., *National Fast. A Discourse Delivered on the Day of Fasting, Humiliation and Prayer, appointed by the President of the United States, January 4, 1861.* Richmond, 1861.
"Westmoreland," *The "Peace Convention," at Washington, and the Virginia Convention, at Richmond, February 9, 1861.* N. p., 1861.
Virginia Political Pamphlets: Miscellaneous Collection. 5 vols. (Virginia State Library).
Views of the Constitution of Virginia, contained in the essays of "one of the people"; and in the letters of Messrs. Robinson, Macfarland, Morson, and Patton in reply to a communication, from many citizens of the Richmond district. Richmond, 1850. I.
Willey, W. T., *Speeches before the State Convention of Virginia on the Basis of Representation; on county courts and county organization and on the election of judges by the people.* Richmond, 1851. I.
Fisher, Elwood, *Lecture on the North and the South delivered before the Young Men's Mercantile Library of Cincinnati, Ohio, January 16, 1849.* Richmond, 1849. III.
Meade, R. K., *Speech to his constituents of the 2nd Congressional District of Virginia on the subject of Restricting Slavery in the Territories of the United States, August, 1849.* N. p., 1849. III.

V. CONTROVERSIAL LITERATURE

"Barbarossa" [John Scott], *The Lost Principle; or the Sectional Equilibrium; How it was Created—How Destroyed—How it May be Restored.* Richmond, 1860.
Bledsoe, A. T., *An Essay on Liberty and Slavery.* Philadelphia, 1856.
Botts, John Minor, *The Great Rebellion: its Secret History, Rise, Progress, and Disastrous Failure.* New York, 1866.
Buchanan, James, *The Administration on the Eve of Rebellion: A History of Four Years before the War.* London, 1865.
Dabney, R. L., *Defence of Virginia, and Through her of the South, in the recent and pending Contests against the Sectional Party.* New York, 1867.
Davis, Jefferson, *Rise and Fall of the Confederate Government.* 2 vols., New York, 1881.
Dew, T. R., *Review of the Debates on the Abolition of Slavery in the Legislature of Virginia, in the Winter of 1831 and 1832.* Richmond, 1832.
Fitzhugh, George, *Cannibals All or Slaves without Masters.* Richmond, 1857.
————, *Sociology for the South, or the failure of Free Society.* Richmond, 1852.
Hunnicutt, James W., *The Conspiracy Unveiled. The South Sacrificed; The Horrors of Secession.* Philadelphia, 1863.
Olmstead, Frederick Law, *A Journey in the Seaboard Slave States, with Remarks on their Economy.* New York, 1863.
Parker, Granville, *The Formation of the State of West Virginia and other Incidents of the Late Civil War.* Wellsburg, W. Va., 1875.
Pollard, E. A., *The Lost Cause; a new Southern History of the War of the Confederates.* New York, 1868.
————, *The First Year of the War.* Richmond, 1862.
————, *The Life of Jefferson Davis, with a Secret History of the Southern Confederacy.* . . . Philadelphia, 1869.
Ruffin, Edmund, *Anticipations of the Future to Serve as Lessons for the Present Time.* Richmond, 1860.

——————————, *The Political Economy of Slavery*. Richmond, 1857.

Slaughter, Philip, *The Virginia History of African Colonization*. Richmond, 1855.

Smith, W. A., *Lectures on the Philosophy and Practice of Slavery, as exhibited in the Institution of Domestic Slavery in the United States: with the Duties of Masters to Slaves*. Nashville, 1856.

Stephens, Alexander H., *A Constitutional View of the Late War Between the States*. 2 vols., Philadelphia, 1868-1870.

Stuart, A. H. H., *The Present Revolution; Its Causes and its Consequences, and the Duties and Responsibilities which it has imposed on the People, and Especially the Young Men of the South. An Address delivered before the Literary Societies of the University of Virginia, June 29, 1866*. Richmond, 1866.

Tazewell, L. W., *A Review of the Proclamation of President Jackson of the 10th of December 1832, in a Series of Numbers originally Published in the "Norfolk and Portsmouth Herald," under the Signature of "A Virginian."* Norfolk, 1888.

Tucker, Nathanial Beverly, *The Partisan Leader. Reprint from the first print of 1836 when published under the name of Edward William Sidney and printed by Duff Green with erroneous date of 1856*. Carleton, New York, 1861.

Wilson, Henry, *Rise and Fall of the Slave Power in America*. 3 vols., New York, 1872.

Wise, Henry A., *Seven Decades of the Union. The Humanities and Materialism illustrated by a memoir of John Tyler*. Philadelphia, 1881.

Wolfe, Samuel M., *Helper's Impending Crisis Dissected*. Philadelphia, 1860.

VI. Published Diaries, Memoirs, Reminiscences, and Correspondence

Allan, Elizabeth Preston, *Life and Letters of Margaret Junkins Preston*. Boston, 1903.

Ambler, C. H., ed., *Correspondence of Robert M. T. Hunter, 1826-1876*. (American Historical Association *Annual Report* for 1916, II). Washington, 1918.

——————————, *The Life and Diary of John Floyd, Governor of Virginia, an Apostle of Secession, and the Father of the Oregon Country*. Richmond, 1918.

Bagby, George W., *John M. Daniel's Latch-Key, A Memoir of the Late Editor of the Richmond Examiner during the War*. Lynchburg, 1868.

Pease, T. C., and Randall, J. G., eds., *The Diary of Orville Hickman Browning*. (Illinois State Historical Library *Collection*, XX). Springfield, 1925.

Chestnut, Mary Boykin, *A Diary from Dixie*, edited by Isabella D. Martin and Myrta Lockett Avary. New York, 1905.

Claiborne, John Herbert, *Seventy-five Years in Old Virginia*. New York, 1904.

Conway, M. D., *Autobiography and Experiences of. . . .* 2 vols., Boston, 1904.

Daniel, Frederick S., *The Richmond Examiner during the War; or the Writings of John M. Daniel, with a Memoir of his Life, by his brother. . . .* New York, 1868.

"The Diary of a Public Man, Unpublished Passages of the Secret History of the American Civil War," *North American Review*, CXXIX, 125-149, 259-273, 375-388, 484-496.

Dickinson, John R., *Speeches, Correspondence, etc., of the late Daniel S. Dickinson of New York*. 2 vols., New York, 1867.

Foote, Henry S., *Casket of Reminiscences*. Washington, 1874.

Goode, John, *Recollections of a Life Time*. Washington, 1906.

Hall, John, *Forty Years Familiar Letters of James W. Alexander, D.D., Constituting, with the notes, a memoir of his life*. 2 vols., New York, 1860.

Hamilton, J. G. deRoulhac, ed., *The Papers of Thomas Ruffin*. (North Carolina Historical *Publications*) 4 vols., Raleigh, 1918-1920.

Hay, John, *Letters of . . . and Extracts from Diary*. 3 vols., Washington, 1908.

Jameson, J. F., ed., *Correspondence of John C. Calhoun*. (American Historical Association *Annual Report* for 1899, II). Washington, 1900.

Jones, J. B., *A Rebel War Clerk's Diary at the Confederate States Capitol*. 2 vols., Philadelphia, 1866.

"A Page of Political Correspondence, Unpublished Letters of Mr. Stanton to Mr. Buchanan," *North American Review*, CXXIX, 473-483.

Phillips, U. B., ed., *The Correspondence of Robert Toombs, Alexander H. Stephens, and Howell Cobb* (American Historical Association *Annual Report* for 1911, II).

Washington, 1913.
Pryor, Mrs. Roger A., *Reminiscences of Peace and War.* New York, 1904.
Robertson, Archibald T., *Life and Letters of John Albert Broadus.* Philadelphia, 1901.
Rowland, Dunbar, ed., *Jefferson Davis, Constitutionalist, his Letters, Papers, Speeches.*
10 vols., Jackson, Mississippi, 1923.
Tyler, L. G., *Leters and Times of the Tylers.* 3 vols., Richmond and Williamsburg,
1884-1896.
White, W. S., "A Diary of the War, or What I Saw of It," *Contributions to a History of the Richmond Howitzer Battalion.* Richmond, 1883.
Wise, John S., *Recollections of Thirteen Presidents.* New York, 1906.

VII. Manuscript Sources

(a) Manuscripts in the Confederate Museum, Richmond, Va.:
    Thomas L. Broun Paper. 1 letter.
    Judge John A. Campbell Papers. 7 pieces.
    Minutes of a Public Meeting held in Essex and King and Queen Counties February 1, 1861. 1 piece.
    Telegrams in the North Carolina Room from North Carolina troops to Governor Ellis, April 17-24, 1861. 10 pieces.
    Diary of Cornelius Walker of Alexandria from January 1, 1861, to December 31, 1865. 1 vol.
(b) Manuscripts in the Library of Congress:
    Diary of Edmund Bates; John Bell Papers. 1 vol.; Jeremiah S. Black Papers;
    Benj. F. Butler Papers; William M. Burwell Papers. 18 letters; Richard K.
    Cralle Papers. 1 vol; Samuel W. Crawford Papers. 1 vol.; John J. Crittenden
    Papers, X-XXV; John Floyd Papers. 30 letters; James H. Hammond
    Papers, 1849-1861; George F. Holmes Papers, 1824-1892; Joseph Holt Papers,
    XXVII; Franklin Pierce Papers; Diary of Edmund Ruffin, 1856-1865. 14
    vols.; A. H. H. Stuart Papers. 22 pieces; John Tyler Papers, III-IV; The
    Van Buren Papers, VI; Gideon Welles Papers, XLIII.
    Miscellaneous papers including letters to and from the following:
    John S. Barbour, D. H. Conrad, John B. Floyd, J. D. Imboden, R. E. Lee, C. G.
    Memminger, John S. Millson, William C. Rives, John C. Underwood, Henry
    A. Wise.
(c) Manuscripts in the Virginia State Library, Richmond:
    R. Y. Conrad Papers, 1856-1861. 40 letters.
    Manuscripts in the Colonial Dames Case including broadsides and private letters
    on the Brown raid.
    Executive Letter Books, 1856-1861. 3 vols.
    Executive Papers of Henry A. Wise, 1858-1859. About 20 boxes.
    Executive Papers of John Letcher, 1860-1863. About 20 boxes.
    Executive Papers of Francis H. Pierpoint, 1861-1863. 3 boxes.
    Miscellaneous Letters and Papers, 1859-1861. About 12 boxes.
    Preamble and Resolution offered in a Mass Meeting . . . of Botetourt County,
    December 10, 1860. 1 piece.
(d) Waitman T. Willey Papers (in possession of Miss Lilly Hagan, Morgantown,
    W. Va.).
(e) J. D. Davidson Papers, 1847-1861 (in McCormick Agricultural Library, Chicago).
(f) Herbert, Hilary A., Grandfather's Talk About his Life under two Flags (in possession of Professor K. C. Frazer, University of North Carolina, Chapel
    Hill, N. C.).
(g) Nathaniel Beverly Tucker Papers (in possession of Mr. George P. Coleman,
    Williamsburg, Virginia).
(h) University of Virginia Collections:
    Joseph C. Cabell Papers; Miscellaneous Papers.

282 THE SECESSION MOVEMENT IN VIRGINIA

SECONDARY MATERIAL

I. General and Local Histories

Barringer, Paul B., Garnett, J. M., and Page, Rosewell, *University of Virginia, Its History, Influence, Equipment and Characteristics with Biographical Sketches and Portraits of Founders, Benefactors, Officers and Administrators.* 2 vols., New York, 1904.

Bell, L. C., *The Old Free State. A contribution to the History of Lunenburg County and Southside Virginia.* 2 vols., Richmond, 1927.

Callahan, J. M., *History of West Virginia.* . . . 3 vols., Chicago, 1923.

Hagan, John M., *Sketch of the Election and Formation of the State of West Virginia.* . . . (Reprint of West Virginia's Supreme Court's *Reports*, I). Charleston, 1927.

Hall, Granville D., *The Rending of Virginia, a History.* Chicago, 1902.

Hall, Granville D., *The Two Virginias. A Romance of American History.* Chicago, 1915.

Hart, A. B., ed., *The American Nation. A History from Original Sources by Associated Scholars.* 28 vols., New York, 1906.

Lewis, Virgil A., *West Virginia, Its History, Natural Resources, Industrial Enterprises and Institutions.* Charleston, 1904.

————, *Third Biennial Report of the Department of Archives and History of the State of West Virginia.* Charleston, 1911.

Peyton, J. Lewis, *History of Augusta County, Virginia.* Staunton, 1882.

Rhodes, J. F., *History of the United States from the Compromise of 1850.* 7 vols., New York, 1888-1913.

Schouler, James, *History of the United States of America, under the Constitution.* 6 vols., New York, 1880-1899.

Waddell, James A., *Annals of Augusta County, of Virginia, with Reminiscences; Biographical Sketches; a Diary of the War 1861-5; and a Chapter on Reconstruction.* Richmond, 1886.

Johnson, A. L., ed., *The Chronicles of America Series.* 50 vols., New Haven, 1921.

II. Monographs and Special Works

Alexander, Gross and others, *A History of the Methodist Church South, The United Presbyterian Church, the Cumberland Presbyterian Church, and the Presbyterian Church, South, in the United States (American Church Historical Series, XI).* New York, 1911.

Ambler, Charles H., *Sectionalism in Virginia from 1776 to 1861.* Chicago, 1910.

————, *A History of Transportation in the Ohio Valley, with Special Reference to its Waterways, Trade, and Commerce from the Earliest Period to the Present Time.* Glendale, 1932.

Auchampaugh, Philip G., *James Buchanan and His Cabinet on the eve of Secession.* Lancaster, Pa., 1926.

Ballagh, J. C., *History of Slavery in Virginia* (Johns Hopkins University *Studies in History and Political Science*, XXIV). Baltimore, 1902.

Boucher, C. S., *The Nullification Controversy in South Carolina.* Chicago, 1916.

————, *The Secession and Coöperation Movements in South Carolina, 1848-1852* (Washington University *Humanistic Studies*, V. Pt. II, No. 2), 1918.

————, *South Carolina and the South on the eve of Secession, 1852-1860* (Washington University *Humanistic Studies*, VI, Pt. No. 2), 1919.

Bowers, James Carr, *Slavery and Secession Sentiment in Virginia, 1860-1861.* M.A. Thesis at the Universiy of Virginia, 1928.

Brenaman, J. N., *The History of the Virginia Conventions with the Constitution, 1867-68.* Richmond, 1902.

Brown, W. G., *The Lower South in American History.* New York, 1902.

Bruce, Kathleen, *Virginia Iron Manufactures in the Slave Era.* New York, 1931.

Cole, Arthur C., *The Whig Party in the South.* Washington, 1913.

Collins, Winfield H., *The Domestic Slave Trade of the Southern States.* New York, 1904.

Craven, Avery O., *Soil Exhaustion as a Factor in the Agricultural History of Virginia and Maryland, 1606-1860* (University of Illinois *Studies in Social Sciences,* series I, vol. XIII). Urbana, Ill., 1926.

Crawford, Samuel W., *The Genesis of the Civil War. The Story of Sumter 1860-61.* New York, 1887.

DuBois, W. E. B., *The Suppression of the African Slave-Trade to the United States of America.* New York, 1904.

Dumond, Dwight L., *The Secession Movement, 1860-61.* New York, 1931.

Dunaway, Wayland F., *History of the James River and Kanawha Company.* New York, 1922.

Freeman, D. S., *The Attitude of Political Parties in Virginia towards Slavery and Secession, 1846-1861.* Ph.D. Dissertation, Johns Hopkins University, 1908 (in possession of Mr. Freeman).

Gaines, Francis P., *Southern Plantation: a Study in the Development and the Accuracy of a Tradition* (Columbia University *Studies in English and Comparative Literature*). New York, 1924.

Gray, Lewis C., *History of Agriculture in the Southern United States to 1860.* 2 vols., Carnegie Institute of Washington, 1933.

Hall, G. D., *Lee's Invasion of Northwest Virginia in 1861.* Chicago, 1911.

Hamer, Philip May, *The Secession Movement in South Carolina. 1847-1852.* Allentown, Pa., 1918.

Howe, D. W., *A Political History of Secession to the Beginning of the American Civil War.* New York, 1914.

Hubbell, Jay B., *Virginia Life in Fiction.* New York, 1922.

Hungerford, Edward, *The Story of the Baltimore and Ohio Railroad, 1827-1927.* 2 vols., New York, 1928.

Ingle, Edward, *Southern Sidelights. A Picture of Social and Economic Life in the South a Generation Before the War.* New York, 1896.

Jenkins, William S., *The Political Theories of the Slaveholder.* Ph.D. Dissertation, University of North Carolina, Chapel Hill, N. C., 1927.

McGregor, James C., *The Disruption of Virginia.* New York, 1922.

Munford, B. B., *Virginia's Attitude Toward Slavery and Secession.* New York, 1910.

Norwood, John N., *The Schism in the Methodist Episcopal Church 1844: A Study of Slavery and Ecclesiastical Politics.* New York, 1923.

Phillips, U. B., "The Literary Movement for Secession," *Studies in Southern History and Politics inscribed to William Archibald Dunning . . . by his former pupils the authors,* 31-60. New York, 1914.

——————, *American Negro Slavery; A Survey of the Supply, Employment and Control of Negro Labor as Determined by the Plantation Regime.* New York, 1918.

——————, *Life and Labor in the Old South.* Boston, 1931.

Pullian, D. L., *The Constitutional Conventions of Virginia from the Foundations of the Commonwealth to the Present Times.* Richmond, 1901.

Reizenstein, Milton, *The Economic History of the Baltimore and Ohio Railroad, 1827-1853* (Johns Hopkins University *Studies in Historical and Political Science,* series XV, Nos. 7-8). Baltimore, 1897.

Riley, B. F., *A History of the Baptists in the Southern States East of the Mississippi.* Philadelphia, 1898.

Royall, William L., *A History of Virginia Banks and Banking Prior to the Civil War: With an Essay on the Banking System needed.* New York, 1907.

Russell, John H., *The Free Negro in Virginia, 1619-1865.* (Johns Hopkins University *Studies in History and Political Science,* series XXXI, No. 3). Baltimore, 1913.

Russell, R. R., *Economic Aspects of Southern Sectionalism, 1840-1861.* Urbana, Illinois, 1924.

Scrugham, Mary, *The Peaceable Americans of 1860-1861; A Study in Public Opinion.* (Columbia University *Studies in History, Economics and Public Law,* XCVI, No. 3). New York, 1921.

Shryock, Richard H., *Georgia and the Union in 1850.* Durham, N. C., 1926.

Smith, Edward C., *The Borderland in the Civil War.* New York, 1927.

Swaney, Charles B., *Episcopal Methodism and Slavery with Sidelights on Ecclesiastical Politics.* Boston, 1926.

Sweet, William W., *The Methodist Episcopal Church and the Civil War.* Cincinnati, 1912.

————, *The Story of Religion in America.* New York, 1930.

Van Deusen, John G., *Economic Bases of Disunion in South Carolina.* New York, 1928.

White, Melvin J., *The Secession Movement in the United States, 1847-1852.* New Orleans, 1916.

Whitfield, T. M., *Slavery Agitation in Virginia, 1829-1832* (Johns Hopkins University Studies in Historical and Political Science, new series X). Baltimore, 1930.

Willey, William P., *An Inside View of the Formation of the State of West Virginia with Character Sketches of the Pioneers in that Movement.* Wheeling, 1901.

Woodson, C. G., *Disruption of Virginia.* Ph.D. Dissertation. Harvard University, 1913.

III. MAGAZINE ARTICLES

American Historical Review. New York, 1895-.........

Ambler, C. H., "The Cleavage Between Eastern and Western Virginia," XV, 762-780.

"The Change of Secession Sentiment in Virginia in 1861" (Letters of Judge E. C. Burke and Bishop Otey from November 23, 1860 to August 22, 1861), XXXI, 82-101.

Dodd, William E., "Chief Justice Marshall and Virginia," XII, 776-787.

Foster, H. D., "Webster's Seventh of March Speech and the Secession Movement, 1850," XXVII, 245-270.

Hunt, Gillard, "Narrative and Letter of William Henry Trescott, Concerning the Negotiations between South Carolina and President Buchanan in December, 1860," XIII, 528-556.

"From the Autobiography of Herschel V. Johnson, 1856-1867," XXX, 311-337.

Siebert, W. H., "Light on the Underground Railroad," I, 455-463.

Transactions of the Alabama Historical Society. 5 vols., Montgomery.

Herndon, D. T., "The Nashville Convention of 1850," V, 203-307.

Atlantic Monthly. XXXV, Boston, 1875.

Magruder, Allan B., "A Piece of Secret History; President Lincoln and the Virginia Convention of 1861," XXV, 438-445.

The John P. Branch Historical *Papers* of Randolph-Macon College. Richmond, 1901-1908.

Anderson, D. R., "R. M. T. Hunter," II, 4-77.

Dodd, W. E., "John Taylor, of Caroline, Prophet of Secession," II, 214-252.

Ellis, Henry G., "Edmund Ruffin: His Life and Times," III, 99-123.

Prettyman, E. B., "John Letcher," III, 314-349.

"Letters of Thomas Ritchie—Glimpses of the Year 1830," I, 147-151.

"Spencer Roane—Reprint from the Richmond *Enquirer*," I-II.

Spann, J. R., "William Andrew Smith, D. D.," IV, 347-363.

Smith, E. J., "Benjamin Watkins Leigh," I, 286-297.

The Conservative Review; a Quarterly. Washington.

Goode, John. "The Virginia Secession Convention of 1861," III, 75-89.

Mississippi Valley Historical Review. Cedar Rapids, Iowa, 1914-.........

Boucher, C. S., "In *Re* that Aggresive Slaveocracy," VIII, 13-79.

Cole, A. C., "The South and the Right of Secession in the Early Fifties," III, 376-399.

Sioussat, St. George L., "Tennessee, The Compromise of 1850, and the Nashville Convention," II, 313-347.

The Nation: A Weekly Journal Devoted to Politics, Literature, Science, and Art. XXIX, New York.

Welling, J. C., "The Proposed Evacuation of Fort Sumter," XXIX, 383-384.

Richmond College Historical *Papers.* 2 vols., Richmond, 1915-1917.

Webster, Clyde C., "John Minor Botts, anti-Secessionist," I, 9-37.

Wilkinson, A. N., "John Moncure Daniel," I, 73-95.

Wingfield, R. S., "William C. Rives, a Biography," I, 57-72.

Woodfin, Maude H., "Nathaniel Beverly Tucker," II, 9-42.

The South Atlantic Quarterly. Durham, N. C., 1902-........

Bean, William G., "An Aspect of Know-Nothing—The Immigrant and Slavery," XXIII, 319-334.

Carnathan, W. I., "The Proposal to Reopen the African Slave Trade in the South, 1854-1860," XXV, 410-429.

Dwire, Henry R., "The New York *Times* and the Attempt to Avert the Civil War," II, 273-280.

Ellis, H. G., "The Influence of Industrial and Educational Leaders on the Secession of Virginia," IX, 372-376.

Fitzgerald, O. P., "John M. Daniel and Some of his Contemporaries," IV, 13-17.

Hall, Wilmer L., "Lincoln's Interview with John B. Baldwin," XIII, 260-269.

Newberry, Farrar, "The Nashville Convention and Southern Sentiment of 1850," XI, 259-273.

Rowland, Major Thomas and Kate Mason, "Letters of a Virginia Cadet at West Point, 1859-1861," XIV, 201-219, 330-347; XV, 1-17, 142-156, 201-215.

Tandy, Jeanette Read, "Pro-Slavery Propaganda in American Fiction of the Fifties," XXI, 41-50, 170-178.

Southern Historical Association *Publications.* 11 vols., Washington, 1897-1907.

Cobb, Thomas R. R., "Correspondence of . . . , 1860-1862," XI, 147-185, 233-260, 312-328.

Hunter, Andrew, "John Brown's Raid," I, 165-195.

Southern Historical Society *Papers.* 44 vols., Richmond, 1876-1923.

Tyler's Quarterly Historical and Genealogical Magazine. Richmond, 1919-.........

The Virginia Magazine of History and Biography. Richmond, 1893-.........

William and Mary College, *Quarterly Historical Magazine.* Williamsburg, 1892-.........

IV. BIOGRAPHIES AND BIOGRAPHICAL STUDIES

Ambler, C. H., *Thomas Ritchie, A Study in Virginia Politics.* Richmond, 1913.

Anderson, D. R., *William Branch Giles; a Study in the Politics of Virginia and the Nation from 1790 to 1830.* Menasha, Wisconsin, 1914.

Bancroft, Frederick, *The Life of Williah H. Seward.* 2 vols., New York, 1900.

Beaty, John O., *John Esten Cooke, Virginian.* New York, 1922.

Bell, John W., *Memoirs of Governor William Smith, his Political, Military, and Personal History.* New York, 1891.

Capers, Henry D., *The Life and Times of C. G. Memminger.* Richmond, 1893.

Coleman, Mrs. Chapman, *The Life of John J. Crittenden with Selections from his Correspondence.* 2 vols., Philadelphia, 1871.

Connor, Henry G., *John Archibald Campbell, Associate Justice of the United States Supreme Court, 1853-1861.* Boston, 1920.

Craven, Avery, *Edmund Ruffin, Southerner. A Study in Secession.* New York, 1932.

Curry, Charles, *John Brown Baldwin* (in possession of Mr. Charles Curry, Staunton, Va.).

Curtis, George T., *Life of James Buchanan Fifteenth President of the United States.* 2 vols., New York, 1883.

DuBose, J. W., *Life and Times of William Lowndes Yancey.* Birmingham, Alabama, 1896.

Feuss, C. M., *The Life of Caleb Cushing.* 2 vols., New York, 1923.

Gordon, Armistead C., *Memoirs and Memorials of William Gordon McCabe.* 2 vols., Richmond, 1925.

————————, *William Fitzhugh Gordon, a Virginian of the Old School: His Life, Times and Contemporaries, (1787-1858).* New York, 1909.

Hambleton, J. P., *A Biographical Sketch of Henry A. Wise with a History of the Political Campaign in Virginia in 1855.* Richmond, 1856.

Harris, Wilmer C., *Public Life of Zachariah Chandler, 1851-1875.* Lansing, Mich., 1917.

Hoge, Peyton H., *Moses Drury Hoge: Life and Letters.* Richmond, 1899.

Hughes, Judge Robert W., *Editors of the Past, a Lecture delivered before the Virginia Press Association at Annual Meeting at Charlottesville, June 22, 1897.* Richmond, 1897.

John, Rev. J., *Memoirs of Henry Augustus Washington, Late Professor of History, Political Economy, and International Law in William and Mary College, Virginia.* Baltimore, 1859.

Johnson, Thomas Cary, *The Life and Letters of Robert Lewis Dabney.* Richmond, 1903.

King, Joseph L., *Dr. George William Bagby. A Study of Virginian Literature, 1850-1880.* New York, 1927.

[Mason, Virginia,] *The Public and Diplomatic Correspondence of James M. Mason with some Personal History by his Daughter.* Roanoke, 1903.

Merritt, Elizabeth, *James Henry Hammond, 1807-'64* (Johns Hopkins University *Studies in Historical and Political Science,* series XLI). Baltimore, 1923.

Peyton, John L., *Memoirs of William Madison Peyton of Roanoke.* London, 1873.

[Pollard, E. A.], *The Early Life, Campaign and Public Services of Robert E. Lee; with a Record of the Campaigns and Heroic Deeds of his Companions in Arms, by a Distinguished Southern Journalist.* New York, 1871.

Robertson, Alexander F., *Alexander Hugh Holmes Stuart, 1807-1891—a Biography.* Richmond, 1925.

Scott, Robert E., "Robert Eden Scott," Fauquier Historical Society *Bulletins,* series I, 78-92. Richmond, 1921.

Stearns, Emeline Lee, *John M. Daniel and the Confederacy.* M.A. Thesis, University of Chicago, 1928.

Strider, Robert E. L., *Life and Works of George William Peterkin.* Philadelphia, 1929.

Trent, William P., *William Gilmore Simms.* Boston, 1892.

Tyler, L. G., *An Address delivered at the Virginia Polytechnic Institute on April 25, 1913 . . . on Edmund Ruffin.* Roanoke, 1913.

Tyler, Lyon G., *Encyclopedia of Virginia. Biography.* 5 vols., Washington, 1915.

Villard, Oswald Garrison, *John Brown, 1800-1859, a Biography Fifty Years after.* Boston, 1911.

White, Horace, *The Life of Lyman Trumbull.* Boston, 1913.

White, Laura A., *Robert Barnwell Rhett, Father of Secession.* New York, 1931.

Wise, Barton H., *The Life of Henry A. Wise of Virginia 1806-1876.* New York, 1899.

INDEX

Abingdon *Democrat,* 187.
"Address to National Democracy," 108.
African slave trade, Virginians' hostility to reopening, 131, 164, 235, 249.
Aikien, F. A., 208.
Alexandria *Gazette,* 100, 121, 246.
Alleghany highlands, 2.
Allen, J. J., 138.
Ambler, Marshall, saves Secession Convention, 200.
Amelia County, 94, 138, 186.
Anderson, Fulton, Mississippi's representative to Virginia, 161.
Anderson, J. R., president of Tredegar Iron Works, 200.
Anderson, Robert, major at Fort Sumter, 136.
Anticipations of the Future, 71, 74.
Augusta County, 209, 216, 230.
Aylett, Patrick H., editor of *Examiner,* 62; saves Secession Convention, 202.

Bagby, George W., 78.
Baldwin, J. B., 180. *See also* Baldwin-Lincoln interview.
Baldwin-Lincoln interview, 183, 192-195, 267.
Baltimore and Ohio Railroad, 7, 8, 211.
Baltimore Convention. *See* "Constitutional Union Party" and National Democratic Convention of Baltimore.
Barbour, James, 174; leader of legislature in 1861, 142, 253; on election of February 4, 1861, 154-155; leader of moderates in Convention, 160; advises Seward, 169; report to Secession Convention, 179-180.
Barbour, B. J., 151.
Bates, E. W., 194; on conservatism of Lincoln, 170, 249.
Battelle, Bishop Gordon, 235.
Baugham, J. H., 268.
Baylor, George, 165, 245.
Baylor, Jacob, 111.
Bayly, T. H., on Compromise of 1850, 38.
Bedinger, Henry, 44.
Bell, John, 102, 110; votes received in 1860, 115-118.
Belmont, August, and Seward, 252.

Benning, H. T., Georgia's representative to Virginia, 161.
Bledsoe, A. T., 71, 78.
Blow, George P., on nullification, 21.
Blue Ridge Republican, on election of 1859, 61-62.
Bocock, T. S., candidate for Congress in 1851, 43; on right of secession, 43-44.
Border-states conference, 130, 131, 165, 186, 190, 197, 199, 200, 201, 204.
Boteler, A. R., 91, 132, 172.
Botts, John M., 48; candidate for Congress in 1851, 44; on right of secession, 44; on Lincoln's election, 122; Baldwin-Lincoln interview, 193; on Lincoln's call for troops, 209; on Kansas-Nebraska bill, 277. *See also* Whigs.
Boycot of Northern goods, discussed, 40-41; a remedy for Brown raid, 93; voluntary associations for carrying out, 94; effect on North, 239.
Branch, Thomas, 177, 187, 245.
Breckinridge, John C., 109; significance of votes for, 115-118.
Breckinridge party, not for secession, 112; on Lincoln's election, 113. *See also* Democratic party and Presidential campaign of 1860.
Breckinridge press, on Lincoln's election, 121-122.
Broadus, J. M., 175.
Brockenbrough, Judge John, 57; report on Peace Conference, 174.
Brooklyn, 137, 146.
Brooks-Sumner episode, 51; *Kanawha Valley Star* on, 51-52.
Brown, John, 85, 86. *See also* Brown raid.
Brown raid, 65; early reaction to, 86; North's reaction, 87-88; North blamed for, 87; excitement in Virginia, 89-91, 237, 238; investigation of, 92-93; effect on secesssion sentiment, 91, 96, 100-102; non-intercourse resolution, 92, 94.
Brown, W. G., 119.
Bruce, George W., 271.
Buchanan, James, message to Congress, December, 1860, 132; reception, 132; policy toward Sumter, 136-137.
Buchanan's Cabinet, and forts, 136. *See also* Federal forts.